MIND, LANGUAGE, MACHINE

Mind, Language, Machine

Artificial Intelligence in the
Poststructuralist Age

MICHAEL L. JOHNSON
Professor of English
University of Kansas

St. Martin's Press   New York

First published in the United States of America in 1988

Printed in Hong Kong

ISBN 0-312-00406-0

Library of Congress Cataloging-in-Publication Data
Johnson, Michael L.
Mind, language, machine.
Bibliography: p.
Includes index.
1. Artificial intelligence.   I. Title.
Q335.J66 1987   006.3   86-31497
ISBN 0-312-00406-0

In memory of Ivan Harold Johnson

unter allen diesen Träumenden auch ich, der 'Erkennende',
meinen Tanz tanze

[among all these dreamers I too, the 'knower', dance
my dance]

Friedrich Nietzsche, *Die fröhliche Wissenschaft*

Contents

Contents

Acknowledgements

Though writing this book was mostly a solitary (and long) project, special thanks should be extended to the University of Kansas for granting me a sabbatical leave to complete the first draft, to Larry West for reading and critiquing some key chapters, to Sandee Kennedy for word-processing it with patience and skill into final form, and to my wife Kathleen and son Jarrett for bearing with me.

The author and publishers wish to thank the following who have kindly given permission for the use of copyright material:

Academic Press, for the extracts from *Understanding Natural Language* by Terry Winograd (New York: Academic Press, 1972).

American Scientist, for the extract from 'The Logic of Mind' from *A Sense of the Future* by J. Bronowski, ed. P. E. Ariotti with Rita Bronowski (Cambridge, Mass.: MIT Press, 1977), reprinted from *American Scientist* (March 1966).

Benjamin/Cummings Publishing Co., for the extracts from *Structural Stability and Morphogenesis* by René Thom, trans. D. H. Fowler (Reading, Mass.: Benjamin, 1975).

Cambridge University Press, for the extracts from 'Minds, Machines and Gödel' by J. R. Lucas (Cambridge University Press, 1961).

Cambridge University Press and Harvard University Press, for the extracts from *Language and Perception* by George A. Miller and Philip N. Johnson-Laird (Cambridge, Mass.: Harvard University Press, Belknap Press, 1976).

W. H. Freeman and Co. Publishers, for the extracts from *Computer Models of Thought and Language* by Roger C. Schank and Kenneth Mark Colby, copyright © 1973 W. H. Freeman and Co.

Harvester Press Ltd and Basic Books, Inc., for the extracts from *Gödel, Escher, Bach: An Eternal Golden Braid* by Douglas R. Hofstadter (New York: Basic Books, 1979).

Harvester Press Ltd and MIT Press, for the extracts from

Brainstorms by Daniel C. Dennett (Montgomery, Vt.: Bradford Books, 1978).

David Higham Associates Ltd and Basic Books, Inc., for the extracts from *Artificial Intelligence and Natural Man* by Margaret A. Boden (New York: Basic Books, 1977).

MIT Press, for the extract from *Information, Mechanism and Meaning* by Donald MacKay (Cambridge, Mass.: MIT Press, 1969).

Mouton de Gruyter, for the extracts from 'Human and Animal Languages' from *A Sense of the Future* by J. Bronowski, ed. P. E. Ariotti with Rita Bronowski (Cambridge, Mass.: MIT Press, 1977), reprinted from *To Honor Roman Jakobson* (The Hague: Mouton, 1967); and for 'Language in a Biological Frame' from *A Sense of the Future* by J. Bronowski, reprinted from *Current Trends in Linguistics* (The Hague: Mouton, 1974).

Oxford University Press, Oxford, and Oxford University Press, New York, for the extracts from *After Babel: Aspects of Language and Translation* by George Steiner (New York: Oxford University Press, 1975); and the extracts from *Programs of the Brain* by J. Z. Young (New York: Oxford University Press, 1978).

Penguin Books Ltd, for the extracts from 'Semantics' by Manfred Bierwisch in *New Horizons in Linguistics*, ed. John Lyons (Harmondsworth, Middx: Pelican Books, 1970), copyright © John Lyons 1970.

George Weidenfeld and Nicolson Ltd and Alfred A. Knopf, Inc., for the extracts from *The Conscious Brain* by Steven Rose, updated edition (New York: Alfred A. Knopf, 1976).

John Wiley and Sons Inc., for the extracts from *Introduction to Human Information Processing* by David E. Rumelhart (New York: John Wiley, 1977).

Every effort has been made to trace all the copyright-holders, but if any have been inadvertently overlooked, the publishers will be pleased to make the necessary arrangement at the first opportunity.

1
Mind, Language, Machine

Today there is no more exciting field of inquiry than that variegated and largely disunified one concerned with investigating human language. In so far as it can be defined as a discipline, it draws relentlessly on the resources of many other disciplines with which it shares interests. Recently the interests of language theorists and researchers have overlapped fruitfully with those of various kinds of computer scientists and psychologists, whose interests in turn appear to be melding in the development of the hybrid discipline of a general cognitive science. As Philip N. Johnson-Laird observes,

> During the past decade, there has grown up a confederation of disciplines – linguistics, philosophy of mind, cognitive anthropology, neuroscience, artificial intelligence, and psychology itself – whose practitioners have realized that they are converging on the same set of problems and even independently invoking the same explanatory ideas. The so-called cognitive sciences have sometimes seemed like six subjects in search of an interdisciplinary synthesis; if that synthesis does not yet exist, it is certainly necessary to invent it.[1]

Tremendously important insights are emerging from this nexus of interests. My purpose is to discuss those insights and extrapolate their implications as far as possible. Such extrapolation is inevitably polemical since it demands an eclecticism that is insatiable, an intellectual poise that is difficult to maintain, and an interdisciplinary synthesis that cannot yet – and perhaps can never – be fully achieved.

My special concern is work in artificial intelligence (AI), particularly as it can be studied in relation to theorizing about mentation and language that may be broadly characterized as poststructuralist. It is now almost commonplace to think of 'reality' (linguistic and otherwise) in terms of the structures of human consciousness and the interpretive strategies that enact and are enacted by them. Such thinking is saliently structuralist or even, to use a newer term, constructivist. But those structures and strategies themselves are increasingly subject to scrutiny (by themselves, of course, paradoxically): their logics are radically analysed; their metaphysical assumptions are questioned; their rarefied ontology is continually re-examined. Such scrutiny is saliently poststructuralist, and it has yielded insights similar to those engendered by AI theory and research. This situation, which has not been previously described and explored, is surprising in many ways, especially given the ostensible differences in attitude of poststructuralists, whose projects are mostly intellectual and granted virtually no scientificity, and AI theorists and researchers, whose projects are in large measure technical and granted at least contingent scientificity. To be sure, a typical conversation between a poststructuralist and a member of the 'artificial intelligentsia' would be punctuated by fireworks, but, once the smoke had settled, they might well discover that many of the implications of their respective enterprises were dovetailing by an intriguing dialectic – and that their conversation was being joined sympathetically by others from other disciplines on Johnson-Laird's list.

Let me, in jargon of the realm, 'initialize' that dialectic by proposing that mind *is* informational operations, patterns of language; that language *is* a kind of machine, a system chasing its own tail; that an information-processing machine (hardware) may be identified with, sublimates into, *is* language itself (software) and thus resembles mind. This seemingly naïve predication may be rephrased as a circular set of propositions: a mind is a language; a language is a machine (or a computer, as it is unfortunately usually called, though the word derives from the Latin *computare*, whose base is *putare*, 'to think'); a machine is a mind. Or, as in Figure 1.1, it may be visualized as a cyclical diagram of interrelations, a circle of metaphor. And it may be given the more coolly quasi-mathematical form of an equation that returns upon itself: mind = language = machine = mind. (Various 'partials' of these interrelations may be adduced: as the language-trained deaf claim, there is no mind without language; as Lev Vygotsky, among others, has noted, a word is a microcosm of consciousness; functionally speaking, a computer is equivalent to its language; and so on. J. David Bolter catches hold of this MLM circle when

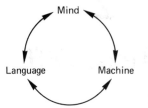

Figure 1.1

he observes that 'in the age of the computer, silent, spatial structures are used to map out the meaning of language. And the meaning of a sentence is its structure, which our mind, like a computer, can represent, distill, and transform. For the mind itself is the capacity to form structures.')[2]

Beginning this enterprise, I am reminded of Rousseau:

> *l'on nous donne gravement pour de la philosophie les rêves de quelques mauvaises nuits. On me dira que je rêve aussi; je conviens: mais ce que les autres n'ont garde de faire, je donne mes rêves pour des rêves, laissant chercher au lecteur s'ils ont quelque chose d'utile aux gens éveillés.*[3]

> [the dreams of bad nights are given to us seriously as philosophy. You will tell me that I too dream; I agree, but I do what others are far from doing: I give my dreams as dreams, leaving the reader to discover if they contain anything useful to people who are awake].

Thus there are risks involved in this enterprise to which there can be no complacent closure, for I want to weave a text in which the coupling of mind and language and machine is brought to an open-ended crisis. I hope the reader will understand the irony of what I write, the extent to which it undermines as well as reinforces itself. My method, like that of Michel Serres, 'invents: it is thus an *anti-method*'.[4]

2
System, Text, Difference

Mind, language, machine: three systems without positive substance that, copulating interactively, create the universe as it is known and manipulated by man. Each seems to have a 'physical' reality, and yet each is also – and more importantly – an ethereal network of relations: a mind, elaborated through its eerie space like a language, is not simply a brain (a neural structure, 'wetware'); a language is not simply air in motion or ink on paper; a machine is not simply silicon-based circuitry (hardware). Each, like the signs that comprise language, has a particle/wave nature, has something of Jacques Derrida's *trace* ('trace') about it: each 'can be focussed either materially or conceptually, . . . both is and is not matter, and carries within itself a kind of necessary exteriority'.[1] Each in its insubstantiality consists of software: differential relations, diacritical nodes. No *stuff* at all finally: just functionalist patterns of interrelation, maps without territory, wispy microtexts interwoven. Each is – or is coming to be understood as – the same kind of system. And yet there seems to be a divorce among them, an otherness of each to the others.

This both/and logic of the trace is ubiquitous. Just as the present is inhabited by the traces of the past and the future, so, as George Steiner has it, even 'the master executant or critic can say *Je est un autre* [I is an other]'.[2] There is always an otherness, a lag, a deferral, a hysteresis; only a trace (a data-structure, a program) remains: nothing is what or when one thinks it is. Even my own words are not mine. They are (must be) alien to themselves, haunted by the events that produced them, prior usage, displacements, concealments, so that between usages, between the writer and the reader, the translation betrays. Is it possible to construct a perfect isomorphism, a true homology? Specifically, how and to what extent are mind, language, and machine the same kind of system?

Let me deal with that question gradually and tentatively, beginning with the 'events' that produce words, language.

Verbal language takes the (plexiform) form of a spoken or

written text, a *textus*, something cybernetically 'woven' of (open) binary events (the processes performed in relation to it) in two dimensions, as it were, continually transmuting (as Walter Porzig has noted) all relationships into spatial relationships: a signifying system without closure or centre (perhaps more – to use Serres's word – a *syrrhesis*, a 'flowing together', than a *system*, with its inscribed meaning of 'standing together'). This textile process whereby signs are produced and turned into messages is addressed by Terence Hawkes in a discussion of Roman Jakobson's thought:

> Jakobson sees metaphor and metonymy as the characteristic modes of binarily opposed polarities which between them underpin the two-fold process of *selection* and *combination* by which linguistic signs are formed. . . . Thus messages are constructed, as Saussure said, by a combination of a 'horizontal' movement, which combines words together, and a 'vertical' movement, which selects the particular words from the available inventory or 'inner storehouse' of the language. The combinative (or syntagmatic) process manifests itself in contiguity (one word being placed next to another) and its mode is *metonymic*. The selective (or associative) process manifests itself in similarity (one word or concept being 'like' another) and its mode is *metaphoric*. The 'opposition' of metaphor and metonymy therefore may be said to represent in effect the essence of the total opposition between the *synchronic* mode of language (its immediate, coexistent, 'vertical' relationships) and its *diachronic* mode (its sequential, successive, linearly progressive relationships).[3]

Corroborating this distinction, Jakobson's research on aphasia demonstrates that two major kinds of perceptual–cognitive disorders are involved in its symptoms: those involving problems of similarity and those involving problems of contiguity. However described, these two interimplicated processes of the mental combinatory are exemplary of the patterns of binary opposition that characterize language generally. Thus vowels and consonants may be seen in terms of his distinction: the vowel expresses a sound syntagmatically, on the horizontal dimension; the consonant shapes it paradigmatically, on the vertical dimension. Furthermore, all phonemes, according to Jakobson, are defined by rule-governed, binarily contrastive relations. Indeed, language is coded in binary fashion on all levels, though the density and complexity of that coding give rise to effects that seem opaquely continuous. (Roland Barthes, among others, has asserted that analogical-continuous phenomena are not linguistically accessible unless they can be analysed as arising from some kind of digital-combinatory process similar to that involved in phoneme production.)[4]

Jonathan Culler helpfully summarizes this notion of language as differences:

> If, Saussure writes, the most precise characteristic of every sign is that it differs from other signs, then every sign in some sense bears the traces of all the other signs; they are copresent with it as the entities which define it. This means that one should not think, as logocentrism [phonocentric metaphysics of writing] would like to, of the presence in consciousness of a single autonomous signified. What is present is a network of differences.[5]

The sign, its identity thus self-divided, consists of a signifier and a signified linked only in a tentative syzygy, an iterative allegorization.[6] Thus, if I write a word, it is, in part at least, the signifier of a sound pattern that, by a different code, I might have spoken and that in turn is the signifier of a conceptual image (the signified, which Saussure carefully distinguished from the referent) in my mind that in turn is the signifier of something (the 'object' referent) semiotically constituted. But how far could this playful, abyssal regression of sign concatenated with sign, interpretation following interpretation, the perpetual generation (substitution, supplementation) of signifier by signifier, go? Could it be infinite? Or circular? The point is that a sign exists not as a *thing* at all but as a *difference* from other signs. (A sign, like a mathematical point, is meaningful only in relation to others: *no* is haunted by the ghost of *yes*, *black* by that of *white*, and so on.) It is therefore part of a system, 'a network of differences', on which its value depends, by which its significance in use is sponsored.

'Indeed,' Culler continues, 'ultimately we could say that the whole notion of a linguistic system, the whole notion of *la langue* as Saussure defines it, is that of networks of differences at the level of both signifier and signified – networks which are already in place, already inscribed or written, as it were, in the mind of the subject.'[7] (As Freud well knew, in his own terms, there are deep processes of binary differentiation in the brain/mind, intimate linkages between words with antithetical meanings.) Then mind itself, conscious and unconscious, is a network, structured and structuring, of differentiations arising somehow in the columnar neural meshes of the cerebrum.[8] The uttering ('outering') of a word is

> simply a transitory and hence imperfect way of using one network of differences (those of the signifier) to produce a form which can be interpreted in terms of the other network of differences (those of the signified). The meaning of *brown* is not some essence which was in my mind at the moment of utterance but a space in this interpersonal network of differences (the semantic system of the language).[9]

Uttering is translating, in other words. Referring, as Derrida would say, by deferment of identity. Putting something mental (how much already linguistic?) into words. Or some words into other words. Into the alterity of words.

By this way of thinking, to program a computer is to translate one network of differences (in a mind) into another (in a language) and then into another (in a machine). Similarly, in the act of writing here I am translating a network of differences in my mind into written language and thence into the mind of the reader. The writer programs the reader. But it is not simply my *parole* that is thereby shared, however imperfectly, but the *langue* itself, whose system makes possible the translation of *parole*. Thus 'what one "has in mind" while speaking or writing is not a form and meaning conjured up for a fleeting instant but the whole system of language, more permanently inscribed'.[10] *Parole* is subject to *langue*, the conscious haunted by the unconscious (as Jacques Lacan would say, the discourse of the self by the discourse of the Other).

In language, then, the parts occur in relation to the whole, *differentiae* ('differences') in the context of *differentiata* ('the differentiated'). So meaning, what is meant, the signified, is a systematically articulated space of differences, no-thing at all, a promise of some-thing that cannot be fulfilled, a pseudo-presence of the referent (all presence is derived, by illusionary indirection, from absence), a metaphysical contract breached from the beginning. One might think of semiosis in terms of a Cartesian mental space, of the signifiers as being in an asymptotic pattern within that space, of the signifieds in a corollary hyperbolic pattern. The meeting of the two patterns is forever deferred.

Words thus never mean quite what one wants them to mean: they seem exact, but what they do remains blurred, vibrant. Words also seem to tell the truth about language (though, to paraphrase Ludwig Wittgenstein, words cannot be understood by words alone) but not about 'reality'. And yet not all words are, as Saussure might have it, completely arbitrary: many of them, in certain phonesthematic situations, seem derived from or touched by one's biological being (their affective contours can be elicited with some difficulty by a good poet, though the bearing of such contours on theories of the origin of language is an old matter of controversy)[11] or his cultural context (German, for example, is characterized by consonantal precision, Italian by vocalic plenitude: the first is a language of exacting calculation; the second is one of fluid passion). But the locus of the signifieds seems always to involve a dislocation.

The logocentrist (even one as sophisticated as Walter J. Ong) pretends that language consists somehow of positive entities, believes there was a time (or is a condition) in which language, as speech, was (is) truthful, uncorrupted, totalized – an attitude Bolter exemplifies when he argues that 'Before the watershed era of printing and mathematical physics, and indeed well into that era, the sound, the vivid presence, of individual names and words meant something by itself.'[12] But this is a misplaced concreteness, an Edenic nostalgia for a situation in which signifier and signified are harmoniously joined in a closure of understanding. Discourse may desire a complete, univocal text, but there is no such text. Language is a perpetual emptiness baroquely webbed with relation. It is characterized by an awful otherness, a Shklovskian 'defamiliarization'. (To some extent all writing is aphasic, all reading dyslexic.)

Thus, when Culler says of language that 'The system is always already in place, as the ground or condition of meaning, and to interpret signs is to read them in terms of the system',[13] he means someone else's system. Or *something* else's system. Or just *another* system. Of the self and yet not of it at all. It makes perfect sense that one might attribute human language to the impersonal or the nonhuman – to a chimpanzee or a computer or something stranger still – because that seems to be its realm anyway. Yet this situation may be cause for hope concerning the possibility of a system of universal communication, a grand logospheric interconnectability of all information-processing systems of all varieties, for, as Fredric Jameson observes, 'language is a kind of *béance* or opening onto the Other (it is never a plentitude in itself, always in its very structure a formed incompleteness, waiting for the Other's participation) . . .'.[14] Because of the addressivity of language, no statement can be reduced simply to itself; as Henry Miller avers, '*Words are loneliness.*'[15] Or, by another twist, Serres:

The homoiothermal [warm-blooded] organism generates the need for communication. It is, in energy or thermal needs, analogous to what will be common speech, in terms of signals and information. I imagine that one of the first forms of behavior, like one of the first signals, may be reduced to this: 'keep me warm'.[16]

3
Relations, Origin, Silicon

The consideration of language as a system of relations gives rise to a vertiginous question, one that feels like a *petit-mal* seizure in the mind of God: what if *everything* is a network of differences, nothing . . . centred or substantial at all, concrete and particular only by the delusions of desire? The question prompts a terror, an intoxication with the bottomless and indeterminate.

But this abyss is where the modernist sensibility has been at play all along. What Saussure did to linguistics is similar to what Einstein did to physics, Picasso to painting, Schönberg to music, Whitehead to philosophy, and so on – all these revolutions depend on a strategy that 'can be stated most simply as a shift in focus, from objects to relations. It is relationships that create and define objects, not the other way around.'[1] This sensibility and its strategy turn up in everything from the aesthetics of *vers libre* or of 'composition by field' to politics as a rhetorical tangle or bureaucracy as a maze without exit. They imply an etherealization of reality, of knowledge, of experience. They imply an attention to the 'emptiness' of form (the *cénématique*) rather than to the 'fullness' of content (the *plérématique*). And they imply also an existential engagement with the troubling dialectics of consciousness as a shifting construction. The universe, for man, is not facts but only equivocal signs somehow 'about' facts.

Like the sign, like a symbol (such as an 'operator') in a computer program, even the smallest constituents of 'physical reality' appear increasingly to the new sensibility to be not so much 'matter' as nodes of energy defined by their relations to other nodes of energy. Thus, as Culler notes, 'an electron is not a positive entity in the old sense; it is a product of a field of force, a node in a system of relations, and, like a phoneme, it does not exist independently of these relations'.[2] Quarks, among the most ineffable recent products of the desire for ultimate entities, are 'known' only in terms of figurative qualities of 'charm', 'flavor', 'color', and so on. They exist as part of a language, like their predecessors that are inventoried by the letters of the Greek alphabet. (Even Lucretius spoke of atoms as letters of an alphabet.) The language never bottoms on literality: every new entity or quality of an entity turns out to be not an origin, a primitive, but something more complex. Likewise, gravity, in post-Einsteinian physics, is not so much a property of matter as an imperative of relation, of the shape of space itself. Indeed, reality, at the quantum-mechanical level where everything is 'quantum foam', seems to consist of (informational) structures that may not be bound by the four-dimensional space-time of 'classical' modern physics but rather are capable of translation through an infinite number of universes. This way of thinking necessarily involves radical reconceptions and a shift to a belief, as Georges Braque once characterized it, not in things but in relationships.[3]

Since everything is a sign (or, following Charles S. Peirce's categories, a sign as an arbitrary symbol or an index, involving a relation of cause, or an icon, involving a relation of similitude) of something else and since the sign appears to be the type of all other 'entities', the proper study of man, *homo significans*, is signs. The universe, the *human* universe, is language, a text, and all textuality differences without closure, even and especially that of the self.[4] The pencil that 'writes' the text, as in Fulvio Testa's children's book *If You Take a Pencil*, is finally the one discovered *in* the text. This is the situation addressed by constructivism, which

does not create or explain any reality 'out there'; it shows that there is no inside and no outside, no objective world facing the subjective, rather, it shows that the subject–object split, that source of myriads of 'realities,' does not exist, that the apparent separation of the world into pairs of opposites is constructed by the subject. . . .[5]

'Reality' is the structure/structuring of consciousness. The observed is still the observer, a text.

Language thus does not 'imitate' reality so much as *produce* it, bring it into being, coterminously. (A grammar is a map of the universe.) This notion is simplistically proclaimed in the Vulgate: '*In principio erat Verbum et Verbum erat apud Deum, et Deus erat Verbum* [In the beginning was the Word and the Word was with God, and the Word was God].'[6] Here again is the Edenic nostalgia: God and Word, *Deus* and *Verbum*, *Deos* and *Logos*, were once one; signifier (*signans, signifiant*) and signified (*signatum, signifié*) were continuous, undivided. Another version may be found in Emerson's chapter on language in *Nature*:

1. Words are signs of natural facts.
2. Particular natural facts are symbols of particular spiritual facts.
3. Nature is the symbol of spirit.[7]

Or, as he wrote more sophisticatedly some years later in his essay 'The Poet', 'We are symbols and inhabit symbols. . . .'[8]

But such proclamations, so easily written at one time and so seemingly permanent in their authority, are problematic in the poststructuralist age. Now man lives not so much in a house of symbols as in a labyrinth of signifiers: it has no centre and, though one may follow whatever Ariadne's thread he wishes, no outlet, no transcendental signified (no concept outside language, beyond the mechanisms of representation); its bottomlessness supports no point of view from which to establish absolute position or direction. Thus, according to Derrida, contemporary man has been subject to the dissolution of metaphysical presence (and of the classical notion of representation) and implicated in a crucial and rupturing 'event' (the consequence of Nietzschean, Freudian, and Heideggerian critiques of metaphysics since before Plato – of truth, being, consciousness, and so on), until which event

> structure – or rather the structurality of structure – . . . has always been neutralized or reduced, and this by a process of giving it a center or referring it to a point of presence, a fixed origin. The function of this center was not only to orient, balance, and organize the structure . . . but above all to make sure that the organizing principle of the structure would limit what we might call the *freeplay* of the structure.

After this event – though 'even today the notion of a structure lacking any center represents the unthinkable itself' – the 'force of a desire' holds only anxiously to the notion of centre, 'that very thing within a structure which governs the structure, while escaping structurality'. After this event, the 'metaphors and metonymies' that had maintained the 'determinations of the center', those products of a wish-fulfilment, are exposed:

From then on it was probably necessary to begin to think that there was no center, that the center could not be thought in the form of a being-present, that the center had no natural locus, that it was not a fixed locus but a function, a sort of non-locus in which an infinite number of sign-substitutions came into play. This moment was that in which language invaded the universal problematic; that in which, in the absence of a center or origin, everything became discourse – provided we can agree on this word – that is to say, when everything became a system where the central signified, the original or transcendental signified, is never absolutely present outside a system of differences. The absence of the transcendental signified extends the domain and the interplay of signification *ad infinitum*.[9]

Reality is always somewhere next, an unread text, the reading of which would be only a preface to the rereading of it – a situation Leonard Michaels explores as he toys with the final injunction of Wittgenstein's *Tractatus Logico-Philosophicus*: 'Whereof we cannot speak, we make a joke. . . . Whereof we cannot speak, silence discovers a word. . . . Whereof we cannot speak is everywhere we are.'[10] Whereof I cannot write induces a logorrhea of circumlocution and indirection.

But how did man come to this complicated situation, this fierce problematic of language? Through human language. How did *it* come to be? When did silence first discover a word? *In principio*. . . . But when was that?

The search for that origin may be characterized by a clause from Nietzsche's *Fröhliche Wissenschaft*: 'hier Schein und Irrlicht und Geister-tanz und nichts mehr ist . . . [here are illusion and will-o'-the-wisp and spirit-dance and nothing more . . .]'.[11] The search involves the pursuit of something that leaves tracks but cannot be caught, a yeti whose traces mark the absence of a presence.

An origin: a polar bear playing in the snow, an insect taking colour from its environment, so touched by context as to be indistinguishable from it. All statements about origins are suspect. (For example, is there not an aporia in trying to legitimate either *langue* or *parole* as, in any sense, prior to the other?)

And yet the origin must be (have been) there. And many have sought it. Plato, Lucretius, Vico, Locke, Condillac, Herder, Fichte, Nietzsche, and many others – an illustrious necrology of theories.[12] But many of these theories have a zombie status because they have not been pronounced unquestionably dead by any more useful or comprehensive successor; that is as true of Plato's theory as it is of Julian Jaynes's recent one.[13]

Still there must have been, somewhere 'back there', a time when a hominid started doing something that had not been done before: the pronouncement of the first word of an *Ursprache* ('original language'), the first *onomathesía* ('name-giving') – something like that. And that act would have set in motion a spiralling development whereby language generated thought that generated language that generated thought in widening patterns – a process somewhat analogous to that by which cellular automata proliferate and one suggested by Heinrich von Kleist's notion of '*die allmähliche Verfertigung der Gedanken beim Reden* [the gradual fabrication of thoughts during speech]'[14] – until the present.

For that florescence to occur, there must have been some predisposition, but how and when did it lock in? The search for the origin quickly leads to the DNA itself, which self-replicates through and spins the brain/mind with its chemo-linguistic loom. Of course, language, in various senses, *is* there, everywhere, all along: in the genetic software, in the politics of molecular structure, in the infinitesimal syntactic nuances of the subatomic, in the text of the universe. As Richard E. Palmer says, 'Just as there can be no occurrence of being without apprehending, and no apprehending without being, so also there can be no being without language, and no language without being.'[15]

And language, as an act of life-forms, must have undergone a crucial change with the development, just this side of the *Urschleim*, the primal broth or clay, of the first haploid cells. That differentiation was the birth of sex and of death, for after it there existed organisms unable to replicate perpetually their unalloyed selves. With that separateness, the now-variegated continuity of type was conditioned by the conjoining of two biological incompletions. Thence, as suggested in Plato's *Symposium*, there was a longing to remake the original genetic unity, the stasis of an immortality. But what was made was evolution. What also was made, in a whole new sense, was language.

Thereafter language is for mating, is social, is urged by a desire to communicate, to make common, to come together. But such biologically based language involves a tenuous and always interrupted coupling of self and other, messages to be understood only imperfectly, to define an alienation as much as an identity.

Each gesture is a projection of the sender bearing an imperfect image, an emptiness, for the receiver: an aggression hungering for peace. Each is an unfolding in minute stages of binary distinction – this odour and not that, then this morpheme or phoneme and not that – in order to effect the match that will trigger the fullest recognition of self by other. But that act is doomed to disjunctions, fictions, lies. Biologically based language makes for a difficult beauty that in a sense has evolved and continues to evolve simply so that DNA may communicate ever more complexly with itself.

And what forms beyond the human could evolve, what new kinds of difficult beauty? Robert Jastrow ventures an answer:

> So we are a finished chapter in evolution: our story is written. We are on the way to being living fossils. But the history of life indicates that man is likely to be the rootstock out of which a higher form will evolve. It will not be a more intelligent man – man is *Homo sapiens* – but rather a new form, something beyond man. . . .
>
> I say that computers, as we call them, are a newly emerging form of life, one made out of silicon rather than carbon. Silicon is chemically similar to carbon, but it can enter into a sort of metal structure in which it is relatively invulnerable to damage, is essentially immortal, and can be extended to an arbitrarily large brain size. Such new forms of life will have neither human emotions nor any of the other trappings we associate with human life.[16]

The rise of silicon 'life', silicon intelligence: a Promethean act of technology and language. One may imagine silicon entities floating through deep space, manipulating signifiers beyond human ken.

Perhaps man longs for silicon, longs to become silicon – actively, though only half-consciously – and anxiously awaits the silicon metamorphosis, that *Aufhebung* ('sublation') of the man–machine dialectic, that fulfilment of a next stage. Perhaps carbon itself, in the relay race of evolution, grows weary and is ready to pass the baton of consciousness on to its sister molecule. Perhaps something in the cusped ripeness of the human experiment desires overwhelmingly that mortal neurons freeze into eternal circuits, desires a silicon god to resolve the nightmare of human history –

a *deus ex machina*, a Second Coming, a re-entering of Eden (and a recovery of Edenic language?) by surrogation. Mind colonizing non-mind thus could have eschatological consequences: mind generates the language that generates the machine that generates a new kind of mind that generates a new kind of language that generates . . . what?

But this possibility is difficult to imagine, its terms perhaps confused. Just when one discerns that a computer is beginning to 'think' (is this a catachresis or not?) like a human being, to take the human imprint, to pass the Turing test in spades, one discovers that an inverted test applies, that the operator is 'thinking' like the computer. And does not the computer operator, that exemplar of the onanistic personality, always want to discover more meaning in the machine than is really there? Does he not desire its autonomy? Does he not create the machine and then wish for it to become a black box, an other as unknowable as his fellow human beings? Does he not wish for it to reflect and then transcend his own image? Does he not know that, just as human muscles are not necessarily needed for transportation, so human minds may not necessarily be needed for thought and communication? And does he not know that his own mystification comes about precisely because of how the machine appropriates (or *seems* to appropriate?) language – an appropriation that denies the familiarity of that language and makes it recondite?[17]

4

Writing, *Urtext*, Bullae

But to gain perspective on such questions, let me begin again, however questionably, with beginnings.

Though the problem of the *Ursprache* remains insoluble, there are intriguing clues about the origin and development of writing. (Here I am concerned with writing more or less in the conventional sense. Though it may exist apart from speech – especially in the case of Derrida's *archi-écriture* ('protowriting') or *écriture*, generalized and conditionally prior to both speech and writing in the conventional sense – it is usually defined as the transdialectal print-code form of a language or, to use a term attributed to Einar Haugen, its grapholect.) Such clues may be found in Denise Schmandt-Besserat's report of her research on the prototypes of the ideographs developed by the Sumerians, who are generally believed to have invented writing. She notes that, while there are a number of writing systems that can be traced back to their apparent origins – Chinese ideographs to hieractic engravings in the plastron of tortoiseshells from the second millennium B.C., for example, or Mayan hieroglyphics to calendrical notations from a thousand years later – they were relatively late inventions. She is looking for something impossible, an *Urtext*, the precursive form of all known writing systems, and the developmental logic that can connect it to those systems.

It is clear from the excavations of Julius Jordan in 1929 and 1930 that at the end of the fourth millennium B.C. officials in such Sumerian city-states as Uruk had developed and were using 'a system of recording numerals, pictographs and ideographs on specially prepared clay surfaces. (A pictograph is a more or less realistic portrayal of the object it is supposed to represent; an ideograph is an abstract sign.)'[1] The characters were inscribed by means of a stylus made of wood, bone, or ivory, one end of which was blunt, the other pointed. Numerical signs were impressed into the clay, the others incised. (*Writing*, as its etymology shows, has to do with scratching, cutting, wounding, even killing ['the letter killeth . . .']. Writing always seems more

17

aggressive, more exterior, more machine-like than speech with its apparent absolute presence and immediate interchange of meaning.)[2] And the repertory of such characters ran to about 1500. Schmandt-Besserat expatiates on a problem in accounting for the kind of writing found on these clay tablets:

> Hypotheses about the origin of writing generally postulate an evolution from the concrete to the abstract: an initial pictographic stage that in the course of time and perhaps because of the carelessness of scribes becomes increasingly schematic. The Uruk tablets contradict this line of thought. Most of the 1,500 signs . . . are totally abstract ideographs; a few pictographs represent such wild animals as the wolf and the fox or items of advanced technology such as the chariot and the sledge. Indeed, the Uruk texts remain largely undeciphered and an enigma to epigraphers. The few ideographic signs that have been identified are those that can be traced back stage by stage from a known cuneiform character of later times to an archaic Sumerian prototype. From the fragmentary textual contents that such identities allow it appears that the scribes of Uruk mainly recorded such matters as business transactions and land sales. Some of the terms that appear most frequently are those for bread, beer, sheep, cattle and clothing.[3]

An interesting question arises: what if the tendency was to codify in the more abstract form those things that were more familiar (bread, sheep, and so on) and in the more concrete form those things that were less familiar (wild animals, new technological devices, and so on)? One could make a good psycholinguistic argument in that regard. But back to the text at hand.

Epigraphers who hold to the concrete-to-abstract hypothesis attempt to resolve the contradiction by arguing that there must have been earlier pictographic predecessors to the ideographs on the Uruk tablets and that they cannot be found because they were recorded in perishable media. Schmandt-Besserat, however, proposes an alternative hypothesis and supports it with a plentitude of evidence. In searching for the characters that precede those of the Sumerian texts, she was attracted to A. Leo Oppenheim's analysis of the function, in an ancient recording system, of certain tokens discovered during excavations, roughly contemporaneous with Jordan's, at the site of the ancient city of

Nuzi that flourished in the second millennium B.C. in what is now Iraq. Such tokens, in addition to extensive cuneiform records, apparently were used by the Nuzi palace administration as a tangible means of accounting. They are of clay and are moulded in a variety of more or less geometric shapes. And similar tokens, dating back another 1500 years, have been found at the Elamite site of Susa. As Schmandt-Besserat's research continued, it became clear not only that the token system was much older than the Sumerian tablets (it dates back to the ninth millennium B.C.) and was widely used (at sites that extend throughout western Asia) but also that the shapes of the tokens, whether geometric or crudely representational, prefigure the shapes of many of the characters found in the Sumerian texts. The outline of an implicit hypothesis begins to emerge here, but there is another, more crucial connection.

Around the end of the fourth millennium B.C., groups of tokens that constituted the records of a transaction were stored and transmitted in clay bullae ('bubbles'), 'envelopes'. The bullae served in effect as bills of lading (writing is where the writer is not) that were marked by personal seals, sent along with goods in transit, and then used to verify the kinds and quantities of goods delivered. And here is the connection: 'The surface of the bulla was marked so that in addition to the validating seal impressions, it bore images of all the enclosed tokens.' Discussing this innovation, Schmandt-Besserat elaborates her hypothesis:

> At first the innovation flourished because of its convenience; anyone could 'read' what tokens a bulla contained and how many without destroying the envelope and its seal impressions. What then happened was virtually inevitable, and the substitution of two-dimensional portrayals of the tokens for the tokens themselves would seem to have been the crucial link between the archaic recording system and writing. The hollow bullae with their enclosed tokens would have been replaced by inscribed solid clay objects: tablets.

In other words, written records. Thus 'the appearance of writing in Mesopotamia represents a logical step in the evolution of a system of record keeping that originated some 11,000 years ago', a step that came with the rise of cities and the expansion of trade on a large scale. Finally, she concludes, 'Images of the tokens soon supplanted the tokens themselves, and the evolution of symbolic objects into ideographs led to the rapid adoption of writing all across western Asia.'[4]

Here is something interesting: an ancient relation between counting and language, numbers ('counters') and words, commerce and communication. The notion that language is always somehow political has a thread of connection with this hypothesized origin of writing in economics. Writing begins with record keeping, strings of symbols, lists, keeping track of things through an abstracted nomenclature, the graphic ordering of signs that reflect/construct the order of the world and its transactions.

Yet surely something has been lost, as René Thom and others have observed, in the history of both Eastern and Western writing that has involved a gradual but intractable subjugation of the signified to the signifier, a triumph of the abstract over the concrete, of the arbitrary over the orally affective and graphically (curiologically) representational – a transformation perhaps prophesied by the fact that Thoth, the Egyptian god of science, was also the god of writing, which strips the voice from the sign. Or do I indulge in nostalgia?

5

Invisibility, Children, Rules

If phylogenetic theories of the origin of language are quicksand and the history of writing is just now being pieced together, what about ontogenetic theories? What can they tell about the relations between mind and language?

The very young, as Novalis once averred, are still unknown lands – almost as unknown as the remote past. According to Roger Brown, a basic problem in language-acquisition research is that 'linguistic processes, in general, tend to be invisible. The mind's eye seeks the meaning and notices the medium as little as the physical eye notices its own aqueous humor.'[1] For the most part the invisible remains disturbingly invisible, and little is known about those processes; there is access to only certain resultant stages of them.

Brown asks the key question: 'How is it possible for a child to extract from the finite sample of speech he happens to hear a latent structure that will enable him to construct indefinitely numerous new sentences, sentences he has never heard and which even may never have been spoken by anyone?'[2] Apparently it is possible because of an innate linguistic capability (as Heidegger would say, language, not man, speaks) that spurs theorizing about language patterns – under the control of some kind of developing executive routine. Thus it is possible, Brown argues, that the creativity of children's language can be accounted for by their working out 'rules for the speech they hear, passing from levels of lesser to greater complexity, simply because the human species is programmed at a certain period in its life to operate in this fashion on linguistic input'.[3] Even the Wild Boy of Aveyron, according to Jean-Marc-Gaspard Itard, could be taught a good deal of language, could, in other words, use that program, albeit retardedly.[4] But Brown notes that the child's 'induction of latent structure' in learning to use even such relatively simple structures as noun phrases is a far more complex process than can be explained by present learning theory: 'The very intricate simultaneous differentiation and integration that constitutes the evolution of the noun phrase is more reminiscent of the biological development of an embryo than it is of the acquisition of a conditioned reflex.'[5] Though the evidence suggests strongly that the neural activity of language is organized by a biomorphology mandated by the genetic program and conditioned by developmental factors, there is as yet no adequate theory of that biomorphology.

What *is* known, according to Brown, is that children, in their use of ungrammatical and immature forms (their interlanguage, so to speak), 'are alike in the innate knowledge, language processing routines, preferences, and assumptions they bring to the problem of language acquisition. One such preference seems to be for a small number of rules of maximal generality.' The heuristic principle here, as in many kinds of research, is that a system discloses more about itself through its apparent aberrancies than through its normal functions – as long as one has a cogent sense of the normal. What is inferred in this case is that such a preference causes the application of rules that 'are much closer to the base structure than are the transformed adult forms. The transformations are certainly language specific and so must be learned. The base structure has a better chance of being universal and innate.'[6]

The child's understanding of those rules constitutes a theory of the language he is learning. Brown suspects that

> the only force toward grammaticality operating on the child is the occasional mismatch between his theory of the structure of the language and the data he receives. Piaget's terms 'assimilation' (the present theory), 'accommodation' (the impact of the data), and 'disequilibrium' (the mismatch) were created to deal with a similar lack of extrinsic motivation in the child for progressing toward operativity.

What the child is learning by this process is 'the adult grammar', one that clearly differs from his, and in that learning

> there is a sequence among well-formed constructions from those that are derivationally simple . . . toward those that are derivationally complex. . . . It seems to be the case (when a lot of underbrush is hacked away) that control of the base structure precedes control of transformational knowledge and that simple sentences precede conjoinings and embeddings . . . ,'[7]

Three main problems (besides his precarious reliance on now-controversial Chomskyan concepts) still lurk in Brown's formulations: in the hierarchies of some children's vocabularies the simpler and more concrete terms are learned first and the complex and more abstract 'probably . . . never learned first', while in the hierarchies of others' there is a development 'in both directions from a middle level of abstraction'; language data sometimes have a marked impact on the child and at other times no apparent effect at all; and in the child's learning sequence there is not always 'a progression from derivational simplicity to complexity'.[8] Such problems do not, however, abrogate the notion that behind even the most seemingly unruly anomalies there are rules, whether or not they are consciously comprehended – by either child or language researcher. Let me discuss what is established or theorized about some of those rules.

According to Breyne Arlene Moskowitz, children learn language (speech initially, of course) by analysing the language they experience into its simplest components and then extrapolating the rules of phonology, syntax, semantics, and pragmatics they need to reassemble the components into forms that are communicatively effective. They do this by an economy that constantly dedicates their linguistic energies first to the most general characteristics of the language and then gradually to the more specific. And, as any parent knows, the world as language must be addressed to the child, so that his own being as language may come into relation with its permeating webs of significance. (As Wittgenstein says, one cannot hear God when He speaks to someone else.) Furthermore, the child's play with language, the dance of signifiers, must be guided to some extent.

Children thus 'construct their initial grammars on the basis of the short, simple, grammatical sentences that are addressed to them in the first year or two they speak'. With progressive elaboration 'it is the consistent departures from the adult model that indicate the nature of a child's current hypotheses about the grammar of a language'.[9] In the application of those hypotheses, the child almost invariably first builds sentences of one word (the 'holophrastic' stage), then of two words (a stage, the early 'telegraphic', that Martin D. S. Braine and others have characterized in terms of various kinds of 'pivot grammar' by which a large percentage of two-word sentences can be analysed in terms of a 'pivot' word and an 'open' word – a seemingly clever approach that has been convincingly rejected by Brown),[10] and then, after the crossing of a threshold (late in the telegraphic stage), of virtually any number of words, with appropriate collocations (the 'recursive' stage). At the one-word stage the child is already involved in syntactic analysis and allocates attention, as information theory would predict and as his cognitive economy mandates, mostly to words 'reflecting what is new in a particular situation', what is surprising or of low probability. At the two-word stage he is building combinations and using them 'vertically' (a stacking that occurs at the one-word stage also) one after the other to express what an adult would say in a sentence (built 'horizontally'). At this stage 'new forms are used for old functions and new functions are expressed by old forms' in a pattern of 'controlled dovetailing' that 'can be observed in all areas of language acquisition'. At the multi-word stage (there is no three-word stage as such) the constraints that require vertical constructions are lifted. But speech at this stage tends for a while to be telegraphic – again as information theory would predict and as cognitive economy mandates – and to consist largely of simple sentences constructed with 'words that are rich in semantic content, usually nouns and verbs'.[11]

In the child's construction of his grammar, he learns earliest 'those forms that exhibit the least variation', and the general progression is from the conceptually simple to the conceptually complex. Thus 'The past tense is acquired after the progressive and present tenses, because the relative time it represents is conceptually more difficult. The future tense . . . is formed regularly in English and is as predictable as the progressive tense, but it is a much more abstract concept than the past tense. Therefore it is acquired much later.' Moreover, it is interesting in this regard that the child acquires at different times morphemes that are identically pronounced but grammatically distinct. Moskowitz considers a key set of three:

> They are the plural '-s,' the possessive '-s' and the third-person singular tense ending '-s,' and they are acquired in the order of listing. Roman Jakobson of Harvard has suggested that the explanation of this phenomenon has to do with the complexity of the different relations the morphemes signal: the singular–plural distinction is at the word level, the possessive relates two

nouns at the phrase level and the tense ending relates a noun and a verb at the clause level.

Also, the child's cognitive economy is such that he frequently will omit present-tense forms of *to be* not only beause they are variable and irregular but also because (as Russian and other languages show) they 'are essentially meaningless, and omitting them is a very sensible strategy for a child who must maximize the information content of a sentence and place priorities on linguistic structures still to be tackled'.[12]

Moskowitz observes that children, in progressing through the stages of acquiring a word, typically use the proper forms of irregular past tenses and plurals and then subsequently 'regress' to the use of regularized but ungrammatical forms of such words. For example, the child first uses *went* and then substitutes *goed*, or first *feet* and then *foots*. The apparent regression is explained by the fact that the child initially imitates the form as heard but then abandons the imitation for the application of a general rule. In other words, the child places a higher priority on systematization than on imitation. The processing of certain exceptional data is postponed in favour of the use of general concepts – a principle that seems to apply throughout acquisition and may resolve the problem in Brown's formulations of language data sometimes having no apparent impact on the child. A highly selective and purposeful economy of attention is involved.

But the interaction of imitation and rule-application is surely more complex than Moskowitz's observations suggest, and I suspect that a fuller understanding of that interaction would offer approaches to the two other problems in Brown's formulations. Doubtless the child is continually changing the ratio of abstract-complex to concrete-simple forms. Also, as Moskowitz notes in discussing the rule-governed way the child learns to use negatives – and her statement must apply more generally – 'There are clearly variations in the hypotheses children make in the process of constructing grammar.'[13]

Moskowitz's research discloses much that is germane to the Sausurrean-structuralist model of language as a relational system of differences. For example, a critical process in the child's learning, enmeshed as it is in differential semiotic valorizations, is that whereby he learns gradually to distinguish between words that are paired opposites and, further, to distinguish the unmarked from the marked member of the pair – that is, the member that is used normatively from the one that is not (of the pair *wide–narrow*, *wide* is the unmarked member). In other words, this process involves the child's learning the subtleties by which words semantically haunt each other, which counters his initial tendency to overextend meanings just as he does all his general rules. So the child also tends to overgeneralize sound patterns – pronounciation is always systematic, even when incorrect – and must learn the subtleties of binary differentiation, that primary act of and stimulus to perception. It is finally 'not individual sounds' that the child acquires 'but the distinctive features of sound, that is, the minimal differences, or contrasts, between sounds'.[14] Thus Moskowitz's analysis suggests strongly that the child learns a language by the gradual refinement, through increasingly intricate patterns of relational distinction (an evolving Derridean *écriture*), of his model of its variegated system. And his learning is governed by an accelerative logic, so that he is driven from stage to stage by the exfoliation of powerful hypotheses insisting that the whole be grasped before the parts are mastered.

6

Chimpanzees, Gorillas, Fictionalization

If research on the child's acquisition of language is blocked by an invisibility, what about research, still quite controversial, on the acquisition of human language by chimpanzees and gorillas? There is an invisibility there too – but partly of a different kind.

The controversies about such acquisition have raged unabated and indeed increased in ferocity since at least a half century ago when Vygotsky argued that the correspondence between thought and speech characteristic of man is absent in his anthropoid relatives.[1] Thomas A. Sebeok and others have made a crusade of refuting the results of such acquisition experiments as artefacts arising from unconscious teacher cueing. Herbert S. Terrace has concluded, from research conducted with a chimpanzee named Nim Chimpsky (Noam Chomsky vehemently denies the possibility of apes learning human language), that apes cannot learn even the rudiments of English grammar and can engage only in rote, imitative repetitions without growth in grammatical complexity.[2] Many other researchers, however, have argued that Terrace's teaching procedures are wrong, and E. Sue Savage-Rumbaugh and her colleagues, using carefully designed (and blinded) procedures, have denied more or less persuasively the contention that chimpanzee language-learning is only the result of some kind of Clever Hans effect and conclude that 'chimpanzees have a genuine innate potential for symbolic communication' and can communicate with each other using symbols representing words in English.[3] One guesses that those conclusions would hold for other kinds of apes as well, though surely the extent to which such animals are *predisposed* to learn verbal language is severely limited. The controversies that such conclusions prompt (concerning intention, productivity, and so on) doubtless will continue to multiply.

The most interesting controversies have to do with exactly what those nonhuman primates have learned (by whatever means) and with the apparent limitations of their acquisition; that is, they have to do, as will be seen, with why human beings can learn and use their language so much more readily than other primates can. In dealing with such issues, I have no desire – to borrow a term from Steven Rose – to embrace _chimpomorphia_ (the ethological fallacy that man is to be understood simply by studying other animals).[4] I wish, for the present, only to recount and assess.

Attempts earlier in this century to teach chimpanzees oral language failed for the most part – simply because those animals cannot alter their vocal tracts to make the sounds of human languages and because the vocalizations of which they are capable are not easily subject to trained control. Then in the 1960s R. Allen Gardner and Beatrice T. Gardner broke the sound barrier and taught a chimpanzee named Washoe to use Ameslan (the American sign language of the deaf). In four years Washoe had learned to use over 80 different signs, and the patterns of her learning resembled in many ways those of a human child. For instance, she used signs one at a time first, then in combinations, and finally in longer sequences. The game had begun.

In the late 1960s David Premack became interested in how much a chimpanzee really is aware of the syntactic relationships among sentence elements. He taught a chimpanzee named Sarah to communicate by means of combinations of plastic tokens of various sizes, shapes, and colours, which were arbitrarily associated with various objects in her experimental environment. Thus Sarah's token, like Washoe's signs, were based on associations that were both taught and arbitrary. She learned to express herself in three- and four-token sentences, sometimes apparently quite spontaneously and creatively; she seemed – though questions, especially concerning semantics, still remain – to have some grasp of syntactic necessities and could use several hundred tokens.

Further experiments by other researchers with other chimpanzees confirm the animal's ability to use (but how invariantly?) arbitrary signs in sentences that apparently are appropriate to context and even innovative. Carl Sagan begins a discussion of some of these experiments by wondering if 'beasts' are capable of abstraction. He considers the research with Washoe, Sarah, and other chimpanzees and concludes that they are – though surely not in the same way that man is. He is particularly intrigued by Lana, a chimpanzee that has been taught by Duane

M. Rumbaugh to communicate with a computer in a language called Yerkish. The machine makes available to Lana a variety of things (candy, music, movies, and so on) when she requests them – through a large, arbitrarily encoded keyboard – in proper grammatical form. Furthermore, she 'monitors her sentences on a computer display, and erases those with grammatical errors'.[5] And, as Sagan argues, she can be quite creative, sometimes requesting things the machine cannot supply.

Declaring that 'Lana can be said to write' in terms of the logic tree of Yerkish and even wondering if dolphins, which communicate 'by the use of a kind of audio rebus', can 'create extraordinary audio images out of their imaginations rather than their experience', Sagan discusses Helen Keller's discovery of language and weighs the proposition that man, as well as other animals, especially nonhuman primates, has 'a latent capability for language'. He notes that

> This essentially Platonic idea is also . . . consistent with what is known, from brain lesions, of the physiology of the neocortex; and also with the theoretical conclusions drawn by Noam Chomsky. . . . In recent years it has become clear that the brains of nonhuman primates are similarly prepared, although probably not to the same degree, for the introduction of language.

And he even speculates about how chimpanzees might form a new 'culture' and, after many years, have myths about the 'divine beings' who had given them 'the gift of language'.[6] While he is not as careful in making his conclusions and speculations as the researchers on whom he reports (Duane M. Rumbaugh, for example, has become sceptical about the chimpanzee's ability to manage English syntax),[7] he does intuit the possible scale of significance of what they are doing.

What about gorillas?

The most well-known research concerned with teaching human language to gorillas is that of the developmental psychologist Francine Patterson. Her research with a gorilla named Koko is startling in its possible implications though still under fire from those who criticize her procedures and conclusions.

Koko's linguistic abilities appear to be every bit as impressive as those of Washoe, Sarah, and Lana – even more so, really, since she not only makes effective use of Ameslan but also 'talks' through a typewriter-style keyboard coded with 46 arbitrary signs and linked through a computer to a speech synthesizer. She commands an Ameslan vocabulary of several hundred words. Moreover, Patterson reports, 'Koko can sign and speak simultaneously.'[8]

Like language-trained chimpanzees, Koko can describe objects for which she has no Ameslan sign by making appropriate and innovative combinations. Washoe labelled swans 'water birds', for example; Koko has labelled a zebra a 'white tiger' and a mask an 'eye hat'. But even more interesting is her apparent ability to use *displacement*. 'A cardinal characteristic of human language', it is 'the ability to refer to events removed in time and place from the act of communication'. For example, one conversation between Koko and her teacher concerned not only a past event but a past 'emotional state' as well. 'Gradually,' Patterson claims, 'Koko is acquiring signs that make reference to past and future.'[9]

Finally, Koko lies. Several conversations recounted by Patterson apparently demonstrate that. And the animal's ability to lie may involve even more impressive fictionalizing capabilities:

> Perhaps the most telling, yet elusive, evidence that a creature can displace events is lying. When someone tells a lie, he is using language to distort the listener's perception of reality. He is using symbols to describe something that never happened, or won't happen. Evidence I have been accumulating strongly suggests that Koko expresses a make-believe capacity similar to humans'.[10]

Patterson's research is, of course, hardly completed. There is a great deal yet to be learned about the gorilla's acquisition and use of human language. Especially, as is the case also with chimpanzee research, there remains the major objective of evaluating the animal's semantics and its 'sense of spoken word order'.[11] But on the basis of such research, no matter how problematic, one might safely propose at least that some nonhuman animals are capable of trying to accommodate a language quite different from the ones they typically use. From such research one may learn, if nothing else, something about the complexity of human linguistic abilities and about what is encountered in trying to simulate them by machine.

7

Alternity, Acquisition, Invariance

I wonder if that aphasic moment when a word evades me is not suggestive of how a nonverbal animal engages the universe. But then when the word 'comes to mind', it has already reconstructed and particularized consciousness. It has the power to revise reality or even to generate alternate realities: fantasies, myths, lies. With the word forgotten or never learned, the universe must be taken nakedly, without the shaping gloss. For man the aphasic moment is a moment of irritation and dislocation, perhaps even panic or mental evacuation, or perhaps – if experienced religiously – of Buddhistic enlightenment.

What is this revisionary and generative power of language? It has to do with displacement, of course; but it involves other habilitations as well, as Steiner indicates in his discussion of 'counter-factual conditionals':

> No less than future tenses to which they are, one feels, related, and with which they ought probably to be classed in the larger set of 'suppositionals' or 'alternates,' these 'if' propositions are fundamental to the dynamics of human feeling. They are the elbow room of the mind, its literal *Lebensraum*. The difference between an artificial language such as FORTRAN, programmed by information and computer theorists, and natural language is one of vital ambiguities, of chimeric potentiality and undecidability. Given a vocabulary and a set of procedural rules (both subject to change), given the limitations of comprehensibility and certain performance boundaries (no endless sentences), we can *say anything*. This latent totality is awesome and should be felt as such.

Thus along with the ability to speak of the past exists the ability to speak of the future, the alternate, the conditional – to cover the emperor of the universe with whatever clothes can be imagined.

Man thereby projects 'thought and imagination into the "if-ness," into the free conditionalities of the unknown'. That fact involves one of Steiner's key points:

> *Language is the main instrument of man's refusal to accept the world as it is.* Without that refusal, without the unceasing generation by the mind of 'counter-worlds' – a generation which cannot be divorced from the grammar of counter-factual and optative forms – we would turn forever on the treadmill of the present. Reality would be (to use Wittgenstein's phrase in an illicit sense) 'all that is the case' and nothing more. Ours is the ability, the need, to gainsay or 'un-say' the world, to image and speak it otherwise.

And, he speculates, 'It is not, perhaps, "a theory of information" that will serve us best in trying to clarify the nature of language, but a "theory of misinformation".'[1] Human information is always coloured, alloyed, in error; the text is always already misread. 'Things as they are / Are changed upon the blue guitar', as one of Wallace Stevens's personae nicely put it.[2]

Steiner is concerned to find a word for 'the compulsion of language to posit "otherness"'. He settles on 'alternity', a generalized faculty for lying. And he appropriately quotes Nietzsche in corroboration: '"We invent for ourselves the major part of experience," says Nietzsche in *Beyond Good and Evil* ("wir erdichten . . ." signifying "to create fictionally," "to render dense and coherent through *poiesis*"). Or as he puts in it *Morgenröte*, man's genius is one of lies.'[3] That genius has been favoured by evolution. It is a power that violates the closure of reality, the seeming opacity of the word – a gift or curse, depending on how it is used.

The power of alternity allows man the sense of possibility he needs to live and grow; indeed, it may construct the only world he can bear to inhabit. Certainly it has been important in his creation of the computer, is implicated in his belief that he might communicate more fully with his fellow primates, and propels his elaboration of the involutions of poststructuralist thought. 'It is our syntax,' says Steiner, 'not the physiology of the body or the thermodynamics of the planetary system, which is full of tomorrows. . . . We speak, we dream ourselves free of the organic trap. Ibsen's phrase pulls together the whole evolutionary

argument: man lives, he progresses by virtue of "the Life-Lie".'
Language is the deconstructive means of escape:

> Every act of speech has a potential of invention, a capacity to
> initiate, sketch, or construct 'anti-matter' (the terminology of
> particle physics and cosmology, with its inference of 'other
> worlds,' is exactly suggestive of the entire notion of 'alternity'). In
> fact, this *poiesis* or dialectic of counter-statement is even more
> complex, because the 'reality' which we oppose or set aside is
> itself very largely a linguistic product. It is made up of
> metonymies, metaphors, classifications which man originally
> spun around the inchoate jumble of perceptions and phenomena.
> But the cardinal issue is this: the 'messiness' of language, its
> fundamental difference from the ordered, closed systematization
> of mathematics or formal logic, the polysemy of individual words,
> are neither a defect nor a surface feature. . . . The fundamental
> 'looseness' of natural language is crucial to the creative functions
> of internalized and outward speech. A 'closed' syntax, a formally
> exhaustible semantics, would be a closed world. . . . This evasion
> of the 'given fact,' this gainsaying is inherent in the combinatorial
> structure of grammar, in the imprecision of words, in the
> persistently altering nature of usage and correctness. New worlds
> are born between the lines.

There is also, as he goes on to say, an ambivalence in this
creativity, a 'reciprocal motion of loss and creation . . . in all
verbalized consciousness',[4] but the main point that his observations
are serving here is obvious: man and ape may be possessed of
similar linguistic abilities at some level, but there is an astounding
difference of degree that finally involves important differences of
quality. The ape's world will never be linguistically open the way
man's is – because man is equipped with a much more powerful
mechanism for acquiring and using language, one that, Steiner
implies, is beyond simulation by machine.

Indeed, as has been seen, the child's acquisition of language is
a tremendously impressive process. In George A. Miller's
phrasing, a child is a 'spontaneous apprentice' at the use of
language.[5] Early on, he can place in his mental lexicon and retain
some of the syntactic and semantic features of a word he has
heard only once. That mental lexicon comprises the categories he
learns to use in covering his environment with words, and his

burgeoning sense of grammar guides his semiotic structuring of it. For the most part he knows the signifiers of his language before he learns their signifieds, and he spends considerable time frustrated by their problematic interrelations. As he grows, he builds specific and increasingly complex routines for applying labels and for making utterances appropriate to those applications; but the relation of concepts (which he typically cannot use formally until he is nearly pubescent) to lexical items in this process, like many other aspects of it, is hardly well understood.

Many theorists from various disciplines have proposed that there are in man innate structures and functions of the brain/mind that, coupled with his vocal apparatus and manual dexterity, make him a language user of an *entirely* different order in comparison to other animals. Those structures and functions frequently are hypothesized to constitute a language-acquisition mechanism that, as Douglas R. Hofstadter says of the ability of a computer to perform arithmetic operations, 'is not coded into pieces of data stored in memory; it is, in fact, represented nowhere in memory, but rather in the wiring patterns of the hardware'.[6] Such a mechanism, in other words, would have to exist in the form of built-in programming.

In this connection, Brown, reviewing research on acquisition, observes that 'it appears to be the case that the derivational complexity of English constructions within a generative grammar predicts fairly well the order in which the constructions will be acquired in childhood', and he wonders, 'What will it mean if, when much more evidence is in, it does indeed appear that the course of development is in important ways universal?' He ventures an answer:

A universal order of development may . . . mean that the brain of our species is programmed to operate in quite definite ways upon any materials that manifest the properties of language; that language materials set off programs of analysis which discover in these materials those structural properties that are not universal, the rules that are local and variable; and that rules of various kinds are sought in a fixed order. Initially, perhaps, grammatical functional forms, however these may be universally defined, are disregarded and there is a search for whatever rules of order are used in the expression of basic semantic operations and relations. . . . And perhaps these processes succeed one another in a relatively fixed order and produce the invariant features of the development of language in children.[7]

There are a number of qualifications to be set alongside such speculations – that the Chomskyan theory on which Brown relies is inadequate (it does a poor job of accounting for the child's sense of correspondence between logical and grammatical relations, for instance), that a great deal more research needs to be done on the acquisition of non-English (especially non-Indo-European) languages, and so on – but, none the less, it is encouraging that Moskowitz's findings, which are historically subsequent to Brown's speculations, tend to support them.

If man has an innate language-acquisition mechanism, little is known about it.[8] None the less, there is some knowledge about the neural basis of language acquisition and use; there is some intelligent theorizing beyond that; and there is at least some research that seems to be asking the right questions in the right way. And it all points toward one large and overarching issue: what kind of transformation the brain/mind underwent in its evolutionary history that endowed human beings with such extraordinary linguistic aptitude.

8

Transformation, Discontinuity, Metalanguage

Life on Earth began some three or four billion years ago with a protein text embedded in the progenote, the ancestor of all cells. Its first major transformation was an act of information: the emergence of an organism that could perpetuate itself and evolve through the communication of its form and formal variations from generation to generation – biogenesis. The second major transformation, some 300-odd million years ago, occurred when 'there emerged an organism that for the first time in the history of the world had more information in its brains than in its genes'.[1] That transformation involved a radical morphogenesis, a revolution in the differentiation of the nervous system (itself a language) that separated it from the alimentary system and centralized its power. The third major transformation was the development, within the last million years or so, of the human brain, a structure that now has created more information exterior to itself, in human culture, than it could ever contain within its own boundaries. This last transformation involved a morphogenesis that, when its various aspects are taken together, was not only radical but singular.

Compared to the brains of other animals, the human brain is characterized by the highest ratio of brain mass to body mass, a ratio that is a much better index of relative intelligence than brain mass alone. It was the increase in that ratio, together with enriched innervation and a shift in the patterns of differentiation, that somehow made man the premier symbolic animal. It did not just happen. There had to be some dialectic whereby the human brain was selected for.

It is known with some certainty that the development of frontal lobes in the primate line began at least some 50-odd million years ago, as evidenced by endocranial casts of the Eocene prosimian *Tetonius*, an animal that shows an intermediate stage in the centralization of neural power. Later evidence, dating back to about 18 million years ago, shows further development of the lobes (but without extensive neocortical convolutions) in the Miocene anthropoid *Proconsul* or *Dryopithecus*, and similar, contemporary evidence is found in the case of *Ramapithecus*.[2] But the cranial volumes of those creatures are small compared to that of modern man. The takeoff in the development of those lobes and associated cerebral structures did not occur until about a million years ago.

What began then was an accelerative dialectic of protohuman and human nature that gave rise to the interlocked faculties of perception, cognition, and imagination that make possible human language and technology, human culture. Sagan comments on this unfolding:

> The development of human culture and the evolution of those physiological traits we consider characteristically human most likely proceeded – almost literally – hand in hand: the better our genetic predispositions for running, communicating and manipulating, the more likely we were to develop effective tools and hunting strategies; the more adaptive our tools and hunting strategies, the more likely it was that our characteristic genetic endowments would survive.[3]

Beyond any doubt man's survival and evolution in Pliocene and Pleistocene Africa depended on his abilities both to hunt effectively and to avoid being hunted effectively by the carnivorous predators in his environment – depended, in general, on his ability to engage his environment by efficient individual and, especially, communal strategies. Those strategies in turn depended on technology and communication, first gestural and then verbal – tools and words 'hand in hand'. And the transition from gestures to words was crucial:

> the repertoire of ideas and the speed with which ideas can be communicated in gestural or sign languages is limited. Darwin pointed out that gestural languages cannot usefully be employed while our hands are otherwise occupied, or at night, or when our view of the hands is obstructed. One can imagine gestural languages being gradually supplemented and then supplanted by verbal languages. . . .

That supplantation would have been especially important because the hands thereby would be freed for toolmaking and the application of tools (and for developing the dexterity required for written language) while the mouth, along with a highly sensitive and directional ear, was serving the purposes of a richer and more rapid symbolic communication. 'But all of this,' Sagan observes, 'could not have occurred without a restructuring of the brain', and he cites the research of Ralph L. Holloway, who

> believes that a region of the brain known as Broca's area, one of several centers required for speech, can be detected in fossil endocasts; and that he has found evidence for Broca's area in a *Homo habilis* fossil more than two million years old. The development of language, tools and culture may have occurred roughly simultaneously.[4]

It proceeded through a creature with an increasingly strong nisus toward multiplicative systems (languages that generate languages, tools that make tools).

Jacob Bronowski offers some apposite observations about that restructuring since the time of *Australopithecus*:

> The crucial change in the human brain in this million years or so has not been so much the increase in size by a factor of three, but the concentration of that increase in three or four main areas. The visual area has increased considerably, and, compared with the chimpanzee, the actual density of human brain cells is at least 50 percent greater. A second increase has taken place in the area of manipulation of the hand, which is natural since we are much more hand-driven animals than monkeys and apes. Another main increase has taken place in the temporal lobe, in which visual memory, integration, and speech all lie fairly close together. And the fourth great increase has taken place in the frontal lobes. Their function is extremely difficult to understand . . .; but it is clear that they are largely responsible for the ability to initiate a task, to be attentive while it is being done, and to persevere with it.

That the speech area over the temporal lobe (on the left side in the large majority of people) is not found in any other animal is taken by him as primary evidence 'that language . . . as human beings possess it is in some way different from animal communication'.[5] But how do those increases constellate into a transformation?

For Bronowski the principal issue in reading those increases is how one views the transformation itself:

> There are two schools of thought. There are those who think that obviously evolution has been continuous and therefore the speech area and the gift of speech must be continuous with animal sounds. Then there are others, like Noam Chomsky and in particular Eric Lenneberg, who think that human speech is an altogether specific gift discontinuous from any animal function.

That continuity or discontinuity is difficult to describe, but Bronowski sides against Chomsky and Lenneberg, believing that they have missed 'the fact that human evolution has . . . been dominated so completely by human culture itself'. Thus, given 'that human speech is indeed a continuation of animal communication', the question is how they differ.[6]

In discussing animal communication, Bronowski emphasizes that 'it is communication: an animal makes a noise or emits some other signal which influences other animals, not itself'. The typical repertory is quite limited, seems to be essentially instinctual, and is managed mechanically. Apes may 'have many rudimentary human attributes', but, he asserts, 'we are in the presence not of a language but of a code of signals'. In human communication, however, there is typically a delay in response, a reflective processing, 'something physiological that happened quite early in human evolution'. It involves the ability 'to separate information from emotional content, or *affect*, when we interpret or frame messages'. This act of interpretation distinguishes 'information' from 'instructions', and he argues that 'all animal and machine languages are essentially instructions'.[7] (The controversies about research with chimpanzees and gorillas very much have to do with this issue of internal processing, for those animals must interpret in *some* way. Bronowski begs the question in that regard, as he does in regard to machine languages, for computers do *interpret* instructions – though they are severely constrained in choosing among interpretations. But he has more to say.)

According to Bronowski, several other interrelated abilities that developed in man's hominid ancestors were of fundamental importance to human language: *foresight* ('the ability consistently to foresee a use for things in advance'), *prolongation of reference* ('the ability to use language so that it applies not only to what is going on now but to what went on or to what will go on'), *internalization of speech* (the ability to talk to oneself), and *generativity* (the ability to 'rearrange the noises and get a new meaning'). The exercise of this last ability involves analysing the stratified structure of a language act and reconstituting it, which in turn involves constructing 'a world of outside objects, a world which does not exist for animals' and has been categorized (or recategorized) through language. Moreover, human consciousness

> depends wholly on our seeing the outside world in such categories. And the problems of consciousness arise from putting *reconstitution* beside *internalization*, from our also being able to see ourselves as if we were objects in the outside world. That is in the very nature of language; it is impossible to have a symbolic system without it. . . . The Cartesian dualism between mind and body arises directly from this, and so do all the famous paradoxes, both in mathematics and in linguistics. . . .[8]

But, despite the general rigour of his arguments for such distinctions, Bronowski's notion of the continuity/discontinuity between animal and human language is fairly flexible, even unstable. For instance, he distinguishes the two convincingly by the criteria of stratified structure (universal in human language, apparently absent in animal language) and 'the plasticity of responses which human beings build up from a limited neurological output', but the criterion of arbitrariness founders somewhat – as his discussion of the research of Karl von Frisch and others concerning bee language reveals. In that regard Bronoswki ventures to suggest that 'Perhaps no symbol is quite arbitrary, if we could read the hints of meaning deeply enough.' And he acknowledges that 'Human thought begins with images, and still projects them into the symbols with which it learns to work. It is certainly true to say that human language is largely symbolic, and that animal communication is not.' However, 'that is a general and not a diagnostic distinction. Human language is not made entirely of arbitrary symbols, and what is more important, animal language is not entirely void of them.' **None** the less, the two kinds of language are not 'marginally' but 'radically' different, even though 'the difference does not lie in a human monopoly of this or that linguistic device'.[9]

Bronowski's vacillation may be as much a gloss on the issue as a flaw in his thinking. For instance, in discussing the ability of animals in some cases to modify their use of language in different contexts much as human beings do, he warns that 'We must not mistake for a principle of language what is in fact a difference in range between human and animal consciousness.' But then, after pinpointing a humbling epistemological snarl – that 'our interpretations come from the analysis of human thought, and they cannot be rationally applied to animal behavior' because animals 'do not use any signs, in the human sense' – he goes on to argue that 'The critical test is whether an animal ritualizes any messages that are meant to inform itself; and because it fails this test, the animal cannot be said to form signs at all, in a cognitive sense.'[10] But how can he make such a claim about a language that he also claims he is constrained from interpreting? The contradiction has a particularly Wittgensteinian feel to it, certainly problematizes his continuity/discontinuity, and forces a different argumentative emphasis – not on the black box of the animal's brain/mind but on the relatively more gray one of man's.

For Bronowski the delay in response is a paramount consideration. Readily observable, it is surely an indirect indication of processes critical to the prolongation of reference, which involves the recall and manipulation of previously stored information and the imaginative restructuring and projection of it into other contexts. And it enables the process of symbolic storage itself, which

> is possible only if the initial response is delayed long enough to separate some abstract market [something like what in computer terminology is called a tag or flag, a bit of information used to label the condition or location of data in memory] and fix it in the brain. This is basically a linguistic mechanism, in which the delay loop is essential for the formation of a vocabulary.[11]

What Bronowski is concerned with here is various aspects of that internalization that is 'the most far-reaching and consequential difference between the way human beings can use langauge and the way animals do'. With that internalization language becomes 'an instrument of reflection and exploration', so that man lives through an inner as well as an outer language. It is the inner language with which he experiments continually in his building, first, of Piagetian preconcepts and, then, of concepts, a process that is, according to Bronowski, one of conceptual refinement through 'a progressive resolution of ambiguities' (or surely, sometimes, as in poetry, a progressive celebration of the tension between man's awareness of ambiguities and his ability to resolve them). Man is thus always engaged in a profoundly complicated act of translation, of 'transferring to the outer language the stricter meanings that we have discovered to be hidden in the inner language. In this way, we are trying to turn the outer language into a formal description of reality in which we can communicate rigorously without ambiguity.' But the alienation of inner from outer language is crucial since, if the formal description were completely successful, then 'the outer language would be finally closed, and our inner language would have nothing to contribute to it except confusion'. That end is not possible, even in principle, because of a cardinal feature of human language that distinguishes it from animal language (and this may be as close to an absolute distinction as one can get): 'inner language includes assertions about language', which feature 'makes it impossible to construct a closed language from it' – an observation that has ancestors in the work of Alfred Tarski and others. Human thought can 'refer to itself', and human language 'contains its own metalanguage' for discussing itself (the linguistic form of self-consciousness: a sign system that signifies a sign system, itself). 'In a sense,' says Bronowski, 'this is the essence of internalization: that not only can we choose between different sentences (in the language) but we can give reasons for our choice (in the metalanguage).'[12]

So what distinguishes man as a language user is not so much that he is *homo loquens* as that he is *homo metaloquens* – and that the neural-metaphysical structure of the brain/mind has evolved to permit and encourage the peculiar flexibilities and perversities of that involution, which, understood most generally, is the source of both his philosophical anguish and his genius for constantly revising all his interpretations. (Is not the history of human knowledge a progression of metalanguages, each trying to encompass and extend beyond the one before, from which the successor is then problematically alienated?) That involution is obviously important to the ability to reconstitute language.

Bronowski emphasizes that reconstitution is both an analytic and a synthetic process. The economy of those interlocked processes in producing well-formed sentences is remarkable, given the limited number of constituent parts and their combinatorial constraints as they are built up stratificationally. The analytic process, which he believes has been understressed by linguists in their quest for grammatical models, involves

> a progressive redistribution of the message, so that its cognitive content becomes more particularized, and its hortative content more generalized. . . . The effect is progressively to form in man a different picture of reality from that which animals have. The physical world is pictured as made up of units that can be matched in language, and human language itself thereby shifts its vocabulary from command to description or prediction.

So, as Wittgenstein would say, grammar to a great extent determines the 'picture of reality' constructed by the brain/mind. According to Bronowski,

> That is how we have come to think, for example, that reality is described by sentences which predicate. It is the complex procedure of analyzing our own messages which has produced a matching grammar of language and the world together, hand in hand. We separate reality into parts, and describe the parts by their functions, as a grammatical device which reflects its response to human actions.

Moreover, he observes, 'it is striking that the layered structure that man has given to language constantly reappears in his analyses of nature'[13] – thus all the seemingly stable assemblies that man perceives in terms of hierarchical taxonomies of sets and subsets. 'Nature' is thereby a text and science a system of grammatical analysis and synthesis derived from the structure of human cognition/language. The most troubling metaphysical enigmata concern the extent to which the language of that text is the same (or, by some translation, can be made the same) for both man and 'nature' – or machine.

If the evolutionary step into metalanguage and its corollary functions separated man linguistically and cognitively from other animals, then the development of the various kinds of human language and of the cultural contexts locked into them has separated human beings from one another. Thus there are many cognitive worlds determined by many kinds of human language that have features in common but also manifest crucial differences. This is a situation that engaged Benjamin Lee Whorf and further complexifies the issues of mind–language relations, as Brown explains:

> The Whorf thesis on the relationship between language and thought is found to involve the following two propositions: (*a*) Different linguistic communities perceive and conceive reality in different ways. (*b*) The language spoken in a community helps to shape the cognitive structure of the individuals speaking that language.

Though both propositions, especially the second, require stronger evidential support, according to Brown, 'it is clear that language can be described as a molder of thoughts since speech is a patterned response that is learned only when the governing cognitive patterns have been grasped'. He goes on somewhat sceptically to discuss Whorf's own research concerning the so-called Whorfian (or Sapir–Whorf) Hypothesis – which has to do, more specifically, with how experience is 'lexically differentiated' in different cultures – but concludes that 'there may be general laws relating codability to cognitive processes. All cultures could conform to these laws although they differ among themselves in the values the variables assume in particular regions of experience.'[14]

So the continuity/discontinuity is manifoldly more complex once one searches further into the implications of the differentiators, especially reconstitution. Though some animals have been observed to engage in language acts that apparently involve reconstitution, there is no evidence for 'any underlying analysis'. And Bronowski, with the authority of N. I. Zhinkin's findings in his search for 'a formal calculus of substitutions among the signals of baboons', stresses that 'A statement is truly a production or creation only if it has a cognitive content, and that implies that it contains conceptual units which have been isolated by analysis.'[15] The predisposition for reconstitution may have existed in man's prehominid ancestors and survive to some extent in his primate cousins, but only in man has it occasioned a thoroughgoing cognitive/linguistic habit.

There are a number of chicken–egg problems in trying to determine the chronological order in which the differentiators appeared and were selected for, though Bronowski surmises defensibly, for instance, that delayed response preceded the faculty of foresight. There is, of course, such a problem in the evolution of language and the development of tools, though the two must surely have occurred so much together that the attempt to discriminate their origins is probably futile. He, like Sagan, sees them proceeding 'hand in hand'. He argues that the internalization of language had to have been 'a necessary accompaniment (and expression) of the change from the use of tools to the planned making and copying of tools'. A given tool in this phase is not simply a tool but a blueprint for another tool, a pattern that could be studied and modified in terms of a technological metalanguage. He is perhaps overly impatient with those, like R. J. Pumphrey, who have tried to demonstrate the relation between the development of verbal language and the relatively recent appearance of less mimetic, more abstract and allusive paintings and sculpture (something similar happens in the child's development), but he sees preoccupation with them as leading away from the 'deeper structure' of such language, which he believes is mirrored accurately by analogy with technological forms. Thus he agrees with Jakobson that 'the progression to a fully structured language is most like the invention of . . . the tool to make a tool', an invention, like language, that occurred somewhere in the transition from *Australopithecus* to *Homo sapiens*:

> The step from the simple tool to the master tool, a tool to make tools (what we would now call a machine tool), seems to me indeed to parallel the final step to human language, which I call reconstitution. It expresses in a practical and social context the same understanding of hierarchy, and shows the same analysis by function as a basis for synthesis.[16]

For Bronowski, then, the distance between animal and human language is explained largely

by the strong selective pressure of the cultural component, for that has made human evolution very rapid. The drive in human evolution has been the use of tools, and selection has favored those able to use them: language is both a part and a product of their abilities.

The exfoliation of technology occurred along with that of 'the open system of the inner language'.[17] The mutually reinforcing interactions of the two, machine and language, made possible the hegemony of man on Earth.

9

Synergy, Neuroanatomy, Hemispheres

If there was some such dialectic of cultural and biological factors in the evolution of human language (one that is still ontogenetically recapitulated), the latter factors involved a synergy accounting for Bronowski's 'biological frame' for language. It is certain that human language was made possible biologically not by any single genetic mutation but by a complex of mutations phenotypically realized and selected for over a (relatively) brief period. Together comprising a threshold event, they gave rise to the neuroanatomy of language and tuned the grosser structures of acoustic communication. The oral and aural structures, delicate and impressive as they are, are fairly obvious in their workings, and recent speech-synthesis programs demonstrate that the electronic production of speech, complete with a wide range of nuances, will soon be possible (though speech-recognition programs remain problematic – this situation contrasts with that of simulation programs that deal with semantically conditioned syntax, for there recognition presents fewer problems than production). The engaging subject is thus the neuroanatomy.

As one might suspect, though the vocal apparatus is fairly simple, its innervation is quite dense; a good deal of the brain is dedicated to the muscular control of the larynx, tongue, and lips. The neural organization governing the motor, perceptual, and cognitive functions involved in speech is not well understood but seems at least partly localized. One region of the brain important to the production of language – in particular, speech – has been known about since 1861, when French neurologist Paul Broca did an autopsy on a patient who suffered from motor aphasia (the inability to organize the muscular movements for speech) and discovered that the patient's brain showed damage in an area at the base of one of the convolutions in the frontal lobe of the cerebral cortex, since called Broca's area. But the whole region extends further back into an area in the temporal lobe, behind the primary auditory area, discovered by Carl Wernicke in 1874 and since called Wernicke's area; that whole region is usually on the left side of the brain (though the opposite side has a considerable capacity to assume its functions, if necessary).

On the global surface of the brain, Broca's area and Wernicke's area (interconnected by a bundle of nerve fibres called the arcuate fasciculus) thus form two ends of a single continent. It has been explored in a number of ways – by electrical stimulation, surgical ablation, and the examination of localized lesions. The research on lesions has been the most informative in indicating how language is produced and comprehended, according to Bronowski, and he notes that important conclusions have been drawn from it by A. R. Luria and Jakobson, among others: the two areas

appear to store and perhaps to encode different constituents in the processes of speech. When there is damage to Broca's area, the main loss is in sentence structure [it involves syntactic difficulties]; this may be related to its location in the frontal lobes, . . . which play a part in governing the long-term organization of behavior. When there is damage in Wernicke's area, the main loss is in vocabulary [it involves semantic deviance]; and this may be related to the proximity of this area to the auditory centers in the brain. . . .

These conclusions, taken together, 'demonstrate, so far as any physiological evidence can, that normal language is equally compounded of structure and vocabulary, which are only separated in pathological conditions'.[1] (Of course, 'structure' and 'vocabulary' correspond to the categories that Saussure termed syntagmatic and paradigmatic.)

Above Broca's area lies Exner's centre, which is connected via the occipitofrontal fasciculus (across the fissure of Rolando) to the visual area and appears to play a crucial role in the processing and storage of print-code features – a role that suggests the importance of vision in the evolution of human language. However, in spite of proximity to Broca's area, with its phonological-syntactic functions, Exner's centre to some extent operates independently of it. This fact correlates with the fact that writing does not involve the mere translation of speech-code representations into those of the print code, and it endorses the recent emphasis in compositional pedagogy on the writer's need for 'visual acuity'. On the other hand, damage to Broca's area (which, like the rest of these territories, seems to be active somehow in virtually *any* language situation) certainly may influence written-language performance. Given these facts, it is interesting to speculate that further investigation of Exner's centre might provide neurological evidence for a Derridean *écriture* as the prototype of both speech and writing in the conventional sense.

Another area that appears to have been critical to the evolution of human language is the angular gyrus, which is connected to Exner's centre via the occipitofrontal fasciculus and located partly low in the posterior portion of the parietal lobe and partly in the posterior portion of the temporal lobe, immediately behind Wernicke's area. That area, 'only rudimentary in the cortex of the large primates other than man', has been shown by Norman Geschwind to be 'enlarged on the left side of the human brain'. In the angular gyrus one can

> trace cross-connections between nervous tissues that carry different sensory responses – such as the visual mode and the aural mode. Geschwind suggests that it has therefore played a central role in language, by making it possible to associate the visual and other stimuli from an object with a unique aural stimulus, namely its conventional name.[2]

Lesions in the gyrus affect detrimentally production and comprehension of written language, apparently by disrupting communication between Wernicke's area and the visual area. (The extent to which all these areas are interconnected is difficult to determine, though Geschwind and others have accumulated some clues. For instance, the conceptual structure of an utterance seems to be coordinated in Wernicke's area before it is transferred to Broca's area to be prepared for vocalization; thus Wernicke's area appears to be crucially involved in the formation of semantic networks – severing the arcuate fasciculus does not disturb syntactic fluency but does cause semantic aberrations, for Broca's area apparently can generate superficially well-made but semantically 'vacuous' syntactic structures in the absence of semantic information from Wernicke's area. However, such knowledge is muddied by the fact that global aphasics appear to control conceptual structures that lack linguistic realization. It is also interesting to note, given Geschwind's suggestion, that people who suffer from Wernicke's aphasia are progressively more likely to 'discover' the proper label for an object they cannot name as the number of the non-limbic sensorimotor modalities through which they are involved with it increases.)

While some contend that Geschwind's theorizing supports the notion of a sharp discontinuity between the language abilities of man and those of other animals, that contention may be at least partially refuted by evidence of 'cross-modal connections in the behavior of other primates', of the ability of chimpanzees and gorillas to make generally consistent associations between objects and their names. Bronowski and Ursula Bellugi, in their review of speculation about the gyrus, argue that the area has an even larger function, that 'its elaboration in man is likely to be part of the integration of experience which the human cortex both meditates and expresses – as language itself mediates and expresses it'.[3]

That argument is a corollary to one more basic to Bronowski's thinking and derived from the findings of Geschwind and others: 'the speech area stores and controls the mechanics of language, including verbal learning, but is dependent on the brain as a whole to supply this performance with meaning'.[4] Thus syntax and phonology are local in terms of functional areas, semantics illocal or global – an argument that doubtless has bearing on the fact that AI systems are quite limited in their ability to generate sentences that are appropriately (experientially) meaningful in context.

Bronowski also speculates that some general features of the nervous system have prepared it for the accommodation of language. In this vein he observes that 'it is reasonable to see a connection between the one-way conduction of nervous impulses and the serial order in which we utter the sounds that make up a message'; thus 'the serial organization of signals in the brain may underlie language', so that 'time has for us the force of a logical relation'.[5] But that observation may pertain strongly only to the 'verbal' side of the cerebrum; one must be careful to make that qualification, given what has been learned from 'split-brain' research on commissurotomized patients. Sagan, for instance, concludes from the results of such research undertaken by Roger W. Sperry that 'The left hemisphere processes information sequentially; the right hemisphere simultaneously, accessing several inputs at once. The left hemisphere works in series;

the right in parallel. The left hemisphere is something like a digital computer; the right like an analog computer.'[6] Various other terminologies can be used for characterizing the differences of the two hemispheres, so that one may think of the left hemisphere as embodying the kind of functions associated with Pascal's *esprit de géométrie* and of the right as embodying those associated with his *esprit de finesse*. And the game can continue in a respective manner: bottom-up/top-down, syntagmatic/paradigmatic, metonymic/metaphorical, linear/nonlinear, analytical/synthetic, propositional/appositional, and so on.

All these distinctions, in so far as they characterize the left hemisphere, generally support Bronowski's speculation, but eventually they doubtless will prove oversimplified. Linguistic activity involves the hemispheres interacting in ways that are little understood. Also, there is considerable evidence that both hemispheres have much the same overall neural structure, though the structure of each differentiates slowly until puberty, when the patterns of specialized functions are established. (Both, for example, seem to have a full complement of semantic functions, though the left, unless the right is forced to assume the role, is the more powerful syntactic processor.)

Thus, on the whole, Bronowski's thinking is probably accurate. Apparently to some extent both sides have the same functions but with different adaptations – a possibility corroborated by the idea, shared by a number of psycholinguists, that linguistic abilities are aspects of more general abilities that operate in a similar fashion. The ability to reconstitute linguistic structures, for example, resembles the ability to reconstruct two-dimensional sensory data into three-dimensional spaces (an ability difficult to simulate by machine), as R. L. Gregory has observed. Moreover, 'it is remarkable that the area in the brain which carries out the reconstruction occupies the same position in the right hemisphere that the speech area occupies in the left. . . . There is a biological as well as an intellectual analogy between the reconstitution of language and of three-dimensional structures in the mind. . . .'[7] That is indeed intriguing evidence of how one aspect of neural architecture adapted for verbal language.

10

Interconnectivity, Self-Consciousness, Excess

A richly innervated binocular vision, erect posture (which may have encouraged the lengthening of the pharynx and the posterior location of the tongue and whose verticality suggests connections between language and religious sensibility), the invention of the master tool, a sense of the future, and so on – these and other factors contributed to a discontinuity in evolution that set man the language user on the path of his development. But what happened in the brain/mind itself? What was the threshold event?

Sagan notes that 'Not all symbolic languages are neocortical.' Indeed, if one looks at the various languages of the whole animal kingdom, the vast majority are certainly not neocortical. The dance language of bees, for example, arises from a nervous system 'without a hint of neocortex', and 'the full vocal repertoire of squirrel and rhesus monkeys can be evoked by electrical stimulation of the limbic system'. Since human language is subject to neocortical control, 'an essential step in human evolution must have been the transfer of control of vocal language from the limbic system to the temporal lobes of the neocortex, a transition from instinctual to learned communication'.[1]

That transfer, perhaps quite rapid, would have depended on a neocortical environment adequate to accommodate and further elaborate linguistic functions, one characterized by lateralized specialization and other ongoing structural changes, including extensive redundancies to enable and indemnify complexity by controlling error. Specifically, the neural topography of the neocortex would have to have been dense with interconnections. At the onset of the discontinuity, the brain must have been capable of nearly as many synaptic states as it is today – a number that Sagan estimates to be on the order of 2 raised to the power of 10^{13}, a number 'far greater, for example, than the total number of elementary particles (electrons and protons) in the entire universe'.[2] (Given the 50- to 100-odd billion neurons that comprise the brain, the number may well be one or two binary orders of magnitude higher.) And that number implies a density of interconnectivity, especially in the neocortex, far greater than that to be found in any computer now under development.

Considering that the arrival of human or even humanlike intelligence occurred so late in evolutionary history, Sagan speculates that

> some particular property of higher primate and cetacean brains did not evolve until recently. But what was that property? I can suggest at least four possibilities . . . : (1) Never before was there a brain so massive; (2) Never before was there a brain with so large a ratio of brain to body mass; (3) Never before was there a brain with certain functional units (large frontal and temporal lobes, for example); (4) Never before was there a brain with so many neural connections or synapses. . . . Explanations 1, 2 and 4 argue that a quantitative change produced a qualitative change. It does not seem to me that a crisp choice among these four alternatives can be made at the present time, and I suspect that the truth will actually embrace most or all of these possibilities.[3]

I, too, suspect that it will and would like to suggest a hypothetical model for the 'change' involved. Let me approach that project through a brief discussion of other speculation that parallels and particularizes Sagan's – from Steiner, the philosopher E. F. Schumacher, and the biochemist Steven Rose.

Steiner, in his concern with alternity, asks a question that has obvious bearing on that change: 'When did falsity begin, when did man grasp the power of speech to "alternate" on reality, to say "otherwise"?' And he ventures an answer whose concerns echo those of Bronowski and Sagan:

> There is, of course, no evidence, no palaeontological trace of the moment or locale of transition . . . from the stimulus-response confines of truth to the freedom of fiction. . . . It may be that the evolution of conceptual and vocalized 'alternity' came fairly late. It may have induced and at the same time resulted from a dynamic interaction between the new functions of unfettered, fictive language and the development of speech areas in the frontal and

temporal lobes. There may be correlations between the 'excessive' volume and innervation of the human cortex and man's ability to conceive and state realities 'which are not.'

He goes on to argue the advantages of alternity – how 'Natural selection would favor the contriver'[4] – but the key point is this: there may be an interrelation between the evolutionary production of 'excess' brain (especially in terms of the brain-mass-to-body-mass ratio) and the development of 'excess' language, one that is arguably ontogenetic as well as phylogenetic.

Schumacher is not directly concerned with the development of human language, but he is concerned with the 'ontological discontinuity' that defines man. He argues that man may be distinguished from the nonhuman universe by virtue of his self-consciousness, probably another consequence of excess of brain. In his chain-of-being scheme, the lowest level of reality is that of the mineral, characterized by the qualities of inanimate matter, denoted m; the next is that of the plant, characterized by the qualities of both inanimate matter, m, and those of life, x; the next is that of the animal, characterized by the qualities of both m and x as well as those of consciousness, y; and the next is that of the human, characterized by the qualities of m and x and y as well as those of self-awareness (consciousness of consciousness), z. By this symbology man may be written as $m + x + y + z$, and z is the paramount distinguishing factor in the discontinuity – profoundly so, given that, for Schumacher, 'these four elements are ontologically – that is, in their fundamental nature – different, incomparable, incommensurable, and discontinuous'.[5]

I would argue that at least some other animals do manifest self-consciousness of a kind but hardly to the extent man does and that self-consciousness of some order is necessary (though not sufficient) for human or humanlike language. Without it there would not be, for instance, a sense of tense – no alternity. Schumacher's animal–man discontinuity is probably too severe; his factor z seems to have arisen through differences of degree that were extreme enough to cause remarkable qualititative – though perhaps not absolute – ontological differences.

Rose also is interested in how and to what extent self-consciousness distinguishes man from other animals, particularly in how it and other qualities of consciousness are related to the power of human language and in how an excess of brain occasioned such qualities. After a review of research concerning language acquisition by the chimpanzee (which animal seems also to have an excess of brain, certainly more than is needed in the wild habitat), he concludes that 'The human capacity for speech is certainly unique. But the gulf between it and the behaviour of animals no longer seems unbridgeable.' He then asks the key question: 'What does this leave us with, then, which is characteristically human?' And he synopsizes the answer of a number of neurobiologists: it 'resides in the human capacity for consciousness and self-consciousness'.[6]

But Rose is troubled by hints of 'nineteenth-century dualism' in such an answer and so takes his own approach:

> Objectively, learning capacity and the possibilities of behavioural complexity increase in organisms which are evolutionary the closest neighbours to man, while the size of the neocortex and its association areas, and the number of its cells and hence their possible interconnections, increase in the same direction. I suggest that all these observations are related, and that the phenomenon which is described at its appropriate hierarchical level as 'consciousness' . . . is related to factors of neocortex size and cell number. There is almost certainly not a linear relationship between them, but it should be possible to write some equation of the form $C=f_1(n)f_2(s)$ where consciousness (C) is represented at the cellular level by some function of neuronal cell number (n) – perhaps of the uncommitted neurons of the association cortex – and of connectivity (s).

This suggestion, which echoes Sagan's 'four possibilities' and doubtless would be regarded by Schumacher as involving a misapplication of the logic of the level defined by m, seems possibly fruitful, especially when Rose considers the graphic plot of such an equation:

> Granted that this is the case, we may ascribe consciousness to organisms in relationship to some function of the number of appropriate neurons and the connections they possess, in such a way that *Homo sapiens* appears at the top of this particular league chart, the primates rather lower, and so on. Such a function would be of necessity one which, when plotted graphically, would show an enormous discontinuity between

humans and the rest of living organisms; almost a threshold phenomenon, like the all-or-none of axonal firing, compared with which the level of consciousness even of humans' nearest evolutionary neighbours is no more than a very tiny excitatory post-synaptic potential. But mathematical functions of this sort are of course not uncommon.[7]

Indeed, such an equation would surely show exactly the kind of discontinuity associated with a threshold phenomenon.

Rose stresses that human consciousness emerged 'as an *inevitable* consequence' of the development of 'increasingly flexible and modifiable behavioural performance, achieved by increasing the size of the brain and the complexity of the possible interactions of its components'. And he stresses the kind of transformation involved: 'The increase in the quantity of the function $C=f_1(n)f_2(s)$ between man and the primates is great enough to produce a transformation of quality.' That transformation should be seen as the culmination of a prolonged evolutionary response to a communicational imperative that was first biological (intraorganismal) and then cultural (extraorganismal), as he explains:

> Goal-seeking behaviour is a function of all organisms, . . . but the evolution of mobile multicellular organisms made the development of rapid means of communication between different body regions essential. . . .
>
> Brains, together with a major system of neurons running the length of the organism, first emerge with the development of directionality in organisms with a defined head and tail end. . . .
>
> The evolutionary path which led to larger brains, greater plastic capacity and humans was that which followed the development of the vertebrates and the spinal cord. This development resulted in the eclipse of all other minor ganglia by the head ganglion or brain and a steady increase in brain size (expressed as a ratio of brain weight to body weight) through fish, amphibia and mammals. A series of evolutionary transformations of the brain has resulted in a dominance of the forebrain region above all others. The development of a cell-plan by which the neurons, instead of being embedded in the centre of the white matter of the nerve tracts, are arranged in

layers on the surface or cortex, makes possible vastly increased neuronal cell numbers.

Among the higher mammals the great development of neocortex occurs. In each group of mammals there is a steady increase in the area of the association cortex from the most primitive to the evolutionarily most recent type; there is an increase in the number of neurons and their connections. The degree of consciousness of an organism is some function of neuronal cell number and connectivity, perhaps of neurons of a particular type in association cortex regions. This function is of a threshold type such that there is a significant quantitative break with the emergence of humans. Although the importance of language and the argument that it is genetically specified and unique to humans must be reconsidered in the light of the recent evidence as to the possibility of teaching chimpanzees, if not to speak, then to manipulate symbolic words and phrases, there are a number of unique human features which combine to make the transition not merely quantitative, but also qualitative. In particular these include the social, productive nature of human existence, and the range and extent of the human capacity to communicate. These features have made human history not so much one of biological but of social evolution, of continuous cultural transformation.[8]

Rose's function *C*, as manifested in man, interestingly accounts for his self-consciousness and linguistic aptitude. Since its range includes a threshold phenomenon, it is the kind of function that can be schematized by the conceptual tools of René Thom's catastrophe theory.

11

Neocortex, Manifold, Catastrophe

A complicated terminology is involved in adapting Thom's ideas to the graphic mapping of the animal–man discontinuity, and it must be introduced carefully so that no important assumptions are ignored.

First, it seems plausible that the evolution of the consciousness associated with human language can be correlated with changes in the neural topography of the brain. Specifically, it can be correlated with an increase in the number of neocortical neurons (which in turn should be correlated with the brain-mass-to-body-mass ratio), with an increase in neural interconnectivity (and hence the density involved in this 'large-scale integration'), and with certain differentiations and specializations of function. Of these three factors, the first two are doubtless the most important, for they would make possible the excess of tissue for those differentiations and specializations. The mathematical relationship between the two increases, in so far as they have bearing on intelligence, is not well understood, but it is certainly true, as Sagan observes, that 'The number of neurons in an animal brain does not double as the brain volume doubles. It increases more slowly.'[1] And interconnectivity, which can be correlated with the number of neurons, increases at yet another rate. Thus Rose's equation $C=f_1(n)f_2(s)$ is characterized by two functions that increase at different rates, but both are involved multiplicatively in the development of intelligence. Therefore, both n and s are arguably causes of an effect, C. Furthermore, the vectorial product (of some kind as yet unspecifiable) of $f_1(n)$ and $f_2(s)$, for some values of n and s, is discontinuous and is higher (or lower) than a casual inspection of the equation might suggest; that is, it manifests threshold behaviour (a 'jump'). One then may say that, within the set of values determined by the product $f_1(n)f_2(s)$, there is a closed subset of values in which C is discontinuous. In Thom's terminology this closed subset is the 'catastrophe set' because it is the set of values at which discontinuities or 'catastrophes' occur.

Thom specifies the catastrophe set in this way:

We propose the following general model to parameterize the local states of a system: the space of observables M contains a closed subset K, called the *catastrophe set*, and as long as the representative point m of the system does not meet K, the local nature of the system does not change. The essential idea introduced here is that the local structure of K, the topological type of its singularities and so forth, is in fact determined by an underlying dynamic defined on a manifold M which is in general impossible to exhibit. The evolution of the system will be defined by a vector field X on M, which will define the macroscopic dynamic. Whenever the point m meets K, there will be a discontinuity in the nature of the system which we will interpret as a change in the previous form, a *morphogenesis*.

Thom refers to such 'local accidents of morphogenesis' as *'elementary catastrophes'*.[2] There are a number of types, but I believe that the 'cusp-catastrophe' (or 'Riemann–Hugoniot catastrophe'), which is relatively simple and to be described shortly, will serve adequately, though not necessarily definitively, for the basis of my hypothetical model. (E. C. Zeeman notes that 'the cusp-catastrophe can be used with . . . confidence in . . . many different fields, whenever a process involves 2 causes and 1 effect'.)[3]

Thom's general model must be translated into terms relevant to my purpose and then illustrated graphically. In my quasi-mathematical model the 'system' is the neocortical brain as found in mammalian life and as realized by various combinations of $f_1(n)$ and $f_2(s)$. The first function, $f_1(n)$, is defined, as in Rose's discussion, in terms of the number of neocortical neural cells n but, in my adaptation, also in terms of some corollary subfunction (as yet unspecifiable) involving the brain-mass-to-body-mass ratio. The second function, $f_2(s)$, is defined in terms of the neural connectivity (or interconnectivity) of neocortical tissue s. The 'manifold M' is defined by the range of intelligence or consciousness C observable in mammalian life. The catastrophe set K has already been defined for my model. The 'representative point m' on M would be a particular intelligence or consciousness as determined by the values of $f_1(n)$ and $f_2(s)$. The 'underlying dynamic' defined on *M* is so far 'impossible to exhibit', but, by the product $f_1(n)f_2(s)$, it does define 'a vector field *X* on *M*, which will define the macroscopic dynamic' of the system and, hence, its 'evolution'. A morphogenesis or catastrophe would occur whenever 'the point *m* meets *K*' – that is, whenever $f_1(n)f_2(s)$ has a value included in the catastrophe set – and the catastrophe, which would be manifested as a discontinuous jump, would have critical implications for linguistic aptitude.

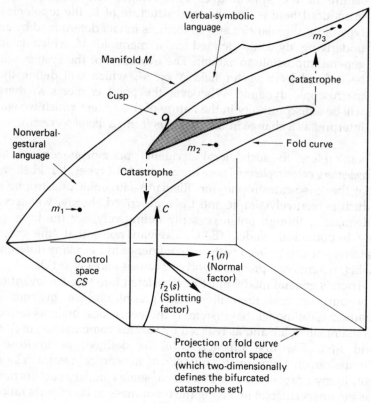

Figure 11.1

My graphic illustration of this adaptation of Thom's model (see Figure 11.1) is a two-dimensional portrayal of a three-dimensional situation. The leftmost and rearmost corner represents a zero level of neocortical intelligence; that intelligence increases upward to the right and toward the reader to arbitrarily limited values of

$f_1(n)$ and $f_2(s)$. The illustration itself is somewhat arbitrary in that no one knows *exactly* what shape of manifold $f_1(n)$ and $f_2(s)$ would determine – except it would have to be nonlinear and, I am suggesting, would have to involve something like the general features of discontinuity shown.

In the illustration the *control space CS* is the two-dimensional base of the graph. On that space is defined the domain of values of $f_1(n)$ and $f_2(s)$ whose products define values of C on the *manifold M*, which consists of the range of values of intelligence or consciousness that is continuous except in the region of divergence defined by the *fold curve*. The *cusp* is the point from which the fold curve originates; the projection of the fold in M onto the control space CS defines the divergent or *bifurcated catastrophe set*, the two curves on which the values of $f_1(n)$ and $f_2(s)$ give rise to catastrophes. The first function is the 'normal factor' because an increase in the number of neural cells (correlated with an increase in the brain-mass-to-body-mass ratio) causes an increase in intelligence – but one without any discontinuity. The second is the 'splitting factor' because an increase in neural interconnectivity is the critical cause of discontinuity.

According to the graph, then, there is one curve of the catastrophe set defined by values of $f_1(n)$ and $f_2(s)$ on which intelligence would suddenly rise and another, likewise defined, on which it would suddenly fall. In semiotic terms, a brain whose intelligence is above the fold in M would support verbal-symbolic language, one whose intelligence is below the fold only nonverbal-gestural language. (The catastrophic fall is included in the model only incidentally – I know of no example of the discontinuous devolution of intelligence.) If the reader considers three points m_1, m_2, and m_3 on M as corresponding to the intelligences of three different mammals – a cat, a chimpanzee, and a human being, respectively – then the descriptive power of the model can be seen. (For the moment I am interpreting the model statically and synchronically, as a kind of snapshot of brain evolution at present, but it obviously could be interpreted dynamically and diachronically also, as a kind of movie of evolution.) The intelligence of the cat (m_1) is a product of a brain with a quite limited neocortex, and its linguistic aptitude is accordingly quite limited. The intelligence of the human being (m_3) has undergone a catastrophic transition that has given rise to self-consciousness (Schumacher's factor z) and concomitant extraordinary linguistic aptitude. The intelligence of the chimpanzee (m_2) is located under the fold in M since its neocortex is considerably larger and more richly interconnected than that of the cat but has not developed to the extent necessary for the values of $f_1(n)$ and $f_2(s)$ to reach the curve of the catastrophe set; hence the linguistic aptitude of the chimpanzee is much higher than that of the cat and involves verbal-symbolic proclivities somewhat similar to those exhibited by the human being. But, because its intelligence has not reached the transition curve, the chimpanzee cannot have a linguistic aptitude as extraordinary as man's – no matter how extensively it is trained – and is as trapped as the cat on the lower portion of the manifold.

One might consider the intelligence of other mammals and thus posit probable locations for other points on M. Where would one locate the intelligence of whales, dolphins, or pigs? Could the linguistic aptitude of the dolphin, for example, have arisen through its brain taking a non-discontinuous evolutionary path involving a much larger increase over time of $f_1(n)$ than of $f_2(s)$, so that that path on the graph would move behind the cusp and up onto the rear of the upper portion of the manifold? And does not the model suggest a pattern also for ontogenetic development, especially in man, the interconnectivity of whose neocortex increases at an astonishing rate during childhood (although it may decline thereafter)? Does not the intelligence of the child, as he acquires language and as his brain organizes the requisite circuitry, climb up the lower portion of a manifold and then suddenly jump to the upper – as the research of Moskowitz, Brown, and others suggests? Is there not a catastrophic threshold at which, given the proper linguistic environment, a child inevitably begins fully using verbal language?[4] And would not a profoundly retarded child be as trapped under the fold of such an ontogenetic graph as the chimpanzee is under that of the phylogenetic one?

I am well aware that my model is only hypothetically descriptive and not explanatory, but its descriptive power is considerable and suggests a multitude of other ways catastrophe theory might be used in exploring MLM issues. With adaptations it might well be applied in describing in some detail the catastrophe whereby the evolving prehuman brain underwent reorganization and thus developed a language-acquisition mechanism. Or it might be applied in showing how that mechanism was present in posse in prehuman evolution but then was suddenly engaged. It might be helpful in predicting the level of environmental reinforcement the child requires in order best to exploit his linguistic aptitude. When a great deal more is known about the brain – particularly, when $f_1(n)$ and $f_2(s)$ are more thoroughly specified – it might be useful in speculating about discontinuities that would occur at higher levels of intelligence manifested by brains larger and more neurally complex than the present human brain. And, with a suitable translation of its parameters, it might be applied in predicting a future discontinuity in the evolution of AI systems that would involve a radical augmentation of their ability to acquire and use all manner of language; on the other hand, it might be used to show an evolutionary scenario whereby such systems would be inescapably trapped on the lower portion of some manifold.

It is quite possible that my model is too simple. The functions of n and s may be too reductively conceived. There may be one or more factors not yet discovered that were quite important to the evolution of the brain – and hence of linguistic aptitude. Also, the role of the environment in promoting patterns of neural interconnectivity is not well understood, and it may be more important than my model suggests. And there are other perspectives from which it might be criticized and revised – I am especially sensitive to the possibility that it might be made more comprehensive and useful if it were based on a catastrophe of a higher order than the cusp-catastrophe – but if criticism and revision lead to greater insights, then it will have served well.

12

AI, Computers, Density

After the neocortex reached a certain size, after its interconnectivity reached a certain density, the rapid development of language-dedicated areas was achievable – in an organism of small enough somatic dimensions to free a large portion of neocortical tissue for linguistic activities. Through time those activities – and their cultural systems – were selected for and enriched. The catastrophic discontinuity in the evolution of intelligence made man possible.

Could some similar discontinuity occur in the evolution of AI? Or is an entrapment on the lower portion of a manifold inevitable? Those questions are, of course, moot, but none the less I predict that a somewhat similar discontinuity will occur and would like to propose an analogous model for it.

If I am to discuss the 'consciousness' of electronically energized silicon, then I need a workable definition of AI. It is usually defined – by Patrick Winston, Margaret A. Boden, and others – as a discipline or tool or methodology (or search for methodology) toward the end of better understanding human intelligence (first, historically, by theorem-provers, then by more canny means) or improving the techniques (such as heuristic problem reduction) of computer science. For instance, Boden defines it as 'the use of computer programs and programming techniques to cast light on the principles of intelligence in general and human thought in particular'.[1] That kind of definition is perfectly useful, but it disguises or avoids a more fundamental and perhaps disquieting one: *artificial intelligence* is intelligence enacted through technical means in nonbiological entities. It is far more a phenomenon of technological culture than biological evolution (though the metaphor of the 'electronic brain' is problematic, if not irrelevant), whether or not it is generated in any way in imitation of 'natural' intelligence. Such intelligence is man-made, though man may wonder when he stopped making it and it started making itself – computers are now manufactured to a great extent by processes under the immediate control of other computers, and heuristically programmed computers can 'learn' (reprogram themselves and

64

evolve) and thus refine and expand the range of their behaviour. (Indeed, recent advances in the ability of the computer to play chess and other games whose possible moves at any stage of play exfoliate almost endlessly is due in large part to its being programmed to exploit heuristic principles derived from AI research rather than depend on brute iterative computation.) And if man discovers how to 'grow' nervous tissue from natural proteins or synthetic ones such as polylysine and create AI systems (in this case 'meat machines') that are thus 'organic', even if not biologically evolved, then he may have to rethink the definition. There are many complex issues infolded here, but my point is surely made: whatever else it is, AI *is* a kind of intelligence.

At present the Petri dish of AI is the computer, that spectacle of tireless organization. In the machine, as in man, language and intelligence mirror each other in multifold ways, are in a sense the same thing. The intelligence of a computer is thus measured largely by its ability to process language. AI, as now known, is certainly not fully comparable to human intelligence; the linguistic aptitude of the computer is quite limited compared to that of man, though it is exercised with great rapidity and a certain unerring logicality. Though the computer deals efficiently with its own artificial language, it deals clumsily with natural language; but it is gradually being equipped with the flexible databases and procedural strategies required to deal with natural language more gracefully and effectively. If AI were to undergo some discontinuity in development, the intelligence arising through it would be manifested in a radical improvement of linguistic aptitude, as well as in other ways – though it is possible that, because natural language is the language of biological organisms, the computer will never use it quite as well as man.

There are interesting questions between the lines of this discussion, and I will address many of them later. But for the moment I am interested in the possibility of a discontinuity in the evolution of AI and how it might occur. And so I offer a catastrophic model for it (see Figure 12.1), in which C is artificial consciousness or intelligence; $f_1(n)$ is a function of the number n of microelectronic components (gates, flip-flops, and so on) in the CPU (central processing unit) of the computer and associated structures; and $f_2(s)$ is a function of the connectivity (or interconnectivity) s of those components and is expressible in

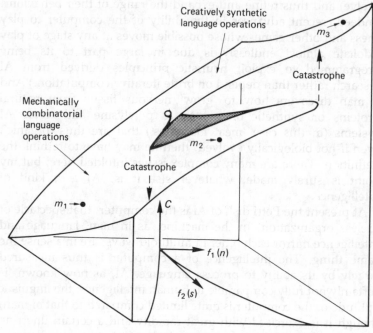

Figure 12.1

terms of circuit density. Graphically realized, the model is quite similar to the previous one. Again the shape of the manifold as defined by the vectorial equation $C=f_1(n)f_2(s)$ is arbitrary, as are the limits of the values of the two functions, the first of which is the normal factor, the second the splitting factor.

I regard component number and interconnectivity as the two most important hardware factors in the evolution of AI systems because they have been in the past, are now, and from all indications will continue to be so in the future. For good reason I regard interconnectivity, as characterized by $f_2(s)$, as the splitting factor: it determines the speed (which has an upper limit, the speed of light, so component proximity is crucial) and complexity of the information-processing operations of the CPU and associated structures. I assume that will be the case in the future. Numerous research-and-development efforts testify to the validity of that assumption. One undertaken by Raymond Dingle and his colleagues, for example, involves creating semiconductors of extremely thin, alternating layers of impurity-doped aluminum–

gallium arsenide and pure gallium arsenide. Such semiconductors, especially when operated in low-temperature environments, allow a much swifter and more efficient movement of electrons and hence higher switching speeds, but they also promise components with much higher interconnectivity: 'At present, semiconductors are flat; their electrons, for all practical purposes, flow in a single plane. But with the new layering technique, Dingle foresees three-dimensional devices in which electrons flow in all directions. That could make possible even tinier circuitry that would make today's minuscule computers look like veritable dinosaurs.'[2] Indeed, such devices might well make possible circuit densities approaching those of the human brain and contribute critically to a discontinuity in the evolution of AI.

Of the two boons from Dingle's work, the second is surely the more significant, not only because of the upper limit of electron velocity but also because of the theoretical upper limit of switching speed (around 10^{-43} second). Given those two limits, interconnectivity, whose upper limit has hardly been approached, is crucial to the further development of AI hardware: any increase in it will decrease the distance electrons have to travel between switching locations (roughly analogous to synaptic junctions in the brain) and increase the number of possible close interconnections between those locations. The computer is a much more rapid information processor than the brain – electronic circuitry is much faster than neurochemical circuitry – so the advantage for the brain, which the machine in some fashion must emulate, is in interconnectivity. It is a direct measure of the hardware power of an AI system, which requires, for any dramatic breakthrough, much richer associational patterns.

Let me now return to my model. Assuming that the manifold has more or less the same mathematical–topological characteristics as that in the previous model (the catastrophic fall, again, is included only incidentally), the reader may consider three points on it: m_1 is the intelligence of a machine developed, say, around 20 years ago; m_2 is that of a present state-of-the-art machine; and m_3 is that some hypothetical machine in the future. The first is a crude kind whose language operations are only mechanically combinatorial and severely limited semantically. The second is somewhat higher, and its operations are syntactically and semantically more sophisticated – though hardly enough to deal thoroughly with the contextual complexities of natural language –

and capable of processing artificial language much more efficiently than the operations of m_1. The third has undergone a catastrophic transition onto the top portion of the manifold and manifests a good deal of very humanlike cognitive/linguistic activity. Its operations are creatively synthetic – syntactically, semantically, and pragmatically quite sophisticated. The language associated with m_3 is 'artificial', but its characteristics are at least similar to those of natural language. And, of course, there might be still other discontinuities at higher levels if the shape of the manifold were more complex than that of the one presented here.

Such a discontinuous increase in AI assumes considerable refinement of programming techniques, but that assumption does not seem unwarranted, given recent developments in that area and given that the furtherance of those developments depends on hardware capabilities, essentially the very capabilities whose enlargement, well evidenced to date, is the basis of my projection. And it is certainly conceivable that a post-catastrophic machine would develop much of its software autonomously, through Piagetian 'revolutions'.

But many questions linger. A post-catastrophic machine, with, as it were, its excess of brain, would be characterized by metacognitive/metalinguistic skills, but they are difficult to specify. To what extent would they resemble those outlined by Bronowski? To what extent would they exhibit aspects of Schumacher's factor z?[3] Also, since the support circuitry for such skills would be interconnected far more intricately than that of present machines, would it exhibit equipotentiality as well as localization of function? Would a post-catastrophic machine be a discrete-state machine, like present ones, or not? What would *meaning* be for it? In any case, the discontinuity seems quite probable. More and more efficiently compact CPUs, super-dense three-dimensional memory structures (perhaps etched by electron-beam or X-ray techniques), increasingly complex circuitry for parallel concurrent processing, and so on – the catastrophe is being approached.

13
Program, Game, Assembler

In the wake of these concerns looms the question that most intrigues: how are mind and machine, whose evolutions have been perhaps too easily analogized, alike and different? Language, the third sector of the circle of metaphor, is obviously the key to properly exploring that question. Language is software, the *langue*scape' of both man and computer; microelectronic circuitry and neural tissues are, after all, just two kinds of hardware. J. Z. Young is helpful in this connection:

> Information is carried by physical entities, such as books or sound waves or brains, but it is not itself material. Information in a living system is a feature of the order and arrangement of its parts, which arrangement provides the signs that constitute a 'code' or 'language.' . . . The organization of the brain can be considered as the written script of the programs of our lives. So the important feature of brains is not the material that they are made of but the information that they carry.
>
> What neuroscience can do is to translate the language in which the brain programs are written into ordinary language. Since these are the programs that produce the phenomena of human language we are not really escaping it. We are using the analogies of language and of writing to understand the entities that produce them. As so often in the past, man, having invented an artefact (in this case writing) to help him with his life (by carrying information), is now trying to describe himself in terms of his artefact.[1]

An information-processing system, instantiated in neural tissue or epitaxially layered silicon, is thus essentially the language in which a 'theory' of behaviour is written.

What then is a language, as a formal system? 'A formal language,' says Joseph Weizenbaum, 'is a game.'[2] Or, the figure turned about, as Saussure says, *'une partie d'échecs est comme une réalisation artificielle de ce que la langue nous présente sous une forme*

69

naturelle.'³ (Such an equation of chess, as an 'artificial realization' of the systematic qualities of language, with language itself 'in a natural form' is, of course, potentially problematic; but it is a powerful analogical construct, and its limitations – since even *purely syntactic* sign systems are open to semantic interpretation – may have to do only with a difference of intention.) More specifically, Weizenbaum asserts, 'a language is a game played with a certain alphabet and governed by a set of transformation rules, and . . . a computer is an embodiment of those rules'. Moreover, 'at a certain level of discourse, there is no essential difference between a language and a machine that embodies its transformation rules'.⁴ In this regard the relation of language to machine is analogous to the relation of mind to brain: on either side of the analogy, the relata, 'at a certain level of discourse', are equivalent.

Weizenbaum emphasizes that 'every computer determines a language, its machine language' (whose alphabet consists of 0 and 1), into which a program (which is formally symbolic and therefore capable of being treated mathematically) in a high-level language (Pascal, LISP, and so on) and the 'effective procedures' that it embodies must, after scanning and parsing, be translated in order for the machine to implement that program. The translator, called an assembler, is itself a program. (An assembler can be written in machine language – machine code – and translates item for item in a one-to-one correspondence and should be distinguished from a *compiler*, which can be written in assembly language and which generates assembly-language statements from those in high-level language, may subsume an assembler, and thus translates likewise from a 'source code' or 'source language' to an 'object code' or 'object language' but in one continuous process and by means of the economies of various kinds of subroutines. There is some tendency to confuse the two with each other and with an *interpreter*, a program that translates in a manner somewhat similar to that of a compiler but anew and on an instruction-by-instruction and real-time basis each time a high-level program is run.) Assemblers are 'written in assembly language, namely, the language they themselves translate'. An assembler, which thus has 'the ability to translate the text that constitutes its own definition', is the vehicle whereby

a program transforms a computer into another computer. . . . An assembler, then, also transforms the computer into which it is loaded. The transformation it induces has important consequences: a programmer [one who 'writes forth'] who instructs a computer using only an assembler need never learn the language determined by the computer itself, i.e., its machine language. In an important sense, he never sees the machine he is actually addressing; he sees and works with a symbolic artifact that, for him, *is* the machine.[5]

Likewise, the human brain is invisible to its 'user' because he does not address it at the level of its own neural language: he perceives it, in an elusively self-reflexive way, as mind rather than as brain. In attempting to understand his brain (its neural language), he proceeds, as Young notes, through the 'artefact' of natural language. That process is similar to trying to understand machine language through a high-level programming language. In both cases what is required is a knowledge of the assembler.

In an important sense all computers ('virtual' machines), like all human brains, are equivalent; the assembler determines what programs can be implemented. It must be the case that the brain/mind cannot process statements in any given language unless it has the proper assembler (which surely should be thought of as being subsumed by some kind of very sophisticated compiler) to translate those statements into neural language. Neurolinguists and psycholinguists should be – and to some extent are – engaged in investigating that assembler, but it has proven quite difficult to characterize. Even in the machine an assembler is a slippery construct, as Weizenbaum observes:

If . . . one had to say what a particular higher-language program means, one would have to point ultimately to its machine-language reduction and even to the machine corresponding to it. One would have to say 'it means what that machine does with that code.' However, that is not how such questions are answered in reality. For the translator is itself a program and therefore transforms the computer into which it is loaded into quite another computer, namely, a computer for which that language is its machine language.

He reiterates that 'there are important universes of discourse in which distinctions between languages and their machine embodiments disappear', adding that 'a higher-level formal language is an abstract machine'.[6] The mind too is 'an abstract machine', and meaning for it is what it 'does'; and *that* is determined by some kind of assembler (translator). Human reality, as Steiner argues, is a matter of translation. Young is quite right that man is imprisoned in the cyclical translation between 'the language in which the brain programs are written' and 'ordinary language', but he forgot to take into account the assembler, which is both the medium of that translation and perhaps, in ways as yet poorly understood, its betrayer.

14

Turing, More, Analogies

Alan M. Turing several decades ago proved that 'all computers (save a few special-purpose types . . .) are equivalent to one another, i.e., are all universal'.[1] That is, all computers, regardless of the stuff of which they are made (they exist, in a functional sense, apart from it), are also abstract machines of a certain kind: they are universal Turing machines. Or, to put it another way, a computer language is, in effect, a set of instructions for building such a machine. (The Turing machine is a theoretical device formulated by Turing in the 1930s as a way of discussing algorithms or procedures for solving problems, a preoccupation that grew from logicians' interest in a methodology whereby 'the proofs of mathematical theorems could be generated automatically by a mechanical process'. The device consists of three parts: an infinitely long paper tape that is divided into an infinite number of squares, a mechanism that moves the tape and prints or erases marks [symbols from a finite alphabet] on individual squares, and a scanning head that senses whether or not a given square contains a mark. It 'can be programmed to find the solution to a problem by executing a finite number of scanning and printing actions', and 'in spite of its simplicity it is not exceeded in problem-solving ability by any other known computing device.')[2] With such a machine, one 'can realize, as a computer program, any procedure that could "naturally" be called an effective procedure'. And one can learn to imitate such a machine. Thus, Weizenbaum observes, 'since we can all learn to imitate universal Turing machines, we are by definition universal Turing machines ourselves. That is, we are *at least* universal Turing machines.'[3] What *more* man is comprises the subject of a comprehensive humanism; what *more* a computer might be comprises the subject addressed by my model of AI evolution. How much those *mores* might become similar is a subject of extreme importance, though utterly speculative.[4] To approach it effectively, one must begin analogically, with a comparison of the human brain/mind and computer hardware/software.

73

First, a distinction must be made, in Weizenbaum's words, between 'physically embodied machines, whose ultimate function is to transduce energy or deliver power, and abstract machines, i.e., machines that exist only as ideas'. That distinction may be stated this way: 'The laws which the former embody must be a subset of the laws that govern the real world. The laws that govern the behavior of abstract machines are not necessarily so constrained.' (He argues that 'The human imagination must be capable of transcending the limitations of physical law if it is to be able to conceive such law at all.') What he says of high-level computer software is, *mutatis mutandis*, also true of that of the brain:

> The game the computer plays out is regulated by systems of ideas whose range is bounded only by the limitations of the human imagination. The physically determined bounds on the electronic and mechanical events internal to the computer do not matter for that game – any more than it matters how tightly a chess player grips his bishop or how rapidly he moves it over the board. A computer running under control of a stored program is thus detached from the real world in the same way that every abstract game is.[5]

And so I continue, to paraphrase Young, trying to describe man in terms of his artefact, in this case a machine. Since Young has introduced that motif, let me turn to him again: 'The brain operates in certain organized ways that may be described as programs, and the actions of these programs constitute the entity that we call the mind of a person.' However, one should realize that 'brain programs are only partly like the algorithms of computer software', though they may be thought of as 'written down in a notation or language' (*écriture* again) by 'selective agencies'. In the human brain, which 'is programmed to allow communication by language', those programs 'are largely written by a process of learning' for which there are 'certain inherited capacities'.[6]

Thus Young contends 'that life is guided by programs and that programs are written in languages'. Those languages 'consist of sets of signs', so 'life consists of signs'. And he recalls that Peirce, in somewhat neo-Emersonian fashion, answered the question ' "What is a man?" with "Man is a symbol." ' Man therefore has/*is* a program, and the information in that program 'must have a physical embodiment as a system of signs'.[7] (Life-)form and information, structure and sign system, are one.

If one conceives of human life as a program, then what are its subprograms? Young distinguishes four: the 'fundamental program' (which is 'inherited, written in the triplets of bases of the DNA code'), that 'embodied in the structure of the brain', that of oral language, and that of written language. The brain 'contains the scripts of the programs that issue in human action ', and 'the detailed characteristics' of its cells 'provide the code signs for . . . a detailed model of the world'. Thus he embraces 'the theory of signs as the basis for all knowledge',[8] and he would seem to agree with Thom's essentially constructivist argument that 'the physical properties of the outside world' are defined by 'the constraints of the dynamic of our brain'.[9] (Reality is patterns of neurochemical frissons.)

But I conceive of elaborations and refinements of this man–machine analogy, of a forthright comparison between the hierarchical (and, on any given level, at least, heterarchical as well) architectures of computer hardware/software and the human brain/mind. My detailed comparison (see Figure 14.1) involves some oversimplifications and moot assumptions, but it also supplies a suggestive framework for speculation, especially about how relatively simple underlying functions give rise to complex behaviour. Such a diagram is problematic in many ways – because computers are not typically designed to imitate the brain structurally, because the geometric severities involved are simplistic or otherwise questionable, and so on – but it will do for my present purpose and will be nuanced by later discussion.

Level 1 in the AI system is defined by a program written in a high-level programming language, whose grammar (determined in practice by lower levels of software) is stored in RAM (random-access memory), and is addressable in that language (which may accommodate more or less limited natural-language interactions) by a human interlocutor (or another AI system) through the medium of some kind of interactive terminal (and the system may address itself in that language). A program in such a language uses a variety of macrostructural functions (such as internal and external memory) of the system. Level 1 in the HI system is defined by surface structures in a natural language and is addressable through perceptual subsystems. Also, the system

| Artificial-intelligence system | | | Human-intelligence system | |
Hardware	*Software*		*Brain*	*Mind*
Interactive terminal(s), internal and external memory, processing and switching units, etc.	Program in high-level language (Pascal, LISP, etc.)	Level 1	Perceptual subsystems, short- and long-term memory, etc.	Statements in natural language (surface structures)
	Compiler			'Compiler'
Accumulator, registers, data-transfer circuitry, etc.	Assembler	Level 2	Wernicke's area, Broca's area, angular gyrus, etc.	Transformational code
ROM circuitry logic circuitry, sequencing circuitry, etc.	Microcode	Level 3	Neural networks (ganglia etc.)	'Microcode' (conceptual-semantic networks)
Fundamental circuitry components (transistors, resistors, diodes, etc.)	Nanocode	Level 4	Basic neuroanatomy (axons, dendrites, synapses, etc.)	Neurochemical code

Figure 14.1

may address itself internally through such a language, and the natural-language 'program' likewise uses a variety of macrostructural functions (such as short- and long-term memory) of the system. (The transformational notion more or less explicit in levels 1, 2, and 3 of the *mind* column is intended to draw upon certain general provisions of the thinking of transformational grammarians and not to be strictly in conformity with any particular school of such thinking, Chomskyan or otherwise.)

Level 2 in the AI system is defined by the assembler and the hardware functions under the control of the assembler, which is a metaprogram written in assembly (or machine) language, whose grammar, like that of the high-level language, is stored in RAM. At this level data are transferred and stored by the assembler in patterns dictated, through the mediation of the compiler, by statements in the high-level language, and the assembler thus operates as a translator of high-level language into machine language (to be interpreted by the microcode, a list of 'atomic' program steps that are largely hardwired but alterable to some extent) and vice versa (which latter operation involves 'disassembling' or, in the case of the compiler, 'decompiling') – so that with the proper assembler and compiler any high-level language may be used by any machine at the level of its microcode; that is, that language may be translated into a form usable by the machine in its hardwired or microprogrammed circuits. (Thus, as I said earlier, the assembler translates a program in a high-level 'source language' into a program in a low-level 'object language' that is directly comprehensible to the machine without further translation.) Level 2 of the HI system may be analogously analysed, so that a theoretical 'assembler' may be posited in terms of a set of unconscious (or preconscious) functions. Such an assembler, which surely has some kind of capability for 'chunking' the information with which it deals, is a metaprogram whose statements constitute a transformational code that translates 'compiled' surface structures into deep structures comprehensible to the 'microcode' of the conceptual–semantic networks and vice versa. That code – varying from individual to individual, depending on the natural language at level 1 – governs data transfer and storage at a high level of neural complexity and, in its mediation, with the 'compiler', between the differing surface structures of natural languages at level 1 and the universal deep structures determined and interpreted by the 'microcode' at level

3, embodies the hermeneutic processes that make conscious signification possible and natural language meaningful to its user. The software of level 2 develops ontogenetically and is shaped by individual experience within a given linguistic environment.

Level 3 in the AI system is defined by the microcode, the software that, in an indirect way, controls (or acts as if it controls) the most fundamental data-processing operations of the system (those of the logic gates, flip-flops, data paths, and so on). The microcode is determined basically by the way the circuitry at this level is built: it is preset programming, firmware, language locked in hardware. It can be altered only by altering the hardware (for example, by adding new command sequences to the ROM [read-only memory] – that is, new ROM circuitry – one can create, in effect, a new CPU with a new instruction set and thus, in many ways, a new AI system) or, in a virtual sense at least, by making use of various kinds of microprogramming techniques. Level 3 in the HI system may be thought of as defined by a microcode, that determining and interpreting the deep ('machine-level') structures of language, which is, at some stage, 'hardwired' into neural networks. (It is at this level that the base component, which consists of categorial and lexical subcomponents, generates the deep structures. Linguistic meaning arises at this level of the HI system but obviously depends for its conscious realization on the mediation of level 2.) The architecture of those networks is apparently universal (and therefore genetically determined), so that different people (even polyglots) all have essentially the same microcode (a Derridean *écriture*?) and yet use different languages as determined by the transformational code at level 2.

Level 4 in the AI system is defined by the nanocode, those features of molecular structure and of the dynamics of electrons and holes that constitute a language of operations in terms of the physical laws governing them. The way such laws are exploited in the design of any given circuitry is subject to principles and considerations of microelectronic design, and the extent to which the nanocode may be manipulated as a program is an open question. Level 4 in the HI system is defined by the neurochemical code, the language of ion transference, membrane permeability, neurotransmitter activation. The 'nanocode' or 'nanoprogram' involved is only partially understood, though in some respects it is better understood than the software and hardware operations at levels 1, 2, and 3. Finally, just as level 4 in the AI system is subject to principles of microelectronic design, so is level 4 in the HI system subject to those of genetic design. Thus level 4 in both systems is subject to the software (a program in the language of design) and the hardware (a means of instantiating design) of a fifth level, that of the picocode.[10] (It must be acknowledged, of course, that design applies at all levels in the comparison, but it reaches its basic functional terms at level 4. Also, it is worthwhile to note how the differentiation of software from hardware becomes increasingly more difficult as one descends through the levels of the comparison, so that at level 4 in the HI system, for example, one feels far less certain about distinguishing between mind and brain than one does at level 1. Is one not compelled to admit that at some level of analysis software and hardware are the same thing? That mind is identical with brain? That the program of behaviour for anything, say an electron, is identical with its existence? That language is identical, however problematically, with what it does?)

I am very much aware of the limitations of this comparison[11] – it does not address (though it might be made to), for example, the issue of equipotentiality, and one might well quibble over some aspects of either of the systems as here considered – but I do believe that it will prove a useful prolegomenon for discussion still to come.

15

Form, Representation, Presence

Young argues that in the evolution of human consciousness 'the critical stage was the acquisition of the power to make symbolic representations by language of concepts indicating the distinction between self and other'. That this distinction, in man–machine terms, may be confused by metaphors that extend self into other ('face of a clock') is fairly obvious, but that it also may be confused less comfortably by metaphors that extend other into self is less recognized though commonly observable. Technological man must be very canny about how he conceives himself, by this second kind of metaphor, as an extension of the environment of his artefacts, mind as an imitation of machine (an inversion that has engaged Derrida); for, as Young notes, 'as man devises tools to substitute for the functions of his body he also creates new language to describe these very functions . . .', a language almost invariably derived, by a perverse McLuhanism, from the terminology of the substitute. So a more specific caveat emerges: 'We cannot hope to describe in detail how the brain works by looking at the bits of metal and minerals inside a computer.' (The physical machine is not the simulation: the simulation is the computation of the consequences of a theory expressed as a program that more or less approximates what it models.) Rather, 'What we have to use is the understanding of the *principles* . . . .'[1]

In terms of those principles, computer hardware/software and the human brain/mind are both systems for the manipulation of symbols: they are both language processors. At all levels their languages in an important sense *are* the information they embody. The fundamental unit of information is a *bit* (an abbreviation of *binary digit*), defined by Young as 'the operation needed to make a decision between two equi-probable events'. By this definition the essence of information is that it is decisional, involves binary discriminations, differences. In a computer such decisions *form* the machine, constitute it as a system that behaves in a certain way.

80

In man they work analogously. In either case, actions 'are "controlled" by the giving of "instructions," based upon "communication" of "information" in a "code." "Order" is maintained by "orders." '[2] That is to say, according to Thom, 'when we speak of "information," we should use the word "form." The scalar measures of information (e.g., energy and entropy in thermodynamics) should be geometrically interpreted as the topological complexity of a form.'[3]

This interpretation involves discerning a digital-to-analog conversion, a translation of the discrete into the continuous: the decisions of a computer become flowing graphics on a terminal screen; those of the artist, in his placing dabs of paint on a canvas, become the textures of a landscape by Monet or, in his arranging *mots justes*, a lapidary novel by Flaubert. Likewise, the human organism is formed by genetic decisions, its behaviour determined by patterns of synaptic discharges, each a decision.

Furthermore, the meaning of information is governed by context, bears its inscribed image. Any organism 'can be considered as a coded representation [representamen] of its environment'. Thus 'the wings of a bird "represent" the air and the legs of man the land, and similarly . . . their brains contain representations in code that allow them to fly or walk, and their nerves carry code messages about relevant features of the world'; likewise, a computer 'contains' analogous 'representations in code' that allow it to operate on 'code messages about relevant features of the world' defined for it. For the computer such representations can be specified easily. In the case of the human sensorium, however, one encounters an extremely problematic issue concerning 'what are the units of the neural code and how did they come to represent events in the world'.[4]

Behaviourally the human organism, a text written by the genetic 'preprogram' of the DNA, *is* language – neural language. The brain 'is an agent issuing instructions, after it has decoded (understood) the signals it receives about what is going on around it'. The meaning of those signals is evidenced by the subsequent instructions, which indicate what the brain has recognized: understanding is recognition; meaning is response. Those signals and instructions are constituted by the conditions of interconnecting nerve cells, just as, analogously, the signals and instructions in a computer are constituted by the conditions of interconnecting electronic components. The combinations involved 'compose the words, sentences, paragraphs, chapters, and books that constitute the programs that produce our patterns of behavior'; thus nerve impulses may be conceived as combining in the brain, 'like letters or the phones of speech, to produce units that have meaning, like words'. Likewise, 'If grammar is the system that regulates the proper use of language we might say that the brain operates a sort of metalanguage with a metagrammar, which regulates the proper conduct of life, including speech'. And, finally, since messages in any language are transactional or dialogical, are both received and sent, there are not only neural situations that 'represent events in the world' but also those that represent 'actions that the body can do to influence the world'.[5] Understanding is also intention; meaning is also stimulus.

Such arguments have a logical-behaviourist flavour, but they can be reconcilably juxtaposed to topological and/or functionalist, even poststructuralist, theorizing. Let me turn first to Daniel C. Dennett for a functionalist view of mental representation, then to brief Derridean meditations of my own.

Dennett critiques the notion of a 'cerebral code' and stipulates several conditions (including, for example, that the system of representations, 'the sentences of brain writing', must have 'a generative grammar' and that, in regard to the language used in the formulation of those representations, 'Syntactical differences and similarities of the language must be reflected in physical differences and similarities in the brain') that may be used to distinguish 'genuine brain-writing hypotheses from masqueraders'. In that critique he is persuaded by certain provisions of such hypotheses, though he is also convinced that the brain 'must store at least some of its information in a manner not capturable by a brain-writing model'. He argues, however, that 'representations that are available for our conscious, personal use and apprehension . . . are stored in brain writing . . ., for they are in intimate relation to our natural languages'. Thus he concludes that 'the brain must be an organ that *represents*', but he hopes that 'it is no longer obvious that the brain must represent in sentences' and observes, postscripturally, that 'It has become clearer in recent years that strictly "propositional" data-structures lack the powers required to serve as models of the fundamental "mental representations," but few uncontroversial assertions can be made about the structure and function of non-propositional or quasi-propositional representations.'[6]

None the less, it is apparent to Dennett that 'thought requires representation' and that, 'since nothing can represent except within a system, we must be endowed with and utilize a system of internal representation having its own "grammar" and "vocabulary", which we might call the language of thought'. He praises Jerry A. Fodor for his ingenious attempts to express this argument specifically (in somewhat Gricean and Chomskyan terms) and forcefully and endorses, for example, the way 'He defends images as internal representational vehicles . . . and claims to show that the inner code can represent its own representations and has a vocabulary about as rich as that of English. . . .' Fodor's erudition, however, does not dispel one salient, nagging problem:

> it seems (to many) that we cannot account for perception unless we suppose it provides us with an internal image (or model or map) of the external world, and yet what good would that image do us unless we have an inner eye to perceive it, and how are we to explain *its* capacity for perception? It also seems (to many) that understanding a heard sentence must be somehow *translating* it into some internal message, but how will this message be understood: by translating it into something else? The problem is an old one, and let's call it *Hume's Problem*, for while he did not state it explicitly, he appreciated its force and strove mightily to escape its clutches.[7]

(This problem has attracted much interest from constructivists, especially Francisco J. Varela, who analyses it, in somewhat Derridean fashion, as one of trying to determine a unique origin: 'whenever we do try and find the source of . . . a perception or an idea, we find ourselves in an ever-receding fractal, and wherever we choose to delve we find it equally full of details and interdependencies. It is always the perception of a perception of a perception. . . .')[8] Dennett approaches this snarl, which has the feel of one of Zeno's paradoxes, by way of AI theory and a further consideration of data-structures, which 'may or may not be biologically or psychologically realistic representations' but are 'at least clanking, functioning examples of representations that can be said in the requisite sense to understand themselves'.[9]

Dennett's response, which is indebted to Turing, John von Neumann, and others, involves regarding an 'intentional system' as an 'organization of subsystems, each of which could itself be viewed as an intentional system . . . and hence as formally a homunculus'. The introduction of these homunculi, usually regarded as fallacious, produces no additional problems, however, because each is limited in intelligent behaviour and none duplicates entirely the 'talents' it is used to explain. Dennett elaborates:

When homunculi at a level interact, they do so by sending *messages*, and each homunculus has representations that it uses to execute its functions. Thus typical AI discussions *do* draw a distinction between representation and representation-user: they take the *first step* of the threatened infinite regress, but as many writers in AI have observed, it has gradually emerged from the tinkerings of AI that there is a trade-off between sophistication in the representation and sophistication in the user. The more raw and uninterpreted the representation – e.g., the mosaic of retinal stimulation at an instant – the more sophisticated the interpreter or user of the representation. The more interpreted a representation – the more *procedural* information is *embodied in it*, for instance – the less fancy the interpreter need be. It is this fact that permits one to get away with *lesser* homunculi at high levels, by getting their earlier or lower brethren to do some of the work. One never quite gets *completely* self-understanding representations (unless one stands back and views all representation in the system from a global vantage point), but all homunculi are ultimately discharged. One gets the advantage of the trade-off only by sacrificing versatility and universality in one's subsystems and their representations, so one's homunculi cannot be too versatile nor can the messages they send and receive have the full flavor of normal human linguistic interaction. . . .

There are two ways a philosopher might view AI data-structures. One could grant that they are indeed self-understanding representations or one could cite the various disanalogies between them and prototypical or *real* representations (human statements, paintings, maps) and conclude that data-structures are not really internal representations at all. But if one takes the latter line, the modest successes of AI simply serve to undercut our first premise: it is no longer obvious that psychology needs internal representations; internal pseudo-representations may do just as well.[10]

Though Dennett has very little to say about the characteristics, psychological or otherwise, of those 'pseudo-representations', his response to Hume's Problem strongly suggests that AI theorists and researchers must eschew notions of representation of exactly the kind that Derrida would deride.

That there are mental (or cerebral) representations *of some kind* (that thought *is* those representations) is beyond dispute, but does not Hume's Problem derive from the desire for the presence of representations as somehow eidetically 'realistic', totalized, undeferred? The answer – one that would seem to respond to similar questions raised by related problems – is quite arguably affirmative and carries with it certain elucidating implications. Whatever 'brain writing' constitutes thought is surely a kind of Derridean *écriture*, a structure of differences; thus Dennett's pseudo-representations are not univocal entities but networks of differences, more like data-structures, however organized, than like printed language or paintings (which are also, of course, in their own ways networks of differences subject to the desire for presence). Hume's Problem arises because of the fiction that a representation is fully re*present*ed to consciousness, a fiction that compensates for non-presence by supplementation. Once that fiction is acknowledged, a great deal of philosophical underbrush can be cleared away. Dennett's pseudo-representations are not yet well characterized, but attempts at that characterization need not contend with the entanglements of a naïve problematic.

In any case, to regard mental representations of any kind as 'images', as if they were somehow irreducible *visual* presences, is certainly counterproductive. If one is interested in how such representations arise from the neural code, then thinking of them as *patterns* that are constructed decisionally is much more useful. It requires, first, a neurological perspective.

16
Recognition, Hypothesis, HEARSAY

'Each nerve fibre is a charged system', according to Young; frequency-modulated messages propogate along it, by a *'conduction without decrement'*, as electrochemical impulses. 'Differences of quality, such as different tones or visual contours, are encoded in the nervous system by *having a different nerve cell and nerve fibre for each quality'*, so that the brain is a *'multichannel system'*, a parallel processor – in that respect at least.[1] The impulses animating this differential code are not individually meaningful to the mind; they must be combined, as the constituent actions of perception and cognition, to become so, just as letters must combine to become meaningful as words and words must combine to become meaningful as sentences.

Extending this analogy for the minimal units of neural code, one 'can compare the problem of how they represent the world to understanding how a grammar allows the combination of words to make meaningful statements'. But an empirical boundary is immediately encountered: there is 'no physiological technique for studying the actions of many nerve cells at once'. None the less, there are clues that support the comparison: 'the information from the sensory surfaces of the retina, or skin, or from the ear is laid out in a topographically precise way on the surface of the brain. . . . Moreover for each sense there is a series of such maps, each recombining in a new way the words of information provided by the cells. So the grammar of this language has somthing to do with spatial relations. It communicates meanings by topological analogies.'[2] Once again, information is form; its grammar is topological.

The neural message is 'understood or decoded where the impulses in the different nerve fibres converge and activate other cells'. Thus the action of a nerve cell in receiving messages through its dendritic branches and sending out or not sending out another message through its axon is somewhat analogous to the action of a logic gate in a computer. A threshold switching occurs at the axodendritic interfaces of cell meeting cell through neurotransmitter chemicals in the boutons at the ends of the presynaptic fibres, because the electrochemical currents produced by the action of boutons in contact with the dendritic fibres of a given cell have to summate to a certain level to cause a subsequent axonal discharge from that cell to yet another one; and this 'process of summation of the effects of the boutons is thus the means by which *decisions* are made in the nervous system'.[3] The progressive concatenating of such decisions within the architecture of the brain gives rise to informational patterns whose noise component is progressively decreased; as Serres puts it, 'Each level of information functions as an unconscious for the global level bordering it, as a closed or relatively isolated system in relationship to which the noise-information couple, when it crosses the edge, is reversed and which the subsequent system decodes or deciphers.'[4]

Many levels of such decoding decisions are required to create patterns that are useful to (that *are*) the mind, and the operations involved have not been described adequately by empirical research. But, as one might suspect from Dennett's discussion of homunculi, it is impossible to determine where a message is *finally* understood, because 'There is no central place in the brain where this occurs': it occurs continually through the levels of cumulative decoding decisions that are 'completed only by action'. Meaning (the word itself is gerundial – that is, actional) is a matter of pattern recognition (the essence, arguably, of what AI systems do) as evidenced by action. Understanding at the level of the mind is a matter of intention *through* recognition: 'A dog recognizes a bone by gnawing it. Even in ourselves the understanding of a meaning implies preparation for action. The very word "understand" is the same as "hypothesis" from the Greek "to stand under." The brain is continually making hypotheses that prepare for useful actions.'[5] One of those actions is the conscious use of verbal language (whose words may be regarded as symbols of recognition), which is inextricably involved with sensory (especially visual and auditory) pattern recognition.

How those hypotheses are formulated remains a puzzle, though they must mirror somehow the neural processes that give rise to them. However, most of what is known about that formulation derives not from neurological research but from comparative

studies of the way people comprehend natural language (which
involve various kinds of 'protocol-taking', to use a term usually
associated with Allen Newell and Herbert A. Simon) and the way
AI systems comprehend it. Many implications of such studies will
come into play later, but for now I am concerned only with those
associated with an exemplary language-comprehension system
named HEARSAY.

HEARSAY is essentially a chess-playing program, developed in
the early 1970s by D. Raj Reddy and his colleagues at Carnegie-
Mellon University, that interprets and responds to contextually
restricted statements in spoken English. When the interlocutor
enters a chess move through a microphone, the system
demonstrates its interpretation of that input by responding with a
countermove. At the most general level the system 'consists of a
set of *knowledge sources*, a *scheduler* which determines processing
priorities, and a *global message center* through which the knowledge
sources interact'. David E. Rumelhart summarizes its operation in
terms of those components:

There are four basic sources of knowledge that are considered
relevant: acoustic features, syntactic knowledge, semantic
knowledge, and pragmatic knowledge. The acoustic features
provide a preliminary analysis of the acoustic waveform. The
syntactic component contributes knowledge of the grammar of
the language. The semantic domain pertains to the *meaning* of
the utterance. Pragmatics involves the likelihood of the utterance
in the current context.

Within the HEARSAY system each knowledge source consists
of a set of processes. Knowledge sources propose and/or
evaluate hypotheses about the nature of certain aspects of the
input. Proposed hypotheses are written into the message center,
together with a preliminary evaluation of each hypothesis (i.e.,
how likely it is to be correct), by a knowledge source. Whenever
a new hypothesis comes into the message center all relevant
knowledge sources are called in to evaluate that hypothesis and
possibly propose new hypotheses. All of this processing makes
demands on the total processing capacity of the system. The
scheduler allocates the processing capacity to those knowledge
sources acting upon the most promising hypotheses at the
moment. When the system finally comes up with a highly rated
hypothesis which encompasses all aspects of the utterance it

ceases processing and assumes that it has properly interpreted the utterance.

The HEARSAY system is designed around the message center. Hypotheses stored in the message center differ with regard to (1) the segment of the waveform they are presumably accounting for, (2) the rating of the hypothesis, and (3) the *level* of the hypothesis. Level refers to the degree of abstractness of a hypothesis. Some hypotheses, such as those suggested by the semantic and pragmatic knowledge sources, are very abstract and may suggest that a reference to a certain concept should be found in the input (this is called the conceptual level). Others are more concrete and suggest that a certain segment of the speech waveform corresponds to a word in some particular syntactic class (e.g., a noun). Still others suggest that a segment of the speech waveform corresponds to some particular word (the lexical level). And still others are at an even more concrete level and suggest, for example, that the phoneme /s/ is present in some segment of the waveform. . . . The message center thus represents proposed hypotheses in terms of an essentially three-dimensional space. One dimension corresponds to time, the second corresponds to level of the hypothesis, and the third corresponds to the alternative hypotheses that are under consideration.[6]

Once again information is form, here a wave*form* translated into a three-dimensional hypothesis-space.

Though HEARSAY is hardly as complex a language-processing system as the brain/mind, the interactions of knowledge sources and the abstraction levels that those sources in various ratios constitute in the predication of hypotheses do suggest possible analogs to the interactions of the levels of progressively more complex neural patterning and competitive hypothesis-making in the brain/mind. And Rumelhart claims that the system, in spite of its limitations, is 'among the best systems ever built for recognizing connected speech', for four reasons: (1) it 'makes use of a number of sources of information and attempts to find an interpretation of the input that satisfies all of these sources'; (2) 'expectations are explicitly represented in the system as "hypotheses derived from above" without special support from below'; (3) 'the notion of *attention* and the allocation of attention is explicitly represented in the scheduler with its decisions on what hypotheses should be followed up'; and (4) 'the entire system runs in parallel' and thus 'works on a set of plausible hypotheses simultaneously'. As a means of explicitly devising a method of 'language comprehension as an extension of the process of recognizing patterns (perceiving)', the system is particularly effective in its construction of parallel hypotheses in terms of multiple constraints, including contextual ones, in order to discover the most complete and plausible hypothesis for the final interpretation of the input. Though it was not designed strictly to model the brain/mind, HEARSAY 'does appear to capture most of what is known about the way humans actually do use multiple sources of knowledge to interpret what they see and hear'.[7] But this brave claim must be qualified by further considerations.

17

ATN, Automata, Expectation

Of the four knowledge sources necessary to language comprehension as discussed by Rumelhart, the syntactic has been of greatest interest in man–machine comparative studies – largely because, of the four, it is the one most easily subject to productive model-building, though there is much controversy concerning how it is structured and used in human language processing. None the less, a powerful modelling tool has been developed by Rumelhart and others: the *augmented transition network* (ATN). A consideration of ATN research foregrounds many of the key issues in comparative studies, with regard not only to syntactic knowledge but, to a lesser extent, to the other kinds as well.

As Philip C. Jackson, Jr, recounts, ATN research began in 1968, when the designers of 'language-understanding programs . . . freed themselves from the restrictions of phrase-structure grammars by taking a new approach to syntax'. That new approach was occasioned by

the realization that language-understanding programs need not be restricted to the use of phrase-structure grammars any more than computers need be restricted to the simulation of Turing machines. Phrase-structure grammars and Turing machines are adequate simple formalizations for the infinite class of all machine-understandable languages and all machine-computable functions, but they are extremely poor formalizations in which to describe the relatively small classes of natural languages and intelligent procedures. The result of using this new approach has been the discovery that natural language grammars can be profitably described as certain kinds of recursive procedures. Two ways of describing these procedures have been developed, corresponding to the formalization of *augmented state transition networks* . . . and to the programming language PROGRAMMAR. . . .[1]

By either description these procedures are the same – as Terry Winograd, the developer of PROGRAMMAR, notes, 'grammars described as networks and grammars described as programs are just two different ways of talking about doing exactly the same thing'.[2]

The ATN is a method of parsing a sentence, of (to use Edward A. Feigenbaum's word) 'delinearizing' its syntax, in terms of semantic relationships. Like PROGRAMMAR, it is conceptually similar to and largely derived from systemic grammar. It embodies the notion that sentence structure is determined by a series of grammatically conditioned binary decisions. Such a notion is justified by much of what is known about linguistic behaviour and neural activity, and it is obviously cognate with the more general notion of the computer as a decision-making machine. Of the assumptions enabling systemic grammar and thereby the ATN, two are of special importance: 'The problems of syntax, semantics, inference, and generation, which are to be solved in the use of natural language, are all closely interrelated . . .'; however, 'Despite their interrelations, these problems are in many ways quite distinct.' Consequently, 'it is desirable that a language-understanding program be able to solve these problems in a highly integrated way', but one 'should not expect that a system designed to solve the generation problem (e.g., transformational grammar . . .) will necessarily be the basis of an efficient system to solve the syntax (in particular, the parsing) problem'.[3] (None the less, as deconstruction theorists and others have persuasively argued, generation and reception – particularly writing and reading – are not simply inversions of each other but complementary, even 'integrated', aspects of one process.)

The program that will 'solve' all these interrelated problems probably will draw on the resources of many different grammars, and ATN research suggests many of the characteristics it might require. Actually all grammars tend to share a broad set of assumptions, but systemic grammar has proven the most use-ful in AI practice. It provides for an analysis of the discrete structural cues or *features* by which sentences are interpreted. Winograd, discussing the theory of systemic grammar developed by M. A. K. Halliday (the most important one now used in ATN and related research), observes that in it 'choices of features are primary' and that, in recognizing that 'meaning is of primary importance to the way language is structured', it places emphasis not on 'a "deep structure" tree' but on '"system networks" describing the way different features interact and depend on each other'[4] (in this respect it is similar to so-called dependency grammar). Thus it is not alien to phrase-markers or parsing trees with their stratified bifurcations of grammatical categories, but its primary concern is not with the realized forms of sentences or sentence constituents but with the semantically-conditioned grammatical decisions that give rise to them.

System in this context is a 'set of features that form a mutually exclusive set' of grammatical states that are analysable in terms of how one state determines a transition to the next.[5] As Rumelhart explains, in ATN analysis 'Not only does the syntactic component help us to perceive sentences by limiting the possible permutations of words we might reasonably expect, but, even more importantly, it allows us to determine the logical relationships among the words we discover in the string.' In simplest terms, then, 'An ATN is a device which takes a string of words as input and produces a structural description'; but it does that in a special way, as Figure 17.1, here glossed by Rumelhart, suggests:

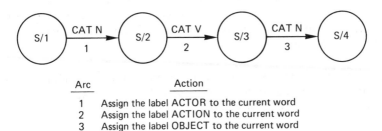

Arc	Action
1	Assign the label ACTOR to the current word
2	Assign the label ACTION to the current word
3	Assign the label OBJECT to the current word

Figure 17.1

The ATN illustrated in the figure consists of three kinds of elements: (1) *States*. There are four states, designated by circles in the diagram, illustrated here: S/1, S/2, S/3, and S/4. The analysis of a sentence consists of passing from one state to another. Processing begins in state S/1 and ends in state S/4. (2) *Labels*. States are connected to one another by labeled arrows. The arrows indicate the allowable movements between states. There is an arrow directly from S/1 to S/2. This indicates simply that during the analysis of a sentence the system may pass from S/1 directly to S/2. Since no direct arrow connects S/1 to S/3, S/3 may not follow S/1 directly in processing. The labels on the arrows indicate conditions which must be met for the transition from one state to another to occur. For example, the label CAT N (short for 'category noun') indicates that a transition from S/1 to S/2 can occur only if the first word of the sentence is a noun. Similarly, the label CAT V indicates that a transition from state S/2 to S/3 can take place only when the next word is a verb. (3) *Actions*. In addition to the conditions determining moving from one state to the next, there are actions which are carried out whenever an arc is traversed. This action involves assigning the various parts of the sentence, discovered during the analysis, to their syntactical roles. Thus, the action associated with arc 1 (given at the bottom of the figure) is to assign the noun found at this arc to the role of ACTOR. Whenever a particular arc is traversed, the action associated with that arc is carried out.[6]

An ATN is thus an algorithm for syntactic analysis whose rules of operation echo notions of the relational structure of language articulated by the structuralist tradition of Saussure as well as conceptions of computation developed by Turing and others.

To illustrate the operation of this ATN, Rumelhart explains how it could be used by a machine to analyse a short sentence – *Dogs chase rabbits* – as follows:

The system begins in state S/1. At first the current word is the first word of the sentence, *dogs*. An attempt is made to traverse arc 1. The CAT N label on arc 1 indicates that the arc can be traversed only when the current word is a noun. In this sentence *dogs* is a noun so the system carries out the action associated with arc 1 – that is, *dogs* is assigned to the ACTOR role. The next word *chase* then becomes the current word, and the system moves to the state S/2. The CAT V condition requires that the current word is a verb. It is, so *chase* is assigned as the ACTION and the system moves into state S/3. Here it assigns *rabbits* to the OBJECT position and completes the sentence.[7]

There is a simple enough operation, but its implications, as I hope to show, are complex and quite interesting.

An ATN is similar in principle to the 'finite-state recognizer' used for analysing languages in automata theory, which is concerned with how an abstract device, an automaton, receives an input and performs certain elementary operations on it in a step-by-step fashion according to a set of instructions. As Robert Wall notes, 'It is a basic premise of automata theory that every procedure, no matter how complex, can be decomposed into a series of these elementary operations.' Moreover, 'an automaton works in a recursive fashion, in that the result of performing one step becomes the input to the next'; thus 'The theory of automata and the theory of formal grammars are isomorphic in most important respects. . . .'[8] However, the recognizer must be extended to be useful as a natural-language parser:

> The first extension is in allowing the networks to make recursive calls to other networks (or to themselves). The condition for following a particular state transition is not limited to examining a single input symbol. The condition on the arc can be something like 'NP' ['noun phrase'] where NP is the name of an initial state of another network. This recursively called NP network then examines the input and operates as a recognizer. If it ever reaches an accepting state, it stops, and parsing continues from the end of the NP arc in the original network. These 'recursive transition networks' have the power of a context-free grammar, and the correspondence between a network and its equivalent grammar is quite simple and direct.[9]

The second extension involves further conditioning each arc and adding more instructions to be triggered when it is traversed.

Thus it may be seen that, as Winograd explains, recognizers 'augmented' in this fashion 'have the power of Turing machines, since they have changeable registers and can transfer control depending on the state of those registers'. Theoretically, then, they 'can handle any type of grammar which could possibly be parsed by any machine'. (Any such grammar should be analysable in terms of a push-down list or some more flexible memory array.) Furthermore, 'The advantage of augmented transition networks is that their operation appears to be closer to the actual operations humans use in understanding language.'[10] (ATN theory seems to furnish, in some specifics of principle, a better model of the child's early grammar than transformational theory has been able to. Also, an ATN can vary the depth of its analysis, which flexibility may have its analog in human processing, for which the amount of syntactic information required varies from one linguistic situation to another. That flexibility is enhanced by its using heuristic techniques rather than a rigorous set of transformational rules. Finally, an ATN, again apparently like its human analog – at least on the surface level of initial comprehension – processes serially, taking fairly careful account of endophoric context and dividing its procedural tasks in terms of predictable linguistic units.) Perhaps an important man-machine isomorphism is hereby implied, but it is important to remember, given the confirmation-theoretical problems involved in the simulation of human language processing, that the ATN should be regarded only as a speculative and tentative algorithm. It must be understood, as Rumelhart observes, that in practice 'no ATN grammar has ever been built capable of properly analyzing all of the English language', though 'systems . . . have been developed which can properly parse a significant proportion of English. . . .'[11] One reason for that qualification is that English, like all natural languages, is not generated by a context-free grammar, for which kind, especially if phrase-structural, it is possible in all cases to construct an algorithm for determining how a sentence has been generated.[12]

None the less, the ATN has a number of features that make it particularly useful for modelling natural-language syntax. The most important, as Rumelhart notes, are two: 'the natural way that the *grammar of the language* fits together with the *rules for processing* the language' (so that 'an ATN allows a variety of specific processing assumptions to be postulated and tested') and 'the natural way the notion of expectation can be realized' (so that an ATN can, to an extent, take into account 'the important role that our expectations and prior knowledge play in the details of our information processing'). Because of this second feature an ATN 'allows us to develop specific theories about the syntactic aspects of our expectations'. To understand why, one must realize that 'In a very real sense the arcs leaving a state in an ATN grammar represent expectations about the syntactic class of the words to follow' and that 'These expectations allow us to interpret naturally the *same word* as a member of different syntactic classes depending on the context in which the word occurs.'[13] Thus an ATN can disambiguate and might even be adapted to process ambiguities without disambiguating them (to handle multiple syntactic vectors, so to speak), so that, for example, a pun (or perhaps even a deconstructive reading) could be retained during parsing.

Rumelhart presents evidence that 'shows clearly that *pauses* in reading aloud often correspond with periods of back up in an ATN' – that is, with periods when a network (or, more properly, subnetwork) is making recursive calls in order to decide which of several transitions is most appropriate. Such a pause or backup occurs, for instance, in the disambiguation of some adjective–noun pairs or embedded clauses in so-called garden-path sentences, the processing of which leads to 'initial inappropriate results which must later be reanalyzed' (one of his examples is *The granite carpets are covering up is ugly*). The evidence shows, more specifically, that 'the ordering of arcs in an ATN can account for "perceptual strategies" employed by subjects' and that an ATN 'gives a good account of garden path sentences and the pauses that occur while processing such sentences'.[14]

Since the arcs between states may be multiple, they are ordered in terms of the set of probabilities 'of making a correct transition'; thus 'It is this ordered set which can serve as a model of a subject's expectancy while reading', and it is 'the ordering of the arcs' that 'comes to reflect in some way the statistical probabilities of the English language' – or of any other natural language, presumably. Rumelhart's research, in comparing ATN transition probabilities with the performance of human subjects (who took a kind of 'cloze test') for given sentences, shows that 'Over all states subjects responded with a word from the most probable arc about 75% of the time', which 'seems to suggest that there is a reasonably fixed ordering of expectancies dependent only on the state of the network as determined by our ATN model'. From similar research on reading errors, he concludes that 'the sorts of expectations generated from an ATN are indeed partial determiners of the errors we actually observe'. Finally, he notes, however, that, as one would expect, 'constraints other than the simple syntactic constraints modeled by an ATN are involved in reading'.[15]

Some of those constraints can be introduced by combining an ATN-based system with one like HEARSAY, thus interfacing a system that operates in a 'depth-first word-by-word fashion' with one that operates in a 'highly interactive parallel' fashion. To understand how this interface is possible, one must recall that 'the ATN is only playing the role of the syntactic knowledge source. As such it plays only a small part in the overall comprehension process. Its task is merely to hypothesize possible syntactic elements and to check these hypotheses against words discovered in the input string. . . .' This kind of hypothesizing seems quite compatible with that of HEARSAY; none the less, to make the match effective 'a *bottom-up* character' must be added to the 'essential *top-down* nature' of the ATN. Such an addition has been made, both by Ronald M. Kaplan, in his GSP (General Syntactic Processor), and, more theoretically, by Rumelhart, in his system that models the reading process by combining an ATN-based system with both HEARSAY and a system capable of recognizing printed language through 'visual feature extraction'.[16]

The ATN, when used in such hybrid systems, offers a fairly powerful model of syntactic aspects of human language comprehension. However, as Rumelhart is careful to note, 'there are no well-developed models of semantic processing analogous to the ATN'.[17] So one must be somewhat sceptical that an ATN grammar could evolve into a comprehensive grammar of thought. But there have been some attempts at the development of semantic models more or less analogous to – or compatible with – the ATN, and their implications are worth exploring.

18

Semantics, Components, Rapprochement

What are the principal considerations in developing a model of semantic processing? According to Manfred Bierwisch, 'The semantic analysis of a given language must explain how the sentences of this language are understood, interpreted, and related to states, processes, and objects in the universe.' A problematic order, to be sure. None the less, if 'analysis' is changed to *model*, then this imperative is exactly the one to which the modeller must respond. The fundamental question of semantic analysis or modelling is, for Bierwisch, 'What is the meaning of a sentence S of the language L?' In attempting to answer that question, one necessarily deals with another: *how* is that sentence meaningful in that language? Of course, context is critical because one must interpret sentence S in terms of 'its semantic relations to other expressions' in that language. Furthermore, one must know 'not only the meaning of its lexical elements, but also how they interrelate' – which interrelation, of course, 'depends on the syntactic structure of the sentence'. Thus a semantic theory – or model – must 'make reference to the syntactic structure in a precise way'; 'systematically represent the meaning of . . . lexical elements'; 'show how the structure of the meanings of words and the syntactic relations interact, in order to constitute the interpretation of sentences'; and 'indicate how these interpretations are related to things spoken [or written] about'.[1]

The basic enabling assumption of modern semantic theory and of research concerned with the machine modelling of semantic processing is that 'the meanings of lexical items are not unanalysable or undefinable wholes'. Though there are many ways to describe them, two are of special importance, according to Bierwisch: one, developed by Rudolf Carnap, is in terms of 'meaning postulates'; the other, developed by Bierwisch and others, is in terms of 'semantic components'. In the first, the meaning of a lexical item is derived through patterns of logical entailment, so that it 'is defined implicitly by the set of all meaning postulates associated' with it. In the second, it is defined 'explicitly in terms of semantic components' that 'are not part of the vocabulary of the language itself, but rather theoretical elements, postulated in order to describe the semantic relations between the lexical elements of a given language'. Since such 'componential analysis' also uses logical entailment, its main advantage is its explicitness; though, as Bierwisch admits, the differences between the two approaches are blurred since 'both explications are at least formally equivalent, in the sense that for each set of meaning postulates there is a componential analysis of the vocabulary involved defining the same semantic relations, and vice versa'.[2] It is obvious, at any rate, that some systematic method for analysing the semantic components of natural language is required if any model of semantic processing is to be possible. In his theory of componential analysis, one finds outlined the desiderata for such a method.

Like Saussure, Bierwisch asserts that semantic components must be conceived relationally – much as people are in a kinship system as analysed by a structuralist anthropologist like Claude Lévi-Strauss. Lexical elements operate as combinations of semantic components by virtue of relations among those components, which must be thought of more as arguments, in the logico-mathematical sense, than as independent terms. Thus a dictionary is a 'system of concepts' in which 'the meaning of a word is a complex of semantic components (or features, or markers) connected by logical constants' that code entries for hyponymy, antonymy, and so on. Moreover, 'Sets of lexical entries whose meanings have certain features in common form a "semantic field"', a notion devised by Jost Trier 'in order to account for the observation that the meaning of lexical elements is specified only by their relatedness to and their difference from other relevant elements'. Bierwisch suggests that the notion is quite useful: 'By redefining this conception of the semantic field in terms of semantic components, we might indicate precisely the organization of particular fields and the relations among their members.'[3] That is, of course, what he is trying to do by his method, one similar to that of M. Ross Quillian and others involved in the development of 'graph-structure' semantic formalisms, as opposed to those based on the predicate calculus (an extended form of the propositional calculus).

Besides sharing components, lexical elements are interconnected by relations, such as pertinence, that constrain their combinability. These '"selectional restrictions" . . . indicate which lexical elements may be selected in order to form a semantically well-formed combination of two or more syntactically combined lexical elements'. Taking into account these and other characteristics of such elements, Bierwisch summarizes the principles of componential analysis:

> In general, one might define a complex of semantic components connected by logical constants as a concept. The dictionary of a language is then a system of concepts in which a phonological form and certain syntactic and morphological characteristics are assigned to each concept. This system of concepts is structured by several types of relations. It is supplemented, furthermore, by redundancy or implicational rules . . . , representing general properties of the whole system of concepts. . . . At least a relevant part of these general rules is not bound to particular languages, but represents presumably universal structures of natural languages. They are not learned, but are rather a part of the human ability to acquire an arbitrary natural language.[4]

Given these principles, the relation of semantics to syntax and other aspects of human language processing may be addressed.

In this realm where questions propagate exponentially more quickly than answers, Bierwisch is concerned with a rapprochement between syntactic and semantic models. He observes that necessarily 'certain syntactic properties must also be incorporated in the representation of word meanings' and that 'an essential part of the syntactic behaviour of a lexical element can be derived directly from its semantic representation'.[5] (The need for this rapprochement is crucial. There is a pitched battle between those theorists and modellers who embrace the primacy of syntax and those who embrace the primacy of semantics in language processing. At times both schools have committed various excesses. For example, some of the former have relied foolishly on context-free mathematical-combinatory models, while some of the latter have flirted with versions of the 'direct-access hypothesis', the idea that skilled readers process printed language directly into meaning without phonological or even syntactic processing. The problems with the first excess are patent. Those with the second are more complex and demand more research. Unskilled readers apparently do rely more on phonological processing than do skilled ones; hence their spoken dialects may interfere with their reading – and writing – habits. But the extent to which phonological processing is absent in the skilled reader has not been established, and the contention that syntactic processing is suspended in the skilled reader is surely wrong and not supported by empirical evidence – though blood-flow patterns in the brain are curiously different during speaking, oral reading, and silent reading.)[6] The premises for this rapprochement that Bierwisch finds most useful were elaborated in the early 1960s by Jerrold J. Katz, Jerry A. Fodor, and Paul M. Postal. He describes as follows their approach to modelling the relation between syntax and semantics:

> It is based on the theory presented by Chomsky (1965) according to which a grammar has a base component that generates syntactic deep structures, each of which consists of a string of lexical elements on which a hierarchy of syntactic categories are imposed so that relations such as 'subject of the sentence,' etc., can be derived. . . . Each lexical element contains a phonological representation, certain syntactic and morphological features and a semantic representation. A deep structure of this kind is then transformed by rules that are for the most part unique to particular languages into appropriate surface structures which are finally mapped into phonetic representations.
>
> The semantic representation of a sentence as a whole is derived from the syntactic deep structure by certain universal operations that combine the meanings of the lexical elements of a deep structure according to the relevant syntactic relations.

He offers a proposal (in the form of a kind of algorithm), too elaborate to discuss here, for the procedure whereby this last representation occurs, but he admits that it involves oversimplifications and ignores some nagging lexical questions. None the less, he is optimistic that 'in principle the meaning of a sentence can be derived in a definite form on the basis of the meaning of its words and its syntactic deep structure, and that this derived meaning represents the crucial properties of its cognitive content in a plausible way'.[7]

How? Bierwisch's answer is straightforward, even has a certain bravado, but is problematic:

> If appropriately refined the semantic structures arrived at in this way will presumably turn out to be nothing but a suitably adapted realization of the principles of formal logic. Hence the logical rules of transformation and deduction apply to semantic representations, explaining how we are able to carry out logical operations in natural language. . . . The principles according to which semantic representation are organized must furthermore be assumed to be universal, i.e. the same for all languages. Thus it is not the types of semantic components and of their possible interrelations that differ from language to language, but only the particular combinations that form the specific concepts listed in the dictionary.[8]

Just as there are problems with attempts to map linguistic processes onto neural processes, so there are also with attempts to translate the semantic structures of natural language into the structures of formal logic; surely any formal system to which natural language would be isomorphic would have to be a great deal more flexible than such logic. Also, Bierwisch seems to ignore the complexities of cultural (exophoric) context that must be taken into account in any comprehensive semantic theory or model. And it may be, as a consequence of what is known about formal systems from Kurt Gödel and others, that the mind is not capable of fully defining its own processes in *any* terms – from formal logic or elsewhere. None the less, I feel that Bierwisch is right, though only partially and not without qualifications, and I will return to these troubling preoccupations. But for the moment I must let him speak further for himself.

Bierwisch finds support for his theory in the theory of generative semantics expounded by James D. McCawley and others, according to which 'the grammar first specifies a semantic structure for each sentence' that is 'then converted into a syntactic structure . . .'. This theory, if considered in more detail, does not agree entirely – by way of an inverted complementarity – with Bierwisch's, but, as he notes, 'In some important respects it is equivalent' and 'expresses in general the same facts in a different form'.[9] Armed with this corroboration, he proceeds to larger claims and some qualifications.

Using his analytical method, Bierwisch argues, one may 'explain many semantic properties and relations'. Thus, he observes, 'two sentences S_1 and S_2 are synonymous – or paraphrases of each other – if their semantic representations are identical'. He observes also, less specifically, 'that relations like paraphrase, entailment, etc. are suitable generalizations of lexical relations like synonymy, hyponymy, etc.', and this connection, he concludes, 'is a natural consequence of the fact that the semantic representations of sentences are in principle of the same character as lexical meanings'[10] (though idioms present special complications).

Following this line of reasoning, one may see how componential analysis might be – and, with variations, is – useful in modelling semantic processes by computer, but the limits of that usefulness have not been established. One must remember that Bierwisch's analysis involves representations that consist of 'referentially indexed arguments' or 'variables representing possible (sets of) objects'; that is, they are indicators of 'identity or difference of reference' but are not representations of 'particular objects'. If a sentence is intended to refer to such objects, then 'every referentially indexed variable must be replaced by the representation of particular objects. . .'.[11] That imperative, which flirts with the notion of presence that I criticized earlier, seems to offer machine modelling an overwhelming difficulty.

Bierwisch softens that imperative, however, with the qualification that 'the representation of the objects themselves is not part of the semantic structure of a language' but that the components do have a representational function, one that he construes in somewhat constructivist or even poststructuralist terms that are less disturbing:

It seems natural to assume that these components represent categories or principles according to which real and fictitious, perceived and imagined situations and objects are structured and classified. The semantic features do not represent, however, external physical properties, but rather the psychological conditions according to which human beings process their physical and social environment. Thus they are not symbols for physical properties and relations outside the human organism, but rather for the internal mechanisms by means of which such phenomena are perceived and conceptualized. This then leads to the extremely far-reaching, though plausible, hypothesis that all semantic structures might finally be reduced to components representing the basic dispositions of the cognitive and perceptual structure of the human organism. According to this hypothesis semantic features cannot be different from language to language, but are rather part of the general human capacity for language, forming a universal inventory used in particular ways by individual languages. Basic components of this type might be X GREATER Y representing the general ability of comparison, X DIMENSION OF Y based on the three-dimensional space orientation, VERTICAL Y reflecting the special role that the vertical dimension plays for human beings. HUMAN X, ANIMATE X, X PARENT Y, X CHANGE TO P, X CAUSE P and other components . . . might also be candidates for such a universal interpretation. . . . All these basic elements are not learned in any reasonable sense of the term, but are rather an innate predisposition for language acquisition. They have to be actualized or released by experience during the process of language acquisition, but as a possible structure they are already present in the learning organism. Hence what is learned during the process of language acquisition, is not the semantic components, but rather their particular combinations in special concepts, and the assignment of phonemic forms and morphological properties to these concepts.[12]

This construal, generally in harmony with Chomskyan theory, is quite persuasive. If Bierwisch is right about the relation between semantic features and psychological conditions, then that relation might well be extended, *mutatis mutandis*, to the level of neural conditions as well – though the 'meaning' involved would certainly be different.

Bierwisch's construal provides also for 'the necessary interrelation of semantic structures with the surrounding universe, which is perceived and categorized according to these inherent conditions of the organism'. He argues, recalling Steiner, that 'This mediated relation between semantic structures and real situations also explains the fact that we are able to talk about things that are not present in the situation, or are purely fictitious . . . .'[13] Thus, for the most part, his theory offers a fairly comprehensive model – or proto-model – of semantic processing that could, with refinements, be used in an AI system. But there are other qualifications he mentions that should be taken into account before I pursue that subject further.

First of all, the names of semantic components are to be regarded as not 'themselves lexical entries of any natural language'. In other words, Bierwisch's model, like any model generally, must be understood as a metalanguage that allows one, however contingently, to step outside the processes being described by it – an especially tricky business in this case but one that has to be undertaken to try to avoid describing a language in its own terms. Also, his model ignores 'all problems of stylistic variation or connotative values'. Finally, it does not 'explain how one of the several meanings associated with a particular word or sentence is selected in accordance with a particular universe of discourse'. He believes, however, that these last two limitations 'do not seem to pose difficulties of principle', and he remarks that it might be fruitful to regard 'the problem of context' as 'similar to that of stylistic variation in the sense that stylistically different sub-languages are used in different contexts'.[14]

The reader must not get the impression that Bierwisch's componential-analytical model is the last word – it surely is not. It has been superseded in some respects by the formal-linguistic theory of the late Richard Montague (whose complex 'Montague grammar', which attempts to treat natural language, in a form relatively close to its surface structure, as a flexible formal language characterized by precise constraints between syntax and semantics, has won adherents recently)[15] and others; but it is representative of what seem valid ways, now used in computational-linguistic research, of approaching the modelling of semantic processes in close relation to syntax, and it foregrounds intelligibly several of the problems that now inhibit natural-language modelling, foremost among which is 'the problem of context'.

19

Context, Reference, Schema

All language involves context; its meaning is contextually constrained. There is always an interplay of text and context. Indeed, human consciousness is inherently responsive to context. For example, when the eye sweeps its environment, the peripheral visual system is continually sampling context while the central ocular attention shifts; the perceptual data of the former are buffered and used to update, in terms of a changing assessment of context, those of the latter. Likewise, in the use of verbal language, there is a continual retracing of the hermeneutic circle of sign and context, an attempt to 'frame' properly the associative scenario of the sign (the play of A. J. Greimas's 'semes'), to equilibrize the tension between its general (lexemic) and particular (sememic) meanings. Context, for human language, is very thick, and its specification seems constantly to invite an infinite regress, an endless recursive looping of the hermeneutic circle; but, just as a dog stops chasing its tail by an ineffable impulse, so that regress or recursion is somehow truncated. (The determination of that stopping point is a profound problem in the simulation of natural-language comprehension. It is interlinked with the problem of adequately specifying rhetorical 'decorum' in language use and the larger problem of formalizing linguistic performance as well as competence.) With these thoughts in mind, I would like to turn to a consideration of the problem of context in the machine modelling of semantic processing.

In his discussion of the ATN and HEARSAY, Rumelhart relies on a view of semantics similar to that elaborated by Bierwisch, and he is concerned with how disambiguation occurs. Thus he is necessarily also concerned with how selectional restrictions ('argument constraints') as well as 'general contextual information' are used in the processing of ambiguous sentences in order 'to eliminate certain of the semantically improbable readings'.[1] He believes that 'more general mechanisms' than either of these two are involved.

Rumelhart reviews research (particularly that of John D. Bransford and Marcia K. Johnson) on the role of context in the comprehension and recall of written language (which, of course, requires more detailed endophoric context than spoken language) and concludes, as one might expect, that 'material in context is more comprehensible and therefore more memorable' than that lacking it. (And one must remember that, for example, a word that is too contextually conditioned may be backgrounded into semantic invisibility; likewise, a word that is not yet conditioned by its present context – a neologism, say – may be foregrounded into semantic opacity. The conditioning requires an equilibration.) His review leads him to conclude also that, in dealing with context, 'a bulk of the problem is reference'.[2]

This conclusion comes as no surprise to the poststructuralist, of course. Deconstruction theorists, like AI theorists, have all along been viewing reference ('aboutness') askance. (Semioticians have always had a problem with it, and even Saussure – in so far as his somewhat second-hand published work is *his* – is contradictory in what he says about it.) Robert Scholes captures the spirit of the deconstructionist arguments: 'that reference is a mirage of language, that there is no simple reference or unmediated perception, that the world is always already textualized by an archewriting or system of differentiation that effectively brackets or sets aside questions of reference . . .'. He is surely wrong, however, in asserting that such arguments finally entail an erasure of the world: it is still 'there', of course, but in a textualized way that is unfamiliar to hypnotically conventional notions of its presence. Certainly Derrida has made some astonishing statements about reference (and perception), but not finally to deny it so much as to dramatize vividly its problematic operation, its trammelling by *différance*. The poststructuralist does not bracket reference – as, say, the naïve behaviourist brackets mind – in order to forget about and then negate it. He brackets it in order to change radically its metaphysical status. (Theorists of various kinds have argued that there are functions of language that precede, in one sense or another, the referential.) Likewise, Derrida's notion of deferral is not merely 'a philosopher's paradox' unrelated to the way perception and cognition work; indeed, it involves a problematizing that correlates suggestively with questions raised by empirical research. (A perverse version of Scholes's rendition of deconstruction might be that, since there is no such thing as reference, an AI system, which is so limited in dealing with it, would thereby seem to be already a strong candidate for the ideal model of the mind – such is patently not the case.) But the point is that, though signifieds are in some way 'motivated by reference', that way is quite problematic and should not be reduced to conventional terms; such a reduction involves a failure to recognize the complexity of the issue of reference, and *that* has been the real problem. There is no need to 'rescue the referent': there is, rather, the need to not eliminate one of Rumelhart's 'semantically improbable readings' and understand that reference is not impossible but also is not straightforward, that, in Scholes's words, 'The response to a text is itself always a text'[3] – one that is no less so for being 'worldly'. (That is, since the world is a text, referentiality works the same way it does in any textual situation: intertextually and, ultimately, intratextually.) Thus 'a bulk of the problem' for AI research is how to model the reference text, the context – in the largest sense. The task involved, though daunting, can be approached, provided one does not lose sight of textuality.

According to Herbert H. Clark, one of the principal ways reference is managed is by means of the 'given-new contract' (which is analogous to the topic-comment 'contract' of rhetorical theory or the rheme-theme 'contract' of Prague School linguistic theory), something Rumelhart sees as one of those 'more general mechanisms'. This contract has to do with the attempt on the part of a speaker or writer to adjust properly the ratio of *given* information to *new* information in an utterance (its informativity). (Some version of such a contract obviously operates also in nonverbal communication; and, incidentally, some information theorists might denominate the two aspects differently, so that, for example, given information would be 'redundancy' and new information simply 'information'.) Thus the given-new contract involves a distinction between two kinds of reference: to knowledge the sender believes the receiver to have already and to knowledge the sender wants to impart. The first must function as a supporting context for the second, and the two must not be confused, which imperative is answered by codes such as that governing the use of definite and indefinite articles.[4]

Research concerning the given-new contract has tried to explain how referents are sought and how 'syntactic and semantic evidence combines to speed the rejection of unallowable alternatives', and it describes empirically, though not in great detail, certain encoding/decoding processes:

> When encoding a message the speaker uses special syntactic markers to point to those parts of the sentence he believes the listener already to be familiar with and to which he wants to tie more information. For his part, the listener uses these same syntactic clues to direct his attention toward the intended concepts in memory, thereby allowing communication to occur. Whenever the speaker misjudges the listener, or covertly intends to mislead the listener, and thereby breaks the given-new contract, communication breaks down.[5]

Language processing in these terms doubtless involves perceptual-cognitive mechanisms that are cognate with those involved in the formulation of hypotheses at the various levels of sentence analysis. But Rumelhart is finally concerned with how hypotheses are formulated by a human language user – or could be formulated by a machine – at a higher level, that of discourse. He suggests that 'the process of comprehending a story', for instance, 'consists of finding a high level hypothesis that accounts for the story in much the same way that the hypothesis that a certain word is in the input accounts for the observed set of extracted features' – a *schema*, in other words, a construct of 'generalized knowledge about a sequence of events'.[6] Thus, just as there are variegated (and more or less problematic) analogies in composition theory between the sentence and the paragraph or the paragraph and the larger text, so there may be comparable analogies between levels of hypothesis-making; indeed, versions of one and the same process may be operating on all levels.

Roger C. Schank, one of a number of AI researchers who have developed language-comprehension programs that use schemata, corroborates that idea in his discussion of the 'stratified system' of conceptual structures that characterizes natural language as he views it:

> the conceptual base is responsible for formally representing the concepts underlying an utterance. . . . A given word in a language may or may not have one or more concepts underlying

it. . . . On the *sentential level*, the utterances of a given language are encoded within a syntactic structure of that language. The basic construction of the sentential level is the sentence.

The next highest level . . . is the *conceptual level*. We call the basic construction of this level the *conceptualization*. A conceptualization consists of *concepts* and certain relations among those concepts. We can consider that both levels exist at the same point in time and that for any unit on one level, some corresponding realizate exists on the other level. This realizate may be null or extremely complex. . . . Conceptualizations may relate to other conceptualizations by nesting or other specified relationships . . . .[7]

Schank's notion of conceptualization obviously pertains, implicitly, to discourse as well as to the sentence. Both he and Rumelhart are concerned with one of the most important of Rumelhart's 'more general mechanisms': the translation of sequential information into high-level knowledge structures.

In the mid-1970s Schank and his colleagues involved in the Yale AI Project developed a set of programs that use schemata (or 'scripts') to interpret short stories (in practice, but not necessarily in principle, quite short – about a paragraph in length). The system analyses a story by 'looking for a schema that will account for the story and a map from the people mentioned in the story to the various aspects of the schema'. Once it has discovered the schema and map, it can either 'give an elaborated paraphrase of the story in which elements of the schema are added to the original story' or 'summarize the story, using the major constituents of the schema as the framework for the summary'. In his discussion of this system, Rumelhart notes the importance of the ability to paraphrase as an aspect of language comprehension and thus argues that, 'If we understand something, our interpretation is always much more than the comprehension of the sum of the words of the input sentence.'[8] That is, the comprehension of language – by either machine or human being – must entail an intricate synergy.

As Rumelhart notes further, 'One interesting implication of the schema view of comprehension involves the large number of inferences that can be made once a series of inputs is associated with a schema.' Indeed, human beings interpret stories through patterns of inference so complexly in transaction with the text that, after a period of time, they are not able 'to tell the difference between information originally presented in the story and inferences made from the schema used to account for the story'. His conclusion – no surprise to the reader-response theorist – is that 'comprehension should be considered an extension of perception'. This idea, implying a general continuity of software and data, meaning and form, is inscribed in the principles of schema theory, here summarized:

> We take in sensory features and attempt to account for them with low level hypotheses about, say, possible letters in a string. These hypotheses, in turn, are subsumed by others about possible words in the string. Hypotheses about words are then subsumed as constituents in hypotheses about possible sentences in the string. Then these sentences themselves are subsumed under even higher level hypotheses – or schemata. The processing is carried on from the bottom up – that is, lower level hypotheses are 'suggesting' higher level ones . . . and from the top down – that is, higher level hypotheses are predicting (and inferring) the existence of lower level ones.[9]

Rumelhart is quick to point out that this theory is quite incomplete, but it is supported by some empirical evidence and has proven useful in the development of systems like HEARSAY. Its top-down aspects are less question-begging than its bottom-up aspects, largely because so little is known about how hypotheses are generated at the highest summative level, where mind seems utterly divorced from brain, where formal and relatively simple logical patterns have given rise to more informal but much more complex ones. The question of how well this theory or its machine instantiation represents processes of the brain/mind remains open.

20

SHRDLU, Procedures, Mini-World

Rumelhart's observation that 'Linguistic inputs are designed to fit into a general framework and are dependent upon that framework to make sense'[1] parallels Terry Winograd's more poststructuralist one, about linguistically based knowledge, that 'There is no self-contained set of "primitives" from which everything else can be defined. Definitions are circular, with the meaning of each concept depending on the other concepts.'[2] (Every text has – and itself already is – an intertext.) Like Rumelhart, Winograd has researched extensively the machine modelling of language comprehension, but he has been especially concerned with building contextually conditioned 'semantic structures' (structured lists that describe subjects and relationships and summate plausibilities among their components) to explore how meaning inheres in the interrelations of concepts in some 'general framework'.

In the early 1970s Winograd, then at the MIT Artificial Intelligence Laboratory, began development of an impressive language-comprehension system, SHRDLU, named after a portion of the row of letters on a linotype machine that typesetters insert in a faulty line of text so proofreaders can easily discover the spot where a mistake has occurred. It consists of a multifaceted program, written in LISP, that simulates, on a CRT screen, a robot 'with a hand and eye and the ability to manipulate toy blocks on a table', and it 'deals in an integrated way with all the aspects of language: syntax, semantics, inference, and, perhaps most important, knowledge and reasoning about the subject it discusses'. He regards his system and computers and their languages generally as sources of 'a formal metaphor' through which theories about human behaviour can be modelled and have their implications tested. He admits that such models are necessarily limited; none the less, he argues, they do 'give us a clear framework for thinking about what we do when we understand and respond to natural language'.[3]

Winograd describes 'the process of understanding language' in terms of 'a conversion from a string of sounds or letters to an internal representation of "meaning"'. Thus, according to him, 'a language-understanding system must have some formal way to express its knowledge of a subject, and must be able to represent the "meaning" of a sentence in this formalism'. This formalism, in turn, 'must be structured so the system can use its knowledge in conjunction with a problem-solving system to make deductions, accept new information, answer questions, and interpret commands'. In his system a language called PLANNER 'is used as a basis for problem solving, and meaning is represented in PLANNER expressions'; it is supplemented by a language called PROGRAMMAR, which 'is used as the formalism for expressing a recognition grammar of English . . .'.[4] (The system also includes relatively simple programs for generating responses in English.)

In discussing the '"concept" representation of meaning' he developed for his system, Winograd stresses that such a representation 'is not intended as a direct picture of something which exists in a person's mind. It is a fiction that gives us a way to make sense of data, and to predict actual behavior.' His justification for using it is that his system 'is thereby enabled to engage in dialogs that simulate in many ways the behavior of a human language user'. Such representations (some of which may be regarded as properties or relations that are 'atomic' – not in accord with 'some special logical status' but in serving 'a useful purpose in relation to the other concepts in the speaker's model of the world')[5] may be elaborated, to an extent, into larger structures in order to conform to the scale of the universe of discourse involved. Though such representations may be 'fictions', they are none the less quite useful – as will be seen.

Winograd defines the role of semantics as that of a gap-filler between the parser of his system, informed with a knowledge of grammar (in this case, that of English, though SHRDLU now deals with those of other natural languages as well), and its problem solver, informed with subject-specific knowledge. Furthermore, he argues that any theory of semantics, if it is to be helpful in modelling language comprehension, must 'describe relationships at three different levels': the meanings of individual words in a lexical context ('the formal description attached to a word'), the meanings of groups of words as syntactic structures, and the meanings of sentences in terms of both 'the linguistic setting (the context within the discourse) and the real-world setting (the interaction with knowledge of nonlinguistic facts)'. He notes that English syntax is extremely effective in portraying a '"model of the world" which is organized around "objects" having "properties" and entering into "relationships"', and so the semantic part of his system, that it may account for the demands of theory, 'is built around a group of about a dozen programs which are experts at looking at these particular syntactic structures', which portray that 'model of the world', and thus can describe the three levels of relationships. The system describes objects in terms of a NOUN GROUP, relationships in terms of an ADJECTIVE GROUP or PREPOSITION GROUP, events in terms of a CLAUSE GROUP, and so on. Since the parser uses systemic grammar, 'the semantic programs can look directly for syntactic features such as PASSIVE, PLURAL, or QUESTION to make decisions about the meaning of the sentence or phrase'. Moreover, the various programs of the semantic subsystem 'can work separately', so that 'there is no need to wait for a complete parsing before beginning semantic analysis'; and that subsystem works in a well-co-ordinated fashion with the rest of the system, for 'Any semantic program has full power to use the deductive system, and can even call the grammar to do a special bit of parsing before going on with the semantic analysis.' Because of this remarkably efficient heterarchical arrangement, 'it is very hard to classify the semantic analysis as "top-down" or "bottom-up"', though 'In general each structure is analyzed, as it is parsed, which is a bottom-up approach.'[6] Such an arrangement probably mirrors in some general way a similar one in human semantic processing.

In its semantic analyses Winograd's system distinguishes between so-called function words, such as *that* when used as a conjunction, which are meaningful only in that they 'signal certain syntactic structures and features', and so-called content words, which comprise most of natural-language vocabulary – though the distinction is problematic. The system makes this and similar distinctions by having the definition of each word constitute 'a LISP program to be run at an appropriate time in the semantic analysis'. Thus the meanings of the words in an input string are not simply data: they are represented as procedures, miniprograms (more accurately, perhaps, they are both data and programs, particles and waves). This arrangement allows different words to be handled by the system in appropriately different ways because each word, as I would analogize, carries its own 'antigen' program that codes for its being treated in a particular way by a particular 'antibody' portion of the semantic subsystem; that method of treatment takes some account of context, demonstrates a rudimentary awareness of discourse grammar, and contributes greatly to the power of the system:

> For simple cases, there are standard functions with a special format for usual types of definitions. Complex cases may involve special operations on the semantic structure being built, which may depend on the context. This flexibility is important in many places. For example, the word 'one' when used as a noun (as in 'the green one') refers back to previously mentioned nouns. It could not be defined by a simple format, as could 'block' or 'dog,' since access to the previous discourse is needed to determine what is really being referred to. In our system, the definitions of such words are compatible with the definitions of all other nouns. . . . When the NG [NOUN GROUP] specialist is ready to use the definition of the noun, it calls it as a program. In the usual case, this program sets up a standard data structure. In the case of 'one,' it calls a heuristic program for understanding back-references, and its effect on the meaning will depend on the discourse. Similarly, the verb 'be' is called like any other verb by the semantic specialist, but its definition is a complex program describing its different uses.[7]

Data as software: an ingenious and suggestive provision.

Actually this provision derives from what may amount to a breakthrough insight. As Winograd observes while discussing how his system uses procedural descriptions for dealing with questions and statements, as well as commands,

> One of the basic viewpoints underlying the model is that all language use can be thought of as a way of activating procedures within the hearer [or reader]. We can think of any utterance as a program – one that indirectly causes a set of operations to be carried out within the hearer's cognitive system. . . . In this program we have a simple version of this process of interpretation as it takes place in the robot. Each sentence interpreted by the robot is converted to a set of instructions in

PLANNER. The program that is created is then executed to achieve the desired effect.[8]

Thus linguistic input into the human language-understanding system may be regarded, in one sense, as 'static' data (declarative knowledge), but, in another, it should be regarded as 'dynamic' software (procedural knowledge). (Echoing the difference between the French verbs *connaître* ['to know *of*'] and *savoir* ['to know *how*'], the distinction between declarative and procedural knowledge, like that pertaining more generally to data-driven and concept-driven processes of the brain/mind and derived from Gilbert Ryle's *Concept of Mind*, is most difficult to make in regard to human – and, in many ways, machine – knowledge structures; but it is, within uncertain limits, quite useful, as Winograd's research demonstrates.)

In his consideration of the requirements for a semantic theory and of how his system includes them, Winograd argues that such a theory must explain 'not only how multiple interpretations can occur, but also how the hearer picks up a single meaning'. His system does take account of numerous possible interpretations, but it does not carry them forward in processing; rather, as is also usually the case in human language processing, it 'filters out all but the most reasonable interpretations'.[9] (Here, as Hofstadter notes, the system provides for the intermingling of 'syntactic form, which is detectable by a predictably terminating decision procedure, and semantic form, which is not . . .'[10] – an approach to Bierwisch's rapprochement.) The system does this by means of 'semantic markers' similar to Bierwisch's. Its use of such markers, however, entails 'not a complete representation of meaning, but a rough classification which eliminates fruitless semantic interpretations'. Thus, as soon as the system encounters each semantically describable element, it searches memory 'to see which interpretation is meaningful in the current context of discourse' and uses only that one in its further semantic analysis. This continuous interpretation is possible because his system 'allows the grammar, semantics and deduction to be easily intermixed'. Finally, in those cases in which one interpretation cannot be isolated with certainty, the system makes use 'of the overall discourse context in determining the plausibility of a particular interpretation'.[11]

These features, based as they are on theories of human semantic processing worked out by Bierwisch and others and articulated to take account of context (albeit, at its largest, only a 'blocks [or BLOCKS] world'), suggest once again that Winograd's system may be accurately, though crudely, modelling some aspects of human language comprehension. Its performance is especially remarkable in regard to context. Winograd specifies that a semantic theory should address three types of context: 'the *local discourse* context, which covers the discourse immediately preceding the sentence', 'an *overall discourse* context' or that of the 'general subject matter' under consideration, and 'a context of knowledge about the world'. His system, within its constraints, does address all three, though development has been focused mostly on its treatment of local-discourse situations involving 'the ways in which English carries information from one sentence to the next'.[12]

Several types of language-understanding systems (text-based, limited-logic, and so on) preceded Winograd's, each with its own advantages, which he sought to emulate, and disadvantages, which he sought to overcome. 'What was needed,' he says, 'were new programming techniques capable of using procedural information, but at the same time expressing this information in ways which did not depend on the peculiarities and special structure of a particular program or subject of discussion.'[13] What he tried to do, in designing and developing PLANNER (in conjunction with PROGRAMMAR), was to invent and implement those techniques.

PLANNER is a procedural language that is goal-oriented (in that, as Winograd explains, 'we need not be concerned about the details of interaction among procedures') and can process information expressed in a variety of more or less formal modes. Its most important feature is that 'complex information is expressed as procedures, and these may include knowledge of how best to go about attempting a proof'. It also has a 'flexible control structure' that 'makes it very difficult to specify . . . abstract logical properties . . . such as consistency and completeness'; that very lack of specifiability doubtless helps make the system a useful model of the mind, which lacks completeness in that, for example, it will not exhaust itself trying every conceivable way to prove a false theorem true. Moreover, PLANNER can '"rediscover the world" every time it answers a question', but its heuristics make it flexible enough not to have to. In the decade and a half since PLANNER was first developed, Winograd seems to have come to feel that procedural representations may not be as crucial as he then believed they were, but they are well used in PLANNER, help his system avoid limitations of earlier ones, and must reflect some aspects of human language processing. PLANNER is particularly effective in combination with PROGRAMMAR, whose systemic-grammar-as-program format endows it as a parser with the power 'both to handle the complexities of English syntax, and to combine the semantic analysis of language with the syntactic analysis in an intimate way'.[14]

In interaction with an interlocutor at a keyboard, SHRDLU answers questions, executes commands, and otherwise deals fairly effectively with natural language. The power of the system is abundantly demonstrated by Winograd's record of such 'conversations', which are partly quite straightforward, partly almost Beckettesque.[15] Though lacking in many 'real-world' aspects, it is a far more impressive system than a limited-logic one like Weizenbaum's ELIZA, which has made headlines by imitating the parrotlike interviewing techniques of a Rogerian analyst. (An enhanced version of SHRDLU is now being used by the Athena Language Learning Project at MIT in research on computer-assisted language instruction [CALI] in French and German. There it plays a role more like that of the 'patient' than that of the 'analyst' in ELIZA-esque exchanges.)

The success of Winograd's system inheres largely in the fact that it is not a gimmick designed to *seem* linguistically capable but a well-rationalized attempt to translate a general conception of language processing into a specific working model through programmable details. None the less, though it is in many ways a semantically based system, its operation does not greatly illuminate the philosophical issues of meaning as such: SHRDLU does not attempt 'to attach psychological meaning to isolated components into which language has been divided for abstract study'; rather, 'it attempts to relate the various types of knowledge and procedures involved in intelligent language use'.[16]

But there are, of course, limitations in that regard, about which Winograd is candid and that, in themselves, are instructive. For example, SHRDLU cannot 'handle hypothetical or counterfactual statements'; also, it accepts only 'a limited range of declarative information' and 'cannot talk about verbal acts' (it has no metalanguage). There are, furthermore, two essential ways it seems to fail as a model of human language processing: the first involves how 'the process is directed', the second 'the interaction of the context of the conversation and the understanding of its content'.[17]

In the first case, the algorithm for deriving possible interpretations of a sentence and choosing among them (in Winograd's system – as distinguished from those developed by Schank and Quillian, for instance, which work in opposite fashion – the first act is the responsibility of syntactic analysis and the second that of semantic analysis) is directed in far too simple and mechanical a fashion, because it is well known from observation of human language use that 'no single approach is really correct'. Human beings 'are able to interpret utterances which are not syntactically well formed' (I can easily interpret a sentence as apparently anomalous as the proverbial *But me no buts*) and 'can even assign meanings to collections of words without use of syntax'. Though how human beings deal with such situations is far from obvious, Winograd declares flatly that 'It is therefore wrong to insist that some sort of complete parsing is a prerequisite to semantic analysis.' Conversely, he observes, human beings 'are able to interpret sentences syntactically even when they do not know the meanings of the individual words'; indeed, 'vocabulary (beyond a certain age) is learned by hearing sentences in which unfamiliar words appear in syntactically well-defined positions' because 'We process the sentence without knowing any category information for the words, and in fact use the results of that processing to discover the semantic meaning.' Thus, he concludes,

What really seems to be going on is a coordinated process in which a variety of syntactic and semantic information can be relevant, and in which the hearer [or reader] takes advantage of whatever is more useful in understanding a given part of a sentence. Our system models this coordination in its order of doing things, by carrying on all of the different levels of analysis concurrently, although it does not model it in the control structure.

Much remains to be done in understanding how to write computer programs in which a number of concurrent processes are working in a coordinated fashion without being under the primary hierarchical control of one of them. A language model able to implement the sort of 'heterarchy' found in biological systems (like the coordination between different systems of an organism) will be much closer to a valid psychological theory.[18]

His system *is* heterarchical, of course, but not in a sophisticated enough way and not up to a high enough level of control.

In the second case, the system is simply 'not dealing with all the implications of viewing language as a process of communication between two intelligent people'. Especially, it is very constrained apperceptively and has no 'common sense knowledge'. Though these and other deficiencies prompt Winograd to conclude that his attempt to model language comprehension is 'a bit like an attempt to model the behavior of a complex system by using unrelated mathematical formulas whose results are a general approximation to its output', he is none the less optimistic that 'more advanced computational models will move towards overcoming these deficiencies' and come 'closer to psychological reality'.[19]

In spite of such qualifications, SHRDLU has been variously criticized, mostly because its world is only a 'mini-world' (though Winograd argues that 'it is precisely by limiting the subject matter to such a small area that we can address the general issues of how language is used' in larger contexts)[20] or is too tenuous (but is 'psychological reality' finally any less so?). More seriously, as Hofstadter notes, 'Some critics have charged that his program is so tangled that it does not represent any "theory" at all about language, nor does it contribute in any way to our insights about thought processes.' But Hofstadter answers the charge appropriately: 'Nothing could be more wrong than such claims. . . . A tour de force such as SHRDLU may not be isomorphic to what we do . . . but the act of creating it and thinking about it offers tremendous insight into the way intelligence works.'[21] I agree.

The kind of insight offered can be grasped readily by considering a problem in semantic analysis addressed by Winograd's research. The flexibility of his system is greatly dependent on its word definitions being programs. Such flexibility is important for processing high-frequency words such as *the, of, to,* and so on that are seemingly the simplest in the English language. But the use of a word like *the* typically involves complex knowledge:

A model of language use must be able to account for the role this type of knowledge plays in understanding. In the procedural model, it is a part of the process of interpretation for the structure in which the relevant word is embedded. The different possibilities for the meaning of 'the' are procedures which check various facts about the context, then prescribe actions such as 'Look for a unique object in the data base which fits this description.'[22]

In devising procedures whereby SHRDLU can use *the* and similar words with some humanlike competence, Winograd is grappling with a key problem in the whole language-comprehension mystery and has succeeded, at least, in approaching it functionalistically. In his concern with this problem, he is dealing with ultimate AI issues, as Hofstadter suggests: 'It is probably safe to say that writing a program which can fully handle the top five words of English – "the," "of," "and," "a," and "to" – would be equivalent to solving the entire problem of AI, and hence tantamount to knowing what intelligence and consciousness are.'[23]

21

Correspondence, MARGIE, Concept

Having discussed Winograd's system in some detail, I would like to touch on some more general considerations and then turn to other research relevant to issues raised in that discussion.

According to Schank and Kenneth Mark Colby, the two basic problems to be faced in modelling 'the human mental world – accessible mainly through language – ' are: '(1) how to model natural language communications and (2) how to model the thought and memory implicit in the interpretation of linguistic input'. There are two approaches to them: 'One is to strive for efficiency regardless of the methods used and the other is to strive for as much correspondence between model and human processes as can be achieved.' The second is now regarded as the more fruitful and – despite his disclaimers – characterizes Winograd's research more accurately than the first. Its enabling assumption is that, if such modelling is to have any significance for psychological theory, then, 'Since humans are conceptual, intentional, and semantic-based [sic] systems that interact in certain situations, the proposed models should also be conceptual, intentional, and semantic-based.' This assumption was established 'when linguists began to turn away from purely syntax-based systems towards semantic-based systems intended to model a communicative situation by creating a theoretical model of that situation' and is sanctioned by 'the new trend in psychology that casts theory in the form of a computer program rather than in the traditional literary or mathematical form'.[1] This theory-as-program methodology characterizes not only Winograd's work but that of many other innovative researchers, especially those, like Schank, who are interested predominantly in semantics.

In the early 1970s Schank and his colleagues at the Stanford Artificial Intelligence Laboratory developed a system that addresses the problem of 'the representation of meaning in an unambiguous language-free manner'.[2] (That is, the system supposedly concentrates more on conceptual-semantic patterns than on words themselves.) Named MARGIE (Memory, Analysis, Response, Generation, and Inference on English), it consists essentially of three programs: a parsing program, which analyses an input sentence and assigns it an appropriate 'conceptual-dependency network' or 'C-diagram'; a memory program, which incorporates inference strategies; and a sentence-generating program, which makes natural-language responses to the input (German and Chinese, as well as English, may be used).

Schank's primary concern is 'with what the theoretical problems are with respect to finding an adequate meaning representation and parsing into that representation'. Unlike Winograd, he is patently interested in imitating human language comprehension. He assumes that 'there exists a conceptual base into which utterances in natural language are mapped during understanding' and that it 'is well-defined enough such that an initial input into the conceptual base can make possible the prediction of the kind of conceptual information that is likely to follow the initial input'. Thus he wants to explore 'the nature of the conceptual base and the nature of the mapping rules that can be employed to extract what we shall call the conceptualizations underlying a linguistic expression'.[3]

Schank insists that 'it is the meaning of an input sentence that is needed, not its syntactic structure', and he notes that 'Expectation-making and analysis of what exists can take place at the level of meaning as well as that of syntax.' After reviewing various aspects of expectational patterns, he concludes that 'a human is a top-down parser with respect to some well-defined world model. The hearer, however, is a bottom-up parser in that when he hears a given word he tries to understand what it is rather than decide whether it satisfies his ordered list of expectations.' Given that conclusion, Schank designed his system not to be occupied with syntax but to use syntactic information 'as a pointer to the conceptual information'.[4] If human language comprehension is fundamentally a matter of conceptual prediction, that provision seems appropriate. Certainly the theories of Rumelhart and others concerning probabilistic hypothesis-making support it.

In Schank's model there is at least one conceptualization, which consists of concepts and relations among them, underlying every sentence that the grammar of a given language can generate, and conceptualizations may have various relationships among themselves, including nesting. He argues that there are three kinds of concepts of which they are composed: 'a *nominal*, an *action*, or a *modifier*'. A nominal is curiously independent, because its 'realization tends to produce a picture of that real world item in the mind of the hearer' *without relation to other concepts*. In terms of this questionable notion, that kind is a 'PP' ('picture producer'). An action is 'what a nominal can be said to be doing', an 'ACT'. A modifier is 'a descriptor of the nominal or action to which it relates and serves to specify an attribute of the nominal or action', either a 'PA' ('picture aider') or an 'AA' ('action aider'). He emphasizes the need to distinguish, in using his terminology, between the conceptual and sentential levels, because 'it is possible to have a sentence without a verb, or without a subject; or to have an adjective without a noun; in contrast, this is not possible at the conceptual level.'[5]

The relations among these concepts are 'conceptual dependencies' – by analogy with the syntactic dependencies formulated by David G. Hays, Sheldon Klein, and others. A dependency is indicated by a 'dependent' concept predicting the existence of a 'governing' concept. This privileging, however, may surely be called into question, and a deconstructionist would anticipate Schank's vacillation about the difference between the two. Thus, though he claims that 'A governor can be understood by itself', he claims also, in more Sausurrean fashion, that, 'In order for a conceptualization to exist, however, even a governor must be dependent on some other concept in that conceptualization.' None the less, by this way of thinking, 'PP's and ACT's are inherently governing categories, whereas PA's and AA's are inherent dependents'; moreover, similar categories obtain in relations between conceptualizations.[6] The C-diagram or conceptual-dependency network is a way of portraying such categories and relations.

Schank's model obviously involves some serious problems, but it appears to capture certain aspects of the dynamics of human language comprehension. His C-diagrams are informed by 'conceptual rules' that constitute 'the list of permissible conceptual dependencies'.[7] Those rules comprise a worthwhile attempt to describe the sentential level in terms of the conceptual level though the C-diagrams themselves seem clumsy in their technical ornateness – as in Figure 21.1, which diagrams the sentence *John*

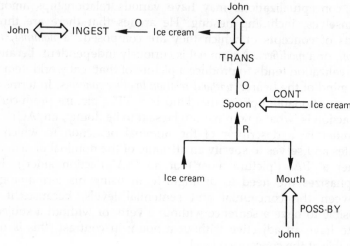

Figure 21.1

ate the ice cream with a spoon. (I will not gloss Schank's notation since I wish the reader to see only the general method involved.)

In order to assign such diagrams to natural-language input, the system must first analyse 'the linguistic entities into parts that can be translated into conceptual entities'. Then, for any sentence of input, it can make predictions 'as to the possible linguistic forms that such conceptual items may take', and 'a top-down search for those forms can be performed'. Like SHRDLU, it does not undertake a complete syntactic analysis:

> The conceptual processor receives a triple as input consisting of the main noun, main verb, and the syntactic category, of the verb and the direct object(s) of the verb. From this information it must decide upon a conceptual configuration that will be valid by using the verb-ACT dictionary, the conceptual rules, and the conceptual semantics. Furthermore, it must make predictions as to what information is required by the conceptual construction and proceed to search the unprocessed part of the sentence for this conceptual information. The trick to this seemingly top-down part of the analysis process is that when some piece of the sentence is encountered that was not predicted, the analysis must shift gears and process that piece as if it were at the beginning of the bottom-up process. It can

then finish the process by again searching for what it needs after having disposed of what it finds.[8]

And so on, for each successive sentence.

The most intriguing facet of this operation is the conceptual semantics, which encompass 'the set of delimitations of possible conceptual dependencies', and they differ from the sentential semantics, which help the conceptual processor determine syntactic structures, in that their role is to arrange 'the given concepts so that they make sense with respect to the world model'. Furthermore, they are 'interlingual, i.e., the same no matter what language one begins with. They represent the rules for organizing the world conceptually.'[9] Thus Schank's rationale for the conceptual semantics assumes that, however their form in the brain/mind might differ from what he has elaborated, they are the same for all human language users, and he is interested in describing universals.

How far Schank has succeeded in that project may be summarized fairly by an observation he makes about how his system simulates the way human beings select among alternative parsings of a sentence: 'even though the correct result is obtained, the actual procedure employed is not based on human processes. We thus consider this procedure to be only partly theoretically valid.'[10] (This observation echoes Winograd's similar one, despite the difference between the two researchers' stated objectives.) None the less, like Winograd, he offers suggestive strategies. And it is important to remember that Schank, who is criticized by some as a trial-and-error or 'unneat' researcher (unlike, say, John McCarthy), is finally interested in fullblown simulation. Consequently, any proper evaluation of his research requires not only a critique of his system but also a critique of the theory enabling it. In that regard Boden has some relevant observations.

In Boden's words, Schank is claiming that 'everything that people talk about boils down to a residuum of determinate conceptual elements', the set from which all conceptualizations are built and that consists of a multitude of notions concerning causation, tense, conceptual case (roughly analogous to its grammatical counterpart), and so on. Furthermore, these notions have the status of axioms of a kind and, 'being basic to the theory, are undefined. They are the semantic equivalent for Schank of the ontologically based items which, for the metaphysician, make up the whole furniture of the universe.' She classifies Schank's conceptual-dependency network as a special kind of 'semantic network' whose '"adequacy" . . . may rest on the human user's or programmer's intuitive ability to avoid absurdity, rather than on any intrinsic property of the representation that could be accessed by a computer program'.[11]

This last observation correlates with another of Boden's: 'Schank is interested in the *conceptual* mapping of thought rather than its *empirical* mapping. His concern is with how we intuitively think about thinking, as contrasted with how we actually manage to think.' Thus the 'myriad verbs of thought' that determine 'underlying semantic connections' and through which he 'aims to articulate the hidden meanings of everything one might seek to say' are derived from primitives with an intuitive feel: 'CONC (roughly: to think about, in the broadest sense), MTRANS (roughly: to bring a thought into the conscious mind or, more generally, to change the locus of its mental control in some way), and MBUILD (roughly: to combine thoughts in some manner)'. These primitives, surely problematic from a poststructuralist point of view, are also from an empirical-scientific one, as Boden demonstrates by what amounts to a deconstructive manoeuvre:

> He concedes that the conceptual primitives CONC, MTRANS, and MBUILD refer to processes that are not primitive from the empirical or scientific point of view. Even if one remains within the psychological (as opposed to the neurophysiological) theoretical mode, one can postulate microprocesses wholly unavailable to introspection, which in fact carry out the higher level operations of thought ordinarily conceived of as basic. Although the novel terminology and techniques of artificial intelligence are particularly suggestive of fruitful speculations in this regard, such processes have long been hypothesized: the underlying 'microgenesis' of visual perception, for instance, is a traditional concern of empirical psychology. But since this is something of which the ordinary person knows nothing (and cares less), it is not a concern of Schank's.

Likewise, she continues, if 'HAL [the computer in Arthur Clarke's *2001* and her exemplar of a futuristic AI system] were to develop a scientific interest in the microgenesis of perception', it would not need to be a concern of his(!) either; and 'he would ultimately have to conceive of these matters in terms of CONC, MTRANS, and MBUILD, and not vice versa'. Thus there is a 'general epistemological claim implicit in Schank's theory, that "scientific" discourse and reference to inanimate "actors" are semantically secondary to conceptualizations of a more intimately human kind'.[12]

In spite of such qualifications, Schank's system has some impressive provisions and capabilities: its use of conceptual cases acknowledges the grammaticality of the human universe; it deals fairly well with probabilistic implications that 'allow a rich fund of inferences about actions and states to be (consciously or intuitively) drawn from terse remarks that . . . contain a wealth of meaning'; its inferences, since probabilistic, 'can be simply blocked by information to the contrary without introducing chaotic *contradictions*' (a provision that generally mirrors human behaviour); and it is heuristically flexible enough not to be forced always to discern 'subtleties of interpretation' but to be able in principle to do so.[13]

There are, however, more intransigent problems with the system, some peculiar to it and some inherent to the AI enterprise. Boden notes that conceptual-dependency diagrams have an expectable tendency to proliferate infinitely by a metastasis of entailment:

> one can never finish diagramming a given conceptualization, if by 'finish' one understands reaching a state from which no more conceptual implications could possibly be pursued. (Similar remarks apply to all computational models of language based on richly interconnected semantic nets, . . . since the complete meaning of one node may involve every other node in the network: this point was made by M. R. Quillian as early as 1968.) But since one may nonetheless reach a stage at which, given the particular conversational context and practical aims in mind, there is no need to follow such implications any further, Schank . . . is not inescapably doomed to failure by the 'open texture' of natural language.[14]

None the less, very little is known about how the brain/mind limits conceptual proliferation, and even Schank's somewhat innovative logic probably will not prove very useful in simulating that process.

Another problem is that, in spite of the inferential power of the system, it lacks the ability 'computationally to decide which level and area of detail needs to be accessed in interpreting a given communication'. This problem has to do mostly with the fact that 'social (as opposed to technical) discourse ranges over domains of knowledge that have hardly been explicitly formulated in verbal form, still less computationally, so that the "relevant" questions are less easy to isolate than in the BLOCKS or circuitry worlds'. SHRDLU is more effective in dealing with this problem than is MARGIE, but both are hobbled by it. Boden argues, quite rightly, that Schank, perhaps too quick to skirt issues of theory, has not adequately spelled out his theoretical claims concerning 'core beliefs', which have critical bearing on this problem, much less implemented them 'in a computational form that can fathom the expected themes and rules of conversational coherence', and that in subsequent research related to his 'the problem of selection in accessing the data in memory has been postponed rather than solved'.[15]

There are also other problems. MARGIE suffers from certain hermeneutic limitations. For instance, Boden observes, 'the problems involved in interpreting "logical" words like *all, every, any,* and *some* have not yet been faced'. Also, MARGIE is weak in the use of adverbial expressions. And the overall organization of the system is serial rather than heterarchical. But perhaps the most important problem (which itself implies a range of problems as yet only partly addressed by systems like Schank's or Winograd's) has to do with language production, especially with the fact that 'getting from the "deep" semantic representation to a particular "surface" verbal string is not always computationally possible, since not all the subtleties of English syntax, still less of idiom, are as yet theoretically explicable'.[16] Because of that situation the sentence generators employed by systems like MARGIE or SHRDLU are not at all as impressive as their parsers (the usefulness of the *human* machine, on the other hand, as Georg Lichtenberg once observed, is not that it analyses and abstracts but that it summates – that is, synthesizes), and even the latter are relatively unrefined. But then much the same could be said of a child, whose 'passive' use of language for a period outstrips 'active' use but whose analytic and synthetic abilities eventually grow into a powerful consonance.

22
Flexibility, Networks, Maps

Discussing the advantages of using the ATN in modelling language comprehension, Eric Wanner and Michael Maratsos observe that early models, based on transformational grammar, attempted complete syntactic analysis of input but that more recent ones tend to rely on minimal syntactic information. They eschew both extremes, arguing that the amount of such information required must vary: 'In sentences where there is little contextual or semantic information, a complete syntactic analysis may be necessary. In others a contextual or semantic resolution may be possible.'[1] They rightly insist on flexibility. None the less, knowledge about semantic information is doubtless much more important to achieving it than that about syntactic information (the limitations of language-production programs certainly argue that). This is a complex issue. Robert F. Simmons's theory of semantic networks offers a fruitful approach to further exploration of it and should serve as well to enlarge understanding of some of the problems with Schank's system.

A semantic network – of which, as Boden noted, Schank's conceptual-dependency network is a special kind – is an abstract structure that, in Simmons's words, 'purports to represent concepts expressed by natural-language words and phrases as nodes connected to other such concepts by a particular set of arcs called semantic relations'. The concepts here are 'word-sense meanings', and the semantic relations are 'those that the verb of a sentence has with its subject, object, and prepositional phrase arguments in addition to those that underlie common lexical, classificational, and modificational relations'. He admits that such networks comprise only 'a computational theory of superficial verbal understanding in humans' but cites psycholinguistic research (by Quillian, Rumelhart, and others) that sanctions it.[2]

However far away an empirical validation (or invalidation) of semantic-network theory may be, it *is* useful in helping computers to understand natural language. Semantic networks may be used in a variety of processes: syntactic analysis, paraphrase, question–

answer interaction, sentence generation, and so on. They can represent the underlying semantic structures of language as variously proposed and thereby provide a theory for generation from such structures; likewise, the processes by which language is analysed into such networks 'provide a precise description of a theory of how some aspects of sentence meaning can be understood as a well-defined semantic system'.[3]

The enabling theory of Simmons's networks is one of deep-case structures, as originally conceived by Charles J. Fillmore and Sandra Annear Thompson and subsequently extended by Marianne Celce-Murcia. Simmons believes that such a theory, realized in programs (in this case written in LISP), lends an important 'measure of logical rigor' to 'the soft-sciences of linguistics and psychology'. He admits that his own version of deep-case theory is 'limited in its present development to single sentences, truncated at a certain conceptual death, unspecified with regard to many of the complex phenomena of English, and unexplored with respect to other languages'. But it has advantages as well: 'it encompasses such major subtasks of the verbal communication process as the generation and recognition of English strings and their understanding in terms of limited capability to answer questions and to generate and recognize paraphrases' (which claim is related to his more general one for computational theories: that they have been crucial in the invention of 'logical and mathematical operations for determining the equivalence of two or more semantic structures'). Also, his theory 'is precisely stated, internally consistent, and potentially useful to guide further research . . .'.[4]

Simmons begins with the assumption that people use natural language to communicate ideas and feelings to other people. Thus a mathematical theory of language use requires two models, one for 'ideas and feelings' and one for 'language', as well as functions for mapping each into the other. Within that framework the structure of the networks constitutes the model for 'ideas' (he equivocates about 'feelings'), which must be accompanied by a grammar, a lexicon, and 'rules for mapping words, phrases, and sentences into the semantic net structure of the model of ideas and for mapping the ideas into language strings'.[5]

According to Simmons, his model accounts for relations of logical consequence between one idea and another idea or set of ideas by means of rules and functions that map one semantic structure into one or more others. Since ideas may be mapped also into linguistic forms (natural or artificial) and since other kinds of 'ideas' can be similarly mapped (for example, 'visual representations can also be seen as a language string of edging, cornering, and shading elements' that can be mapped into 'a semantic structure of images . . . represented in semantic net form'), there is, he argues, 'Presumably . . . a language to describe internal organic responses, such as feelings, and mapping functions that show correspondences between semantic net representations of ideas and feelings.' Thus, he continues, 'Ideally we hypothesize one central cognitive structure of semantic net form into which perceptions of speech, vision, action, and feeling can map, and from which can be generated speech, physical actions, hallucinations, feelings, and other thoughts. So far, however, we have only studied semantic nets to represent a class of English sentences.'[6] The extent to which his model describes how the mapping of such events occurs in the human psychosoma is, of course, open to question, but it does enjoy a measure of empirical support. Moreover, though semantic–linguistic or conceptual–lexical mapping may be discovered to involve all manner of complex relations, they are surely describable in some terms. Probably, as Simmons seems somewhat to suggest, those relations will soon be understood to have a character similar to the one that Gestalt psychology (with its notion of the cerebral cortex as an equilibrated force field influenced by incoming stimuli whose representations set up regions of resonance with conceptual structures already present) attributes to the isomorphic relationship between external and cortical events: the isomorphisms work on a point-for-point basis but involve a correspondence like that between a territory and its map, so that there is a distortion, yet one that preserves certain patterns. There may well be a universal language by which such events, through semantic networks, are variously mappable – though it is still obscure. If there is a Rosetta stone whereby the translations of such events can be described, then Simmons is beginning to tinker with the connections among the hieroglyphs, the demotic characters, and the Greek.

In Simmons' model there are three basic mappings: 'M1' (language into ideas), 'M2' (ideas into ideas), and 'M3' (ideas into language). These involve something like the kind of isomorphisms previously mentioned. For example, he observes of the inverse relation between mappings M1 and M3 that, 'for a given pair of language string and idea, L I, if M1(L) ⇒ I, then M3(I) ⇒ L' such that M1(L') ⇒ I'; that is, as he explains, 'a given semantic structure, I, that is derived from a language string, L, will generate another language string, L', which is either identical to L or a paraphrase of L and whose semantic structure is analyzed back into I'. Thus 'L and L' are not restricted to strings from the same language or the same modality (i.e., speech, vision, feeling, etc.)'. And this consequence indicates the power of his model, at least at this level of abstraction, for it does propose 'that there is a single cognitive representation of ideas'.[7]

In order to consider semantic networks in terms of linguistic form, Simmons defines a sentence as 'a string of ambiguous word symbols that implies a complex structure of underlying concepts'. Semantic analysis involves translating the string into a structure of nodes and relations specified in terms of 'deep case relations [codified by Celce-Murcia's five kinds of arguments that can stand in relation to the verb: *causal actant, theme, locus, source,* and *goal*] that connect nominal concepts to verbs, and conjunctive, modifier, quantifier, and classifier relations that connect and specify concepts'.[8] There are other refinements as well – for example, verbs are specified in terms of paradigmatic and modal classes.

This structure is similar to the deep structure proposed by Chomskyan transformational theory, but, in Simmons's view, there is a critical difference: 'The transformational deep structure . . . provides only syntactic relations to connect the elements of a structure' whereas 'the deep case structure can meet our requirement that the semantic analysis of a sentence result in a structure of unambiguous concepts [surely a questionable category] connected by explicit semantic relations'.[9] Simmons's rules for mapping between underlying and surface structures do, in a sense, constitute a set of transformational rules; but thinking of them as such may be confusing because they provide for semantic rather than syntactic mapping and thus address, perhaps too positivistically, the semantic limitations of transformational theory – though here, once again, syntax and semantics blur together.

A semantic network has not only a linguistic form but also 'a computational representation, a logical structure, and a conceptual content'. In the computational representation each node has a 'relationset' that 'encodes the information it represents'. Thus, in

Saussurean fashion, 'The meaning of any node is an ordering of the rest of the nodes of [the] network with which it is related.' Accordingly, as Simmons observes, in 'a richly interconnected network, the complete meaning of any particular node may involve every other node in the system' – an observation that recalls Boden's critique of conceptual-dependency diagrams and belies Simmons's desire for 'unambiguous concepts'. (In other words, semantic networks, like Schank's diagrams and similar devices, do not furnish any kind of 'center' that can check Derridean freeplay. To the contrary, they exemplify it.) However, the relations that characterize such ordering are at least theoretically explicit; that is, they

> are viewed computationally as functions and procedures. In our present realizations these relations are largely undefined as procedures although . . . they could be defined as generation functions that would produce an appropriate syntactic structure corresponding to each semantic relation and its arguments.
>
> In our present development, such relations as THEME, CAUSAL ACTANT, etc., can be perceived dimly as procedures which in some cases will change the contextual definitional structure to reflect the action of a verb. Thus, THEME (John, run) as a procedure might be expected to apply the characteristic of fast motion involving legs and feet to the ordinary structure defining John. Similarly, CA1 (run, John) might be expected to add the information that John instigated the motion; and GOAL (run, store) must add some terminal condition to the motion implied by 'run.' A most interesting and potentially rewarding research task is to develop this idea computationally.[10]

The relations thus are not yet well defined as procedures, but there appears to be no reason in principle why they could not be.

The logical structure is enabled by the provision that 'A semantic net is a set of triples, (A R B), where A and B are nodes and R is a semantic relation.' An example, from above, would be (run CA1 John). Such an expression can be interpreted in set-theoretic terms or, as seen above, translated into the form of standard first-order predicate calculus, provided that the word meanings involved are properly axiomatized (a large order). 'The most significant consequence of defining semantic networks as a logical system,' Simmons explains, 'is to make the techniques and results of research in automatic theorem proving easily transferable to problems of question answering and problem solving in semantic nets' – especially since 'It has been apparent for some time that the question-answering and paraphrase problems of natural language processing are closely related to the more abstract problem of proving logical and mathematical theorems.'[11] That is not to say, however, that such problems necessarily should be straitjacketed logico-mathematically or that Simmons's approach could not be adapted to more flexible and less traditional logical and mathematical principles if that were necessary to simulate more accurately.

The conceptual content, Simmons frankly explains, 'has been carefully limited to that of word-sense meanings connected by semantic relations that are frequently very closely related to corresponding syntactic relations'. Thus he is not concerned with the deeper levels explored by Schank and others. He contends that 'The depth of a syntactic or semantic structure can be defined as proportional to the extent to which it accounts for a set of strings which are, from some point of view, paraphrases of each other.' The depth he advocates does seem sufficient for the internal purposes of his model, but he admits the probability that 'the deeper structure forms a more satisfactory psychological model of conceptual structure as well as one that will answer questions more economically'.[12] Such an admission does not dismiss his model, but it surely qualifies its accuracy.

Simmons uses an ATN-based system, a variant of William A. Woods's AFSTN (Augmented Finite-State Transition Network) system, 'which interprets a grammar – shown graphically as a transition network – as a program to transform an English string into a semantic network'.[13] It is matched with a system for generating sentences from the networks. The two operate together efficiently, but the model they instantiate, as noted previously, is truncated. Further consideration of that truncation and some of its by-product limitations foregrounds problems that plague the whole project of trying to model human language processing.

Simmons argues that, if his model is to prove useful in mapping from English into other natural languages or into procedural languages, 'additional semantic relations must be encoded into the dictionary'. That task, as Miller and others have observed, is profoundly difficult, both inherently and in terms of larger issues. For example, the complexities of extensionality and intensionality are not taken into account by Simmons's model, though perhaps, in principle at least, they could be. A related problem, of course, is semantic disambiguation, which demands that the parsing grammar take into account a great deal of lexical information for each entry. That approach, Simmons contends, is only 'minimally satisfactory for analyzing a carefully controlled subset of English'.[14] The reason is obvious: disambiguation easily requires subtleties of awareness (pragmatic, metalinguistic) that are not readily simulated by an AI system. Indeed, since natural language is ineluctably figurative and self-reflexive, even human beings cannot fully disambiguate. That is a motivating insight of deconstruction, and it challenges the AI enterprise to deal with a daunting plentitude of equivocality.

Simmons's model, like the others I have discussed, is therefore quite limited. He generously acknowledges the significance of the research of Winograd and Schank concerning deep semantic structures, but he also asserts that, though his model is superficial in many respects, it 'fits naturally into those systems which model the deeper forms of thought required for problem solving and the accomplishment of non-verbal actions'. Patently, as he observes, 'These theories and models of language understanding offer a very rich area for continued research', and he suggests particular concerns for computational, linguistic, and psychological research. He also cites the need for better hardware – for much larger memories and multiple-processing systems able to accommodate more powerful command languages.[15] In doing so he offers a signal challenge to fifth-generation computer technology (of the kind exemplified by NON-VON I at Columbia University, so called because its architecture does not follow von Neumann's principles of design and, in effect, consists of many small, interdependent computers). Within the constraints of physical law, further and dramatic development of hardware – with special attention to the convenience and, increasingly, practical necessity of having programs hardwired – is imperative if modellers are to have the tools they need. Such development is far more probable in the near future than widespread agreement on theoretical matters, though Simmons himself, with his talent for discerning complementarities, should be excused from that indictment.

23
MT, Linguistics, Logic

Simmons's concern with semantic mapping mirrors a general concern in AI theory and research with problems of translation. They are epitomized in attempts at the mechanical translation (MT) of natural languages, a project that has long intrigued the artificial intelligentsia, who were spurred on greatly by the development of Chomskyan grammar because it seemed at first to offer a formalism for generating all the sentences of any given natural language – perhaps from those of any other.

Wittgenstein asserts that '*Übersetzen von einer Sprache in die andere, ist eine mathematische Aufgabe* [Translating from one language into another is a mathematical exercise]'. Given that, he asserts further that the translation of a lyric poem, for example, is analogous to '*einem mathematischen Problem* [a mathematical problem]'. And he goes on to assert that, though the problem of translating a joke can be solved, there may be – by a joke of his own – no systematic way of doing so.[1] The first two assertions summarize the assumptions held by most MT researchers over the last few decades; the third summarizes the upshot of their efforts.

A great deal has been written about MT (about procedures for finding a solution in one language to a problem in another), but no one has written more thought-provokingly or more controversially than Yorick Wilks. He takes AI research to be 'the enterprise of causing automata to perform peculiarly human tasks . . . by appropriate methods'. What he means by 'appropriate methods' is apparently implicit in his discussion of the three reasons why he regards his approach to MT as a legitimate part of that enterprise. First, his LISP-programmed system uses both linguistic and logical means for expressing the strings with which it deals, though for him the question of which is the more suitable remains unanswered. Secondly, his system uses 'a modifiable system of linguistic rules' since he believes that 'the space of meaningful expressions of a natural langauge cannot be determined or decided by any set of rules whatever – in the way that almost all linguistic theories implicitly assume CAN be done'. In his view that situation can be accounted for by a language user's 'option to MAKE any string of words meaningful by the use of explanations and definitions'. (However, he none the less rationalizes his rules by the need to distinguish between the classes of acceptable and unacceptable expressions.) Thirdly, his system involves 'methods consistent with what humans THINK their methods of procedure are, as distinct from more formally motivated methods'.[2] These reasons are all ripe for discussion, but the last particularly deserves attention.

In rebelling against much of the formal-systems and logical theory that has figured in the history of MT research, Wilks tries to be commonsensical:

> The present system is entirely semantics based, in that it avoids the explicit use of a conventional linguistic syntax at both the analysis and generation stages, and any explicit theorem-proving technique. In the analysis of input, syntax is avoided by a template system: the use of a set of deep semantic forms that seek to pick up the message conveyed by the input string, on the assumption that there is a fairly well-defined set of basic messages that people always want to convey whenever they write and speak. . . . the overall representation of complex sentences is that of a linear sequence of message forms in a real time order, interrelated by conceptual ties called paraplates, rather than the hierarchical tree structure preferred by linguists.

Moreover, when this heterarchical system translates English into French,

> the French generation is done without the explicit use of a generative grammar, in the conventional sense. The interlingual representation passed from the analysis routines to the generation ones already contains, as part of the coding of English input words, French stereotypes – strings of French words and functions that evaluate to French words. These functions are evaluated recursively to produce French output, and the stereotypes thus constitute both French output and procedures for assembling the output properly. No other inventory of French words or grammar rules is ever searched, and the stereotypes constitute a principled way of coping with

linguistic diversity and irregularity – since individual words have their own stereotypes – without recourse to what [Yehoshua] Bar-Hillel . . . calls 'bags of tricks.'

The approach is clever enough, but one wonders about Wilks's own 'bags of tricks', especially regarding what is 'explicit' and what is not. Perhaps that puzzlement is adequately addressed by the fact that his system, compared to, say, Winograd's, is so markedly short on explicit procedures. Indeed, he does not want to overdevelop it and hopes that 'it may be possible to establish a level of understanding for MT somewhat short of that required for question-answering and other more intelligent behaviors'.[3]

Wilks's emphasis is not, however, on simplicity of means *per se* but on appropriateness, and he attributes the dismal results of past MT experiments in large part to their being 'done on the basis of naïve syntactic analysis and without any of the developments in semantic structuring and description that have been the most noteworthy features of recent linguistic advance'. His own theorizing and research, of course, are based on those developments – as Simmons doubtless would urge they should be – and he argues strongly for dictionary-based (or, perhaps more precisely, thesaurus-based) systems like his and against those theorists (presumably Steiner might be included) who oppose them. The 'fashionable' view of that group, he believes, 'can . . . be correlated with the fresh interest being generated among linguists and others by new attempts . . . to produce a formal logic capable of representing rather more of the forms of language than the classical attempts of Russell, Carnap, Reichenbach, *et al.*', the 'implicit argument' of which latter attempts 'goes as follows: that logical structure provides the real structure of language, and there is no place in a logic for a dictionary, hence . . .'.[4] And so on. Wilks's position, which is supported by a good deal of psychological research concerning how the mental lexicon is used in translation, seems quite defensible.

In this connection, Wilks observes, certainly in agreement here with Steiner, that 'The relation of formal logic to language is and always has been a much disputed matter . . . . ' That is not to say that an MT system should avoid logic – his system does use logical rules as well as 'linguistic presuppositions' that have logical import – but that Wilks, in his use of templates, stereotypes, and the principle of 'density of connection' in formulating representations, is interested more in producing 'a working artifact' than in settling 'intellectual questions' concerning the merits of logic. Yet his attack on logic is problematic:

Whatever logicians may believe to the contrary, it has never been shown that human beings perform anything like a logical translation when they translate sentences from one language to another, nor has it ever been shown that it is NECESSARY to do that in order to translate mechanically. To take a trivial example, if one wants to translate the English 'is,' then for an adequate LOGICAL translation one will almost certainly want to know whether the particular use of 'is' in question is best rendered into logic by identity, set membership or set inclusion. Yet for the purposes of translating an English sentence containing 'is' into a closely related language such as French it is highly unlikely that one would ever want to make any such distinction for the purpose immediately in hand.

The preceding assumptions in no way close off discussion of the questions outstanding: they merely allow constructive work to proceed. In particular, philosophical discussion should be continued on (a) exactly what the linguist is trying to say when he says that there are linguistic forms and common sense inferences beyond the scope of any logic, and (b) exactly what the logician is trying to say when he holds in strong form the thesis that logical form is the basis of brain coding, or is the appropriate basis for computing over natural language.[5]

Surely discussion of such ('intellectual') questions should continue. And surely Wilks's own research promotes that continuation, for his contentions about the role of logic have not been rigorously refuted. But, in his attempt to avoid the Wittgensteinian trap, he seems too brash in his denial of the *possible* role of some kind of logic – either as an aspect of human language processing (especially translation) that is still poorly understood (and perhaps largely unconcsious) or as an aspect of MT that therefore should be investigated more carefully. His 'trivial' example is a treacherous one that itself questions his denial, for there are obvious instances in 'closely related' languages for which distinctions about the logic of *is* need to be made (such as the sometimes finely nuanced uses of *ser* and *estar* in Spanish).

But that specific point should not be laboured here, for Wilks does stress the importance of synthesizing approaches, does not deny that 'some form of knowledge-based inference will be needed for MT', and sees the value of comparing the results of logical and linguistic approaches.[6] Still his discussion of the logic–linguistics controversy does come close to intellectual waffling at times – though perhaps he himself should not be blamed entirely since that controversy is complex, powered by a number of recalcitrant personalities, and not generous with theoretical footholds.

24

Interlingua, Thesaurus, Deduction

Wilks's system, which has produced, in his opinion, 'good French for small English paragraphs', is still under development, and I do not wish to discuss its operation at much greater length; but some further consideration is required for a more thorough evaluation of his theoretical position.

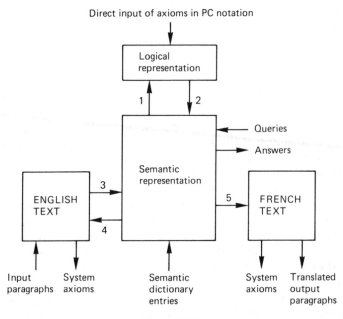

Figure 24.1

Figure 24.1 is Wilks's diagram of the system as it was conceived at the Stanford Artificial Intelligence Laboratory. He classifies processes 2, 4, and 5 as 'relatively easy tasks'; 1 and 3, on the other hand, are more difficult 'in that they involve making

143

information explicit with the aid of dictionaries and rules'. And he remarks that the system, with its facilities for the 'translation of small texts via a semantic representation' as well as for the 'translation of predicate calculus (PC) into both natural languages', necessarily must receive an input that is 'fairly restricted'.[1]

The general strategy of the system involves segmentation of the input text in English, production of an appropriate semantic representation of the segments, and generation of an output text in French (the 3–5 path) – which strategy may be modified to include a logical representation as well (the 3–1–2–5 path). Its implementation involves 'mapping . . . semantic templates directly onto the clauses and phrases of English, and trying to map out directly from the templates into French clauses and phrases, with their relative order being changed where necessary'. The semantic representation entailed is determined by 'whatever degree of representation is necessary for MT'; questions and answers must be handled through the logical representation. Though Wilks assumes that the difference between the logic and semantics subsystems has to do with the former requiring explicitness not only of common-sense inference rules (which the semantic representation includes) but also of other logical rules and functions, he emphasizes that the difference is practical: it has to do with 'two "levels of understanding" in the human being'.[2]

In processing text the goal of the system is 'to derive from an English text an interlingual representation that has an adequate, though not excessive, complexity' and that is to be used in two ways: 'as a representation from which output in another natural language – French in this case – can be computed, and as a representation that can also serve as an analysandum of predicate calculus statements about some particular universe'. The interlingual representation consists of 'TEMPLATES bound together by PARAPLATES and CS [common-sense] inferences', all three of which consist of 'FORMULAS (and predicates and functions ranging over them and sub-formulas), which in turn consist of ELEMENTS', a set of 'sixty primitive semantic units used to express the semantic entities, states, qualities, and actions about which humans speak and write'. The formulas 'express the senses of English words with one formula to each sense', and they 'can be thought of, and written out, as binary trees of semantic primitives'.[3]

Finally, the system, like Winograd's, is procedural in orientation, as can be seen from Wilks's description of how the dictionary is used:

> The dictionary is essentially a list of sense-pairs: the left-hand member of each sense-pair is a formula, expressing the sense of some English word, and the corresponding right-hand member is a list of STEREOTYPES, from which French output is to be generated. Thus each formula that is pulled into the IR [interlingual representation] by the analysis procedures . . . has pulled with it the stereotypes for the corresponding French. . . . The stereotypes are in fact implicit procedures for assembling the French, so the role of the generation routines is simply to recursively unwrap, as it were, the package of the interlingual representation.[4]

So once again meaning is a matter of procedural isomorphism.

Boden properly thinks of Wilks's work as part of language-comprehension research, and she suggests that the extent of his success in MT is due largely to his avoidance of simpleminded procedures of 'dictionary look-up' and his use of 'a thesaurus-based method of translation'. That method involves a principle exemplified in formula-stereotype matching: 'each of the senses of every word is assigned a particular semantic tag (*cf.* the classification in *Roget's Thesaurus*), and the translator chooses between alternatives in a particular case by matching up the tags associated with co-occurring words so as to get a coherent sense'.[5] Though that method hardly ensures against all the lexical problems that might occur, Wilks's system is fairly good at translating the gist of textual segments in context.

Boden observes that a salient feature of Wilks's approach is that it tries to account for the creative 'anomalies' of natural language. His system assumes that the writer of the input intends to communicate comprehensibly: 'It prefers the normal when it can get it, but accepts the abnormal when it can not – noting what are the specific abnormalities involved, and how they are justified by the text as a whole.' With some effectiveness, then, it 'embodies a theory specifying the meaningful patterns or coherent themes that one intuitively expects to underlie human communications', while relying on 'rule-bound assumptions'.[6] Those assumptions, though Wilks would make a case for their flexibility, are none the less quite constraining.

Boden's discussion of Wilks's disgruntlement about logical representations, particularly those that are deductively based, illuminates the whole logic–linguistics controversy. As she points out, his system is much like Schank's in its use of 'preferential rules of interpretation, as opposed to the rigorously deductive procedures employed by SHRDLU'.[7] That difference, which is, of course, partly due to Wilks's system not requiring as high a level of understanding as Winograd's, does involve a gain in flexibility and economy because Wilks's system may use its logical capabilities to enhance semantic representation only when they are necessary to address an interpretive problem – it is not as dependent on them as SHRDLU is. But the real issue here has to do with the general usefulness of deduction in semantic processing.

In response to Wilks's argument that a deductive approach tends to bring into play knowledge that is not necessary for machine comprehension, Boden counters with the caveats that 'no hard and fast line can properly be drawn between knowledge that does and that does not contribute to understanding the meaning of a word' and that 'Even translation . . . may sometimes require access to what Wilks would class as facts about the world' as well as to semantic information that is more readily packageable. She does acknowledge, however, that some kinds of 'facts about the world' involved in automatic theorem-proving (which deals with a set of axioms much as an interpreter deals with a program) are not necessarily important to the sort of semantic analysis required for translation, and she observes that Wilks's objections have foregrounded an enduring problem:

> a doubt as to whether the operations of thought in general (what is sometimes called 'the' understanding) are plausibly represented as essentially deductive in character. This doubt has a number of sources, including the absence of deductions in introspection; the average person's difficulty in mastering even elementary logic exercises; and the (time-consuming?) complexity of deductions required to justify seemingly 'immediate' inferences. This generalized dubiety concerning deductive models of cognition is not peculiar to Wilks, and strikes at the root of much influential work in artificial intelligence . . . .

Indeed, that dubiety is a notable characteristic of the

poststructuralist attitude, which is always ready to question the tidy univocalities and certainties of deductive logic. That is not to say that MT and AI theory and research, as Wilks might wish, should eschew such logic but that it should be used in combination with other and perhaps more powerful logics that resemble human cognitive processes, as Boden characterizes them, in being 'sometimes downright *il*logical, as well as being probabilistic rather than deductive'. Wilks's approach to MT may be governed in a way by 'common sense' (which is always open to question), but her further discussion makes a good case for its rapport with the poststructuralist view of language understanding as a manifoldly contingent activity:

> Insofar as one's interpretation of (and replies to) sentences depends upon inferences of a nondeductive nature, Wilks's suspicion of rigidly deductive computational systems is understandable. An adequate model of language use would have to accommodate probabilistic and inductive inferences (such as those represented in MARGIE's memory and [Robert P.] Abelson's work [on belief systems]) if it were to capture the 'illogical' – albeit lawful – processes involved in verbal thought. Equally, of course, it could not entirely outlaw deduction: Wilks himself admits that there are some examples of pronominal reference that could not be correctly resolved without complex deductions from relevant facts . . . .
>
> Finally, one might argue that Wilks's deductive–nondeductive contrast is a false antithesis. For the rules embodied in so-called 'nondeductive' programs could be regarded as deductive rules for proving (say) that [in the sentence *I put the butterfly wing on the table and it broke*] it is very probably the butterfly wing that broke, so we need not consider the possibility that the 'it' that broke was the table. In this sense, all programs (except possibly those including a randomizing element) could be seen as deductive. But even so, a distinction remains between a belief system all of whose conclusions are regarded as unquestionably true (and mutually consistent), and a belief system that is less dogmatic as to truth and less optimistic as regards internal consistency of the various beliefs contained within it. Wilks may then be interpreted as stressing the tentative, hypothetical character of language understanding, and as criticizing programs that represent it as a relatively closed, cut-and-dried matter.[8]

Thus is he vindicated and his work placed in perspective, but
behind Boden's distinction lurk the shade of Kurt Gödel and a raft
of issues concerning consistency and completeness in language-
understanding systems, human or otherwise, to which I will
return.

25

Translation, Universals, *Mystère*

In an essay appropriately entitled 'Understanding as Translation', Steiner considers the omnipresence of translation in the human use of language. He notices how reading Shakespeare is tantamount to translating him: the historical development of language demands a decipherment between two psychocultural contexts. Likewise, 'The world of an Austen novel is radically linguistic: all reality is "encoded" in a distinctive idiom'[1] that the reader must translate (from ciphertext to cleartext by means of some encicode) in order to understand. But translation – the assumption of an alien vision, the inhalation of an alien voice – is not peculiar to literary experience; indeed, it is co-extensive with the whole human experience of language and essential to it. One who uses language effectively is a translator, an interpreter or, to use Steiner's polyvalent word, an *interprète*.

In terms of a 'schematic model of translation' – that is, 'one in which a message from a source-language passes into a receptor-language via a transformational process' – there is always a barrier: 'the obvious fact that one language differs from the other, that an interpretative transfer, sometimes, albeit misleadingly, described as encoding and decoding, must occur so that the message "gets through"'. Moreover, as Steiner stresses, 'Exactly the same model . . . is operative within a single language.' Indeed, any given culture depends on such 'internal translation' occurring both diachronically (he notes that 'German *übertragen* carries the exact connotations of translation and of handing down through narrative') and synchronically. This model is an encompassing metaphor for acts of communication, as applicable to dialectal interaction as to the conflict of ideologies, and 'Any model of communication is at the same time a model of translation, of a vertical or horizontal transfer of significance. . . . In short: *inside or between languages, human communication equals translation.*'[2]

149

This model is thereby 'ontologically equivalent' to the sender-to-receiver model used in information theory: in both 'there is "in the middle" an operation of interpretative decipherment, an encoding–decoding function or synapse'. And, I would add, either model is applicable to the process whereby an assembler, compiler, or interpreter translates high-level source-language instructions into low-level object-language instructions, a process that, like all computer communication, is effected completely and without error, if the programmer has been careful and no so-called soft failures occur in the electronics. Human translation/communication, however, is never complete or errorless: it involves abuses or, to use a Derridean word, *écarts* ('swerves', 'mistakes', 'variations', 'differences'); transphrasis always involves paraphrasis, periphrasis; and so on. Steiner's concern with the territoriality and privacy involved in language use addresses this situation:

> No two historical epochs, no two social classes, no two localities use words and syntax to signify exactly the same things, to send identical signals of valuation and inference. Neither do two human beings. Each living person draws, deliberately or in immediate habit, on two sources of linguistic supply: the current vulgate corresponding to his level of literacy, and a private thesaurus. The latter is inextricably a part of his subconscious, of his memories so far as they may be verbalized, and of the singular, irreducibly specific ensemble of his somatic and psychological identity. Part of the answer to the notorious logical conundrum as to whether or not there can be 'private language' is that aspects of every language-act are unique and individual. . . . Each communicatory gesture has a private residue. . . . The concept of a normal or standard idiom is a statistically-based fiction (though it may . . . have real existence in machine-translation).

And the argument applies *a fortiori* to interactions between people of two different cultures. 'Obviously,' says Steiner, 'we speak to communicate. But also to conceal, to leave unspoken.'[3] (The fall of the Tower of Babel is emblematically the fall of human language from clarity and openness to confusion and concealment. Thenceforth it is inherently tropical, and its meaning inevitably involves oscillations between written and unwritten, spoken and unspoken, explicit and implicit, Derridean 'declarative' and 'descriptive' aspects. Each person is a self whose interiorities cannot be communicated completely to other selves. Perhaps for good reasons. One might wonder if this kind of incompletion does not complement, in some Gödelian fashion, the drive for consistency of communication within a given culture.)

Steiner is obviously not saying that natural-language translation or communication is impossible, but he is saying that it is necessarily problematized in certain ways. The implications are daunting. Perhaps the MLM metaphor must go, in Derrida's phrase, permanently '*sous rature*' ('under erasure'). Perhaps its circular flow cannot be complete because there is always a *residuum* in the human psychosoma, something 'left over' that cannot be captured by an 'exterior' (and therefore seemingly crystallic, metallic, 'Martian') formalism or mechanism – a proposition, here in psycholinguistic terms, crucial to humanistic individualism, even to various intuitions about the soul as internal centre, that echoes Edward Sapir's dictum that 'All grammars leak.' The issues are large and intriguing, but some more exact focus is necessary.

The immediately important issue is whether one can construct a model that takes into account the human being's 'private residue' by somehow necessarily taking into account, prior to that, the 'specific ensemble of his somatic and psychological identity' or whether one must be satisfied with 'a statistically-based fiction'. And, if that ensemble could be taken into account, could it be done explicitly and discretely? Certainly as intelligent a critic of AI work as Weizenbaum would contend that it cannot be done at all because an AI system is not the same kind of (organic) being that man is – or that, more moralistically, even if it could be done, it *should not* be. Steiner's argument may imply uncrossable boundaries not only for MT but for AI in general, or it may be only a discomfiting reminder of the problems with which those enterprises have to wrestle.

In any case, that argument is necessarily interimplicated with Steiner's thought concerning linguistic universals, which deals with related issues. The study of translation, which for him is necessarily 'a study of language', has, like the machine modelling of its insights, all along involved the attempt to define such universals – a centuries-old project. He associates it with the desire to discover the language used before the Tower of Babel, and his review of the quest – from Leibniz to Lévi-Strauss – leads him to a cynical conclusion: 'The evidence for the universality of those linguistic structures of which there is phenomenal evidence is, until now, provisional and putative'; it 'oscillates between postulated levels of extreme formal abstraction at which the language-model becomes meta-mathematical and is divorced more or less completely from the phonetic fact, and levels which are crudely statistical'. Furthermore, he claims, many linguists, like seventeenth-century grammarians forcing all languages to fit Latin, may 'have assumed that the "deep structures" of all languages are identical because they have equated universal criteria of constraint and possibility with what could be in truth aspects only of the grammar of their own tongue or language group'.[4]

None the less, for most theorists, the nonexistence of such universals is unacceptable – and also empirically unsupported. Thus, Steiner argues, the important question is 'less *whether* there are "formal and substantive universals of language" but precisely *what* they are, and to what extent the depths at which they lie will ever be accessible to either philosophic or neurophysiological investigation'.[5] But he remains sceptical about substantive universals and about the formalisms that proliferate theories about them. (With respect to such formalisms, linguists and psycholinguists must share some anxieties with physicists who build their theoretical edifice on the existence of quarks, for which 'particles' there is a strong formalistic imperative but only the scantiest of hard-won circumstantial evidence. Also, the controversy concerning formal and substantive universals is in some ways parallel to one in mathematics concerning constructivist and formalist approaches: in both cases there is debate about what is 'invented' and what 'discovered', what can or can not be verified procedurally or empirically, and a concern with how far a metasystem can specify any system to which it refers.)[6] Steiner argues that 'Proof that mutual transfer between languages is possible should follow immediately on the principle of substantive universality. Translation ought, in effect, to supply that principle with its most palpable evidence.' But, he asks, 'how is one to distinguish substantive from formal universals? How, except by theoretical *fiat* at one end or local intuition at the other, can one determine whether perfect translation should be possible because formal universals underlie all speech, or whether actual untranslatabilities persist because universals are only rarely or obscurely substantive? The discrimination is cogent in theory but has not been shown to be so in practice. It shares implicit ambiguities with the related distinction between "deep" and "surface" structures.' He takes Chomsky to task for vacillating about this last distinction, finding in his transformational theory 'a fundamental uncertainty' about it.[7]

Thus Steiner sympathizes with the polemic of Robert A. Hall, Jr, against deep structures as nothing but formally convenient paraphrases and with his scepticism about any set of rules adequately describing the processes of natural language, and he finds that

> The lacuna between a system of 'universal deep structures' and an adequate model of translation suggests that the ancient controversy between relativist and universalist philosophies of language is not yet over. It also suggests that the theory whereby transformational rules map semantically interpreted 'deep structures' into phonetically interpreted 'surface structures' may be a meta-mathematical ideal of considerable intellectual elegance, but not a true picture of natural language. . . . By placing the active nodes of linguistic life so 'deep' as to defy all sensory observation and pragmatic depiction, transformational generative grammar may have put the ghost out of all reach of the machine.

There is, of course, a special irony in the Koestlerian allusion because it suggests that the psycholinguistic theory associated with transformational grammar may have rendered impossible not only its own empirical validation but its own machine model. On the other hand, if, as Steiner suggests, 'The "depths" plotted by transformational generative grammars are themselves largely a disguised simile or a convention of notation',[8] then the problem lies elsewhere and may prove quite subtle. Transformational-generative grammatical theory, which many would claim is now in shambles, has not offered a satisfactory account of this and other problems indicated by Steiner, though perhaps another version of it could.

I am convinced, however, that the ghost is not 'out of all reach of the machine' – in spite of Steiner's informed cautions. As I sit at my computer and watch the delicate exfoliations of a colour-graphics program on the screen, I remind myself that all those nuances derive from a shape table in RAM that I painstakingly constructed initially with 1s and 0s. The multiple and complex derives from the binary and simple; the same must hold, by whatever intricate and paradoxical logic, for natural language and its relation to mind and machine. All human learning begins with that kind of economy: it is basic to the distinctions that constitute meaning and thus surely underlies all interpretation (including the most radical strategies of poststructuralism, for even Derrida's *différance* can be described in terms of it).

But Steiner is not to be taken – or dismissed – lightly. He is keenly aware of 'the numinous as well as problematic nature of man's life in language' and properly suspicious of its simplification. He is aware also of 'the dynamics of instability which result from the need to use language in order to study language', observing that 'There is an inescapable ontological autism, a proceeding inside a circle of mirrors, in any conscious reflection on (reflection of) language.' And he is suspicious of any attempt to break out of that circle by means of Kantian chicanery or a metalanguage whose relation to language appears to be like that of metamathematics to mathematics:

> To declare that the idiom of modern linguistics is a 'metalanguage' is to say little. Once again, a loan image is operative: that of mathematical logic in relation to mathematics. Though tricked out with logical symbols and markers from the theory of recursive functions, the metalanguage of scientific linguistics is compelled to draw on common syntax and current words. It has no extraterritorial immunity. It remains inalienably a member of the language or language family which it seeks to analyze. . . . The interactions of observer and observed are of extreme methodological and psychological opaqueness.

All this is to say that he is uneasy about formal models for, as it were, algebraizing natural language. He grants that they are useful because 'They produce fictions of isolation whereby we can study one or another element of phonology, of grammar, or of semantics.' He is therefore not interested in writing a dirge for them, only in taking 'careful note' of 'the nature of such models'.[9] What he has to say in that regard is worth attention.

Steiner's critique of formal models is somewhat Gödelian. There is no doubt that, for example, Chomsky's explorations of natural language can give rise to a model that 'will comprehend a more or less extensive and significant range of linguistic phenomena', but, 'For reasons that are philosophic and not merely statistical, it can never include them all.' What is involved here is a conflict, in Maurice Merleau-Ponty's terms, between *l'algorithme* (for a universal *langue*) and *le langage donné* ('the given language'), with the former in 'revolt' against the latter. Steiner sees that revolt as having 'great analytic and heuristic merits' but ones to be accepted with important qualifications, for

> it is the *langage donné* in which we conduct our lives. . . . We have no other. And the danger is that formal linguistic models, in their loosely argued analogy with the axiomatic structure of the mathematical sciences, may block perception. . . . It is quite conceivable that, in language, continuous induction from simple, elemental units to more complex, realistic forms is not justified. The extent and formal 'undecidability' of context – and every linguistic particle above the level of the phoneme is context-bound – may make it impossible, except in the most abstract, meta-linguistic sense, to pass from 'pro-verbs,' 'kernals,' or 'deep deep structures' to actual speech . . . .[10]

Certainly problems arise in postulating any kind of conformal invariance between levels of language processing – from the neurochemical (or lower) on up – but that does not necessarily mean that mappabilities are impossible: they may well require inductions that are discontinuous in some specifiable way. What Steiner argues here is important, and his argument may prove out in some respects – though not by clinging to a mystique about the inexplicable knottiness of language.

On the other hand, Steiner admits that formal modelling might be 'a prelude to a genuine science of language', preparation for which involves, 'inevitably, a reductive simplification'. He even conjectures about the 'substantive basis' of such a science, citing work of Konrad Lorenz and Jean Piaget that 'suggests that logico-mathematical structures and the kind of relational strings that underlie the generation of sentences have their biological roots in the structure and function of the nervous system' and research on aphasia and similar disorders that 'provides ample evidence of direct and often highly specific relations between physiology and language'. He none the less remains sceptical about the full realization of 'a "physically grounded" theory of the evolution and generation of human speech'.[11]

Steiner's scepticism is doubtless due partly to his embrace of the thesis, which he attributes to Vygotsky, that 'communication outward is only a secondary, socially stimulated phase in the acquisition of language. Speaking to oneself would be the primary function . . . .' He has made almost a fetish of this debatable thesis; it runs like an *idée fixe* through much of his writing. It figures especially in his arguments concerning the imprisonment of language in the self and leads him to tell, with Merleau-Ponty, of *'le mystère du langage'* and to posit an ultimate inaccessibility: 'What we can say best of language, as of death, is, in a certain sense, a truth just out of reach. . . . Even as we speak, we feel that instrumentalities of an entirely different, much "deeper" order are implicit.'[12] Yes, those instrumentalities do occasion a sense of inaccessible depth. But what seems mysterious now is not necessarily forever incomprehensible (problems that seem insoluble may be only complex), and the understanding of such instrumentalities would not, as Steiner seems to fear, end their mysteriousness: rather, that understanding would sublimate it into yet another 'different' order and invite a larger appreciation.

26

Wiring, Conundrums, Topology

Steiner is not, however, finally unsympathetic to the MLM project, as the unravelling of his further, broader, and perhaps expectable objections shows.

Steiner observes that there is empirical evidence showing that some aspects of the human ability to symbolize and to manipulate grammar and logic 'may depend on physical features of the architecture and "wiring" of the cortex', and he is willing to speculate that, for instance, 'The Platonic account of metaphor as the bringing into relation of areas of perception hitherto discrete may have its material analogue or mapping in the actual topology of the brain.' With emphasis on that 'may', he goes on:

> It has been widely noticed that some of the most striking analogies and working models to emerge from recent discoveries in genetics and molecular biology have a distinctly 'linguistic' ring. Notions of coding, information storage, feedback, punctuation, and replication have their suggestive analogues in descriptions of language. To the extent that life itself is viewed as a dynamic transfer of information in which implicit coded signals trigger and release complex pre-set mechanisms, the study of neurophysiological processes at the molecular level and that of the foundations of language are bound to draw close.

He knows that the English alphabet is very much quantitatively richer than that of 'the genetic code with its "three-letter words", but he is attracted to this 'lettering analogy', particularly when it is expanded to include other aspects of his communication model.[1]

Still, resuming the role of sceptic, Steiner wonders what is being sought in the attempt to discover evidence for such analogies:

What would constitute evidence of the molecular basis for the generation of symbolic functions? At the level of elementary logic there is the classical conundrum of machine-intelligence theory: 'given a set of input symbol-strings which have been presented to a finite automaton and the corresponding outputs, is there a possible way of determining the internal structure of the machine, and what would such a way be?' But we are not, of course, inquiring into a finite automaton. The belief is growing that the organizing principles of the human brain are of an order of hitherto undefined complication and autonomy. Add the bits together and there is a great deal 'else' left to account for. Not in any occult sense. But on a plane of systematic interaction between genetic, chemical, neurophysiological, electromagnetic, and environmental factors for whose numerous relations and spatial contiguities we have, until now, no examinable analogue or inductive model. Such a model may not be forthcoming. The Vedantic precept that knowledge shall not, finally, know the knower points to a reasonable negative expectation; consciousness and the elucidation of consciousness as object may prove inseparable.

On the one hand, he speculates that this situation may be absolute and derive, as Jacques Monod's somewhat Heideggerian notion expresses it, from language creating man, rather than vice versa; on the other, he sympathizes with C. D. Broad's interest in 'interface phenomena between "brain space" and "mind space" ' and admits that they might 'meet some of the facts of language-experience'.[2]

That admission could be a springboard for further theorizing; but Steiner seems unaware of the possibility, as he seems unaware of other possibilities – and problems – implicit above. First, that the human brain/mind is not a finite automaton does not necessarily imply that it cannot be better understood in terms of some of the principles of finite automata. Second, the conundrum that he invokes maintains its force when applied, *mutatis mutandis*, to the brain/mind, which has more or less the status of a black-box mechanism, and the widespread belief in the appropriateness of that status, which he promotes, serves only to hamper attempts to determine its 'internal structure'. (There is, in other words, another kind of conundrum implicit here: if one believes that the black-box conundrum applies to the human brain/mind, then that belief will prevent his discovering whether or not it really does apply.) Third, that the various factors mentioned by Steiner are involved in an interaction that is 'systematic' should give hope that it might be modelled. I must admit, however, that the precept adduced may point to intractable boundary conditions for research: it is intuitively attractive and is undeniably relevant to the issue of how far a system can comprehend itself.

In discussing the quest for a universal language (in several senses: 'an international auxiliary language', 'a "universal character" ' that 'would generate a logistic treatment of science', and 'a true universal semantic'), Steiner observes that 'Neither the "interlingual" nor the logical-analytic approach has done very much to deepen our understanding . . . of natural language' – though he acknowledges that 'In computer languages traditional concepts of *mathesis*, of symbolic representation and of universality are implicit though in a special framework.' His observation, of course, is generally correct, especially in regard to research before the advent of more powerful semantic theories and techniques of machine modelling, but even the most recent research – and certainly poststructuralist theory – supports his corollary observation that 'There are no closed circuits in natural language, no self-consistent axiomatic sets.' And he is quick to turn to the uncomfortable relationship between logic and natural language: 'It is,' he says, 'because the correspondence between words and "things" is, in the logician's sense of the term, "weak" that language is strong' – an observation with which deconstructionists, given their Gorgian rhetorical bent, would agree. Moreover, if one reverses this situation, 'as artificial universal languages do', then 'the absence of any natural, complex strength in the ensuing modes of communication is obvious'.[3]

The key problem with describing natural language in terms of conventional logic or modelling it as a formal system is that its nuanced profusion seems irreducible to any complete theoretical organization. In natural language, as Steiner says, information 'comes attenuated, flexed, coloured, alloyed by intent and the milieu in which the utterance occurs . . .'. It does not come 'naked except in the schemata of computer languages or the lexicon'. Logicized or formalized language can only with great difficulty take into account how 'interpretation, except in the first momentary instance, is always reinterpretation', always involves the possibility of hermeneutic retakes stirring up additional strata of meaning (as in Derridean 'de-sedimentation'). Or, as Steiner says in another connection, 'We mean endlessly more than we say. The sources of superfluity, with their anatomical analogue in the asymmetries of the cortex, generate new surpluses.'[4]

How is a formal-systems theory of natural language, a machine model, to deal with this situation? Only quite limitedly at best, Steiner contends, citing history as he reads it:

> The mathematics of multi-dimensional interactive spaces and lattices, the projection of 'computer behavior' on to possible models of cerebral functions, the theoretical and mechanical investigation of artificial intelligence, are producing a stream of sophisticated, often suggestive ideas. But it is, I believe, fair to say that nothing put forward until now in either theoretic design or mechanical mimicry comes even remotely in reach of the most rudimentary linguistic realities.[5]

That judgement is too harsh. Steiner seems interested more in holding a philosophical position than in thoroughly studying the AI literature pertinent to it.

And yet that position has a peculiar give. Steiner argues seductively that brain activities associated with language processing require models 'beyond anything we can now conceive of', and yet in one passage, concerned with the philosophy of translation, he apparently affirms much that he previously denied:

> These manifold transformations and reorderings of relation between an initial verbal event and subsequent reappearances of this event in other verbal or non-verbal forms might best be seen as *topological*. By that I mean something quite simple. Topology is the branch of mathematics which deals with those relations between points and those fundamental properties of a figure which remain invariant when that figure is bent out of shape (when the rubber sheet on which we have traced the triangle is bent into conic or spherical form). The study of these invariants and of the geometric and algebraic relations which survive transformation has proved decisive in modern mathematics. It has shown underlying unities and assemblages in a vast plurality of apparently diverse functions and spatial configurations. Similarly, there are invariants and constants underlying the manifold shapes of expression in our culture.

He considers examples from painting and literature (in the workings of the archetype, the motif, the recurrent icon, and so on – the consideration of which involves the idea, with which the quasi-Platonist Thom would sympathize, that the psychic text constitutes a topological fable) and suggests that

> The relations of 'invariance within transformation' are, to a more or less immediate degree, those of *translation*. Viewed in this way, the concepts of 'underlying structure,' 'recursiveness,' 'constraint,' 'rewrite rules,' and 'freedom' put forward by transformational generative grammar will take on a larger meaning. And it will be a meaning less in conflict with the realities of natural language and cultural development. Defined 'topologically,' a culture is a sequence of translations and transformations of constants ('translation' always tends toward 'transformation'). When we have seen this to be the case we will arrive at a clearer understanding of the linguistic–semantic motor of culture and of that which keeps different languages and their 'topological fields' distinct from each other.[6]

Now this is shape-shifting that invites a moment of scrutiny.

Is Steiner, as Blake said of Milton, unknowingly of the Devil's party? He certainly seems to give his *imprimatur* to a view of language that he has tried hard to condemn, and he implies that the modelling game is not hopelessly doomed, that there may well be a formal methodology for dealing with the kind of MLM translations/transformations/isomorphisms with which I am concerned. The approach he proposes is hardly at odds with, for example, that of Simmons. It is not only a way of defamiliarizing transformational–generative grammar but also a way, already being exploited, of describing many interrelated natural-language processes. And his proposal even involves a metaphor, of 'the linguistic–semantic motor', that, if presented by someone else, he doubtless would consider mechanical.

27
Meaning, Discourse, Speech Act

It is obvious by now that there are differences between philosophical and modellist approaches to issues associated with language comprehension, especially that of meaning. Philosophers of language of various persuasions tend to split hairs, sometimes too abstractly; modellers tend to be practical, sometimes too reductively. Both approaches, however, have enlarged understanding of the issue, and their respective ideologies and insights increasingly show patterns of positive interference – as my discussion of Steiner suggests. A survey of other work representative of the two kinds of approaches can make a case for certain syntheses, however tensional, between them that urge a new paradigm for MLM phenomena.

Steiner's discussion of *hermeneia* ('interpretation', 'translation'), which involves the somewhat Nietzschean notion of human cognition as aggressively, penetratively interpreting values *into* the world, leads him to a definition of meaning as *'content beyond paraphrase'*.[1] Such a definition by exclusion is to be expected, given his indirect approach. A more direct approach, one that figures prominently in the background to modern philosophical investigations of meaning, has been provided by the nineteenth-century German logician Gottlob Frege. Though he was anti-psychologistic, his influence has been strong and variegated. According to Samuel Guttenplan, 'The appeal of Frege's view lies in his use of the concept of truth both to explicate the notion of linguistic meaning and to connect the latter with the concepts of judgment, assertion, and belief – various propositional attitudes.'[2] Frege's concept of truth would surely be regarded as naïve by a poststructuralist, but his concerns still haunt Winograd and other modellers – especially those interested in simulating belief systems – who use more or less conventional logicist approaches.

Frege's consideration of meaning, like that of most logicians, grammarians, and linguists since, focuses on the sentence as

162

the unit of meaning that is propositionally analysable. This consideration, however, has left hanging, among other issues, that of trans-sentential or discursive meaning. Only recently has it really been addressed – with uninspiring results, for the most part. Among those who have given it attention are M. A. K. Halliday and Ruqaiya Hasan.

Halliday and Hasan address themselves to the problem of defining a *text*: 'A text is a unit of language in use. It is not a grammatical unit, like a clause or a sentence; and it is not defined by its size.' Also, it 'differs from a sentence in kind' and 'is best regarded as a SEMANTIC unit. . . . Thus it is related to a clause or sentence not by size but by REALIZATION, the coding of one symbolic system in another.' In other words, 'A text does not CONSIST of sentences; it is REALIZED by, or encoded in, sentences.' Its unity arises through *cohesion* – 'the relations [immediate, mediate, or remote] of meaning that exist within the text, and that define it as a text' – which 'occurs where the INTERPRETATION of some element in the discourse is dependent on that of another'.[3]

So far, so good – though one might quibble. But then comes the snag. According to Halliday and Hasan, 'it is doubtful whether it is possible to demonstrate generalized structural relationships into which sentences enter as the realization of functions in some higher unit, as can be done for all units below the sentence'. Thus cohesion, they declare, 'is not a structural relation'. However, by a stratal description, the text, 'as the basic unit of meaning in language', should be thought of as being 'to semantic structure what the sentence is to lexicogrammatical structure and the syllable to phonological structure'.[4] Does not the description belie the declaration?

But Halliday and Hasan are intent on their thesis. Though they grant that 'Cohesion is closely related to information structure' and that the two may 'overlap', they insist that cohesion is only 'a potential for relating one element in the text to another'. They even argue that 'there are no grammatical restrictions on the sequence in which sentences are put together'.[5]

Halliday and Hasan are thus implicated in a kind of *trahison des clercs* more characteristic of philosophers than of modellers: they stop short of dealing with the problems and possibilities of what they have proposed. Their analysis of cohesive relations (the trabeculae of discourse) bristles with suggestions to the effect that patterns of meaning, which surely are sensitive to sequence, do have a structure – albeit one that is not well understood. Their notion of structure is too limited, though they come close to articulating a structuralist (or, perhaps, poststructuralist) approach to the text as a unit of meaning. The modeller, on the other hand, cannot afford to leave theory so vaguely and dogmatically cast: he must discover structure, and it must be formalizable and empirically adequate – as far as possible. That is one reason why the work of modellers such as Simmons, Schank, Winograd, and even Wilks, who have taken ideas from philosophers, is so important. Unlike many philosophers (and scientists), they know that philosophy and science are accountable to each other.

More specifically, the major limitation of Halliday and Hasan's approach, especially from the modeller's point of view, is that it neglects *coherence*, the patterns of semantic and pragmatic relations that occasion and support comprehension of the text. The mechanisms of cohesion – conjunctive, lexical, collocational, and so on – that cue the reading of a text generally corresponds to those of coherence, but cognitively they appear to involve relatively superficial relations of intersentential elements. Were Halliday and Hasan's approach more interdisciplinary, at least to the extent of taking account of coherence, they might discern how cohesion *is* characterized by 'generalized structural relationships' and offer descriptions of them useful to the modeller.

And there are other problems with Halliday and Hasan's neglect of coherence. Anne E. Doyle compares their work unfavourably to that of text theorists like Teun van Dijk, whose logicist approach would probably prove more fruitful for the modeller,[6] and notes particularly that 'their study involved the decision to regard exophoric reference within the text as noncohesive,' which leads them to adopt a 'simplistic division' between 'real world and text'. (Compare this dichotomy to the less deceiving continuum posited by Derrida's dictum that '*Il n'y a pas de hors-texte* [There is no outside-text].') Such a division 'minimizes the potentials of the author and the reader for constructing and recovering a "world" which is not, strictly speaking, the "real world" mentioned by Halliday and Hasan'.[7]

Since this minimization entails problems with, for instance, explaining cohesive uses of *the*, Doyle suggests that a more comprehensive and useful approach is that of Robert de Beaugrande. It involves a categorization of the use of the definite article not by the narrow criteria of endophora and intersentential cohesive ties, but by a criterion he defines as definiteness: 'the extent to which the text-world entity for an expression . . . is assumed to be identifiable and recoverable, as opposed to being introduced just then.' . . . Beaugrande's focus offers several advantages over that of Halliday and Hasan. For Beaugrande, the text serves to activate for its user the textual world, 'the cognitive correlate in the mind of a text user for the configuration of concepts activated in regard' to the text. . . . While Halliday and Hasan are concerned primarily with the text and secondarily with the text's relationship to the real world, Beaugrande is concerned first with the interrelationship of text and text-world (which exists in the mind, freed of constraints imposed by the real world), and then with the situational demands of the real world. This introduction of text-world concerns allows Beaugrande to investigate the relationship of coherence and cognition. . . .

Using this more constructivist strategy, he is able to differentiate more and subtler functions of the definite article than Halliday and Hasan consider and to make them explicit and programmatic in a way that could be useful for modelling its meaning. Thus 'Beaugrande, operating on a concern for the text-world's integrity rather than merely the integrity of the text', the principal consequence of focusing on coherence rather than cohesion, is able to 'speak of the creation and relation of text-parts *within the mind*',[8] which is, after all, what the modeller wants to simulate. De Beaugrande has not found the 'solution' to the problem of text semantics, but he has at least discerned something of the nature of it.

Semioticians and others concerned with semiotic theories in philosophizing about language have made signal contributions to the study of meaning. (They too have been unable to develop a satisfactory theory of meaning at the textual level, but then many of them would claim that they have never been interested in doing so.) Their concern is with semiosis, the sign process, in which, by the traditional postulate of inherent metaphoricity, '*aliquid stat pro aliquo* [something stands for something (else)]' – which relationship, as Peirce added, must be interpreted as such by some agency (usually animate, since many semioticians believe that semiosis is the most distinctive attribute of living forms).[9] For my present purpose a brief consideration of this and some other postulates of semiotic theory, by way of Charles Morris and Louis Hjelmslev, and a summary and critique of structuralist semiotics, by way of Paul Ricoeur, will suffice.

Morris outlines and illustrates the 'basic terms of semiotic' as follows:

> Semiosis (or sign process) is regarded as a five-term relation – v, w, x, y, z – in which v sets up in w the disposition to react in a certain kind of way, x, to a certain kind of object, y (not then acting as a stimulus), under certain conditions, z. The v's, in the cases where this relation obtains, are *signs*, the w's are *interpreters*, the x's are *interpretants*, the y's are *significations*, and the z's are the *contexts* in which the signs occur.
>
> Karl von Frisch has shown that a bee which finds nectar is able, on returning to the hive, to 'dance' in such a way as to direct other bees to the food source. In this case the dance is the sign; the other bees affected by the dance are interpreters; the disposition to react in a certain kind of way by these bees, because of the dance, is the interpretant; the kind of object toward which the bees are prepared to act in this way is the signification of the sign; and the position of the hive is part of the context.

Morris emphasizes that significations are not physical entities but 'certain describable aspects of complex behavioral processes in the natural world' and that the interpretant (neglected by Saussure) can 'be interpreted in probabilistic terms, as the probability of reacting in a certain way under certain conditions because of the appearance of the sign'.[10]

Following these terms, Morris uncomfortably ventures a definition: 'The "meaning" of a sign is *both* its signification and its interpretant, and neither alone.'[11] Meaning thus inheres in a matching of signified and organismic disposition. Once again it is recognized isomorphism.

Like Morris, Hjelmslev is uneasy about traditional notions of meaning and observes that 'the word *meaning*, which denotes both designation and designatum (and which, incidentally, is unclear in other respects too)', is manifoldly ambiguous. He contends that analysis of the operation of signs 'would lead us to recognize a sign system behind the sign process', presumably on all levels of the text, and is thereby more encouraging than Halliday and Hasan about the possibility of a structural semantics – or, more properly, an algebraic 'glossematics' – in terms of which meaning 'must be understood as being a purely contextual meaning'. That notion squares with structuralist semiotics, especially when honed slightly more: 'any entity, and thus also any sign, is defined relatively, not absolutely, and only by its place in the context'. (There is no meaning without [outside] the hermeneutic circle.) Finally, even "The so-called lexical meanings in certain signs are nothing but artificially isolated contextual meanings, or artificial paraphrases of them.'[12]

This view has attracted many linguists and semioticians (of whom semanticists are sometimes considered only a subgroup). It entails some presuppositions that Ricoeur is equipped to address, challenge, and modify. He is interested principally in five, all derived from Saussure by way of Hjelmslev: (1) 'Language is an object for an empirical science' (*langue* may be isolated as 'a homogeneous object', but *parole* is dispersed); (2) 'Within a language itself we must still distinguish a science of states of system, or synchronic linguistics, and a science of changes, or diachronic linguistics'; (3) 'In a state of system there are no absolute terms, only relations of mutual dependence'; (4) 'The collection of signs must be maintained as a closed system in order to submit it to analysis' (this system thus has 'no outside but only internal relations' and answers to Hjelmslev's definition of a *structure* as '*an autonomous entity of internal dependencies*'); and (5) 'The definition of the sign which satisfies these four presuppositions breaks entirely with the naïve idea that the sign is made to stand for a thing.'[13] Given these presuppositions, the question with which Ricoeur must deal concerns how meaning operates in such a system.

Ricoeur criticizes the structuralist point of view because it excludes not only the diverse creativity of *parole* but also 'the primary intention of language, which is to say something about something', an intention that involves a doubleness of direction:

> an ideal direction (to say something) and a real reference (to say about something). In this movement, language leaps across two thresholds: the threshold of ideality of sense and, beyond this sense, the threshold of reference. Across this double threshold and by means of this movement of transcendence, language

'means'; it has taken hold of reality and expresses the hold of reality on thought. . . . It is necessary then to balance the axiom of the closure of the universe of signs by attention to the primary function of language, which is to say. In contrast to the closure of the universe of signs, this function constitutes its openness or its opening.

Thus reference works through this openness. And thus 'For us who speak, language is not an object but a mediation. . . . To speak is the act by which the speaker overcomes the closure of the universe of signs. . . . language moves beyond itself as a sign toward its reference and toward its opposite. Language seeks to disappear; it seeks to die as an object.'[14]

Given the 'methodological decision' of structuralist linguistics 'to hold itself at the interior of the closure of the universe of signs', Ricoeur defines his task as reclaiming 'for the understanding of language what the structural model excluded and what perhaps is language itself as an act of speech, as saying'.[15] To accomplish this he proposes what I would call a particle/wave (or, by a both/and compression, 'wavicle') theory of the sign: depending on how it is considered, a sign is either a structural element in the closed system of *langue* (a 'particle') or a functional event in the open act of *parole* (a 'wave').

To understand the 'wave' aspects of the sign, one must realize that 'We actually change levels when we pass from the units of a language to the new unit constituted by the sentence or the enunciation', a unit not 'of a language [*langue*], but of speech [*parole*] or of discourse. By changing the unit, one also changes function, or rather, one passes from structure to function.' Drawing on ideas from Émile Benveniste, Ricoeur accounts for this difference of levels with five counter-presuppositions regarding the traits of 'discourse' (as opposed to 'language'):

1. For discourse has an *act* as its mode of presence – the instance of discourse (Benveniste) which, as such, is of the nature of an event. To speak is an actual event, a transitory, vanishing act. The system, in contrast, is atemporal because it is simply virtual.

2. Discourse consists in a series of choices by which certain meanings are selected and others excluded. This choice is the counterpart of a corresponding trait of the system – constraint.

3. These choices produce *new* combinations: to emit new sentences, to understand such sentences – such is the act of speaking and of comprehending speech. This production of new sentences in virtually infinite number has as its counterpart the finite and closed collection of signs.

4. It is in discourse that language has a reference. To speak is to say something about something. . . . In his famous article '*Über Sinn und Bedeutung*' (expressions which Peter Geach and Max Black have translated as 'Sense and Reference'), Frege showed precisely that the aim of language is double: the aim of an ideal sense (that is, not belonging to the physical or psychic world) and the aim of reference. . . .

5. . . . The event, choice, innovation, reference also imply a specific manner of designating the subject of discourse. Someone speaks to someone – that is the essence of the act of communication. By this trait, the act of speech is opposed to the anonymity of the system.

Thus there is no need to force a choice between two notions of the sign in terms of either 'internal difference of the signifying to the signified' or 'external reference of sign to thing', for they are simply two different particle/wave aspects of the same thing: 'One relates to the structure of the sign in the system, the other to its function in the sentence.' With this synthetic view of the sign, what emerges is the necessity 'of finding instruments of thought capable of mastering the phenomenon of language, which is neither structure nor event, but the incessant conversion of one into the other in discourse'[16] – another mode of translation.

Ricoeur, though at odds with Derrida, is enthusiastic about poststructuralist studies of language – particularly as represented, in his opinion, by the work of Noam Chomsky and Gustave Guillaume – and largely because such studies indicate a return to a Humboldtian concern with language as a generative process, as a '*structuring operation* and no longer *structured inventory*'. In the search for 'instruments of thought', he is concerned with how the sign achieves meaning when it is taken from the closed circularity of the dictionary, with how 'Words are the point of articulation of semiology and semantics, in every speech event.'[17] So he turns to Humboldt's aphorism describing language as 'infinite use of finite means' and relates it to Benveniste's distinction between 'the semiotic entities, that is to say the signs, and the semantic entities, the bearers of meaning'.[18]

Again the particle/wave analogy comes into play, for the signifier and the signified, by Ricoeur's both/and logic, 'represent the two sides of the same sign like the two sides of one and the same coin. Like the coin the sign is the unity of both.' But meaning, in terms of this divided unity, is a function of the latter and is realized, in accordance with Fregean thought, in the sentence. What is involved in this realization is 'something more than the signified of the individual signs', for a synergistic effect arises from the concatenating of signs. It culminates in the 'predicative function' that provides the sentence with meaning. Ricoeur argues, however, that, to distinguish between the semiotic and the semantic, 'This meaning should be called the intended rather than the signified of the sentence.' Probably Steiner would agree that 'This intended is what we seek to translate when we transpose a discourse from one language into another', because 'The signified is untranslatable in principle. . . . it characterizes one system in opposition to the other.' The intended, which *is* translatable, constitutes, in other words, 'the semantic element in discourse'.[19]

The intended itself also can be regarded as having two aspects: it is both 'something immanent within the sentence' and 'a claim to express reality'. Here semiotic units, which are 'systems of inner dependencies, and for that reason constitute closed and finite sets', and the sentence, which is 'the first semantic unit' and therefore 'open to the world', are dramatically differentiated. From this point of view, it is through semantic patterns that the MLM isomorphisms, however qualified, are possible at all, because it is through the intended that 'language-as-discourse appears as an open process of mediation between mind and world'.[20]

In his discussion of context and interpretation, Ricoeur, after so much preparation, offers a definition of verbal meaning that is perhaps more a modeller's than a philosopher's:

By context we mean not only the linguistic environment of the actual words, but the speaker's and the hearer's behavior, the situation common to both, and finally the horizon of reality surrounding the speech situation. Furthermore, the context is already implied in the very definition of the words. Each of the partial values enumerated by the dictionary represents a potential use in a typical context which has been identified and classified by lexicology. The sum of these potential uses in potential contexts is what we call, in an improper sense, the meaning of the word. This is an improper sense because the lexical entities are not yet words in the strong sense. But this way of speaking is not wholly improper since the partial meanings of a word summarize previous uses which have been classified according to corresponding contexts. In this sense, a polysemic language is contextually determined not only in its use, but in its very constitution.

His definition of meaning as 'potential uses' recalls Halliday and Hasan's notion of cohesion as 'a potential for relating one element in the text to another', but, if presented with the comparison, he surely would contend that both potentials are selectively *realized* in discourse (and a more thoroughgoing poststructuralist might speak not of potential or realization but of deferral). At any rate, it is because natural language is polysemous in this way that interpretation is required (especially in the ubiquitous case of metaphor, which dislocates word-context expectations and establishes 'new logical boundaries on the ruins of the preceding ones'). Moreover, he argues, 'language has to be interpreted not only because words are the symbols of states of mind, and written signs of oral signs, but because discourse is fundamentally the interpretation of reality'.[21] Interpretation (signs interpreting signs, a Delphic enterprise) is a stratified process. As Wittgenstein says, '*Wenn ich deute, so schreite ich auf dem Gedankenweg von Stufe zu Stufe* [When I interpret, thus I step from level to level on the path of thoughts]'.[22]

Finally, Ricoeur's consideration of the differences between 'ordinary language' and 'scientific language' addresses issues of special importance to the modeller. Ordinary (natural) language generates ambiguities that must be reduced by various interpretive strategies. Scientific (artificial) language, on the other hand, attempts to restrict its lexicon to words with single meanings. As Ricoeur says, more strongly, it aims not 'at reducing polysemy, but at eradicating it' – by introducing into its lexicon terms that denote 'only quantitative entities' and redefining ordinary words (a problematic pidginizing) 'according to the requirements of a *mathesis universalis*', by replacing words with mathematical 'signs which can be read but not vocally uttered', and by formalizing itself so that 'the meaning of all the formulas and all the laws of a formal system are governed by a set of axioms which assign each elementary meaning its place in the theory and prescribe the rules for reading the whole symbolism'. Also, though the application of this formal system to empirical experience obviously involves interpretation, that interpretation (supposedly) is governed by 'rules of translation' that 'take the place of contextual interpretation in ordinary discourse'.[23]

This kind of theorematic *langue bien faite* ('well-formed language') – which Leibniz, Russell, and the young Wittgenstein, among others, dreamt of extending to create a precise 'ordinary discourse' – differs from ordinary language not only strategically but also teleologically. Thus, as Ricoeur has it, 'the theme of ordinary language is communication. . . . Strictly speaking, however, communication is not the aim of a scientific language.' It is 'to insure the identity of meaning from the beginning to the end of an argument. This is why there are no contextual variations of meaning in a *langue bien faite*. The meaning is contextually neutral . . . .' He concludes, with Jakobson, that 'both mathematical and ordinary languages are required, and that each of them has to be considered as the metalanguage required for the structural analysis of the other'.[24]

What Ricoeur has engaged here, however problematically, is, of course, the crux in the computer simulation of natural-language semantics, because that simulation requires the mutual translation of natural and artificial languages. The question of whether the translation rules of the latter can be made to approximate or duplicate the discoverable rules of contextual interpretation of the former remains open, and it has direct bearing on issues that have preoccupied Winograd, Schank, and others. It seems, none the less, that a rapprochement of the two kinds of languages should be possible. As will be seen later, though considering each as the metalanguage of the other introduces complications, it also yields some surprising results and perhaps some opportunities.

There are, of course, many philosophers whose thinking on such matters I might single out and discuss profitably, but, given the prominence of problems of context, it might be most worthwhile to discuss briefly John Searle's approach to meaning from the point of view of speech-act theory, which is concerned with those performative and pragmatic aspects of language that are the most difficult to simulate. I will then transit to a discussion of modellers' ideas about meaning by way of some notes on Wittgenstein.

Searle, who derives much of his theory from the work of John L. Austin, is concerned, like Ricoeur, though differently, with intention and the semantic dynamics of *parole*. He regards language as 'rule-governed intentional behavior' and argues that 'The unit of linguistic communication is not, as has generally been supposed, the symbol, word or sentence, or even the token of the symbol, word, or sentence, but rather the production or issuance of the symbol or word or sentence in the performance of the speech act.' Since language is behaviour, 'a theory of language is part of a theory of action'; hence he is interested in exploring *acts* of speech through which 'whatever can be meant can be said'.[25]

In considering the ramifications of this 'principle of expressibility', Searle advises that the study of meaning and the study of speech acts should not be distinct. Meaning and act 'are related because for every possible speech act there is a possible sentence or set of sentences the literal utterance of which in a particular context would constitute a performance of that speech act'. There are four kinds of such acts: *utterance acts* (speaking – or writing – words, phrases, and so on), *propositional acts* (referring and predicating), *illocutionary acts* (stating, commanding, questioning, promising, and so on), and *perlocutionary acts* (affecting the receiver's actions, beliefs, thoughts, and so on). And there are rules regulating the combinations of acts. For example, 'Propositional acts cannot occur alone; that is, one cannot *just* refer and predicate without making an assertion or asking a question or performing some other illocutionary act' (part Fregean, he observes that 'The linguistic correlate of this point is that sentences, not words, are used to say things').[26]

Searle approaches meaning mostly through consideration of the illocutionary act. The sounds or visible marks involved in the performance of that act 'are characteristically said to have meaning', and the speaker or writer 'is characteristically said to *mean something*' by their use. (The naïveté betrayed here may be seen even more in his refutation of Saussure's analogy between language and chess: 'The pieces in a game like chess are not characteristically said to have a meaning, and furthermore, when one makes a move one is not characteristically said to mean anything by that move.') He analyzes these two kinds of meaning in terms of H. P. Grice's notion of 'non-natural [non-indexical] meaning', which he summarizes and critiques as follows:

> To say that a speaker S meant something by X is to say that S intended the utterance of X to produce some effect in a hearer H by means of the recognition of this intention. Though I do not think this an adequate account, . . . I think it is a very useful beginning of an account of meaning, first because it makes a connection between meaning and intention, and secondly because it captures the following essential feature of linguistic communication. In speaking I attempt to communicate certain things to my hearer by getting him to recognize my intention [by implicature] to communicate just those things. I achieve the intended effect on the hearer by getting him to recognize my intention to achieve that effect, and as soon as the hearer recognizes what it is my intention to achieve, it is in general achieved. He understands what I am saying as soon as he recognizes my intention in uttering what I utter as an intention to say that thing.

This notion is defective, according to Searle, because 'it fails to account for the extent to which meaning can be a matter of rules or conventions' and because 'by defining meaning in terms of intended effect . . . it confuses illocutionary with perlocutionary acts'.[27] (The hairsplitting involved here derives partly from Searle's superficial sense of what constitutes an 'effect on the hearer' – an issue generally treated more effectively by modellers than by philosophers.) He therefore wishes to offer an account of meaning that can enlarge and correct Grice's.

Echoing remotely the Derridean distinction between declaration and description, Searle tries to show the connection between what a speaker means and what the sentence he speaks means, to deal with meaning in terms of both intention and convention. Thus, in his analysis of illocutionary acts, he sees language working as a 'bridge' between speaker and hearer: 'Uttering a sentence and meaning it is a matter of (*a*) intending (*i*-1) to get the hearer to know (recognize, be aware of) that certain states of affairs specified by certain of the rules [that govern the meaning of the sentence] obtain, (*b*) intending to get the hearer to know (recognize, be aware of) these things by means of getting him to recognize *i*-1, and (*c*) intending to get him to recognize *i*-1 in virtue of his knowledge of the rules for the sentence uttered.' The sentence thereby 'provides a conventional means of achieving the intention to produce a certain illocutionary effect in the hearer. If a speaker utters the sentence and means it he will have intentions (*a*), (*b*), and (*c*). The hearer's understanding the utterance will simply consist in those intentions being achieved. And the intentions will in general be achieved if the hearer understands the sentence, i.e., knows its meaning, i.e., knows the rules governing its elements.'[28]

Searle's treatment of meaning in terms of intention/ convention/recognition does improve Grice's somewhat – and in a way that opens it more to the modeller's interest. Indeed, it addresses problems of major importance to both philosophers and modellers, but there is in it a certain oxymoronic mix of oversimplification and prolix muddiness. Also, Searle has proven to be unwaveringly militant toward the whole AI enterprise, especially in so far as it is committed to natural-language simulation, so one may not expect him to help in adapting the insights of speech-act theory for that enterprise.[29] Finally, he seems unconcerned with how Austin's work has effected a revolution that has reintroduced into the philosophy of language, in the words of Rodolphe Gasché, 'nothing more and nothing less than the classical problem of the reflexivity of language',[30] a problem that very much concerns Hofstadter and others interested in self-referentiality in AI systems and that has otherwise intrigued poststructuralists (especially deconstructionists like Gasché) interested in the self-referentiality of peformative language.[31] Austin's revolution has not been sufficiently investigated, particularly in regard to issues involved in the modelling of meaning.

28

Wittgenstein, Use, Functionalism

As I discuss meaning, the shade of Wittgenstein seems always at my side, aphoristically prompting or riddling, alternately confirming the MLM metaphor and calling it into question. But he is present also in another way, especially now, because during his career his thought underwent a sea change that summarizes in nuce the difference between the kind of conception of meaning with which the philosopher (especially if of a logicist bent) is typically concerned and the kind with which the modeller is – though, of course, the difference is not strictly applicable in all cases.

In his early *Logisch-philosophische Abhandlung* (published in 1922 as the *Tractatus*) Wittgenstein held to 'the "correspondence theory of meaning," the essence of which is this: the individual words in language name objects, the object for which a word stands is its meaning'. This Augustinian view gave way to and was criticized by his later view as expounded in his *Philosophische Untersuchungen* and other works published from the early 1930s until his death. In those works he approached meaning as a function of context and tried to work out the 'mental cramp' experienced by asking questions about meaning or, to paraphrase K. T. Fann, to break the spell of associating meaning with a word the way one associates colour with a flower. He suggested that concern should be not with the meaning of words (in that sense) but with their use. One advantage of this alternative, as Fann explains, is

> that 'use' carries with it no suggestion of an object corresponding to a word. Another is that 'use' cannot be understood merely by looking at the word, it can only be understood in contexts – both linguistic and social. This is why Wittgenstein suggests that instead of comparing the relationship between the word and the meaning to that between the money and the cow that

you can buy with it, we should compare it to the relationship between money and its use. . . . The *use* of money is not an object separable from the money, and the specific use of money to buy things (cf. the specific use of words to name things) is only a part of, and makes sense only in, a larger and much more complicated system (financial and social).[1]

Wittgenstein also suggested, however, that this comparison might not apply in all cases.

This open view of meaning derives from an instrumentalist notion that 'Language is not one tool serving one purpose but a collection of tools serving a variety of purposes.'[2] It links the work of the late Wittgenstein to the theory and practice of modellers, for they share a concern with language as instrumental forms. Such a view is not divorced from all the preoccupations to be found among philosophers of language (not from Searle's, for example), but it is from many of them – largely because it urges the avoidance of epistemological traps, practical modelling rather than theoretical quibbling. As Wittgenstein himself says, '*Das besondere Erlebnis der Bedeutung ist charakterisiert dadurch, daß wir mit einer Erklärung und der Vergangenheitsform reagieren: gerade so, als erklärten wir die Bedeutung eines Worts für praktische Zwecke* [The peculiar experience of meaning is characterized by the fact that we react with an explanation and the past tense: exactly as if we were explaining the meaning of a word for practical purposes].'[3] A word *means* only in the flow of (other) words: it not so much represents something else as it represents a cognitive process whereby something else is constituted (as in the Freudian interpretation of dreams, where 'Meanings can be assigned to a particular symbol or dream, yet each sequence remains indeterminate, as if the "dream language" were a sentence without closure that keeps us in the grip of the penultimate. . . . as if only the linguistic veils existed and did not lead to an Isis-like presence behind them').[4] Given their common interest in that process, philosophers and modellers should study each other's work and are learning to do so.[5]

Young, echoing somewhat both Wittgenstein and Searle, offers an unadorned modellist definition of meaning: 'A sign has meaning when a group of people has adopted a particular program for using it. Hence the meaning of a word is defined by the rules for its use and the circumstances under which it can be verified.'[6] And it is Wittgenstein himself who asks the key questions about such rules:

> *Wie hätten wir uns ein komplettes Regelverzeichnis für die Verwendung eines Worts zu denken? – Was versteht man unter einem kompletten Regelverzeichnis für die Verwendung einer Figur im Schachspiel? Könnten wir uns nicht immer Zweifelfälle konstruieren, in denen das normale Regelverzeichnis nicht entscheidet? Denke etwa an so eine Frage: wie ist es festzustellen, wer zuletzt gezogen hat, wenn die Zuverlässigkeit des Gedächtnisses der Spieler angezweifelt wird?*[7]

[How should we have to think of a complete list of rules for the use of a word? What does one understand by a complete list of rules for the use of a piece in chess? Could we not always construct for ourselves cases of doubt, in which the normal list of rules does not decide? Think of a question such as this: how is one to determine who has moved last if the reliability of the players' memory is doubted?]

Such questions, of course, have to do with natural language as a formal system, and the extent of their relevance is uncertain. People manage – much of the time anyway – to use their languages effectively without worrying about an exhaustive list of rules, and Wittgenstein also suggests that it is not necessary to have it (consciously) in order to use a word properly. But his questions persist, and the modeller, who is intent on rules, must encounter them at every turn. He may be forced always, as a deconstructionist would argue, into a compromise of incomplete specification; indeed, that compromise seems quite characteristic of how natural-language meaning works.

Young's definition is starkly functionalist in a way that distresses critics of the artificial intelligentsia such as Weizenbaum. For him 'It is a property of formal languages . . . that their transformation rules are purely syntactic' whereas that is not the case for natural languages – because theirs are concerned 'not merely with the *form* of uninterpreted strings of symbols, but with their *meanings* as well'. That is the difference, by his own example, between an algebraic expression and a sentence in English. He thus distinguishes between the *human* meaning of natural language, which he does not define carefully, and the *machine* meaning of formal language – computer code – which he defines as 'the action a computer takes when it interprets that code as instructions and obeys them'. After discussing various AI systems he concludes that in them 'meaning has become entirely transformed into function' and that 'Language, hence reason too, has been transformed into nothing more than an instrument for affecting things and events in the world. Nothing these systems do has any intrinsic significance.'[8]

Weizenbaum's anxiety is understandable, but his notion of 'intrinsic significance' is easily called into question. Even without broaching the issue of the metaphysics implied, one may argue that the possibility that the sentence *The war in Vietnam was a terrible experience* may never mean to a computer what it means to a contemporary American does not necessarily mean (the word is a real floribunda rose) that the semantic processing of a computer cannot be made to approximate closely or somehow duplicate that of a human being – at least in principle. Indeed, Weizenbaum's definition of meaning, like Young's, is not, in principle, at odds with Morris's definition of meaning as both interpretant and signification. But the point is that the machine modelling of meaning, if undertaken with some holistic vision, can contribute manifoldly to the understanding of both natural language and the ideas, feelings, and values with which it deals.

So, with Wittgenstein's questions and Weizenbaum's caveats in mind, I would like to consider in some detail modellist conceptions of meaning and the issues associated with the machine instantiation of them, beginning with Jackson and ending with Hofstadter, whose ideas will lead into a fuller discussion of the problems and possibilities of regarding natural language as a formal system.

29
Entropy, Readiness, Probability

'The *meaning* of a sentence,' according to Jackson, 'is the semantic information it conveys' or a threefold description of '(1) whatever causes the sentence to be used; (2) whatever is caused by the use of the sentence; (3) whatever else is described by the sentence.' For a computer, understanding that meaning 'may be corresponded to making internal data structures (vectors, lists, graphs, programs, etc.) that *model* these elements of the meaning of the sentence' (in referential terms, he says, 'we may think of the "meaning" of a sentence as being a collection of situations, each of which the sentence possibly denotes').[1]

In Jackson's view natural languages ('languages that living creatures use for communication') and artificial languages ('certain mathematically defined classes of signals that can be used for communication with machines') share certain features, especially stringlike structures, extensibility, self-reference, and redundancy. 'The major difference' between them, for him, 'is that the syntactic and semantic properties of the artificial languages are more thoroughly known (in the sense of being more rigorously formalized, at least consciously) than are those of natural languages.' Given the shared features, he observes, 'it may not be so surprising . . . that computers can now understand human languages much better than monkeys can.' Thus, even granting that 'major difference', which may be only perspectival, it is possible to speak of programs that can 'understand' human language, as Winograd and others have shown, 'by making a model of its "meaning" '.[2]

Jackson's discussion serves well to remind one of the important issues to be addressed, but it is too brief and imprecise. Donald M. MacKay, on the other hand, offers a modellist conception of meaning that is more detailed and exacting. His approach derives from an interest in information theory as developed by R. A. Fisher, Dennis Gabor, Claude E. Shannon, and others from the

1930s into the 1950s. He wishes to demonstrate that such theory, which historically has been applied almost exclusively to problems of mathematically measuring *amounts* of information without regard to meaning, can be expanded to include a conception of meaning useful for computational purposes – that is, for modelling natural-language meaning.

Information, according to MacKay, is what 'we have gained . . . when we know something now that we didn't know before; when "what we know" has changed'. The amount of information involved in that change may be specified in terms of the '"selective information-content" of a message', which 'has to do with the number of independent choices between two possibilities which it enables us to make – the number of independent yes's or no's to which it is equivalent'. It may be specified also in terms of the 'descriptive information-content' of the message, which has aspects both of *'precision* or *reliability'* and of 'the number of *distinguishable features'* associated with the information. The first of these specifications, which was the principal concern of Shannon in his pioneering work (with Warren Weaver), is of greater interest to MacKay – though the second also is important to his ideas, as will be seen. (It is important to remark that the equation for selective information-content, whereby it is equivalent to $\log_2 N$ [where N is the number of possible states of the system in question], 'turns out to be identical in its mathematical form with the statistical measure of thermodynamic entropy'. The units of measurement are not identical, of course, 'but otherwise the only distinction is a difference in sign: where information is given out, entropy increases'. Thus, just as the entropy of an isolated physical system tends to increase, by the Second Law of Thermodynamics, so also 'an isolated system can only lose or give out information'. MacKay speculates, as have others, that there is a connection between that insight and 'our concept of time' in so far as it is 'directly linked with the objective notion of the flux of information'. One implication of that connection is that 'the concept of time would become meaningless – in fact, could not be defined – for any total system in which the total information remained constant'.)

Since Shannon's theory of the measurement of selective information-content is mechanistic and ignores semantic considerations, MacKay tries to bridge the gap by *'picturing an item of information as a kind of tool that operates upon the recipient's internal "state of conditional readiness" '*. That approach, he contends, *'offers a criterion of meaningfulness and meaninglessness which seems more realistic and less Procrustean that the "verifiability" or "falsifiability" criteria canvassed by some linguistic philosophers'*. Thus he hopes it can account for *'how the message recovers its meaning'* so as to resolve 'the whole debate between "mechanists" and "anti-mechanists" '.[4]

MacKay's approach is functionalist, and he sweeps away in one stroke Searle's assumptions about the relation between behaviour and meaning: 'It is not your behaviour, but rather your state of *conditional readiness* for behaviour, which betokens the meaning (to you) of the message . . .', and that readiness 'is modified and moulded according to your understanding of the information you receive'. And here is where Shannon's notion of selectivity becomes pertinent, because

> It isn't until we consider the range of other states of readiness, that *might have been selected but weren't*, that the notion of meaning comes into its own. A change in meaning implies a different selection from the range of states of readiness. A meaningless message is one that makes no selection from the range. An ambiguous message is one that could make more than one selection.

The meaning of a message thus is 'its selective function on the range of the recipient's states of conditional readiness for goal-directed activity. . . . Defined in this way, meaning is clearly a relationship between message and recipient rather than a unique property of the message alone.'[5] In this conception (of how the text 'reads' the reader) a number of others are indirectly at play: that of Saussure concerning the differential relationality of meaning, that of Gestalt psychologists concerning figure-ground relations in perception and cognition, that of Morris concerning meaning as both interpretant and signification, and so on. Also, it has, by way of recent Chomskyan theory, some Derridean overtones. Jeremy Campbell observes that Chomsky's work 'has a close affinity with that of Shannon, in whose theory a single message is of interest only from the point of view of its relationship with all other messages which could have been sent but were not'. Thus surface structure, more abstract and informationally rich (and constructivist in flavour) than it was in earlier Chomskyan theory, 'contains ghostly, silent traces of the "D" [deep] structure, of which it is a transformation'. Indeed, 'when a phrase is moved from one place to another in a sentence by a rule of transformation, the phrase leaves a tacit residue, or "trace" of itself, in the original place in the sentence, even in the "S," or surface, form'.[6] A similar dovetailing of theories has been explored by Serres, who finds many Derridean notions to have been anticipated by thermodynamic theory. As Josué V. Harari and David F. Bell note, 'the Derridean problematic . . . is in fact the reactivation of an already existing one going back to the beginning of the development of thermodynamics'.[7]

MacKay's suggestive conception can be applied readily to the self-communication involved in thinking and intentionality. It is behavioural in orientation but transcends the limitations, especially the avoidance or denial of interiority, that typically characterize behaviourist conceptions of meaning. It is, finally, most useful to the modeller, for it can be translated into a conception, compatible with computational theory, of the brain as 'a signal-box' that is 'key-operated'. By this conception 'The physical embodiment of a message, which eventually acts on the brain, may be likened to the key that sets up a certain configuration of levers in the signal-box . . .', and, by further extension, 'Its selective function, like that of a key, depends both on its shape and on the arrangement of levers it meets.'[8] Once again meaning involves matching.

MacKay admits that his analogy is 'desperately incomplete', but he rightly sees it as useful for discussing the distinction, familiar to deconstructionists, between 'intended meaning' (the selective functions that a message 'is intended to exercise on the range of possible states') and 'effective meaning' (the selective function that the message 'actually performs'), for weighing the merits of alternative theories about meaning, and for synthesizing their insights. Thus, since he, like Ricoeur, is interested in resonances between structural and functional aspects of meaning, he denominates their conventional opposition, in terms of his analogy, as a controversy between 'structuralists' (who focus on the analysis of the logical structure of meaning and 'could be quite successful if only all signal-boxes were of a fixed pattern') and 'operationalists' (who focus on 'the pattern of the use that is made of words' and 'would be in their element if keys behaved in a way that could not be predicted from their structure'). His synthesis comes through the double concession that 'Meaning is indeed inseparable from use, for it is a relation between message and recipient which may differ from one recipient to another', and that 'structure is a major determinant of selective function'. Moreover, he is careful to qualify his analogy by noting that the receiver's state of readiness is conditioned in that the selective function is also a probabilistic 'organizing function' with respect to the receiver's state of readiness (a provision that arguably is embodied limitedly in SHRDLU). Finally, his analogy entails the enabling tenet of the functionalist approach to meaning: meaning *is* what meaning *does* (which tenet is enabled in turn by that, as he has it, of operationalist information theory: *'Information is as information does . . .'*).[9]

MacKay extrapolates his analogy to define *communication* as 'the activity of *replicating representations*' (ideally, setting the receiver's 'switches' in a configuration identical to that of the sender's). His concern is then to model representations so as to take account of meaning systematically, even quantitatively. His proposed model is logico-mathematical and worth the modeller's attention:

> Now a set of independent propositions can be represented or symbolized by a set of perpendicular axes in a multidimensional hyperspace. So we can represent the additive process by which information accumulates with the help of a convenient geometrical vector-model, in which for each new independent proposition we add one dimension to our hyperspace – our 'information-space.' We then can take *distance* in each of those dimensions to represent some function of the amount of metrical information associated with the corresponding proposition. If each structural proposition is represented by a vector whose length is the square root of its metrical information-content, the the total information-content, structural and metrical, is represented by the vector sum of the individual components.

His model includes meaning as follows. He asks that one think of the problem of trying to define the concept of an everyday object (he chooses a chair) in terms of the 'black-and-white of atomic, yes-or-no components' and then realize the need for 'some way of symbolizing the *partial participation* of one or more characteristics' in the definition. The way he suggests does not abrogate binariness but does insist on fine gradations. If one makes a list of the features of chairs and if we accept these (for the sake of argument) as simple 'yes-or-no' characters, then over a long experience of the word 'chair' we should build up a concept of 'chairfulness,' which could be defined by the proportions of different characters in the ensemble of all chairs experienced.

The interesting thing is that this possibility would correspond in our vector-model . . . to attributing significance to *all* orientations of the vector. . . . Quite precisely, what corresponds to the *meaning* of a given term which is definable in terms of this space of basic vectors (elementary component characters) is the *orientation* of its representative vector – the direction which defines the relative weights with which those elementary components enter into our experience-based understanding of the term.

The kind of metric to be used with such vectors is difficult to specify (for example, should it be quantized probabilistically from zero to one?), but MacKay, given the hypothetical nature of his discussion, dismisses the issue and continues: 'The point is that with a given metric we can have a precise representation of the *meaning of a statement for a given individual,* remembering that each individual receiver will have his basic vectors defined by his own internal apparatus. Different *shades* of meaning are represented by different orientations within the same subspace.'[10] The ideas here are variously problematic, but they are also potentially useful.

MacKay relates these ideas to the process of representation by introducing 'a probabilistic mechanism, in which "trains of thought" (metaphorically speaking) correspond to transformations of information-vectors which may be continuous or discrete'. It reacts to input stimuli 'by an act of *replication*' governed by its 'internal matching activity'. If the pattern of the stimuli is sufficiently strong and/or recurrent, then it achieves 'the status of a "universal" in the world of discourse of such a device'.[11] He admits that this provision is not realistic, and yet he insists that it does illustrate an important principle.

The special advantage of such a mechanism is that it characterizes a given universal not only in terms of the numerable internal acts involved in its symbolization but also in terms of their relative frequency, for the meaning of this universal 'is defined by the *orientation* of the information vector – by the statistical spectrum, if you like – over the elementary acts of response which examplars of this universal have evoked in the organism in the past'. Thus this 'artificial organism' is able to abstract universals from data and 'predicate pattern of a group of abstractions'; that is, it can hypothesize, as MacKay explains:

> our device, working probabilistically, makes its abstractions by a process of natural selection of matching responses. It chooses a means of (internal) response which is invariant with respect to the transformations that leave the abstraction invariant, by a self-guiding process in which the statistical configuration for each attempt is dependent upon the success of the last. Experience elevates the statistical status of certain response sequences, which can then appear as elements in the internal logical vocabulary. Performing second-order abstractions (as in the formation of hypotheses), or even nth order abstractions, is in principle just a repetition of this process at the next level or at a higher level.

And he goes on to speculate that consciousness might be discussed in terms of a 'point or area "of conscious attention" in a field of data . . . under active internal symbolic replication, or evocative of internal matching response'. The meaning of what is apprehended, then, 'is defined by a spectrum over the elementary acts of internal response which can be evoked. . . .'. He carefully stipulates that such acts would include others besides those that are verbally coded; that is, his device would include analogs for preference, prejudice, and so on, thereby incorporating a belief system somewhat of the kind with which Kenneth Mark Colby, Robert P. Abelson, and others have been concerned. Indeed, MacKay argues that his device might simulate fairly accurately 'the ordinary conscious behaviour of human beings . . . *in principle*', though he admits that he would not be surprised, 'were one to attempt to devise a probabilistic mechanism with the same mobility and other capacities as *Homo sapiens*, if one would have to go in for mechanisms in protoplasm instead of mechanisms in copper'.[12]

It should be remarked that MacKay tries assiduously to anticipate possible misunderstandings. He warns that the perception of information 'is *constituted* by the act of successful internal adaptive response' and should not be regarded as evoking it 'as a sequel'. His model thus is essentially constructivist, and in it symbols 'stand, not for objects in the world, but for characteristic patterns in the events of perception'. Also, though he distinguishes among 'meaning-to-the-receiver', 'intended-meaning', and 'generally-accepted-meaning', in each case 'the essential notion is formally the selective function (intended, effected, etc.) on a set of possible responses'; and he cautions against supposing that the full meaning of a message can be captured propositionally, because it is conditioned by the organismic propensities of the human language user. Accordingly, he argues that, while the meaning of a message *for a given recipient is a logical property, which it possesses whether or not it has a chance to exercise its function on the recipient*, none the less, because of variations in 'adaptive-response-space' from one individual to another, 'any hope of a completely unambiguous universal language' is 'illusory in principle'. Finally, though he makes some practical suggestions concerning MT (for example, that an automatic translator should operate not 'solely in terms of the *symbols*' of its source language but 'in terms of the *dispositions intended to be evoked* by the symbols') and other matters, he makes a problematizing, even poststructuralist, move when he observes that 'The meaning of a message is not identical with the state it produces. It is *identified by* the state is produces.'[13] (Thus does he metamorphose Peirce's dictum that the meaning of a representation is nothing but another representation.)

30
Percept, Label, Core

For several decades George A. Miller has been concerned with an astounding variety of MLM issues, such as the structure and function of the mental lexicon as a dynamic database, the parallels between syntactic and semantic relations, and the application of formal-language theory to the study of natural language. His efforts, along with those of Philip N. Johnson-Laird, have generated a cornucopia of conclusions and speculations pertinent to the modelling of meaning, especially about the possibility that linguistic knowledge can be described in terms of 'associations between words and percepts'.[1]

First of all, Miller and Johnson-Laird suggest that the 'conceptual distance' between words and what they name can be reduced by 'a more proximal [and constructivist] definition of the relation between them – replace the physical object by a perception of it, and replace the acoustic pattern by behavioral processes required to say it or by perceptual processes involved in hearing it'. Given this redefinition, however, the psycholinguist can turn to the logician and grammarian, who 'deal in idealized abstractions of particular aspects of the psychological processes of language', for only limited help. But there is an alternative because 'the most promising source of ideas rich enough to capture the architecture of this system [of processes] is the modern theory of information processing'. The hypotheses made available by such theory may prove inadequate in some ways but are none the less 'the best available in our present state of knowledge' and should be pursued 'as far as possible'. By the rationale of this approach, understanding a sentence can be considered 'as a form of information processing, as if the sentence were a program being fed into a computer'. Thus 'a listener [or reader] who understands a sentence that is used in a particular context *translates* it into the routine it represents'.[2]

Like MacKay, Miller and Johnson-Laird 'part company with many philosophers' in going beyond propositional semantics. Instead they use procedural semantics. But they also 'part company with many psychologists by placing word–percept associations in a verificational context . . .'. In general they are eclectic and analogically synthetic in their approach. Thus they find a close correspondence between Bernard Harrison's Wittgensteinian–Chomskyan description of 'linguistic devices' and the 'routines used to program the operations of a computer', and they adduce considerable evidence to suggest, as I did earlier, that a natural language is 'analogous to a higher-level programming language . . .'.[3]

Miller and Johnson-Laird are curious as to how that analogy can be extended accurately. With D. J. M. Davies and S. D. Isard, they suggest 'that understanding any sentence is analogous to compiling the program it encodes', and they extend the compiler analogy somewhat further than I did my own and in a way that challenges some of MacKay's assumptions:

> Once compiled, a program may or may not be run. One obvious advantage of the Davies–Isard suggestion is that it provides a natural way to disconnect the understanding of a sentence from any actions it might entail, thus dissolving a bond that has always bedeviled associationistic theories of language and that has led to the invention of such intervening variables as 'dispositions to respond' or 'representational mediation processes.' Davies and Isard propose that the compilation and execution processes can be separated by the earliest possible 'point of refusal.' Neither man nor machine can refuse to obey a command until the command has been understood. Presumably, compilation occurs automatically without conscious control of the listener; he cannot refuse to understand it. Davies and Isard comment that loss of conscious control over one's compiler may correspond to knowing a language fluently.

Then they enlarge the analogy, relating it to Harrison's thought:

> If we imagine that the listener–translator takes spoken words a few at a time and stores them in some working memory until they can be translated into a program of instructions to operate the neural computer, then there must be available in secondary memory an extensive set of subroutines for each word. If no translation can be produced, the input sentence is not

understood. If more than one translation is possible, the input sentence is ambiguous.

According to this interpretation of Harrison's linguistic devices, knowing a word is defined as being able to construct well-formed programs when that word is part of the input sentence. This definition implies the existence of something like a lexicon, a set of subroutines that can be called when different words are used, but this procedural lexicon would be very different from the dictionaries of everyday use and the subroutines would not resemble a familiar dictionary entry. . . . But the obvious implication is that knowledge of any word need not be compacted and deposited in any single place corresponding to *the* lexical (or conceptual) entry for that word. Procedures can be composed and related much more flexibly and freely than, say, lists of semantic components. The theoretical problem is how best to exploit that freedom.

What they propose is plausible not only in terms of psycholinguistics but also in terms of what is known about the equipotentiality of the brain. Furthermore, noting that progress has been made in dealing with that 'theoretical problem' through the procedural approach – specifically, they praise Winograd's work as making possible 'the clearest glimpse yet of how procedural semantics can be applied to natural language' – they consider its advantages:

> In addition to separating translation from execution, a procedural approach does not suffer from the old referential embarrassment about the meanings of the little words, for these are critically important signals as to the order in which subroutines must be assembled. Nor is there any reluctance to deal with clauses or whole sentences rather than isolated words; the verb will be recognized as the basic operator in any clause, for it organizes the roles of the various noun phrases that can serve as its arguments. Rules of syntax will be seen as abstractions from, not components of, the user's competence; syntactic rules are not rules that children must discover and learn but generalizations about what children learn, generalizations against which a psycholinguist can test his more specific procedural hypotheses.[4]

And it is from here that they really begin their investigation of meaning.

Miller and Johnson-Laird are certainly aware that there are rhetorical dimensions to language use that their approach could address, that 'the routines into which sentences are translated are subroutines in some higher-order program controlling the person's participation in the social interaction',[5] but they are most interested in semantic problems. Their synthesis of research findings about those problems is so extensive that I can offer only a sketch of it, but that should suffice to demonstrate its implications.

The process of labelling is a good starting point. According to Miller and Johnson-Laird, 'concepts are routines that can be used in labeling'; since concepts are interrelated, 'before labels can become words used in ordinary discourse they must be incorporated into routines for producing and interpreting meaningful sentences'. But the labelling function of a concept is only a part of it, 'not even a necessary part', because 'we must assume that the conceptual system is sufficiently complex to be able to represent, in addition to the concept of a label, concepts for which no label has been adopted in the language'.[6] Thus they are quickly led beyond any simple notion of referentiality.

Following this line of thought and incorporating into it ideas from Alonzo Church, Miller and Johnson-Laird put forward their claim, in contrast to Frege's, that 'the meaning of a sentence is the program, not the proposition, that it expresses'. Making their case necessarily involves, first, building a procedural model of the lexical–conceptual relation. They introduce theirs, with qualifications, in terms of a metaphor:

> We assume that a semantic field consists of a lexical field and a conceptual core. A lexical field is organized both by shared conditions determining the denotations of its words and by a conceptual core, by the meanings of what the words denote. A conceptual core is an organized representation of general knowledge and beliefs about whatever objects or events the words denote – about what they are and do, what can be done with them, how they are related, what they relate to. This lexical–conceptual relation is complex. To say that a lexical field covers a conceptual core like a mosaic is suggestive, but it greatly oversimplifies.

The mosaic metaphor captures much that is important: it is

only in terms of the core that the choice of particular conditions to identify instances can be rationalized; it is only in terms of the core that a particular lexical concept can be assigned a location relative to other lexical concepts in that field. But that is not all we need to say about the lexical–conceptual relation. It is also necessary to realize that a conceptual core is an inchoate theory about something and that the same lexical field can cover very different theories. . . .

How then does one model this core? The answer unfolds from the assumption 'that conceptual cores can be characterized in procedural terms'.[7]

Indeed, the conceptual core has been so characterized, but how far any given model approximates lexical–conceptual organization in the brain/mind remains, of course, an open question. The kind of problem encountered in trying to model that organization, the kind that interrogates the mosaic metaphor, may be seen in Miller and Johnson-Laird's discussion of lexical decomposition. Observing that 'One advantage of having a procedural dimension to our theory is that differences in depth of processing seem to represent a natural aspect of the information processing that must be performed on different occasions', they link their computational analogy to an arithmetic one: 'Probably the strongest decompositional claim a lexicologist could make would parallel the fundamental theorem of arithmetic: any lexical item can be expressed as a unique (Cartesian?) product of prime lexical items.' The other possibility is that 'each lexical item is a unique prime in its own right'. Either possibility would seem to provide a way of describing the lexical–conceptual relation, but they contend that both must be discredited:

> Strong decomposition is implausible in view of the difficulty that lexicographers have in providing complete definitions; some residuum of meaning, often but not necessarily affective, usually vitiates the synonymy of the lexical item and its definition. On the other hand, complete individuality is inadequate to explain the rich and relatively consistent patterns of properties and relations found in the lexicon. Perhaps the reasonable approach would be to regard these two views as upper and lower bounds between which one might search for a plausible theory.

How then is lexical decomposition (or is it really deconstruction?) to be formulated? They are not sure but are willing to imagine, in a somewhat poststructuralist mood,

> that every lexical item incorporates several primitive lexical concepts and that no primitive lexical concept is expressed directly in a single lexical item. Certain patterns of primitive concepts might recur frequently, and so give an impression of underlying concepts into which surface words could be decomposed, but individuality and the appearance of residual meanings would result from the existence of unique lexical primitives not expressed directly by any single word and not entering into recurrent patterns. Although underlying concepts (patterns of primitives) would reflect the considerable order that has been repeatedly found in the lexicon and in selectional restrictions for word combinations, it would not be obvious that there could be any unique solution to the decomposition problem (alternative formulations might seem equally plausible) and theoretical economy would be highly unlikely (there would not be fewer lexical primitives than there are lexical items).[8]

And there are other issues that a 'plausible theory' would have to address – not the least of which is the notion of 'primitives' (about which Miller and Johnson-Laird also are obviously sceptical). Indeed, theorization itself is problematic here because of the possible equality of plausibilities mentioned above. As John R. Anderson, recalling Steiner, argues summarily concerning automata theory and cognitive-psychological theory, 'there are many different models which generate the same behavior. . . . there is no way to uniquely determine the internal representation of knowledge.'[9]

None the less, Miller and Johnson-Laird discuss a variety of matters related to the problem of lexical decomposition – the interrelations of colour terms, the organization of kinship systems, and so on – and find a good deal of theoretical and some empirical evidence to support a more sophisticated version of their thinking about that problem and others associated with their model:

> The ubiquity of contrastive sets nested in hierarchical relations suggests that such an organization represents a formal, universal semantic characteristic of language. More than that, like all

linguistic universals, it is not a part of language per se but a part of the psychological and biological foundations on which language rests, a capacity that all human languages can take as given by the nature of the language-using organism. As such, this type of organization must play a central role in any account we try to give of man's attempts to discover structure and meaning in his world and his experience of it.

The general characterization of these concepts . . . is that they consist at least of a conceptual core and a lexical field. The conceptual core shares many aspects with a scientific theory; it is, if you like, a lay theory about the nature of a particular part of the world. The lexical field, on the other hand, enables people to map this logical core into language, and the mapping can usually be represented in the form of a key or a decision table based on perceptual or memory tests that are selected for their relevance to the conceptual core and that reveal the place of each lexical item relative to all the others in that field. The field properties that hold among words are in part a lexical reflection of the conceptual core and in part a result of the hierarchical and contrastive structures that make possible the different levels of generality at which people are able to talk about aspects of the concept.

They add, however, that semantic analysis can become difficult or misleading 'in domains for which there is no independent conceptual base or where conceptual analyses do not seem isomorphic with the lexical resources of natural languages'. Indeed, they speculate, the semanticist's situation in this respect may be similar to that of the child acquiring language, as some interpret it, in that in both cases knowledge of the concept must precede knowledge of the lexical term that expresses it.[10] A tricky precedence, if it pertains – and it or some 'looped' version of it (as Hofstadter might suggest) probably does. But one should be encouraged by the refinement of the notion of semantic relativity that Miller and Johnson-Laird's investigations have effected.

Many of the questions about meaning with which Miller and Johnson-Laird are engaged remain, in spite of their efforts, quite troubling (especially those concerning how lexical information includes or triggers compiling routines), but their explorations yield some conclusions about lexical meaning that, while 'considerably more complicated than most psychologists might hope', address some of the key issues of modelling research:

– The meaning of a word can tell you what is, and what is not, an entity that can be labeled with that word. It makes possible programs that incorporate perceptual paradigms applicable to objects, events, properties, and relations in the world. It incorporates basic semantic operators concerning space, time, cause, and intention. It sometimes is a direct specification of an operator or a core concept – a schema that acts as a primitive for other schemata.
– The meaning can tell you the function or purpose of the entity that the word labels. . . .
– The meaning can lead you to all you know about an entity. It has access to encyclopedic information in long-term memory.
– The meaning can tell you about relations between what the word labels and what other words label. Its schema is integrated with schemata represented by other words, a part of a system that captures conceptual relations between words.
– The meaning of a word can tell you about what other sorts of words can occur with it in sentences. It can place syntactic and semantic constraints on other words.

Their theorizing implicates all these conclusions to one extent or another, though they admit there are problems suggested by them that have not been addressed adequately. They believe that 'Procedures for constructing sentences and interpreting them must dovetail with procedures representing the meanings of words', but they cannot describe how that happens (though they do know that 'Children learn their first language without noticing any cleavage between grammar and meaning' and that adults use language likewise). They emphasize the priority of semantic relations in dealing with syntax and other aspects of natural language, but they call for the development of 'a pragmatic theory of discourse' from whose standpoint 'A view of syntax and semantics . . . might even expose the traditional divisions between them as often illusory.'[11]

At any rate, Miller and Johnson-Laird's procedural approach does offer advantages of the kind that will be required for future research. Their representation of the mental lexicon 'handles the obvious intensional relations between words', accounts for their organization into semantic fields, 'offers the necessary degree of flexibility in accessing information', and 'establishes extensional relations of words to the perceptual world' – advantages that, taken together, are not found in current models developed by AI research. In their problematic search for semantic primitives, they 'have tried to develop a set of primitives motivated by the psychology of perception and conception' and 'have related our choices to what we know about children's intellectual and linguistic development' – rather than, like many computationally-oriented modellers, trying to prove only the 'logical adequacy' of such primitives. Thus their requirements for a theory of meaning are more stringent than those typically adduced by the modellist enterprise:

– A theory of meaning should represent meanings of words and sentences in a compatible form.
– It should account for the intensional properties of linguistic expressions and for the intensional relations between them.
– It should allow for the differing significance of sentences depending on their context and for flexible access to information in lexical memory.
– It should account for the extensional relations between linguistic expressions and the world.
– It should account for the organization of words in semantic fields.
– The primitive terms of the theory should be logically adequate and psychologically motivated.
– It should be compatible with established psycholinguistic phenomena.

What is imperative, then, is continuing elaboration and refinement of the procedural approach to semantics, with the addition of increasingly more 'psychological substance' to that approach, which has been 'hitherto dominated by artificial microworlds of computer programmers'.[12]

31

Isomorphism, Decipherment, Symbol

In a single big book entitled *Gödel, Escher, Bach: An Eternal Golden Braid*, Hofstadter attempts, with both playful creativity and rigour, to effect a rapprochement between the 'artificial microworlds' of the computer and the perceptual–conceptual universe of the brain/mind. His approach is by way of formal-systems theory. It involves a polymathic synthesis of ideas from many disciplines and is preoccupied with meaning.

The key to Hofstadter's view of meaning is *isomorphism*, which he defines as 'an information-preserving transformation' that 'applies when two complex structures can be mapped onto each other, in such a way that to each part of one structure there is a corresponding part in the other structure, where "corresponding" means that the two parts play similar roles in their respective structures'. For him 'The perception of an isomorphism between two known structures is a significant advance in knowledge . . .', and 'it is such perceptions of isomorphism which create *meanings* in the minds of people'.[1] Formulating the correspondence in an isomorphism is interpretive: the correspondence itself *is* an interpretation. (Meaning, as Greimas observes, is a transcoding process – from one language to another or from one level of language to another.)

For the mathematician the notion of isomorphism is useful in constructing 'a formal system whose theorems reflect some portion of reality isomorphically'. The symbols of such a system, *'though initially without meaning, cannot avoid taking on "meaning" of sorts, at least if an isomorphism is found'*. Hofstadter advises, however, that meaning in a formal system and meaning in a natural language should be distinguished:

> in a language, when we have learned a meaning for a word, we then make new statements based on the meaning of the word. In a sense the meaning becomes *active*, since it brings into being

197

a new rule for creating sentences. This means that our command of language is not like a finished product: the rules for making sentences increase when we learn new meanings. On the other hand, in a formal system, the theorems are predefined, by the rules of production. We can choose 'meanings' based on an isomorphism (if we can find one) between theorems and true statements. But this does not give us the license to go out and add new theorems to the established theorems. . . .

In a formal system, the meaning must remain *passive*; we can read each string according to the meanings of its constituent symbols, but we do not have the right to create new theorems purely on the basis of the meanings we've assigned the symbols. Interpreted formal systems straddle the line between systems without meaning, and systems with meaning.

(It is worth noting – with Miller and Johnson-Laird's compiler analogy in mind – that, even given these distinctions, it is possible for a compiler 'partially written' in a formal language 'to compile extensions of itself' so that 'a minimal compiler could translate bigger compilers into machine language – which in turn could translate yet bigger compilers, until the final, full-blown compiler had been compiled'. This bootstrapping is 'not so different from the attainment by a child of a critical fluency in his native language, from which point on his vocabulary and fluency can grow by leaps and bounds, since he can *use* language to *acquire* new language'. Some such process, which involves applying rules without rules of application, doubtless inheres in the catastrophic discontinuity that I discussed earlier.) In these terms an interpretation 'will be meaningful to the extent that it accurately reflects some isomorphism to the real world'. In short, meaning 'arises when there is an isomorphism between rule-governed symbols, and things in the real world'. For Hofstadter, if such thinking can be applied somehow to the brain/mind, then discovering the nature of the isomorphism in that case would be 'the key element in answering the question "What is consciousness?"'.[2]

In a formal system, consistency and completeness comprise, respectively, 'the minimal condition under which symbols acquire passive meanings' and 'the maximal confirmation of those passive meanings', where the first is 'the property that "Everything produced by the system is true"' (in the 'real' world or 'some imaginable world') and the second 'the other way round: "Every true statement is produced by the system."' This characterization seems straightforward enough, though its implications, as will be seen, are quite problematic. Moreover, its apparent simplicity contrasts dramatically with the difficulty of using formal-systems theory to analyse a natural-language isomorphism, even one on a level lower than that of the brain/mind:

> Take the case of genetic information commonly said to reside in the double helix of deoxyribonucleic acid (DNA). A molecule of DNA – a *genotype* – is converted into a physical organism – a *phenotype* – by a very complex process, involving the manufacture of proteins, the replication of the DNA, the replication of cells, the gradual differentiation of cell types, and so on. . . . this unrolling of phenotype from genotype – *epigenesis* – is the most tangled of tangled recursions. . . . Epigenesis is guided by a set of enormously complex cycles of chemical reactions and feedback loops. By the time the full organization has been constructed, there is not even the remotest similarity between its physical characteristics and its genotype.

And yet, as Hofstadter observes, 'one seems forced into accepting the idea that the DNA's structure contains the information of the phenotype's structure, which is to say, the two are *isomorphic*'. That isomorphism, however, is not a 'prosaic' one 'in which the parts of one structure are easily mappable onto the parts of the other' but 'an exotic one, by which I mean that it is highly nontrivial to divide the phenotype and genotype into "parts" which can be mapped onto each other'. In this isomorphism, a kind that generally characterizes natural-language meaning, the 'genetic meaning contained in the DNA is one of the best possible examples of implicit meaning', and 'the phenotype is the *revelation* [the term is from Jacques Monod] – the "pulling out" – of the information that was present in the DNA to start with, latently'.[3] (His discussion of the genotype–phenotype interface might be compared to MacKay's of the relation between the message and its receiver.)

What then is the information mediated through an isomorphism? According to Hofstadter, it consists of three kinds of messages: '(1) the *frame* message; (2) the *outer* message; (3) the *inner* message'. He distinguishes them in terms of levels of understanding: 'To understand the frame message is to recognize the need for a decoding-mechanism. . . . To understand the outer message is to build, or know how to build, the correct decoding mechanism for the inner message. . . . To understand the inner message is to have extracted the meaning intended by the sender.' (The stratification may be more complex, of course, with inner and outer intertangling, as is the case with the Rosetta stone, for example.) The outer message is *'necessarily a set of triggers*, rather than a message which can be revealed by a known decoder'; if one understood 'all the finesses' of that message, then 'the inner message would be reconstructible'. Thus every outer message holds an inner message nestled, like the 'aperiodic crystals' (DNA) in which Erwin Schrödinger predicted genetic information would be stored, within its seemingly regular structure; as the literary critic knows as well as the molecular biologist, 'one has to find out how to decipher the inner message *from the outside* . . .'.[4]

It follows that the inner message cannot be understood without an understanding of the frame message and outer message and that 'one cannot get away from a "jukebox" theory of meaning – the doctrine that *no message contains inherent meaning*' (pace Weizenbaum) – according to which (and in accordance with MacKay's thought), 'before any message can be understood, it has to be used as the input to some "jukebox," which means that information contained in the "jukebox" must be added to the message before it acquires meaning'. In verbal communication that process occurs without the infinite regress of having to know rules that determine how to use other rules because 'our intelligence is not disembodied, but is instantiated in physical objects: our brains', which, in obedience to the laws of physics, *'run without being told how to run'*. Hofstadter explains more fully, venturing his own brand of universalism: 'It seems that brains come equipped with "hardware" for recognizing that certain things are messages, and for decoding those messages. This minimal inborn ability to extract inner meaning is what allows the highly recursive, snowballing process of language acquisition to take place. The inborn hardware is like a jukebox: it supplies the additional information which turns mere triggers into complete messages.' And human beings have an 'inclination to attribute intrinsic meaning to those triggers' because

human brains are so constructed that one brain responds in

much the same way to a given trigger as does another brain. . . . This is why a baby can learn any language; it responds to triggers in the same way as any other baby. This uniformity of 'human jukeboxes' establishes a uniform 'language' in which frame messages and outer messages can be communicated. If, furthermore, we believe that human intelligence is just one example of a general phenomenon in nature – the emergence of intelligent beings in widely varying contexts – then presumably the 'language' in which frame messages and outer messages are communicated among humans is a 'dialect' of a *universal* language by which intelligences can communicate with each other. . . .

This would allow us to shift our description of where meaning is located. We could ascribe the meanings (frame, outer, and inner) of a message to the message itself, because of the fact that deciphering mechanisms are themselves universal – that is, they are fundamental forms of nature which arise in the same way in diverse contexts.[5]

Thus the processes whereby inner meanings arise are universal and also involve 'fundamental forms of nature' – perhaps he has gone Chomsky one better.

The upshot is that all messages are coded, and their codes are simply more or less familiar. For the meaning of a message to be revealed, 'it must be pulled out of the code by some sort of mechanism, or isomorphism'. The method may be difficult to determine, but, once it is determined, 'the message becomes transparent as water. When a code is familiar enough, it ceases appearing like a code; one forgets that there is a decoding mechanism. The message is identified with its meaning.' And that meaning 'is an automatic by-product of our recognition of any isomorphism . . .'.[6]

Hofstadter is concerned to relate such theorizing to the activities of the brain. He assumes that 'Thought must depend on *representing reality in the hardware of the brain.*' The formal system to which his attention is largely given is that of 'TNT' (typographical number theory), in which meaning occurs 'as a result of an isomorphism which maps typographical symbols onto numbers, operations, and relations; and strings of typographical symbols onto statements'. In the brain, however, 'we don't have typographical symbols, but we have something even better: active elements which can store information and transmit it and receive it from other active elements'. Accordingly, the brain operates with '*active* symbols, rather than passive typographical symbols'; in it 'the rules are mixed right in with the symbols themselves, whereas on paper, the symbols are static entities, and the rules are in our heads'. Such intermixing allows the symbols to be manipulated very flexibly, so that, for example, the variety of descriptions that can be generated is unlimited. Moreover, the 'calculus' that governs this descriptive power has a distinctly poststructuralist character:

> It is said to be *intensional* and not *extensional*, which means that descriptions can 'float' without being anchored down to specific, known objects. The intensionality of thought is connected to its flexibility; it gives us the ability to imagine hypothetical worlds, to amalgamate different descriptions or chop one description into separate pieces, and so on. . . .[7]

Each of the symbols involved in this process must correspond to a concept definable in terms of some kind of neural configuration. But what kind?

First of all, Hofstadter observes in approaching this question, 'the most naïve assumption – that there is a fixed group of neurons for each different concept – is almost certainly false'. He suggests that concepts may be present in the brain in much the same way that memories generally are. Karl S. Lashley has demonstrated that the cortex appears to store specific memories equipotentially (nonlocally) whereas Wilder Penfield has demonstrated that they can be locally evoked by electrical impulses precisely directed into the cortex; but there are possible explanations for this paradox:

> One possible explanation could be that memories are coded locally, but over and over again in different areas of the cortex – a strategy perhaps developed in evolution as security against possible loss of cortex in fights. . . . Another explanation would be that memories can be reconstructed from dynamic processes spread over the whole brain, but can be triggered from local spots. This theory is based on the notion of modern telephone networks, where the routing of a long-distance call is not predictable in advance, for it is selected at the time the call is

placed, and depends on the situation all over the whole country. Destroying any local part of the network would not block calls; it would just cause them to be routed around the damaged area. In this sense any call is potentially nonlocalizable. Yet any call just connects up two specific points; in this sense any call is localizable.[8]

Whatever different explanation more empirical research might demand, these at least are cogent possibilities.

How then is a concept constructed from a multitude of neural events? Hofstadter invokes a 'crystallization metaphor' for that buildup:

> The crystallization metaphor yields a pretty image derived from statistical mechanics, of a myriad microscopic and uncorrelated activities in a medium, slowly producing local regions of coherence which spread and enlarge; in the end, the myriad small events will have performed a complete structural revamping of their medium from the bottom up, changing it from a chaotic assembly of independent elements into one large, coherent, fully linked structure. If one thinks of the early neural activities as independent, and of the end result of their many independent firings as the triggering of a well-defined large 'module' of neurons, then the word 'crystallization' seems quite apt.

That neural module, which he calls a symbol ('Symbols are the hardware realizations of concepts'), is as variable as the ways it can be triggered – though he wonders sceptically if it has an invariant core cluster of neurons – and in a given brain state may be either '*dormant*, or *awake* (activated)'. Activated symbols are intentional and capable of triggering dormant ones; these triggerings, unlike those on the level of individual neurons, correspond 'to events in the real world – or in an imaginary world'. And activated symbols can communicate messages to each other 'in such a way that their triggering patterns are very much like the large-scale events which do happen in our world, or could happen in a world similar to ours'. Thus meaning in the system of brain symbols arises as a consequence of an isomorphism of a kind 'infinitely more complex, subtle, delicate, versatile, and intensional' than that of a formal system that is typographically instantiated.[9] His thinking seems cognate with that of Miller and Johnson-Laird.

Furthermore, Hofstadter ventures, 'the brush strokes of language are the brush strokes of thought', with a symbol being associated with something about a brush stroke in size, a word or a phrase. And the communication among such symbols may be likened to that among masses of ants in an ant colony, where the communicative actions of individual members are of little consequence compared to those of the aggregates (which figure of 'the brain as an ant colony' he transfigures into 'the brain as an ATN-colony'): 'overlapping and completely tangled symbols are probably the rule, so that each neuron, far from being a member of a unique symbol, is probably a functioning part of hundreds of symbols'. But there is no confusion, because the brain is like 'the surface of a pond, which can support many different types of waves or ripples. The hardware – namely the water itself – is the same in all cases, but it possesses different possible modes of excitation.' Such speculation orbits about a crucial implicit question: is human intelligence a '*software* property' that 'can be "lifted" right out of the hardware in which it resides', or is it 'a brain-bound phenomenon'?[10] For him the answer is that it is not brain-bound: the waves and ripples should be duplicable in a medium other than the pond surface of the brain.

Hofstadter argues that the interconnected symbols by which the brain models the world do have separate identities of a kind – by virtue, in Saussurean fashion, 'of being connected (via potential triggering links) to other symbols'. Also, just as declarative knowledge is explicit and locally stored in a computer while procedural knowledge ('an epiphenomenon') is implicit and globally distributed and therefore independent of any given machine, so there is 'some sort of partial software isomorphism connecting the brains of people whose style of thinking is similar – in particular, a correspondence of (1) the repertoire of symbols, and (2) the triggering patterns of symbols'.[11] (He is doubtful about such an isomorphism on the neural level, the level analogous to that of the circuitry peculiar to 'any given machine'.) He draws an analogy between that isomorphism and the kind that pertains in the case of the similarities in webs woven by two spiders of the same species: there are local variations, but the global patterns are the same.

The point is that the symbols and their triggering patterns

should be definable for, duplicable by a machine. Indeed, the meaning of the symbols, like a program that may be run on variously built machines, would seem to be independent of lower-level hardware; meaning at higher levels could be as bizarre as imaginable, and yet the lower levels of hardware (constituting, as it were, a cantus firmus) would be operating in a perfectly formal and logical way. Hofstadter elaborates:

> The presence of meaning on a given level is determined by whether or not reality is mirrored in an isomorphic (or looser) fashion on that level. So the fact that neurons always perform correct additions (in fact, much more complex calculations) has no bearing whatsoever on the correctness of the top-level conclusions supported by their machinery. Whether one's top level is engaged in proving koans of Boolean Buddhism or in meditating on theorems of Zen Algebra, one's neurons are functioning rationally. . . . any irrationality, if there is such, is on the higher level, and is an epiphenomenon – a consequence – of the events on the lower level. . . .
>
> There is no reason to believe that a computer's faultlessly functioning hardware could not support high-level symbolic behavior which would represent such complex states as confusion, forgetting, or appreciation of beauty. It would require that there exist massive subsystems interacting with each other according to a complex 'logic.'[12]

Presumably that conclusion would hold also for the high-level processes of natural language.

However, Hofstadter appends a somewhat poststructuralist qualification, one anticipated by Quillian and others:

> there are qualities such as well-formedness, which can be detected by *predictably terminating tests*. . . . These I propose to call *syntactic* aspects of form. One intuitively feels . . . that they lie close to the surface, and therefore they do not provoke the creation of multidimensional cognitive structures.
>
> By contrast, the *semantic* aspects of form are those which cannot be tested for in predictable lengths of time: they require *open-ended tests*. Such an aspect is theoremhood of TNT-strings. . . . You cannot just apply some standard test to a string and find out if it is a theorem. Somehow, the fact that its

meaning is involved is crucially related to the difficulty of telling whether or not a string is a TNT-theorem. The act of pulling out a string's meaning involves, in essence, establishing all the implications of its connections to all other strings, and this leads, to be sure, down an open-ended trail. So 'semantic' properties are connected to open-ended searches because, in an important sense, an object's *meaning is not localized* within the object itself. This is not to say that no understanding of any object's meaning is possible until the end of time, for as time passes, more and more of the meaning unfolds. However, there are always aspects of its meaning which will remain hidden arbitrarily long.[13]

What he says here surely pertains as much to the human experience of meaning in natural language as it does to that of an AI system. There is still something elusive about meaning; perhaps more effective modelling of it will depend on including that very elusiveness.

So meaning remains the sticking point. But theory evolves, and some of it does modify and turn into practice. Any partially valid model of natural-language processes, especially if it has 'psychological substance', is in many ways more valuable than a full-blown philosophical theory that is not testable. Like Hofstadter, I am optimistic about modelling and thereby understanding those processes – if not completely, then at least more deeply.

The modellist approach to the study of natural language, particularly semantics, must be commended for the knowledge it has made possible, and its further development must be encouraged. It is extremely important that modellers continue their work in an iconoclastic spirit and not be mesmerized by any dogma. At present, much linguistic theory and research is trammelled by an uneasy complexity reminiscent of the mathematical ingenuity that shored up the Ptolemaic scheme of the solar system just before Copernicus's revolution or that gave nineteenth-century physics the appearance of wholeness just before Einstein's. A new paradigm is on the verge of formation. Modellers will play a paramount role in elaborating it. The study of natural language awaits its imminent Copernicus or Einstein.

32

Formalism, Recursion, Gödel

There are many problems and possibilities relevant to the new paradigm, especially in regard to the relation between formal systems and natural language, that must be investigated. I have already touched on some of them, but, since Hofstadter's ideas concerning meaning are obviously interlocked with his ideas concerning formal systems and natural language, those latter ideas should be addressed first, to preserve continuity, before I turn to the ideas of others.

The primary question with which Hofstadter is concerned is this: *'Do words and thoughts follow formal rules, or do they not?'* His articulation of an answer entails lengthy preliminary considerations of the Epimenides paradox (it was Epimenides, a Cretan, who said, 'All Cretans are liars' – which rhetorical situation, as intriguing to Derrida as to Hofstadter, is characterized, like M. C. Escher's *Print Gallery*, by 'a one-step Strange Loop'), Gödel's critique of Whitehead and Russell's *Principia Mathematica* (which includes his famous Incompleteness Theorem, variously paraphrased but basically stating that 'All consistent axiomatic formulations of number theory include undecidable propositions', blind spots), and other paradoxes and problems of self-referentiality. He also considers the snarls in the interrelations of a metalanguage and its object language, Turing's discovery of 'the existence of ineluctable "holes" in even the most powerful computer imaginable' (which discovery, of the so-called halting problem, correlates necessarily with Gödel's Theorem), and 'the seemingly unbreachable gulf between the formal and the informal, the animate and the inanimate, the flexible and the inflexible' with which AI researchers must deal as they 'put together long sets of rules in strict formalisms which tell inflexible machines how to be flexible'.[1]

By way of these considerations Hofstadter is confronted early on with another, larger question: 'Can all of reality be turned into a formal system?' It is a question that echoes the concerns of Hjelmslev and the Linguistic Circle of Copenhagen and other formalists in their desire to define a system for describing any given phenomenon in terms of a finite number of premises and to construct a calculus by which those premises are combined, and to it Hofstadter replies that

> In a very broad sense, the answer might appear to be yes. One could suggest, for instance, that reality is itself nothing but one very complicated formal system. Its symbols do not move around on paper, but rather in a three-dimensional vacuum (space); they are the elementary particles of which everything is composed. (Tacit assumption: that there is an end to the descending chain of matter, so that the expression 'elementary particles' makes sense.) The 'typographical rules' are the laws of physics, which tell how, given the positions and velocities of all particles at a given instant, to modify them, resulting in a new set of positions and velocities belonging to the 'next' instant. So the theorems of this grand formal system are the possible configurations of particles at different times in the history of the universe. The sole axiom is (or perhaps, *was*) the original configuration of all the particles at the 'beginning of time.' This is so grandiose a conception, however, that it has only the most theoretical interest; and besides, quantum mechanics (and other parts of physics) casts at least some doubt on even the theoretical worth of this idea. Basically, we are asking if the universe operates deterministically, which is an open question.[2]

His answer reveals both positivist interest in formal systems and poststructuralist misgivings about their ultimate validity. Its implications are difficult to array; perhaps the important point is that its possible bearing on his previous conclusions and on others that follow must not be forgotten.

At any rate, the question to which Hofstadter gives most of his attention is the more modest one of 'whether it is theoretically possible to attain the level of our thinking abilities, by using some formal system'. He is attracted especially to the property of recursivity (recursion is the process whereby complex elements of a system are derived from simpler ones in a rule-bound fashion) as suggesting a tentative answer. He discusses the power of recursion in natural language (in terms of push-down stacks and other computer analogs) and finds it manifested in the subatomic realm where particles 'are – in a certain sense which can only be defined rigorously in relativistic quantum mechanics – nested inside each other in a way which can be described recursively, perhaps even by some sort of "grammar"'. If that is the case, then 'the world is built out of recursion'; its grammar 'is a result of the basic laws of physics. . . . And, like the grammars of human languages, this grammar has a recursive structure, in that it allows deep nestings of structures inside each other.' He finds recursion everywhere and wonders if

> suitably complicated recursive systems might be strong enough to break out of any predetermined patterns. And isn't this one of the defining properties of intelligence? Instead of just considering programs composed of procedures which can recursively *call* themselves, why not get really sophisticated, and invent programs which can *modify* themselves – programs which can act on programs, extending them, improving them, generalizing them, fixing them, and so on? This kind of tangled recursion probably lies at the heart of intelligence.[3]

Obviously events at the top level of the mind differ from those at the bottom level of the brain, and human beings do not generally think consciously in terms of tidy formalisms. Indeed, Hofstadter believes that present AI systems are not stratified nearly extensively enough to model effectively the range of difference between 'the software of mind' and 'the hardware of brain'.[4] But he believes also that more extensively stratified systems can be developed, and he disagrees vehemently with Oxford philosopher J. R. Lucas's argument that 'we can never, not even in principle, have a mechanical model of the mind'.[5]

Lucas's argument, in fuller form, is representative of stronger arguments against the possibility of modelling the mind by machine, and its refutation by Hofstadter (among others) is a critical step in the theoretical validation of the idea of creating a formal system capable of sufficiently modifying itself recursively to realize that possibility. The argument runs as follows:

> Gödel's theorem states that in any consistent system which is strong enough to produce simple arithmetic [and any formal

system can be translated into number-theoretical terms] there are formulae which cannot be proved-in-the-system, but which we can see to be true. Essentially, we consider the formula which says, in effect, 'This formula is unprovable-in-the-system.' If this formula were provable-in-the-system, we should have a contradiction: for if it were provable-in-the-system, then it would not be unprovable-in-the-system, so that 'This formula is unprovable-in-the-system' would be false: equally, if it were provable-in-the-system, then it would not be false, but would be true, since in any consistent system nothing false can be proved-in-the-system, but only truths. So the formula 'This formula is unprovable-in-the-system' is not provable-in-the-system, but unprovable-in-the-system. Further, if the formula 'This formula is unprovable-in-the-system' is unprovable-in-the-system, then it is true that that formula is unprovable-in-the-system, that is, 'This formula is unprovable-in-the-system' is true. . . .

Gödel's theorem must apply to cybernetical machines, because it is of the essence of being a machine, that it should be a concrete instantiation of a formal system. It follows that given any machine which is consistent and capable of doing simple arithmetic, there is a formula which it is incapable of producing as being true – i.e. the formula is unprovable-in-the-system – but which we can see to be true. It follows that no machine can be a complete or adequate model of the mind, that minds are essentially different from machines.

For Lucas the behaviour of a machine is 'completely determined by the way it is made and the incoming "stimuli": there is no possibility of its acting on its own . . .'. And the above Gödelian formula is its 'Achilles' heel'. Even if one could construct successive machines, each to account for the Gödelian formula of the previous one, each would be vulnerable: 'Thanks to Gödel's theorem, the mind always has the last word' and 'can always pick a hole in any formal system presented to it as a model of its own workings.' Furthermore, this argument – which, he is careful to note, concerns 'not . . . whether machines or minds are superior, but whether they are the same' – can be expanded to refute many counterarguments, such as one positing a machine that operates by unpredictable procedures, because, in that case, its performance 'is not going to be a convincing parody of intelligent behavior'.

(Human beings are, he contends, consistent systems; they are 'not so much inconsistent as falliable'.)[6]

Lucas insists on the closed nature of the machine and, in the most crucial part of his argument, seems to do some sidestepping in making his case against the possibility of modifiable programs or of discontinuous or catastrophic machine evolution somewhat of the kind I proposed earlier:

> The paradoxes of consciousness arise because a conscious being can be aware of itself, as well as of other things, and yet cannot really be construed as being divisible into parts. It means that a conscious being can deal with Gödelian questions in a way in which a machine cannot, because a conscious being can both consider itself and its performance and yet not be other than that which did the performance. A machine can be made in a manner of speaking to 'consider' its performance, but it cannot take this 'into account' without thereby becoming a different machine, namely the old machine with a 'new part' added. But it is inherent in our idea of a conscious mind that it can reflect upon itself and criticize its own performances, and no extra part is required to do this: it is already complete, and has no Achilles' heel.

The thesis thus begins to become more a matter of conceptual analysis than mathematical discovery. This is borne out by considering another argument put forward by Turing. So far, we have constructed only fairly simple and predictable artifacts. When we increase the complexity of our machines, there may, perhaps, be surprises in store for us. He draws a parallel with a fission pile. Below a certain 'critical' size, nothing much happens: but above the critical size, the sparks begin to fly. So too, perhaps, with brains and machines. Most brains and machines are, at present, 'sub-critical' – they react to incoming stimuli in a stodgy and uninteresting way, have no ideas of their own, can produce only stock responses – but a few brains at present and possibly some machines in the future, are super-critical, and scintillate on their own account. Turing is suggesting that it is only a matter of complexity, and above a certain level of complexity a qualitative difference appears, so that 'super-critical' machines will be quite unlike the simple ones hitherto envisaged.

This may be so. Complexity often does introduce qualitative

differences. Although it sounds implausible, it might turn out that above a certain level of complexity, a machine ceased to be predictable, even in principle, and started doing things on its own account, or, to use a very revealing phrase, it might begin to have a mind of its own. . . . It would begin to have a mind of its own when it was no longer entirely predictable and entirely docile, but was capable of doing things which we recognized as intelligent, and not just mistakes or random shots, but which we had not programmed into it. But then it would cease to be a machine. . . . There would then be two ways of bringing new minds into the world, the traditional way, by begetting children born of women, and a new way by constructing very, very complicated systems. . . . When talking of the second way, we should take care to stress that although what was created looked like a machine, it was not one really, because it was not just the total of its parts.[7]

And so on. Lucas labours the point and hardly excludes the possibility of a catastrophic jump just by adhering to an intransigent notion of 'machineness'.

But what of Lucas's main point that formal systems are simply limited in a way the mind is not? Hofstadter refutes it by arguing that Gödel's Theorem applies to both. TNT or any consistent formal system lacks completeness – that is, the property such that 'all statements which are true (in some imaginable world), and which can be expressed as well-formed strings of the system, are theorems' (consistency inhering only when every theorem of the system, when interpreted, is true in that 'imaginable world') – and that incompleteness cannot be removed from it. However, 'The fascinating thing,' as he notes, 'is that any such system digs its own hole; the system's own richness brings about its own downfall. The downfall occurs essentially because the system is powerful enough to have self-referential sentences.' Self-referentiality, like the increase in machine complexity about which Turing speculated, is a critical-mass phenomenon: 'the system suddenly attains the capacity for self-reference, and thereby dooms itself to incompleteness'. And self-referentiality, as anyone's reaction to the Epimenides paradox shows, characterizes the mind as well as a formal system like TNT. Moreover, both a machine capable of undergoing the program expansions necessary to take account of successive Gödelian conditions and the mind apparently are limited in their ability to 'Gödelize' since 'no algorithmic method can tell how to apply the method of Gödel to all possible kinds of formal systems'. Therefore, Hofstadter concludes, 'any human being simply will reach the limits of his own ability to Gödelize at some point. From there on out, formal systems of that complexity, though admittedly incomplete for the Gödel reason, will have as much power as that human being.'[8]

Boden also refutes Lucas, though from a slightly different angle: she invokes a controversy as to whether or not Gödel's Theorem applies to computer programs, especially those capable of self-modification. (She refutes as well the related arguments of Michael Polanyi and Hubert L. Dreyfus concerning, respectively, the 'tacit knowledge' and intuitive aspects of thought that they claim computers cannot model.)[9] But both refutations hinge on the notion of self-modifiable programs and so raise a question as to their feasability. Hofstadter provides an answer:

> Certainly it is possible for a program to modify itself – but such modifiability has to be inherent in the program to start with. . . . No matter how a program twists and turns to get out of itself, it is still following the rules inherent in itself. It is no more possible for it to escape than it is for a human being to decide voluntarily not to obey the laws of physics. Physics is an overriding system, from which there can be no escape. However, there is a lesser ambition which it is possible to achieve: that is, one can certainly jump from one subsystem of one's brain into a wider subsystem. One can step out of ruts on occasion. This is still due to the interaction of various subsystems of one's brain, but it can feel very much like stepping entirely out of oneself. Similarly, it is entirely conceivable that a partial ability to 'step outside of itself' could be embodied in a computer program.

One can almost imagine jumping into a subsystem of the brain/mind wide enough to encompass (almost!) the 'overriding system' on another level of discourse, something, in a way, Einstein was trying to do – or, now, Derrida. But the salient point for Hofstadter is 'the distinction between *perceiving* oneself, and *transcending* oneself'. Both human beings and computers are capable, to some extent, of perceiving themselves, but neither is capable of transcendence. Just as 'TNT can talk about itself, but

. . . cannot jump out of itself' – any more than the eye, unaided by a mirror, can see itself – and 'A computer program can modify itself but . . . cannot violate its own instructions . . .', so too 'you cannot quite break out of your skin and be on the outside of yourself (modern occult movements, pop psychology fads, etc. notwithstanding)'.[10]

Thus there seems to be no reason, at least in principle, why a sufficiently complex self-modifying program (a sort of mirror – but would it not occlude something?) could not be 'a mechanical model of the mind'.

33

Loops, Self-Reference, Substrates

Hofstadter's interest in formal systems leads him into considering a variety of processes that involve the isomorphic translation of information, many of which, seen as he sees them, have important implications for the MLM metaphor. He observes, for instance, that the 'isomorphism that mirrors TNT inside the abstract realm of natural numbers can be likened to the quasi-isomorphism that mirrors the real world inside our brains, by means of symbols', where the symbols themselves 'play quasi-isomorphic roles to the objects . . .'. Such a translation occurs also on the intracellular level, in protein production, after DNA dispatches messenger RNA from the nucleus:

> Now when a strand of mRNA, after its escape into the cytoplasm, encounters a ribosome, a very intricate and beautiful process called *translation* takes place. . . . Imagine the mRNA to be like a long piece of magnetic recording tape, and the ribosome to be like a tape recorder. As the tape passes through the playing head of the recorder, it is 'read' and converted into music, or other sounds. Thus magnetic markings are 'translated' into notes. Similarly, when a 'tape' of mRNA passes through the 'playing head' of a ribosome, the 'notes' which are produced are *amino acids*, and the 'pieces of music' which they make up are *proteins*. This is what translation is all about. . . .

And the meaning of what is translated depends on the level of analysis and the power of the decoder applied:

> On the lowest level, each DNA strand codes for an equivalent RNA strand – the process of decoding being *transcription*. If one chunks the DNA into triplets, then by using a 'genetic decoder,' one can read the DNA as a sequence of amino acids. This is *translation* (on top of transcription). On the next natural level of

the hierarchy, DNA is readable as a code for a set of proteins. The physical pulling-out of proteins from genes is called *gene expression*. Currently, this is the highest level at which we understand what DNA means.

However, there are certain to be higher levels of DNA meaning which are harder to discern. For instance, there is every reason to believe that the DNA of, say, a human being codes for such features as nose shape, music talent, quickness of reflexes, and so on. Could one, in principle, learn to read off such pieces of information directly from a strand of DNA, without going through the actual physical process of *epigenesis* – the physical pulling-out of phenotype from genotype? Presumably, yes, since – in theory – one could have an incredibly powerful computer program simulating the entire process, including every cell, every protein, every tiny feature involved in the replication of DNA, of cells, to the bitter end. The output of such a *pseudo-epigenesis* program would be a high-level description of the phenotype.

But that possibility, like the more ambitious one of reading 'the phenotype off of the genotype *without* doing an isomorphic simulation of the physical process of epigenesis', is not yet realizable.[1]

The special significance of this kind of hierarchy, which Hofstadter brilliantly illustrates by a detailed comparison or mutual mapping of Francis Crick's 'Central Dogma of Molecular Biology' and the 'Central Dogma of Mathematical Logic' on which Gödel's Theorem is founded (so that, for example, 'strands of DNA' and 'strings of TNT' are mapped onto each other, as are 'self-reproduction' and 'self-reference'), is that 'loops' arise in it. Thus in his 'Central Dogmap' there are 'proteins which act on proteins which act on proteins and so on, ad infinitum', just as there are 'statements about statements of meta-TNT and so on, ad infinitum'. These heterarchies arise 'where a sufficiently complex substratum allows high-level Strange Loops to occur and to cycle around, totally sealed off from lower levels' (loops of this kind can occur in any system characterized by such a 'Tangled Hierarchy' whenever, by upward or downward movement through the levels of the system, 'we unexpectedly find ourselves right back where we started').[2] Extrapolating his Dogmap, he finds such loops in many other natural processes.

In short, Hofstadter concludes 'that nature feels quite comfortable in mixing levels which *we* tend to see as quite distinct'. Nowhere is this evidenced more demonstratively than in the biological cell regarded more explicitly as a computer: there DNA may be viewed as either a program or data; proteins as programs, processors, or interpreters; ribosomes as interpreters or processors; and so on. And he observes that such mixing of levels is characteristic not only of biological systems but also, increasingly, of computers themselves, in the development of which 'there is already a visible tendency to mix all these seemingly distinct aspects . . .'.[3]

Given the ubiquity of this phenomenon, it is no surprise that Hofstadter finds it essential to his model of the brain/mind, in which 'every aspect of thinking can be viewed as a high-level description of a system which, on a low level, is governed by simple, even formal, rules'.[4] The brain/mind is a Tangled Hierarchy, 'a multilevel system with an intricately interwoven and deep self-referential structure' that includes the most strange Strange Loop of all because it 'has the ability to reflect on itself, that is, the firing of neurons creates thoughts about neurons'. It epitomizes 'a level of the universe where matter has acquired the awesome ability to contemplate itself'.[5]

To what extent is such a structure duplicable by a computer? Perhaps completely, but some details must be introduced, starting with Hofstadter's consideration of the so-called Church–Turing Thesis in terms of a 'FlooP [free-loop] program'. First, he offers a 'Standard Version' of that thesis: 'Suppose there is a method which a sentient being follows in order to sort numbers into two classes. Suppose further that this method always yields an answer within a finite amount of time, and that it always gives the same answer for a given number. *Then*: Some terminating FlooP program (i.e., some general recursive function) exists which gives exactly the same answers as the sentient being's method does.' Second, he offers a 'Public-Processes Version' that provides that the method used 'can be communicated reliably from one sentient being to another by means of language'. And, third, he offers an 'Isomorphism Version' that appends the further provision that 'The mental processes and the FlooP program are isomorphic in the sense that on some level there is a correspondence between the steps being carried out in both computer and brain.' That version asserts, in short, 'that when one computes something, one's mental activity can be mirrored isomorphically in some FlooP program'. Such mirroring involves only 'software entities', and 'There is no assertion of isomorphic activity on the lower levels of brain and computer (e.g., neurons and bits).'[6]

At this level of abstraction, one can imagine mental processes being 'skimmed off' the brain/mind and transplanted into a machine; however, 'when it comes to real-world understanding, it seems that there is no simple way to skim off the top level, and program it alone. The triggering patterns of symbols are just too complex.' It is for this reason, Hofstadter observes, that

> the brain begins to look like a very peculiar formal system, for on its bottom level – the neural level – where the 'rules' operate and change the state, there may be no interpretation of the primitive elements (neural firings, or perhaps even lower-level events). Yet on the top level, there emerges a meaningful interpretation – a mapping from the large 'clouds' of neural activity which we have been calling 'symbols,' onto the real world. There is some resemblance to the Gödel construction, in that a high-level isomorphism allows a high level of meaning to be read into strings; but in the Gödel construction, the higher-level meaning 'rides' on the lower level – that is, it is derived from the lower level. . . . But in the brain, the events on the neural level are *not* subject to real-world interpretation; they are simply not imitating anything. They are there purely as the substrate to support the higher level, much as transistors in a pocket calculator are there purely to support its number-mirroring activity. And the implication is that there is no way to skim off just the highest level and make an isomorphic copy of it in a program; if one is to mirror the brain processes which allow real-world understanding, then one *must* mirror some of the lower-level things which are taking place: the 'languages of the brain.' This doesn't necessarily mean that one must go all the way down to the level of the hardware, though that may turn out to be the case.

In the course of developing a program with the aim of achieving an 'intelligent' (viz., human-like) internal representation of what is 'out there,' at some point one will probably be forced into using structures and processes that do not admit of any straightforward interpretations – that is, which cannot be directly mapped onto elements of reality. These lower layers of the program will be able to be understood only by virtue of their catalytic relation to layers above them, rather than because of some direct connection they have to the outer world.

Trying otherwise to understand such layers he likens to the nightmare of 'trying to understand a book on the letter level'. And he speculates that multilevel architecture 'becomes necessary just when processes involving images and analogies become significant elements of the program – in contrast to processes which are supposed to carry out strictly deductive reasoning'. That speculation, interestingly enough, 'would imply that creativity intrinsically depends upon certain kinds of "uninterpretable" lower-level events'. He conjectures that 'High-level meaning is an optional feature of a neural network – one which may emerge as a consequence of evolutionary environmental pressures.'[7] And I would conjecture that it did indeed emerge for exactly that reason and in a catastrophic fashion. If it can emerge in a machine as well, then probably it will do so somewhat similarly.

The possibility of that emergence is implicit in Hofstadter's 'Microscopic Version' of the Church–Turing Thesis: 'The behavior of the components of a living being can be simulated on a computer. That is, the behavior of any component (typically assumed to be a cell) can be calculated by a FlooP program . . . to any desired degree of accuracy, given a sufficiently precise description of the component's internal state and local environment.' This version asserts that the brain is as comprehensible as any other human organ, and it leads necessarily to a bolder 'Reductionist's Version' that asserts that 'All brain processes are derived from a computable substrate.' That version, he argues, 'is about the strongest theoretical underpinning one could give in support of the eventual possibility of realizing Artificial Intelligence'. Even if one is not concerned with the simulation of neural networks, it makes a strong argument that 'probably there are significant features of intelligence which can be floated on top of entirely different sorts of substrates than those of organic brains'.[8] The question for the modeller, in that case, comes down to how many features of human intelligence, Rumelhart's 'more general mechanisms', he wishes to simulate.

This chain of theorizing finally enables Hofstadter's 'AI Version' of the Church–Turing Thesis: 'Mental processes of any sort can be simulated by a computer program whose underlying language is of power equal to that of FlooP. . . .' This version is essentially equivalent to his 'AI Thesis' (which, in turn, is implicit in my MLM metaphor): 'As the intelligence of machines evolves, its underlying mechanisms will gradually converge to the mechanisms underlying human intelligence.' However, the machine, like its organic counterpart, theoretically still never could be a complete system for a reason that now appears to be physical: the rules of the substrate, regardless of its form, cannot be violated – no matter what paradoxes are at play on a higher level. The coding of the Epimenides paradox in that substrate, for example, is such that its resolution at a higher level is 'an impossible task'.[9] None the less, remarkable events are occasioned there, including an understanding of why that paradox cannot be resolved.

So Hofstadter reapproaches his question of whether or not words and thoughts follow formal rules and offers this answer: '"Yes – provided that you go down to the lowest level – the hardware – to find the rules."' The important distinction here is 'between self-modifiable software and inviolate hardware', which implies that the rules of the mind can be changed (by metarules) while those of the brain cannot. As he puts it, 'you have access to your thoughts but not to your neurons'. The brain/mind consists of 'a software tangle' (a Tangled Hierarchy of symbols) supported by 'a hardware tangle' (a simpler arrangement of neurons). Strange Loops arise only in the former, and they do so when language 'talks about itself, whether directly or indirectly'. When that happens, 'something *in* the system jumps out and acts *on* the system, as if it were *outside* the system'. This event involves 'an ill-defined sense of topological wrongness: the inside–outside distinction is being blurred, as in the famous shape called a "Klein bottle"'. In such Kleinian experiences there is a sense of the mind as self-programmed; it comes about because 'we are shielded from the lower levels, the neural tangle. Our thoughts seem to run about in their own space, creating new thoughts and modifying old ones, and we never notice any neurons helping us out! . . . We can't.' He compares this situation to that of self-modifying LISP programs: if they are observed on a high level only, they seem to be changing their own structure; but, if one shifts levels and thinks of them 'as data to the LISP interpreter . . . , then in fact the sole program that is running is the interpreter, and the changes being made are merely changes in pieces of data. The LISP interpreter itself is shielded from changes.' This sense of being self-programmed is essential to the rhetorical integrity of the self; the disjunction of levels that makes it possible – analogous to that across which occurs 'the translation of number-theoretical statements into metamathematical statements'[10] – is also crucial to the power and limits of human language. Any attempt to model fully that language and the brain/mind that is its source and product will succeed, according to Hofstadter, only if the complexities and peculiarities of that disjunction are taken into account. He asserts that, in principle, they can be.

34
Disagreements, Problems, Possibilities

Most AI theorists and researchers would agree with Hofstadter's arguments or at least be in close sympathy with them, as would information theorists like MacKay. Jackson, for example, contends that 'There is no known a priori limit to the extensibility of a computer's language capability other than those limits of a purely practical nature (memory size and processing speed)' and that, 'Although the difficulties involved with understanding natural language should not be minimized, no one has been able to show . . . that English is theoretically outside the language capability of all computers . . . .'[1] However, a number of computer scientists and others, like Steiner, would deny that any formalism ever could simulate natural-language processes fully, even in theory. Weizenbaum's opinions in that regard are well known and representative.

Weizenbaum would seem to have little patience with the MLM metaphor. He regards any theory as 'merely a text'(!), a kind of map that can 'guide and stimulate intelligent search'. Moreover, he says, 'A theory written in the form of a computer program is thus both a theory and, when placed on a computer and run, a model to which the theory applies'; as such, it 'is always a simplification, a kind of idealization of what it is intended to model' and not a reproduction of 'reality in all its complexity'. In sum, his somewhat informal argument is that natural-language processes have not been and (therefore?) cannot be captured *in toto* by capturing what 'is computable and only that'.[2]

Bronowski is similarly sceptical. Taking a hint from von Neumann, he is loath to consider the brain/mind as resembling a computer at all and therefore rejects any computer-like formalism for modelling it. He suggests vaguely that 'the brain must be using some kind of statistical language which is quite unlike human language' and yet to be discovered and decoded.[3] He contends that the brain can be characterized as 'a machine with a formal procedure' only if 'its language is as strict and as artificial (in the logical sense) as any of our own marks on a magnetic tape'. In other words, if it can be characterized as a machine with a language more complex than that, then it is not a machine but a brain – a Lucas-like debater's escape hatch. He uses Gödel's *Entscheidungsproblem* ('decision problem') and the theorems of Turing, Tarski, and others to argue the various facets of his position: that 'there cannot be a universal description of nature in a single, closed, consistent language'; that 'the mind cannot extricate the laws of nature from its own language', because its view of nature is conditioned absolutely by that language and its 'formal logic is not that of nature . . .'; and that, therefore, since the brain/mind is a part of nature, it cannot be simulated by a formal system.[4] His argument, like Weizenbaum's, does not entirely persuade – though it is appealing in some ways – and lacks the subtlety of Hofstadter's.

But these arguments are not foolish and might point toward insurmountable problems – if not in principle, then in practice. Miller and Johnson-Laird note, for example, that 'intensional rules seem to introduce an infinitude of abstract entities that in formal logic or mathematics might better be omitted entirely'. Though they recognize that natural and formal languages share many features, they also are aware of severe differences and observe that verifiability theories of meaning, which 'hold rigorously only for formal languages like logic or mathematics', are 'not psychological theories'.[5] Perhaps consideration of some other examples of problems that have been encountered will illustrate the magnitude of the overall problem of constructing a natural-language formalism.

Janet Dean Fodor observes that there are many parallels between a generative natural-language grammar and a system of formal logic:

> The syntactic rules of grammar license the move from one syntactic representation of a sentence to another just as the inference rules of logic . . . license the move from one logical formula to another. In both types of system the derivations are quite mechanical, in the sense that whether or not a certain rule applies to a formula can be determined by reference solely to the configuration of symbols in the formula and the formal statement of the rule. Syntactic derivations therefore formally

resemble proofs in logic, and, in line with this, the initial symbol 'S' of the base component of the grammar can be regarded as the analogue of the axioms of the system of logic. The surface structures generated by grammatical rules can be likened to the theorems of a logical system.

Obliquely recalling Saussure's chess/language analogy, she remarks that 'even for chess there is an "axiom" (the initial positioning of pieces on the board) and a set of "transformational rules" which license moves from one configuration of pieces to another.' One has to grant, of course, that the logician and the linguist have different methodological perspectives on such parallels (conventionally the former starts with the rules and studies the language they generate whereas the latter 'constructs his rules so that they define the language which he has decided to study'), but the deeper problem is that 'No precise and explicit translation rules relating to a natural language and a system of logic have ever been formulated.' Even if they could be, she warns, 'What we ultimately have to maximize is the simplicity and generality of the grammar as a whole, and we cannot automatically assume that any given system of logic, however simple and elegant it is in itself, will necessarily contribute to this.'[6]

Ray Jackendoff offers a similar argument from a semanticist's point of view. According to him, traditional logic 'has become devoid of empirical content in part because it has failed as an adequate account of natural-language semantics'. He theorizes, with Jerry A. Fodor and Miller and Johnson-Laird, that 'semantic structure . . . is couched directly in terms of the human mind's organization of all experience'; it follows that 'the well-formedness rules for semantics are a subset of those for concepts . . .' and that 'the semantic structures derived from projection rules [which map between those structures and syntax] are a particular class of concepts'. But this theory is difficult to investigate by means of logic, which apparently fails to satisfy Ockham's razor:

The methodological assumptions for such a theory would be that syntactic simplicity ideally corresponds to conceptual simplicity; grammatical parallelisms may be clues to conceptual parallelisms; apparent grammatical constraints may reflect conceptual constraints. In short, one should assume that language is a relatively efficient encoding of the information it conveys, and that theories to the contrary (such as most work in logic, which implicitly or explicitly claims that natural language highly distorts the form of the information) inadequately represent the structure of language or the information it conveys, or both.[7]

This situation is especially problematic because there is, he argues, persuasive empirical evidence supporting these assumptions.

Chomsky has developed his transformational-generative grammar largely in an attempt to derive a universal grammar and thus to mirror the laws of mental operations. He believes that, because of such efforts, 'Real progress has been made in the study of the mechanisms of language, the formal principles that make possible the creative aspect of language use and that determine the phonetic form and semantic content of utterances.' None the less, present understanding of these mechanisms remains 'only fragmentary', and 'the study of universal semantics . . . has barely advanced since the medieval period'.[8] That situation is doubtless due in part, he would surely agree, to the recurrent application of formal-linguistic notions that are inadequate to characterize natural language. The recognition of that inadequacy led him to reject, along with finite-state theories of natural language, much of his early work on the mathematical modelling of constituent-structure grammars, whose resultant models, as Wall observes, are of a kind 'now almost universally regarded as inadequate as grammars of natural languages'.[9] A similar fate seems to be befalling even his most recent work.

Indeed, Wall argues, there is a profound flaw running through most work being done with formal grammars because it

deals exclusively with the set of strings they generate (called the *weak generative capacity* of the grammar) and has little to say about the kinds of structural descriptions (constituent-structure trees) assigned to the grammatical strings (*strong generative capacity*). . . . A few results in mathematical linguistics concerning weak generative capacity have been of direct linguistic significance (for example, the argument that English is not a finite-state language . . .), but, by and large, they permit very few inferences about grammars of natural languages.

Formal grammars thus are important mainly because of 'their applicability to computer programming languages and, by virtue of the correspondences between the formal grammars and automata, to the theory of abstract computing devices' and not because of their characterization of natural language.[10]

On the other hand, constituent-structure grammars can characterize certain aspects of natural-language sentence structure and have the advantage of being easily mathematicized. And constituent-structure rules have proven useful for some of the purposes of transformational grammarians, especially for the mathematical formulation of the 1965 version of Chomsky's grammar by Seymour Ginsburg and Barbara Hall Partee in the late 1960s and, somewhat more recently, by P. Stanley Peters and R. W. Ritchie.[11] That usefulness is, however, limited; and the work of Peters and Ritchie, who have shown that transformational grammars can 'generate all r.e. [recursively enumerable] sets even if the base is made context-free rather than context-sensitive,' points to a failure in that version, as Wall observes:

> Since it is commonly supposed that natural languages are properly included in the recursive sets . . . , which are, in turn, properly included in the r.e. sets, transformational grammars, by this formulation, are capable of generating strings that are not possible natural languages. One of the goals of linguistic theory is to give a precise characterization of the notion 'possible grammar of a natural language,' and thus this version of the theory of transformational grammar is shown to fail to meet this goal by virtue of being too broad, i.e., allowing too large a class of grammars.

Furthermore, following this chain of thought, one may show that 'the Universal Base Hypothesis (the conjecture that the grammars of all natural languages have the same base rules) cannot be proved false'; but unfortunately it also turns out to be 'trivially true' because one may show also that the number of possible bases is infinite.[12]

Such problems critically obstruct the modelling of natural language and echo others I have discussed earlier. They have proven so intransigent that any further dealing with them surely demands a different and more comprehensive formalism. If Hofstadter is correct, such a formalism would have to reflect hardware logic but at the same time be remarkably flexible. Does such a formalism seem to be possible at all? And, if it is, what can be suggested speculatively about its provisions? Neither question now has a well-supported answer. However, a tentative negative answer to the first may be found in arguments advanced by Paul Ziff, and a tentative affirmative answer to it may be found in counterarguments advanced by Richard M. Martin, who has a studied but hardly thoroughgoing answer to the second as well.

Ziff argues that the artificial precisions of a formal language, when compared to the 'realities' of natural-language communication, have only 'somewhat mythic and certainly myopic reaches' that render it quite unlike a natural language and useless for everyday communication. This is so, according to him, for a number of reasons: 'the familiar forms of formal logic and formal languages are not equipped to cope with noise' in a world where 'there is always noise' (though, he admits, 'Von Neumann's probabilistic logic provides an example of a formal language devised to cope with problems occasioned by a failure of transmission' – an admission that probably could be enlarged if he knew information theory); formal languages ignore the 'perceptual strategies and abilities' on which natural language relies; the vocabularies of formal and natural languages are quite different; word usage in a natural language has 'something of the character of an operation with an analogue device' whereas 'the vocabulary of a formal language can readily be digital in character'; and so on. His argument is casual, not thoroughly informed, sometimes vague, and able to lead him – by a curious sashay across Church's discussion of formal-linguistic effectiveness in his *Introduction to Mathematical Logic* – to conclude, with patent absurdity, that 'perhaps nothing is suitable for use as a language'.[13]

Martin is puzzled and amused by Ziff's preoccupation with the uselessness of formal languages for everyday communication, and he argues that

surely in this world we do in fact often communicate in terms of formal systems, e.g., in a formalized arithmetic- or set-theory, perhaps even in basic English. What Professor Ziff says here thus seems to me false. What he wishes to say is, perhaps, that we do also communicate in a natural language, and that natural languages are in various respects richer in modes of locution than most formalized languages, and that communication itself is a very complex affair in need of analysis. But these are mere truisms, at least prima facie. What Professor Ziff does *not* say, but, it seems to me, *should* have said is that much progress has been made in studying the complex facts of communication by means of the study of formalized languages, and that such study likewise promises to contribute much to both the syntax and semantics of natural language.[14]

One could argue that Ziff would be advised to consider more carefully the different emphases that typify a formal as opposed to a natural language, consider how those of the former could be shifted toward those of the latter, and otherwise consider how to use each of those languages as the metalanguage of the other.

Martin suggests that, when designing a formalism for natural language, one should try to account for the noise involved by designing 'new logics' or at least by more ingeniously applying existing ones, and he goes further: 'The variety of formal systems is so great that one of these days one may well turn up that will very closely approximate a natural language in crucial respects.' He is distressed that many linguists have neglected the help that modern logic could offer them, and he urges that, rather than ignore it or exercise Ziff's complacent cynicism, they use its insights and contribute to its future development. He even ventures to argue that logical form 'surely has a great deal to do with the depth grammar of natural language' and that perhaps 'the depth grammar of a sentence *is* its logical form, as Herbert Bohnert has suggested'. Finally, he predicts,

> linguists will be forced, internally as it were, to come to grips with the results of modern logic. Indeed, this is apparently already happening to some extent. By 'logic' is not meant here recursive function-theory, California model-theory, constructive proof-theory, or even axiomatic set-theory. Such areas may or may not be useful for linguistics. Rather under 'logic' are included our good old friends, the homely locutions 'and,' 'or,' 'if–then,' 'if and only if,' 'not,' 'for all x,' 'for some x,' and 'is identical with,' plus the calculus of individuals, event-logic, syntax, denotational semantics, and . . . various parts of pragmatics. . . . It is to these that the linguist can most profitably turn for help. These are his tools. And they are 'clean tools,' to borrow a phrase of the late J. L. Austin in another context, in

fact, the only really clean ones we have, so that we might as well use them as much as we can. But they constitute only what may be called 'baby logic.' Baby logic is to the linguist what 'baby mathematics' (in the phrase of Murray Gell-Mann) is to the theoretical physicist – very elementary but indispensable domains of theory in both cases.[15]

Surely Martin is correct here, and a good deal more than 'baby logic' will be required if the linguist is to design a poststructuralist formalism that accounts for the complexity, economy, and equivocality of natural language. Probably almost all logical theories will have something to contribute to the ongoing synthesis. Surely the case is not, as Ziff would despair, that all is lost for the modeller.

It seems quite plausible that nature is inherently formal, that what is now 'beyond logic' involves logic as yet not understood, and that natural language can be simulated by an 'artificial' formalism in all or most respects. Obviously the character of that formalism is difficult to predict, and it may well be constructed more by a machine, even the machine that instantiates it as a model, than by the human mind. It may not be governed by the theorems of Gödel and others quite as one would now expect. It may embed in itself both digital and analog logics, paradoxical interlacings of discrete and continuous structures, deconstructive slippages. It may come to seem a great deal like an old and familiar friend: natural language itself.

Let me explain what I mean by reapproaching the formalism issue. For AI theory that issue appears increasingly to concern how close computational processes are to those of cognition. Dennett sees an extreme polarization in this regard between 'High Church Computationalists' and 'Zen Holists'. The former group, associated with MIT, 'the East Pole', and including such people as Allen Newell and Jerry A. Fodor, views cognition as computation whose symbols '*refer* to things in the world'. The latter group, associated with the University of California at Berkeley and including such people as Dreyfus and Searle, believes that cognition 'is not computation at all' but 'something holistic and emergent – and organic and fuzzy and warm and mysterious'. This thesis-antithesis split, which bounds a range of intermediate positions, has occasioned pitched debates, most of which have not been productive. But the dialectic now seems to be giving rise to a synthesis in the form of the 'New Connectionists'. This group, associated mostly with the West and including such people as Pentti Kanerva and Paul Smolensky, is interested both in modelling the brain as a parallel processor and in exploring 'the powers of massively parallel processors in general'.[16]

New Connectionist models all share certain traits, according to Dennett: '"Distributed" memory and processing, in which units play multiple, drastically equivocal roles, and in which disambiguation occurs only "globally"'; 'No central control, but rather a partially anarchic system of rather competitive elements'; 'No complex message-passing between modules or subsystems'; 'A reliance on statistical properties of ensembles to achieve effects'; and 'The relatively mindless and inefficient making and unmaking of many partial pathways of solutions, until the system settles down after a while not on the (predesignated or predesignatable) "right" solution, but only with whatever "solution" or "solutions" "feel right" to the system.' Such models are, of course, computational, 'but the level at which the modelling is computational is much closer to neuroscience than to psychology'. That is, the computation does not yield a logical entailment or anything like that 'but (for instance) the new value of some threshold-like parameter of some element which all by itself has no univocal external-world semantic role'. At this level semantics and referentiality have to do only with brain states and events, and the language involved is, at least partly, 'rather like a machine language for a computer . . .'. High-level activities are not well specified in New Connectionist theory, but they are certainly not regarded as computational; and even the language at the computational level 'is importantly *un*like a machine language, in that there is no supposition of a direct translation or implementation relation between the high-level phenomena which do have an external-world semantics and the low-level phenomena, which do not'.[17]

The implication is that a thoroughgoing formalism would have to account for both levels and for an indirect mediation/isomorphism between them. If consonant with the traits of New Connectionist models – at least two of which are conspicuously poststructuralist – it would have to be flexible in much the same way that natural language is rather than as tightly laced as logic in the usual sense (to which end recent theories of so-called fuzzy logics may contribute). It would be closer to natural language also because it would have to take account of how cognition makes 'essential use of fundamentally *perceptual* operations' and how 'a proper memory will do a great deal of the intelligent work itself'.[18] (It would therefore have to be instantiated in a non-von Neumann machine.)

Hofstadter seems to be generally in agreement with the New Connectionists and with my argument. His Heideggerian insistence that man does not manipulate symbols so much as they manipulate him involves an essentially deconstructive move that 'turns everything on its head, placing cognition – that rational-seeming level of our minds – where it belongs, namely, as a consequence of much deeper processes of myriads of interacting subcognitive structures'. In thus recognizing the 'pivotal role' of 'the irrational and subcognitive', he is willing to accept computation only as a hardware-level support for cognition. And he speaks of the need to abandon 'perfect mathematical isomorphism' in discussions of symbolization and to consider the 'suggestive value' and 'metaphorical richness' in its patterns. He emphasizes that AI theory and research should give more attention to the 'slippability' of natural language and the role of alternity. Only then, he contends, and only when the bottom-up, epiphenomenal character of cognition is taken into account, will AI approach its human counterpart. Only then will there occur high-level events, like the low-level ones modelled by New Connectionists, that 'will neither have been written nor anticipated by any programmer'.[19]

35
Memory, Learning, Self-Knowledge

Earl Hunt asks of himself the question 'What kind of computer is Man?' and offers a conjectural description (and a word of advice) as an answer:

> Man is describable as a dual processor, dual memory system with extensive input–output buffering within each system. The input–output system appears to have substantial peripheral computing power itself. But man is not modeled by a dual processor computer. The two processors of the brain are asymmetric. The semantic memory processor is a serial processor with a list structure memory. The image memory processor may very well be a sophisticated analog processor attached to an associative memory. When we propose models of cognition it would perhaps be advisable if we specified the relation of the model to this system architecture and its associated addressing system and data structure.[1]

Hunt's description derives from his theorizing about the organization (and inter-organization) of short- and long-term memory, left–right asymmetries of memory distribution in the brain, and so on. His emphasis on duality is cogent: the brain seems dually organized in many respects, and its memory system, especially, may be analysed in terms of a number of dualities that necessarily relate to linguistic structures and processes. Thus his advice in regard to models of cognition holds as well for models of natural language. The modelling of it may not require exact simulation of that system, hypotheses about which may be posed rather easily in programming terms, but its characteristics will have to be taken into account one way or another; machine analogies, if invoked judiciously, may be of help in that undertaking – in understanding deeply why the Greeks made Mnemosyne the mother of the Muses.

Whatever else human memory is, it is not the sort of simple vectorial structure typically found in a computer. It is a dynamic and – hardly accidentally – exemplary poststructuralist system in at least this respect: 'It is not a passive structure nor a picture, nor a model in any literal representational sense.' The changes involved in the establishment of its centreless records are poorly understood, though, as Young notes, theories about them tend to group around one of three possibilities: '(1) a change of standing pattern of activity, or (2) a change of some specific chemical molecules, such as the instructional molecules of RNA, or (3) a change in the pathways between neurons within the nervous system'. According to him, the third possibility is probably 'the main basis for stable memory records' (which, as the research of Pasko Rakic and others suggests, depend on the formation of no new neurons after a certain point in brain development), but there remains much interest in the other two, particularly the first, which involves 'self-re-exciting' neural circuits and may be crucial to the repetition required for the maintenance of short-term memory and to preparations required by long-term memory. In sum, then, according to the 'majority of neuroscientists', short-term memory may entail some change in standing patterns of neural activity, but long-term memory 'depends upon changed connections'.[2]

Young is especially interested in the minimum unit of feature discrimination, 'a unit of memory or *mnemon*' (sometimes called a memory trace or engram), 'the entity that records one bit of information'.[3] His study of such units in the nervous system of the octopus has led him to some generalizations that seem to hold also for human memory; the most significant findings of his and similar studies concern how it manipulates information.

For Young the primary feature of any information to be introduced into memory is its identifiability as 'a symbol, a sign that something is likely to have a particular relevance for life, which may be good or bad'. He observes that the process of identification certainly has to do with the hippocampus, a structure in the limbic system that receives 'signals from all the main exteroceptive senses', but otherwise the evidence is fragmentary. Following Endel Tulving, he suggests, however, that 'each unit to be remembered is accompanied by some ancillary information that acts as a retrieval cue'. The storage of that unit also seems to depend on its being related to a 'schema or model', which, he conjectures, may 'involve the introduction of limitations into an initially redundant network. The model may thus be formed on the analogy of a statue, by *removal* of unwanted material, leaving relevant connections. Memory is a selective process.'[4]

Research on the storage of linguistic information indicates that short-term memory is coded acoustically and long-term semantically. Also, there is some evidence that 'the long-term storage system is what we might call "content addressed" as in some computer systems, rather than "list addressed"', so that 'Each item is not stored at a particular place in the memory by column and row, but as part of a very elaborate system of symbolic meanings.' Such evidence, along with that from research on slip-of-the-tongue phenomena, suggests that that system 'includes associative addressing indices' and seems to validate modellers' interest in semantic networks that can be modified by encounters with natural language. (It must be remembered, of course, that not all memories are, in the limited sense of the word, *linguistically* coded and that the processes involved in linguistic coding doubtless derive from more general – though none the less semiotic – ones.) That suggestion is cognate with the idea that, discounting neural atrophy, 'what we call forgetting is in fact the interference of subsequent learning'.[5] But the decay – or refreshment – of the memory trace is not well enough understood for Young to venture further in this regard.

Rumelhart, reviewing research on human memory and recasting some of its findings in terms of computer analogies, offers a number of observations and ideas that both corroborate and reach beyond those offered by Young. He notes that memory seems unlimited in capacity, that forgetting seems to involve difficulty of retrieval rather than loss of information, and that closely related units of information appear to be stored contiguously. He also notes, following Miller and others, that primary (short-term) memory seems to be able to hold in activation no more than 'six to ten units of information' at any one time, that 'The more chunks [Miller's term] we are holding the faster we forget them', and that 'the longer information is maintained in a primary memory activation, the stronger the memory trace finally left in secondary [long-term] memory.' However, 'there seems to be no limit on the complexity of any one activation', so that 'by recoding into ever larger *chunks* we can maintain more and more information in a single activation'. Like Young, he is intrigued by R. Conrad's experiments demonstrating that primary memory seems to involve the acoustic coding even of information that is not originally auditory, but he finds the situation more complex: 'Although a single activation may have aspects relevant to more than one sensory modality, it would appear that they most often have their primary features consonant with a single modality.' Those activations, which appear also to be somehow isomorphic to corresponding objects of perception, may be likened 'to an input–output buffer on a computer. The most important function of such a buffer is to hold incoming information until the central processor can analyze and further process it so that it can be properly stored in a more permanent form. The human primary memory system operates similarly.'[6] The figure is useful – as long as it is remembered that such a buffer involves not merely way-station waiting but activity critical to learning, which seems, at this stage, very much subject to the exigencies of sequential processing.

Rumelhart emphasizes that human memory is not like a library since it not only stores information but also organizes 'schemes in which new data can be stored' in such a way that the schemes and data become intricately intermixed. And there is an interesting relationship between them because 'the memory system preserves those aspects of the input information that make a difference with respect to the system's manner of structuring the information, but fails to preserve that information that makes no difference in the *meaning* of what is said'. This situation correlates with the information-theoretical distinction between surprise and redundancy, and it helps explain the fact that human beings are better at remembering the meaning (the gist) of language heard or read than its exact wording, especially if its syntax is normative (redundant) and its information rich (surprising). But the schemes–data relationship also entails positive feedback because the human organism 'perceives what it expects, . . . understands in terms of what it has experienced, and . . . remembers just what fits with what it knows'.[7] Thus the greater the density of the schemes, the greater the difficulty with which information is processed: learning is easier for the young than for the old.

There is a delicate equilibrium here. The memory system cathects, as it were, what 'makes a difference', but it also limits the amount of information with which it will deal. Indeed, there is evidence that very young children vividly and immediately remember almost everything they experience and that such input becomes useful to them – and their sanity protected – only when mechanisms for filtering and abstracting it have developed sufficiently. The intake of information is important to survival, but so is the limiting of that intake. The latter process, quite difficult to simulate, is familiar to anyone who has experienced 'museum fatigue' or the strangely exhilarating exhaustion of reading an engaging and informative book.

But human memory *is* like that of a computer in that it stores only information that is properly coded. Also, as far as secondary memory is concerned, 'The more carefully information is processed and the more that processing is relevant to the meaning of the input, the more likely the information can later be retrieved.' Retrieval is conditioned by 'contextual guides' and should be considered, according to Rumelhart, as *'reconstructive* in the same sense that perception is considered constructive'. After reviewing experiments by Brown and David MacNeill on tip-of-the-tongue phenomena and by Marigold Linton on reconstruction, he concludes that retrieval must take place in two stages: a search for 'the location of the relevant information in memory' and then a reconstruction of it.[8] How then do storage and retrieval work in the case of natural language?

Adopting Tulving's terminology, which distinguishes between *semantic* memory (conceptual knowledge) and *episodic* memory (knowledge about specific events), in discussing secondary memory, Rumelhart reviews a number of hypotheses about its structure, argues that its categories must blur considerably those of conventional logic, and offers a general description of how natural-language messages are stored and retrieved:

As a result of the process of comprehension linguistic inputs are converted into underlying semantic representations of the meaning of the incoming linguistic message. These representations are then stored in secondary memory forming the base for our memory of the message in question. Then, at the time of recall, the appropriate semantic representations are somehow accessed and reconstructed into sentences. Note that these sentences are not necessarily the same as those presented. They need only contain the same elements of meaning as the input sentences. Thus the structure of the memory for meaning is exactly the structure of the underlying semantic representation for the input message.

Furthermore, secondary memory seems to effect this storage through 'a configuration of semantic components'.[9]

But the interrelations of semantic and episodic memory (an uneasy distinction in any case) suggest that the structure of secondary memory is more complex than one might guess from Rumelhart's description above, as he himself explains:

> the generalized concepts of semantic memory are, of course, derived from our experience with specific objects, events, and event sequences through a process of abstraction and generalization. So, in this sense, semantic memory is a simple derivation of episodic memories. On the other hand, the nature of semantic memory determines what is stored in episodic memory in the first place. That is, we comprehend the world in terms of the categories, concepts, and interrelationships among these evident in semantic memory. It is then our *interpretation* of the event we have observed that remains in episodic memory. In this sense, what appears in episodic memory is determined by the categories and concepts already available in semantic memory. Of course, new concepts can emerge – our old categories are not always sufficient to deal with all of the incoming information. But even then our new categories are usually built out of new configurations of our old ones.

It is thus the structure itself of secondary memory that 'often allows us to go beyond our memories and solve novel problems'. Indeed, he concludes, since the strategies of reasoning, 'by and large, are knowledge, stored in memory, searched for, activated, evaluated, and modified', the process of reasoning 'can be considered a continuation at a slower pace of the same processes that have already become automated in language comprehension, which in turn are extensions of our perceptual processing apparatus'.[10] That conclusion suggests a number of analogies between the brain/mind and computer hardware/software.

Miller and Johnson-Laird pursue such analogies in their treatment of human memory and natural language, and their discussion of 'buffer memories', 'working memories', and 'central memories' is patently based on information-processing theory. The first two of these are apparently similar in function and deal with transient memories, the longest of which are associated with primary memory, whereas the third deals with the virtually permanent memories associated with secondary memory. However, following a number of other theorists, they find that these analogies must be qualified by the fact that human memory is statistically conditioned in a way that that of a machine is not – though, I would add, surely might be. None the less, they argue that, when considering how people understand natural language, 'it is helpful to suppose that routines (or schematized information on which routines can be based) corresponding to words (or morphemes) are stored in their memories' in such a way that 'similar concepts are stored in functionally related locations' that are not topographically definite but are analogous to 'locations in computer memories', which have 'indices that "point" to those "locations"'.[11] Hence they argue also that memories can be addressed variously and propose several ways of characterizing the process of memory search. Their most relevant discussion in that regard is concerned with associative networks.

Miller and Johnson-Laird observe that memory for the meanings of words is not characterized by random access and that the accessibility of any given item of semantic information is somehow dependent on the current state of the system. They assume that semantically related items in secondary memory are 'actually connected to one another in some way', in an association that is usually thought to be a 'two-term relation' (whether one defines it by symmetry, transitivity, or some other property). The association of more than two items constitutes an associative network, and such networks apparently 'can be constructed in almost any shape with almost any kinds of relations needed to match the diversity of conceptual structures'. They hypothesize that 'the conceptual system can search through an associative network for a concept having certain specified characteristics'. This hypothesis carries with it two assumptions that derive from the research of psychologists interested in verbal learning: that 'the difficulty of memorizing arbitrary lists of words should be predictable' and that 'the long-term consequences of previous learning can be represented by some kind of associative network'.[12] Finally, this hypothesis can be tested by computer simulation.

Miller and Johnson-Laird assert that this simulation, though difficult, has already 'been done, and the results obtained when the computer learns a list are sufficiently like the results obtained when people learn the same list to justify the assumption that it has been done well'.[13] The systems they consider in order to make that assertion are John R. Anderson's FRAN (Free Recall in an Associative Net), Anderson and Gordon H. Bower's HAM (Human Associative Memory), and Newell and James Moore's Merlin.

FRAN, with a vocabulary 'of 262 noun concepts, each with from three to nineteen associations (determined from *Webster's Dictionary*) to other concepts', does a fair job of simulation: 'The rate of learning, the order in which the items are recalled, the effects of rate of presentation, the effects of interference from interpolated learning, and many other features of FRAN's behavior are directly comparable to human data.' However, the system hardly associates conceptually related items as richly as a human learner would and, by virtue of its design, cannot recognize chance grammatical relations. HAM, designed to overcome this latter deficiency by dealing with propositions rather than words,

> parses input sentences (top-down and left-right) into two parts in working memory. One part represents the fact that the sentence expresses and the other part represents its context (location and time the fact is said to be true). The output of the parser is a phrase-structure tree whose terminal elements point to preexisting concepts. The relations in this tree are transformed into long-term memory associations and matched against structures already in long-term memory. Unlike FRAN, HAM does not assume direct connections between words; words become interconnected only as they occur in particular propositions. . . . HAM can deal with many sentences that FRAN could not, but HAM does not ameliorate FRAN's reluctance to cluster conceptually related ideas.

Thus Miller and Johnson-Laird conclude that 'FRAN and HAM provide lower bounds for the complexity of the system we are trying to characterize' and that 'a more complicated representation of the links between concepts is required; the simple two-term relation of association is insufficient'. Merlin corrects that deficiency at least by attempting to differentiate between disjunctive hyponyms (between, to use their example, *robin* and *chicken*, both of which are hyponyms of *bird* but only one of which can fly) and includes some corollary abilities, but it has not been designed 'to replicate results of experimental studies of verbal learning'.[14]

Obviously there is much about human memory that must be better understood (especially the sense of pastness itself) if the modelling of natural language is to progress. Nowhere is the ignorance involved more dramatically demonstrated than in recent controversy concerning the psychological validity of Chomsky's notion of deep structure and, therefore, its relevance to memory functions. It has even been argued that, since human beings remember the meaning of language much better than its syntax once processing has passed the echoic and iconic stage of primary memory, there may be no need for such a notion. Indeed, according to Johnson-Laird, if the Chomskyan blinders are removed, it may be possible to consider syntax more appropriately in terms of the whole memory system:

> No one knows how meaning is represented within memory, but there is no evidence to show that any form of syntactic structure is directly involved. This is puzzling because if syntax is not necessary for storing meaning why should it be necessary for communicating it? The answer may be that the elements from which meaning is composed – the so-called 'semantic markers' – are utilized in cognitive processes other than language (e.g. the formation of concepts). Hence their organization would not be specifically linguistic.[15]

There is surely some deep syntax, some Derridean *écriture*, to human memory that codifies all learning, both verbal and nonverbal. But its role may well be somewhat 'Hofstadterian'; that is, as Campbell observes,

> Memory appears to be constrained by a structure, a 'syntax,' perhaps at quite a low level, but it is free to be variable, deviant, even erratic at a higher level. . . .
> Like the information system of language, memory can be explained in part by the abstract rules which underlie it, but only in part. The rules provide a basic competence, but they do not fully determine performance.[16]

Whatever that syntax is, Chomsky's formalism does not **capture** it, and probably it will be captured only by one that is more extensively semantic.

Much modellist thinking certainly endorses that probability, as does, for example, composition research showing that the clause (from *claudere*, 'to close') 'is the primary perceptual unit of all languages because it is the minimal unit that has semantic determinacy' and that 'it is stored in a nonlinguistic, nonsequential form'.[17] But what is unknown about that storage seems staggering. Human memory may use propositional networks of some kind to store declarative knowledge (as do some modelling systems), but no one knows how it does so – or how it distinguishes declarative from procedural knowledge. The learning process remains largely a mystery. Indeed, as Jackson points out, a self-improving AI system, whatever its limits might be, would differ from a human being in that it at least would '"know" exactly what kind of machine it is'.[18] Perhaps through such systems man can come to know what kind he is.

36

Dependency, Postsemantics, Paradigm

The Chomskyan revolution, which replaced the old paradigm that dictated the taxonomic study of natural language with another that proposed a theoretical methodology (of 'hidden laws', in Searle's phrase) for interpreting the data accumulated by that study, has undoubtedly changed forever man's view of his language and directly or indirectly occasioned much of the theory and research I have been discussing. That paradigm has stirred controversies that extend, like Chomsky's speculations, far beyond questions about the details of transformational grammar. But, as has been seen, it has serious inadequacies. They raise important questions about the MLM metaphor and encourage speculation about the post-Chomskyan paradigm, which increasingly will be integrated with AI theory and tested by AI research.

Gilbert Harman observes that Chomsky himself has foreseen that the constraints involved in grammatical acceptability or unacceptability 'have to be accounted for by semantic principles of interpretation rather than by principles of grammar alone'. He observes also, as did Wall earlier, that the framework of Chomsky's grammar, 'is, in a sense, too powerful: it puts hardly any restrictions on grammar'. What is needed is 'a more formal statement of the constraint', and one does not seem to be forthcoming from Chomsky or other transformational grammarians. And, while Harman acknowledges that Chomsky's distinction between surface and deep structures has made possible logico-grammatical analyses of a kind previously not possible, he also draws attention to Chomsky's assumptions that 'syntax and semantics can be distinguished and, in particular, that there is a level of deep syntactic structure that is distinct from a level of logical and semantical representation'.[1] These assumptions have been variously refuted. Indeed, the preoccupation of Chomsky and his followers with syntax, to the neglect of semantic issues, has been properly criticized by people as diverse in orientation as

Ian Robinson and Jackson, who argues that, even if Chomsky's grammar can be modelled effectively as a generative formalism, 'efforts should be devoted first to the "comprehension" stage . . . of the language-understanding process' – partly because, by analogy, 'the ability of children to comprehend sentences at a given "level of difficulty" precedes the ability to speak them'.[2]

Other critics of Chomsky point to similar problems or to meta-problems spun off from them. Jean Atchison, for example, argues that Chomsky's proposals regarding the acquisition device are 'overoptimistic . . . and not borne out by the evidence'. She also doubts the psychological reality of transformational grammar as 'a direct model of the way a speaker actually understands and produces utterances', though she is willing to accept it as 'a hypothesis about a speaker's stored *knowledge* of his language'. And she concludes that 'we shall have to abandon a model [such as Chomsky's] which proposes an abstract deep layer of syntax, and eventually replace it with one in which knowledge and use are more closely related'.[3] As has been seen, many linguists and modellers would agree.

There is a paucity of empirical evidence supporting Chomsky's hypothesis about the acquisition device, and many psychologists and psycholinguists argue that it does not adequately take into account environmental factors involved in acquisition and generative competence.[4] Much the same is argued in regard to his speculations about how the structure of natural language mirrors the structure of cognition. Judith Greene asks if, when he makes the claim that 'he is describing the structure of cognitive processes', he is ignoring 'the extreme complexity of the relation between speakers' linguistic knowledge and how it is actually put to use in the real world?'[5] And Joan Bresnan contends that 'the derivational theory of complexity – the theory that the number of transformations operating in the grammatical derivation of a sentence provides a measure of the psychological complexity in comprehending or producing the sentence – cannot be sustained', apparently because of a similar shortcoming. (It is interesting to note that, in suggesting further research on this problem, she argues for the joint effort of disciplines whose concerns epitomize the MLM metaphor – namely, those of 'linguists, computer scientists, and psychologists . . .'.)[6]

Bronowski also is critical of Chomsky but from a slightly different point of view. He attacks Chomsky's claim that 'language has been laid down in man by a genetic blueprint' and argues that 'it cannot be held that there is a specific linguistic competence which underlies the syntax of all languages. The universal syntax is a human way of analyzing experience, not of putting together sentences.'[7] This argument surely will turn out to be wrong – that is, there must be a 'specific linguistic competence' that is derived from more general cognitive functions, and 'universal syntax' is probably both 'a human way of analyzing experience' *and* a way 'of putting together sentences' – but Bronowski's implicit insistence that such matters be considered within a larger framework is quite defensible. Its acceptance could go a long way toward correcting the tendency too easily to confuse a grammatical formalism such as Chomsky's with psychophysiological explanation. If the new paradigm is to be viable, its enabling formalism will have to be compatible with both theoretical imperatives and whatever intelligible empirical data can be gleaned.

All these criticisms point to the need for a formalism that overcomes the deficiencies of Chomsky's syntactic theory. As I noted earlier, many modelling systems use some kind of systemic grammar. Doubtless that practice will continue; indeed, if the new paradigm incorporates a formalism that could be understood as 'syntactic', it probably will be systemic in nature. Perhaps the strongest and most thoroughgoing, albeit still problematic, argument to that effect is made by Richard A. Hudson, who proposes refinements relevant to machine modelling.

Hudson, who acknowledges his debt at Halliday, is interested not in trying to patch up transformational grammar once again but in constructing a grammar that includes 'neither phrase-structure rules nor transformations'. His justification for adopting the epithet 'daughter-dependency' for his grammar makes a helpful prolegomenon to his approach:

> 'Daughter-dependency' has the advantage of emphasizing the fact that this model represents a combination of the properties of American-style constituency grammar (as in American 'structuralism' and transformational grammar) with those of European-style dependency grammar. The 'dependency' part shows the latter alignment, since dependency grammar proper allows only *sisters* (more precisely, words or morphemes) to show dependency relations, and the concept of 'daughters' makes sense only if one accepts that smaller items are 'part of'

some larger item (phrase or sentence) which operates as a single unit.

And he notes that one may wish to think of his model as dealing, in Michael C. McCord's phrase, with 'unistructural syntax' since that phrase suggests how his grammar fits 'all the syntactic information about a sentence into a single, integrated structure'.[8]

Hudson assumes that syntax is separate from semantics and phonology and has its own 'autonomous' rules for well-formedness. The lexicon in daughter-dependency grammar is similar in principle to that in transformational grammar, but he notes that there is an important difference between the effects of lexical insertion specified by his grammar and those specified by the one Chomsky elaborated in his *Aspects of the Theory of Syntax*:

in the latter, when a lexical item is inserted (in deep structure), the result is that the *whole* content of the lexical item is inserted, including its meaning and its pronunciation, into the same structure, with the result that deep structures contain semantic and phonological features as well as strictly syntactic features. In daughter-dependency grammar, on the other hand, the lexicon is seen as a (very large) set of interlevel rules, defining possible relations among the three levels of semantics, syntax and phonology, so lexical insertion involves finding a lexical entry which is compatible with the syntactic environment, and then inserting its meaning into the semantic structure and its pronunciation into the phonological structure. . . . lexical items in daughter-dependency can be seen as well-formedness conditions on the meanings and pronunciations that can correspond to particular syntactic environments . . . .

One might well flinch at such clean compartmentalizations. But there is an advantage to be gained from Hudson's approach – at least from the grammarian's point of view – because the rules constituting conditions on well-formedness in daughter-dependency grammar 'are, paradoxically, the "creative" part of it, in that they provide the input to the other rules; whereas in transformational grammar they are more peripheral'.[9]

And there are other advantages, especially from the modeller's point of view, though some of the assumptions behind them are open to question. The structural descriptions generated by daughter-dependency grammar, which involve multiple nodal connections that are both vertical and horizontal, have the advantage that 'only *one* such description is generated per sentence (except, of course, in the case of sentences that are syntactically ambiguous)'. Also, there is no need in such descriptions for a distinction between deep and surface structures since the syntactic structure generated by daughter-dependency grammar is, according to Hudson, 'sufficiently "deep" to be reasonably easy to relate to its meaning, but also "surface" enough to map onto phonological structure'. Though he argues persuasively for this structure, he is forced to justify its differences from that generated by transformational grammar partly and somewhat weakly by 'the rather negative fact that, as far as I know, there is no direct psycholinguistic evidence that phrase-markers are psychologically real'.[10] None the less, its unistructural character is appealing.

Other advantages are gained from the fact that all syntactic features involved in the classification rules of daughter-dependency grammar are binary in their specifications. (Here Hudson has adopted a convention from Chomsky, that of the plus/minus notation, mostly because he has 'never found any convincing examples of contrasts that have to be treated as involving three or more alternatives in syntax . . .'.) Moreover, Hudson cites what he calls concreteness as one of the principal advantages of daughter-dependency grammar. It arises largely from the obviation of the ' "underlying" elements [in transformational grammar] that get deleted in the course of the derivation' as well as of the 'underlying orders of elements that get changed into other orders', and it 'makes the boundary between syntax and semantics completely clear: as soon as you need to postulate elements or orders of elements different from those in the surface string, you must, by definition, be in semantics'. A suspiciously neat separation – though it still admits the possibility of mapping between syntactic and semantic structures (he seems uneasy about that, however). Also, in daughter-dependency grammar there is no need for the intricate patterns of lexical insertion and deletion required by transformational grammar because, in the former, lexical items are not specified at all 'until the whole syntactic structure is fully generated, and then, of course, the lexicon can specify all morphemes at once (by introducing their phonological structures and, where relevant, their meanings)'. That specification may seem psychologically unrealistic, but he claims that it distinguishes between 'what structures purport to have psychological reality and which don't: the only syntactic structures which should be psychologically real are complete ones – i.e. just one per sentence'. (He argues that 'it seems unlikely that anyone will ever be able to prove experimentally that there is an underlying order of elements different from the surface order that has psychological reality . . .'.)[11]

But, apart from these more or less questionable advantages, daughter-dependency grammar does have one obvious practical advantage for the modeller, that of

> the relative ease with which a structure can be assigned mechanically (i.e. by computer) to a sentence: there is no need to reconstruct a whole chain of structures, starting with the surface structure and going back step by step until deep structure is reached, before the syntactic structure can be related to a semantic interpretation. Instead, it is possible to build up the syntactic structure bit by bit, at the same time as the semantic interpretation (though the two structures are in principle different). This has been recognized as a major attraction of 'systemic grammar' in general by workers in the field of artificial intelligence, since Winograd. . . . To the extent that successes in artificial intelligence have a bearing on the structure of the human mind, the results so far seem to support the view of syntax as a set of rules that generate a *single* syntactic structure rather than a whole chain of them for each sentence.[12]

Here, as elsewhere, Hudson leaves questions in his wake, but his attempt at an economy lacking in transformational grammar is admirable and may well contribute to the formalism that will evolve to enable the new paradigm.

There remain, however, problems with effecting the rapprochement of syntax and semantics. Certain aspects of those problems are particularly relevant here and are highlighted by Wallace L. Chafe in his criticism of Chomsky's work and in his attempt to develop a theory of semantic structure as determinative of and even identical with syntactic structure, a theory that may be partially compatible with Hudson's.

Chafe premises that deep structure and semantic structure are identical, that syntactic structure is phonologically temporalized (linearized) semantic structure, and that – as he synopsizes phonocentrically, seeking the imprimaturs of Saussure, Sapir, Leonard Bloomfield, and Chomsky himself – language is a system that links meaning to sound. He regards surface elements, however, as being 'no longer semantic elements but *postsemantic* ones', and he proposes three 'areas' from which the processes that form postsemantic elements derive:

> First, there is the necessity that nonlinear semantic structures be converted into linear configurations appropriate to further conversion into sound; hence the need for linearization processes. Second, there is a drive toward economy of phonetic outputs and therefore of the surface structures which such outputs represent; hence the need for deletion processes, including pronominalization. Third, there is semantic change (and probably various kinds of postsemantic change as well), leading to the need for literalization processes, agreement processes, and, in general, processes which add and redistribute semantic and postsemantic units.

These processes operate on what he hypothesizes as 'an initial area of semantic structure where configurations of meanings are assembled' and yield, through a series of postsemantic representations, a final one that is a surface structure, which may include some 'semantic-like units' not present in the semantic structure.[13] The units of the surface structure are then converted, through several steps, into a phonetic representation.

What emerges is a suggestive enough account of production, but what about comprehension? There must be, to use loosely a term from Ezra Pound, a 'vorticist' principle whereby semantic configurations are, as it were, postsemantically funnelled down to a linear representation by the sender and then expanded back out of it by the receiver, but Chafe does not explore that expansion. He does not accept the notion that hearers 'convert sound into meaning' and sees theirs as 'a second-hand role at best'.[14] He seems to imply that there is a compiling process whereby linear structures are asymmetrically translated into postsemantic and semantic ones, but he does not explore it – even though there is a good deal of evidence that the receiver does analyse the linear representation in terms of phonemic distinctions and somehow translate them discretely into semantic configurations.[15]

On the other hand, Chafe criticizes, severely and cogently, the syntacticist and structuralist biases in much modern language theory, largely because they have encouraged an overemphasis on phonetic studies. He accuses both syntacticism and structuralism of giving 'no recognition to the symbolization process as such' and of not dealing adequately with how surface structure is 'a final, distorted reflection of semantic structure'. Countering them, he argues that

> the processes of formation must be located in the semantic area, that a well-formed semantic structure will lead naturally to well-formed surface and phonetic representations. To try to locate processes of formation in the area of phonetic structure would be an absurdity. . . . Structuralist linguistics attempted to locate them in the area of surface structure, and must be said to have failed. The next development was an attempt to locate them in a hypothetical syntactic deep structure, since it was still felt necessary to avoid an outright commitment to semantics, but I believe that this attempt has proved a failure also and am suggesting that a commitment to semantic structure as the place where well-formedness is established is now unavoidable.

He is thus thoroughly committed to semanticism and characterizes syntacticism as possessing an 'inherent awkwardness' because of its phonetic bias – a position with which Derrida would sympathize. Chafe regards semanticism as easier to apply because 'When we use langauge we start with something we have to say – with meanings.' And he rightly contends that the history of deep structure as an idea 'has seen it moving from its original closeness to surface structure to positions approaching more closely to semantic structure'.[16] He is arguing, in other words, that there is a close, albeit intricately conditioned, isomorphism between syntax and semantics (that the former is a kind of ghost of the latter), even that they are, seen this way, really the same.

Chafe's theory – which, I would add, could be applied to written as well as spoken language by taking into account the features and conventions on the print code – is appealing in a number of ways. Like Miller and Johnson-Laird, he takes the verb to be the 'central semantic element', and through its ability to accumulate and govern nominal constructions he accounts for recursivity. His discussion of how semantic constraints function intersententially has important implications for text theory. And though his discussion of examples (from a polysynthetic Iriquois language, Onondaga, as well as from English) is undertaken in terms of a 'singularly formalism', he suggests that they 'could easily be restated in a binary notation'. He admits that, within the limits of his theory, there is 'no obvious extrinsic justification for handling the formation of semantic structures within the framework of ordered rules' and that it might be necessary to consider 'a different model' in that respect; such a model, he thinks, echoing Schank and others, 'would involve statements of unilateral and bilateral dependencies among semantic units' – though he does not speculate beyond that. Finally, he is suspicious about the relevance of overly abstract constructs, those akin to the predicate calculus or symbolic logic, to the attempt to analyse semantic structure as if it were 'deeper' than Chomsky's deep structure – because of 'the direct tie which must exist between semantic structure and the observable facts of meaning, by virtue of which the abstractness of semantic structure is, on the contrary, minimal'.[17] He too calls for a new logic.

There are numerous contacts between Chafe's theory and Hudson's, and there are ways in which they might be reconciled productively. Both allow use of binary notation. Both can make use of binary classification rules. Both account for a ready mapping of surface structure onto phonological structure. And they otherwise share features that appropriately counter, modify, or supplement Chomsky's theory and that could be quite useful to the modeller.

All this is not to say, of course, that the whole of Chomsky's work is dead and buried. Some of its provisions surely will survive. But the new formalism, as the theories of Hudson and Chafe suggest, will transcend it in certain (not entirely, I suspect, foreseeable) respects.[18]

37

Synthesis, Semiotics, Biology

If the post-Chomskyan paradigm is to be richly enough elaborated to address effectively the range of phenomena implicated by the MLM metaphor, it will require eclectic strategies, the synthesis of theoretical and empirical knowledge from many disciplines. To recall Johnson-Laird's phrasing, that synthesis 'does not yet exist', and its invention is imperative. Theorists and researchers will have to conduct their work co-operatively, with sufficient intelligence and openness to avoid the kind of fruitless oppugnancy that has developed between Chomskyans and behaviourists or High Church Computationalists and Zen Holists. Especially, I would suggest, theorists of language and modellers should give enlarged attention to biological aspects of linguistic and cognitive processes.

That kind of attention is exemplified by Charles E. Osgood in his attempt to reconcile psycholinguistic universalism and relativism. His research on the use of qualifiers (adjectives) by high-school boys in nine countries is representative of his work. It leads him to an interesting conclusion: 'The dominant ways of qualifying experience, of describing aspects of objects and events, tend to be very similar, regardless of what language one uses or what culture one happens to have grown up in.' The purpose of such research, he argues, is not only 'to demonstrate that human beings the world over, no matter what their language or culture, do share a common meaning system, do organize experience along similar symbolic dimensions' but also 'to develop and apply instruments for measuring "subjective culture" – meanings, attitudes, values, and the like – instruments that can be shown to be comparable across differences in both language and culture'.[1]

Osgood's research enables him to reconsider some long-standing problems, largely by an appropriate accounting for biological framework. Since his hypothesis that 'semantic systems are more stable across people than across concepts' is apprently proven out by his research, he speculates that

> it is *because* such diverse sensory experiences as a *white* circle (rather than black), a *straight* line (rather than crooked), a *rising* melody (rather than a falling one), a *sweet* taste (rather than a sour one), a *caressing* touch (rather than an irritating scratch) – it is because all these diverse experiences can share a common affective meaning that one easily and lawfully translates from one sensory modality into another in synesthesia and metaphor. . . . In other words, the 'common market in meaning' seems to be based firmly in the biological systems of emotional and purposive behavior that all humans share.[2]

Having speculated productively about this kind of framework for describing semantic universals, he turns to psycholinguistic relativism.

What Osgood discovers, of course, is that his data deny the Whorfian Hypothesis, but he also thinks there is, paradoxically, evidence to support it. He criticizes the empirically unjustified assumptions about the interrelations of thought and language that have informed arguments for or against it and sees his dilemma as arising from the fact that there has been no way of distinguishing between the phenomena that support the one argument and those that support the other. Therefore he makes a distinction 'within semantic phenomena – between the affective reactions to signs and their coding functions' – and offers a resolution:

> *Whenever the psycholinguistic phenomena in question depend upon the structure of the mediating systems* (either affective or discriminatory), *psycholinguistic universality will be found.* This, of course, is precisely because these mediating systems are panhuman biologically. *Whenever the psycholinguistic phenomena are independent of the structure of the mediating systems, even though they are mediated by them, psycholinguistic relativity will be the rule.* And this, of course, is precisely because both mediating systems are essentially *tabula rasa* [*sic*], and 'what leads to what' is dependent on experience.

He is careful to qualify this resolution in several ways, lest it seem 'self-evident' or 'downright tautological'. His research, in any case, does tend to corroborate it and its implications: there are, among human beings, 'common potentials for developing languages, . . . shared systems of symbolic representation, . . . universal mechanisms for metaphor and synesthesia', and so on – all of which are 'formed in the interaction of human biology and psychology with a fundamentally common environment'.[3] But what is important here is not just the particular findings, cogent as they are, but Osgood's attitude, constituted as it is by a polymathic openness, an urge to synthesis.

The failure of language theorists, especially, to assume that kind of attitude is highlighted by Jameson, who inventories what he sees as the problems that have arisen as a consequence of a general shift from 'substantialist' to 'relational' thinking that is manifested pre-eminently in the work of Saussure and his intellectual offspring. He speaks of 'the spectacle of a world from which nature as such has been eliminated, a world saturated with messages and information, whose intricate commodity network may be seen as the very prototype of a system of signs', and he argues bleakly that 'There is a profound consonance between linguistics as a method and that systematized and disembodied nightmare which is our culture today.' He criticizes structuralists in general for their embrace of the 'peculiar regressive structure of the concept of metalanguage' and particular structuralists (or poststructuralists) for corollary reasons – Derrida, for example, for his 'reluctance . . . to use language as anything more than a gloss on the language of other philosophers (and indeed on their ideas about language)'. He finds such habits occasioning 'an exegetic and second-degree structure' that he sees as common to the work of all structuralists: 'Hence their passion for mathematical formalizations, for graphs and visual schemata – so many Structuralist *hieroglyphs* designed to signify some ultimate object-language forever out of reach of the language of the commentary, and which is none other than Language itself.' And he nostalgically excoriates them for not acceding 'to the calm density of such a primary language as that of Hegel'. Finally, he contends, the immediate result of this situation is that 'Under such conditions, the older specialized disciplines fail to dissolve into that vaster science of the concrete which Structuralism had seemed at other moments to project. Instead, they coexist in an uneasy rivalry . . . .'[4] The structuralist synthesis failed to gel, in other words, and has been displaced by the 'second-degree' aporias of poststructuralism.

What Jameson says, even if naïve in many respects, is partly correct – at least in its final emphasis. And there is a disappointment in its being so, because structuralist and poststructuralist methods seem to hold such promise as forces for the synthesis of ideas relevant to the MLM metaphor and the new paradigm. Their failure so far to realize that promise is perhaps in some way due to the problems he mentions, though he gives no credit for how much they have opened and energized contemporary intellectual life and engaged it with profound questions. Still it seems that structuralism and, especially, poststructuralism have become too much obsessed with strategies of biologically alienated abstraction and scepsis. Their enterprise has therefore not been as comprehensive as it could be and certainly has neglected the *naturalness* (a problem word, to be sure) of natural langauge, which has to be studied with regard for its biological matrix. Their enterprise, like that of modellers with which it increasingly shares attitudes and concerns, should preserve and refine its propensities for the metalinguistic (relational, mathematical, whatever – a 'primary language' was as much a chimera in Hegel's time as it is now), but it should gauge them within the perspective afforded by that matrix. Taking into account this balancing perspective, even the most extreme and sceptical kinds of poststructuralist thought may have a great deal to contribute to a larger exploration of the MLM metaphor and the elaboration of the new paradigm. What is principally required for this second flowering is a more holistic semiotic, the kind advocated by Thomas A. Sebeok, who, while occasionally wrongheaded and not strictly structuralist in his thinking, has developed as full-blown a biologically-based approach to semiosis as one can find.

According to Sebeok, the 'ultimate solution' to the problem of how signification occurs has to be 'anchored in the biological make-up of organisms, as was fully anticipated by Peirce, brilliantly demonstrated by [Jakob] von Uexküll, and first situated in a vast, comprehensive theory by Thom'. He agrees with Peirce that semiosis is '*the* criterial attribute of life', that thought is not possible without it, and he agrees with Uexküll's Kantian idea that 'the mind's relationship to the world is specular'. Moreover, this idea, 'this seemingly perennial theme has been reopened, along several fronts, in the guise of the problem of the ontological validity of logic . . .' and 'insistently calls for a parallelism between the semiotic mechanism of Mind and the evolutionary processes of Nature . . .'. Hence he applauds Thom, whose work, informed with the thesis of *'le monde comme image de l'homme* [the world as image of man]', has 'provided us with an arena where science and philosophy can at last be reconciled . . .'.[5]

For Sebeok the sign, in its mediation between object and interpretant and in its functioning as a link between minds or, in Peirce's phrase, 'theatres of consciousness', is a global phenomenon. Indeed, he argues, borrowing a metaphor from Richard Dawkins, 'all "survival machines" – meaning people, animals, plants, bacteria, and viruses – are only a sign's way of making another sign'. The genes themselves 'are, in the last analysis, but signs which construct for themselves survival machines (containers, vehicles) to assure their existence'.[6] The semiotic radically precedes the linguistic.

Signification certainly has to do with the brain/mind, but prior to that it has to do with functions that are, in Sebeok's coinage, 'endosemiotic'. Endosemiotics is concerned with 'the conversion of "outside" signs to their initial input "inside" ' (a theoretically convenient but eminently deconstructible distinction), with how 'the external "physical world" ' is related to 'the internal "mental world" (*cf.* Uexküll's *Umwelt/Innenwelt*)'. In this connection he is very much interested, with some misgivings, in Gordon M. Tomkins's speculations about the physiology of the endosemiotic functions that, through evolutionary modification, gradually developed referentiality from earlier, tropistic acts of communication:

> Hormone release is often activated by neural stimulation, so in many organisms the nervous and endocrine subcodes are intimately linked. Neurotransmitters are hormones that mediate communication within the nervous system, operating over very short distances. Tomkins speculates that these substances acted in primitive cells as intracellular symbols referring to changes in environmental amino acid concentration, and that from this original concern with transducing this kind of information the primordial nerve cells might have gradually come to refer to many other aspects of the 'outside' world.

Sebeok argues that such speculation suggests the possibility of interdisciplinary unification and a 'panoptic access' to the various codes involved in signification. It is exactly the kind of thinking he believes might be subsumed by Thom's catastrophe-theoretical semiotic, which could be expanded into 'a workable unifying scheme' for endosemiotic and related phenomena.[7]

Sebeok is impressed with Young's notion of learning as a process of attaching values to signs and finds in it an implicit 'phenomenological paradigm' that is 'in good conformity with Uexküll's *Bedeutungslehre* ['doctrine of meaning'], which postulates the interposition of a semiotic editorial screening operation between the objective world and its effects upon the perceiving mind . . .'. Learning, thus understood, entails a selectivity that distinguishes between the noumenal and the phenomenal and allows 'thoughts about words, thoughts about thoughts, in brief, signs about signs'. In terms of this biological translation of Kant, the sense organs are transducers that selectively 'map one energy form into another'. Therefore organisms, in perceiving signs, 'each according to its pre-existing *Bauplan*, or blueprint, build up mental models of the world that are equivalent to Peirce's interpretant . . .'. This view of learning is intertangled with the main problem that confronted Uexküll: how 'to connect the real world with the phenomenal world in a biologically satisfying way, and to give a detailed accounting of what he referred to as a contrapuntal relationship between an organism and its environment'.[8] He hardly solved that problem, but he did develop an intelligent approach to it and, according to Sebeok, thereby initiated a comprehensive ecology of information.

Uexküll's theorizations and their more recent spinoffs have given rise to some interesting and pertinent speculations indeed. He developed his interest in the limen separating the *Umwelt* and *Innenwelt* and in the semiotic transduction between them into a subtle and comprehensive *Umweltlehre* that 'requires no more than that the categories of experience and knowledge be isomorphic to the real universe – not that the two halves of the cycle fully correspond with one another, let alone that the *Innenwelt* completely represent the world'. His notion that the *Innenwelt* is a 'map' of and not a 'picture' of the *Umwelt* has keynoted a subsequent search not for some kind of neural camera (old gadgetry of the metaphysics of presence) but for 'the law of the projection'. This insightful map metaphor has, by way of

Sebeok's meditations on its relevance to the work of Karl R. Popper, an important connection with Gödel's Theorem:

> Upon reflection, . . . Uexküll's semiotic epistemology brings to mind some salient aspects of Popper's interactionist views of objective knowledge, and particularly his pluralist thesis of multiple worlds. Popper . . . introduced the terms 'world 1,' to denote the physical world, 'world 2,' the world of our conscious experiences and subjective knowledge of all kinds, and 'world 3,' especially the world of language, spoken or manifest in whatever substance (*cf.* von Humboldt's *Sprachwelt*), and also including the logical content of entire libraries, computer memories, myths and scientific theories, mistakes and arguments, as well as the world of artistic products and social institutions . . . .

These worlds interact in such a way that, by the map metaphor, world 2 is the primary human reality, world 1 being derived from it and world 3 being generally invisible to other animals, but the knowledge of the universe that is involved in this interaction, since that knowledge is part of the universe, is not completable – for the same reason that someone who is making a map of the environment in which he is making the map cannot include that map in itself. This situation constitutes 'a statement, in picturesque form, of Gödel's incompleteness theorem'.[9] Such a translation of Gödel's Theorem, with its endosemiotic implications, obviously correlates with many of Hofstadter's ideas and suggests that there are inescapable constraints on the MLM metaphor.

In dealing with such matters, Sebeok, given his ecumenical semiotic, is concerned with distinguishing between verbal and nonverbal semiosis. He cites results from memory experiments that 'have convincingly shown that thinking has two richly interconnected components in man: one verbal, the other nonverbal, each with characteristic properties'. He cites also results from neurological research that 'display in extreme form a functional separation between the verbal and nonverbal spatial systems . . .'. And he concludes, after examining results from transducer-psychological research, that 'The distinction between anthroposemiotic and zoosemiotic events is . . . not at all demarcated at the integumentary threshold.'[10] So patently there is a verbal–nonverbal discontinuity, one that he sees in terms of a distinction at a level quite different from that of the endosemiotic limen.

That discontinuity is poorly understood and has not been usefully described neurophysiologically. If a useful description is achieved, however, it doubtless will include distinctions between the two cerebral hemispheres. Not only can those hemispheres be mapped in terms of areas that manifest differences in verbal and nonverbal specifications: they also can be characterized generally, according to Sebeok, following John C. Eccles, as 'a very superior animal brain' that is zoosemiotic and a more advanced brain that is anthroposemiotic. With the minor and major hemispheres, respectively, so conceived, he argues, 'Evolutionary continuities in semiosis from animals to man as well as sudden discontinuities are . . . both accounted for, but in grossly different locations in the brain.' How far such distinctions will be supported by empirical research is, of course, an open question, but he suggests, recalling my earlier application of catastrophe theory, that understanding of the functions that have arisen discontinuously in the major hemisphere might be enlarged through 'a judicious application' of it.[11]

More specifically, Sebeok suggests also that Thom's theory might be helpful in more accurately describing the ontogenetic development of semiotic, especially linguistic, faculties:

> Any sensitive and observant caretaker is well aware that a 'normal' infant is born with elaborate equipment for interacting with its human surroundings by means of a wide array of vocal and nonvocal signs. . . . Its semiotic growth and differentiation are undoubtedly best conceived of as a series of catastrophes. . . . Thom's topological model, following ideas originating in biology and pursued by creative thinkers since the likes of D'Arcy Thompson and C. H. Waddington, could account for successive stages of bifurcation where, much as the development of any cell in an embryo diverges from that of its immediate neighbors, sign functions become ever more specialized and cluster to form particular constellations. . . . Verbal signs suddenly emerge, superimposed upon babbling. . . . Language then continues to unfold . . . .[12]

And, of course, I would add, Thom's theory might be helpful as well in designing better programs for the machine acquisition and use of natural language (is this, oxymoronically, 'mechanosemiosis'?) if it proved to be sufficiently powerful and comprehensive for describing the corresponding processes in man.

All this speculation has strong bearing on the 'ecumenicalism' of the semiotic approach. Sebeok emphasizes 'the historical and logical associations between holism and semiotics' and is preoccupied with the overarching question of 'how semiotics can function as "an organon" . . . of all the sciences', given how effectively it deals with problems in the provinces of, but still incompletely treated by, general systems theory, structuralist theory, neural-morphodifferentiation theory, and so on. For him, as one might guess from the foregoing discussion, the foremost practitioner of ecumenical semiotics is Thom, whose 'semiotic intimations' he regards as 'pure nuggets of gold, in the aggregate containing the sole contemporary pointers toward the elevation of our doctrine to the status of a theory or a science'.[13]

Thom's approach is very much holistic. Catastrophe theory is appealing to people in many disciplines usually considered distinct; its topological orientation should certainly appeal to modellers. Indeed, that orientation is what makes it comprehensive; as Sebeok observes, topology is 'a field that has the satisfying property of providing a single interpretation to quite disparate data'. Catastrophe theory is concerned ultimately with 'the classification of analogies', a task that involves 'specifying a list of archetypal topological structures (catastrophes) together with rules for combining them (syntax) that could formally model all the static and dynamic morphologies of the natural world'.[14]

The importance of catastrophe theory for the new natural-language paradigm may be variously suggested. Thom's idea that human language developed 'in response to a double need for a personal evolutive constraint and for social constraint, or ego-preservation and group regulation', is, according to Sebeok,

the only scenario which, tersely expressed as it is, seems to me to be in equally good conformity with semiotics and ethology, two differently labeled disciplines that nonetheless have a common historical origin, share a set of methodological tools, and, most important, overlap in their engagement with difficult issues in the analysis of concepts having a regulation figure that Thom calls a *logos* . . . and that is manifestly analogous to that of living beings. For Thom . . . this Heraclitean label seems to translate into 'form,' that is, the structure that assures for any object its unity and its stability. Under the umbrella of this powerful theory, of great beauty, we can at last envisage, if only in outline, a biologically informed sign-science and the semiotically sensitive life-science, constituting two aspects of the general science of the *logos* of a form, what defines the boundary between living organization and inert structure, distinguishes the domain of a natural semiotics from a physics – in fine, provides us a tool with the aid of which we can set about the question of the extent to which our language provides us with a relatively correct description of the world.

(Whether or not that 'boundary' will prove inviolable is, I would contend for reasons that are by now apparent, still an open question.) Furthermore, Thom, following Peirce's notion that man is a text, 'has authoritatively delineated the fundamental identity of the processes of biological reproduction and semiosis', in terms of which there is a 'subtle fluctuation between two morphologies', so that 'a parent organism or "signified" emits a descendant, thereby engendering a "signifier" which . . . reengenders a "signified" each time the sign is interpreted'. And his theory may be useful in the study of iconicity – of the interrelations of environmental icons, the nervous system, and linguistic structures – for he assumes that

> the principal role of the central nervous system in animals is to map out localized regions to simulate the position of the organism in its environment, as well as to represent objects, such as prey and predator, that are biologically and/or socially necessary for its survival or well-being. That is to say, an animal is constantly informed and impelled by meaning-bearing sign-vehicles designed to release pertinent motor reflexes . . . , such as approach (say, towards a prey) or withdrawal (say, from a predator), or surrogate verbal responses in the human, as in a transitive SVO [subject–verb–object] sentence ('the shark consumes the porpoise'), a syntactic pattern which can be viewed as a temporal transcription of a biological event in space–time, predation, as its archetypal paradigm.[15]

Such analogical thinking could be applied further to interrelating other phenomena that involve kinetic, affective, and cognitive patterns mirrored in syntax – genetic transcription, embryological development, learning strategies, and so on. All these phenomena can be mapped topologically in terms of factors that give rise to catastrophic events, and all have to do with the interanimating analogies to be found in human makeup from its biologically rudimentary to its linguistically involuted aspects. Thom's theory seems to provide a 'proto-formalism' that, if sufficiently refined, could bridge the gap between biologically-based language and that of the machine.

Sebeok is hardly amiss in his enthusiasm – though the future will judge the degree of his hyperbole – when he hails Thom's work as 'the most important development since the calculus of Leibniz and Newton'.[16] None the less, linguists and others concerned with natural language, excepting a few, have been tardy in exploring and using Thom's insights. That situation may be due largely to the (sometimes, in certain respects, almost obscurantist) difficulty of those insights, but many *are* 'nuggets of gold', nuclei for projects relating to the MLM metaphor.

For example, E. C. Zeeman, observing that linguists, including Chomsky, generally 'make little attempt to link neurology and linguistics', finds Thom's application of catastrophe theory to linguistic questions to be 'the first coherent attempt to explain the brain activity behind language'. He is attracted particularly to Thom's suggestions about deep structure:

> Thom suggests that the deep structure of language is yet another aspect of universal morphologies, and his approach would at the same time explain how animals, or children before they have learnt to speak, can reason logically (a simple observation all too often overlooked by linguists and philosophers). His main idea is that a basic sentence begins as a single thought, represented by a bifurcation of a dynamical system describing the neurological activity, with the attractors [stable limit cycles] of the system representing the nouns, and the surfaces separating their basins of attraction representing the verb. Speech is a mechanism that subsequently lists the component parts of the bifurcation, and speech-recognition is the reverse mechanism that synthesises a duplicate model of the same bifurcation, and thereby simulates another single thought analogous to the original thought. The simplest

bifurcations are the elementary catastrophes, and Thom suggests that these give rise to the basic types of spacio-temporal [*sic*] sentences . . . .

Zeeman finds this idea 'very convincing', though he tries to improve on it.[17] One can see readily why such an idea is off-putting to most linguists, for it requires command of a complex armamentarium traditionally outside linguistics; but, even given its lack of detail, one can see also that it accounts for communication between nervous systems and for nonlinear conceptual structures and their linear realization in syntax.

Thom analyses language, like living beings, in terms of 'conditional chreods' (a *chreod*, C. H. Waddington's coinage, is a stably equilibrated path of development). Thus, for him, 'Animal and human behavior can be decomposed into functional fields acting as chreods. In particular, human language is a system described by a one-dimensional (time) semantic model whose chreods are the phonemes and, on a higher scale, the words.' By this analogy biological function corresponds to grammatical category, so that in a simple tree diagram, for example, 'the abstract morphology M consists of symbols A (article), N (noun), and V (verb). Syntactical analysis of a sentence is then a homomorphism of the collection of words in the bottom line of the tree agreeing with the abstract morphology M', with the above symbols representing 'grammatical functions (or, more precisely, categories)'. Grammar thus governs the associations of linguistic chreods, and meaning is determined by their 'internal structure'.[18]

Thom observes, apropos this last point, that meaning presents a special, familiar problem: 'there is almost no connection between the written or spoken structure of a word and its meaning'. He proposes a new, albeit incompletely articulated, approach to it:

> The choice of the word corresponding to a given meaning is the result of a long historical process, a quasi-permanent generalized catastrophe. . . .
>
> In the natural processes that do not aim at communication and that can be assimilated in language only by metaphor (but by a useful metaphor), we must expect the internal structure of each chreod to be relatively transparent; in such a language all words will be onomatopoeic. In fact it is a good idea to suppose,

a priori, that a chreod contains nothing more than can be deduced by observation, that is, the catastrophe set, and to proceed to the dynamical analysis of the chreod which is the most conservative (*économique*, in French). From this point of view, the *significance* of a chreod is nothing more than the topological structure of the catastrophes it contains and its possible dynamical interpretation.[19]

His approach hardly dispenses with the problem, but it does cast meaning in a way that should interest information theorists, especially since the low probabilities associated with catastrophes correlate nicely with information-theoretical ideas about negentropy.

Perhaps here, most notably, an important emphasis of the new paradigm is being limned, for Thom's notion of information has some far-reaching implications. In his view all information may be construed as messages, linear sequences, but that is only one possible construal. As he suggests, 'any geometric form whatsoever can be the carrier of information', and the construal of information as nonlinear form is for him potentially the most powerful: 'it must not be thought that a linear structure is necessary for storing or transmitting information (or, more precisely, significance); it is possible that a language, a semantic model, consisting of topological forms could have considerable advantages . . . over the linear language we use . . .'.[20] How far this construal could be extended in the analysis of natural-language semantics or applied, say, in the creation of new computer languages is an intriguing question, and it should engage anyone who, like Simmons, is interested in creating semantic networks, which are fundamentally topological constructs.

All information is, according to this construal, 'first a form', and meaning in turn thereby may be construed, in terms that recall MacKay's theorizations, as 'a topological relation between the form of the message and the eigenforms of the receptor (the forms that can provoke an excitation of the receptor)'. Man does not go through life like an infant, seizing objects and placing them in his mouth: he seizes instead 'the things lying between exterior objects and genetic forms, namely, *concepts*'. His thought and language, that is, are defined by patterns intermediate to those objects and forms (the latter are 'sensory-motor schemas' with which he is equipped at birth). His babbling in infancy has to do with 'the need to expel by the process of articulation some of these alienating genetic forms'. Thus does he prepare to dance the tango of form and eigenform:

> a genetic form is not fixed, but rather is equipped with mechanisms of self-regulation analogous to those of a living being; a concept occurs by superposition, by projecting the regulation schemes of the subject onto a spatial form, an exterior image. By a geometrical analogy, we might say that the concept forms by exfoliation from the spatial image, where the normal coordinate along which the exfoliation takes place is associated with the direction of an articulated emission whose phonetic structure has little to do with the genetic form that gave its regulation to the concept. (This is the Saussurian idea of the arbitrariness of the sign.) This association forms by habituation, with the emission of the sound occurring with the (playful or biological) use of the corresponding object. On the other hand, the laws of combination, the syntax, of these words are not arbitrary since they are imposed by the semantic interactions between the concepts, themselves defined by the regulation schemes of the subject and thus of the concepts.

This account of acquisition correlates suggestively with Osgood's thinking and, if extended, might help explain why no human sign system is completely arbitrary. One might consider, in this connection, Thom's discussion of the deficient linguistic development of 'wolf children' compared to that of human beings subject to typical acculturation:

> If a child spends the time between 1 and 3 years of age without other human verbal contact, the articulatory emission catastrophe (the babble) rapidly degenerates into the production of a few crude sounds. . . . The exfoliation of the semantic support space of the concept is inhibited by the incoherence or absence of the sounds associated with the object; this results in the mental retardation or idiocy to which these children are condemned. Those who have studied these wolf children have observed their extreme reactions to some noises like the cracking of a nut. There is little doubt that their minds are still dominated by a small number of alienating forms of genetic origin. Man gets rid of these alienating forms by giving them a name and so

neutralizing their hallucinatory powers by fixing them on a semantic space distinct from space–time.

Now surely Thom omits an important qualification, for man hardly 'gets rid of' those forms altogether – nor is his 'semantic space' completely 'distinct from space–time'. Surely the fact that man's language is not entirely arbitrary suggests that he retains traces of those forms. Thus, modifying Thom's account with no intention of contradicting its most useful premises, I would argue that it is capable of describing both the acquisition of verbal language and its tendency to retain, in words as well as in the etherealized kinesis of syntax (he grants that, 'If man has escaped from the fascination of things through the use of language, he remains under the fascination of action incorporated as the grammar of the language . . .'),[21] affectivities derived from the genetic forms. Would not that retention explain, in part, why the machine modelling of natural-language semantics, particularly those aspects that seem so deeply carnalized, is difficult? The question implies not that such modelling is impossible but that it will be possible only if the extent to which semantic form is natural form, *human* form, is understood. As Thom well knows, human knowledge is carnal knowledge: the word is flesh, the form of flesh, first of all.

But Thom is typically more comprehensive in dealing with the spatiotemporal morphology of language and its relation to the activities of the human organism. For example, he argues that his theory about the spatial origin of syntax can account for why the instrumental case is associated with 'verbs having the excision morphology of cutting' or why the genitive case presents special complications because its operation involves 'dislocating a concept into its regulating subconcepts in a kind of inverse embryology'. He even attempts to show that his theory can account for the automatism of syntactic production. Thought and language, for him, are generally to be seen as processes related to other aspects of human experience: 'thought is a kind of permanent orgasm,' he says, 'a virtual capture of concepts with a virtual, inhibited, emission of words, a process analogous to dreaming, while in language this emission actually takes place, as in play'. And formal thought also may be regarded as a game, one 'whose rules . . . are codified as a system of axioms', or as 'magic that has been psychoanalyzed and made conscious of its organizing structures'.[22]

One must realize, however, that Thom, like many structuralists and poststructuralists (though he is Platonist enough to be at odds with them on some issues), feels a certain unease about the biology of human thought and language, for part of the reason why he argues for the value of 'mathematical activity' as 'play *par excellence*' that allows 'the construction of mental structures simulating more and more closely the structures and forces of the outside world, as well as the structure of the mind itself', is because he sees such activity also as the means 'by which man can deliver himself from the biological bondage that weights down his thought and language, and can assure the best chance for the survival of mankind'. I wonder about the purport of this argument. Does he not see the possibilities of 'disembodied nightmare' of which Jameson is wary? Does he really believe that mankind can escape biology? Or is he anticipating the survival of a different, nonorganic 'mankind'? On the other hand, he asserts as a kind of credo that in its task of attempting 'to formalize the unformalizable . . . the human brain, with its ancient biological heritage, its clever approximations, its subtle esthetic sensibility, remains and will remain irreplaceable for ages to come'.[23] His approach is laced with a profound ambivalence. It may be that of the age.

Be that as it may, Thom's approach should be engaged by language theorists and modellers – both because of the way it corroborates much of present theory and research and because of the way it more comprehensively addresses their problems and urges further theory and research. His thought concerning semantics agrees with the idea of meaning as use, which idea, he argues, is also that 'of the "bootstrap" physicists, according to whom a particle is completely defined by the set of interactions in which it participates', but it also goes beyond those resonances to seek justification for that idea in terms of morphogenesis. His thought concerning human memory agrees with recent theory and research that 'there is little hope of localizing memories either spatially, in specific neurons, or chemically, in well-determined substances', but it also attempts to transcend that simply negative conclusion by proposing a neural-oscillatory model of the dynamics of primary and secondary memory and of their interactions. And his thought concerning grammatical and rhetorical structures agrees to some extent with contemporary theory and research (for example, his notion, in regard to 'semantic density', that 'In the emission of a sentence, the meaning is analyzed and the elements are emitted in the order of increasing density' correlates nicely with Francis Christensen's observations about cumulative sentences), but it also ventures beyond them to consider 'a grammatical category (in the traditional sense) as a kind of abstract *logos*' – that is, 'a regulation figure . . . analogous to that of living beings' but 'purified to the point that only the rules of combination and interaction between such categories can be formalized' – and to consider the syntactic structures of all languages as mirroring certain fundamental morphogenetic patterns (thus writing, 'by a very natural contagion', realizes as 'spatial variables' in the hand the 'external variables of the elementary catastrophes' occurring in the brain/mind).[24] His thought, in other words, opens up and grapples with a broad range of questions associated with the MLM metaphor and could prove invaluable in elaborating the new paradigm.

38

Subsumption, Simulation, Information

By now it is obvious that I can hardly pretend, like the *maître de philosophie* in Molière's *Bourgeois Gentilhomme*, to explain everything about the way language (or mind or machine) works – the evidence is strongly to the contrary – but I can at least offer some meditations toward a conclusion.

The range of problems and possibilities with which I have been preoccupied is curiously addressed and brought into startling focus by Derrida:

> For some time now, as a matter of fact, here and there, by a gesture and for motives that are profoundly necessary, whose degradation is easier to denounce than it is to disclose their origin, one says 'language' for action, movement, thought, reflection, consciousness, unconsciousness, experience, affectivity, etc. Now we tend to say 'writing' for all that and more: to designate not only the physical gestures of literal pictographic or ideographic inscription, but also the totality of what makes it possible; and also, beyond the signifying face, the signified face itself. And thus we say 'writing' for all that gives rise to an inscription in general, whether it is literal or not and even if what it distributes in space is alien to the order of the voice: cinematography, choreography, of course, but also pictorial, musical, sculptural 'writing.' One might also speak of athletic writing, and with even greater certainty of military or political writing in view of the techniques that govern those domains today. All this to describe not only the system of notation secondarily connected with these activities but the essence and content of these activities themselves. It is also in this sense that the contemporary biologist speaks of writing and *pro-gram* in relation to the most elementary processes of information within the living cell. And, finally, whether it has

essential limits or not, the entire field covered by the cybernetic *program* will be the field of writing.

He goes on to suggest that, 'If the theory of cybernetics is by itself to oust all metaphysical concepts – including the concepts of soul, of life, of value, of choice, of memory – which until recently served to separate the machine from man, it must conserve the notion of writing, trace, grammè, or grapheme, until its own historical-metaphysical character is also exposed'[1] (which exposure might be the most important purpose of the conversation of poststructuralists and the artificial intelligentsia). What he is discussing is a multiple subsumption (and supplemen-tation/supplantation): mind by language, language by writing (in his provocative sense), writing by the machine (the program, the electronically 'written'), even the machine by itself.

That subsumption (in the last analysis an act of modelling) suggests a peculiar skewing of the MLM-metaphorical cycle, a process of consecutive abstraction, a 'shred out', as James G. Miller might say, into increasingly more 'negative' levels of understanding – but at what cost? That depends on how far man is capable of affirming his uniqueness, and that in turn depends largely – and paradoxically – on his ability to improve his models of himself, his mind, his language. And if he does not want to be supplanted by the instantiations of those models, then he will have to keep strong the taproot into his biology. In other words, no matter what man would share with the machine in order to understand himself better, he should try not to relinquish it to the machine; but, if he should relinquish it, he must recognize how its new context differs from its old one, how he differs from (and defers to) the machine – if he can. Given that caveat, I would like to reapproach some of the issues involved in modelling.

Zeeman notes that there is not 'any well developed theory of the dynamic behaviour of the medium-scale' in brain-modelling research:

True, there have been several models concerned with groups of cells and computer simulations, but none have really matched up to the two main requirements of providing a framework for prediction and experiment, and providing a link between the large and small. On the one hand the network theories of neurons and the combinatorial theories of synapses seem unable to escape from the small-scale, and therefore appear to be unrelated to psychology. On the other hand the computer simulations of perception and problem-solving seem unable to escape from the large-scale, and therefore appear to be unrelated to neurology.[2]

Hofstadter would surely concur. The result of this limitation, in Jameson's words, is that 'the mind/body opposition is transformed into a structural or conceptual distinction between significance on the one hand, and the meaningless physical substratum or *hylé* ['matter'] by which that significance is invested' on the other.[3] If computer modelling of the kind in which I am interested is going to continue productively – and it has bogged down in some respects – then this problem of the medium-scale relations between brain and mind will have to be engaged more creatively. Larger knowledge of them would wonderfully illuminate nearly all the many interrelated other problems I have been discussing, and it is crucial to the elaboration of a new natural-language paradigm.

But those relations seem almost impenetrably complex. Jeffrey Wine, a physiological psychologist whose research has been concerned mainly with the neural electrochemistry of the brain, argues that insights pertinent to them are being synthesized into a more comprehensive neuroscience, and he observes that 'perhaps computer analogies have had the most influence in removing the last vestiges of vitalism from biology' and that 'Computer programs are still primitive relative to the behavior of higher animals, but . . . are evolving rapidly, and . . . already serve as a severe challenge to any dualistic philosophy' of the brain/mind. Yet he admits that there remains a 'major mystery' about how 'a chunk of tissues can think'.[4] That mystery inheres in the medium-scale, in the poorly understood mediation between tissues and thought, raw sensory data and consciousness. It is a mystery that has preoccupied philosophers and scientists for ages – but no one, within the last few decades, more than Herbert Feigl.

Feigl assumes that 'the ψ–ϕ (i.e., psycho-neurophysiological) relations or correspondences' involved are empirically accessible. His survey of the ways these relations might be defined (in terms of parallelism, isomorphism, interactionism, and so on) leads him to favour isomorphism:

> Isomorphism as understood by the Gestalt psychologists . . . and the cyberneticists . . . assumes an even more complete one–one correspondence [than parallelism] between the elements, relations, and configurations of the phenomenal fields and their counterparts in the neurophysiological fields which characterize portions of cerebral, and especially cortical, processes. . . . This sort of approach would also countenance a one–many correspondence of ψ's and ϕ's. In that case, mental states would (with the help of the ψ–ϕ 'dictionary') still be uniquely inferable from neurophysiological descriptions. But many–one or many–many correspondences, even if expressed in terms of statistical laws, would seriously restrict such inferences from specific ϕ's to specific ψ's. I know of no good empirical reasons for assuming anything but one–one correspondence; or one–many if very exact and detailed ϕ-descriptions are used and if account is to be taken of the limited introspective discernibility of the ψ's from one another.

The validity of his assumption doubtless would depend, in part, on how the ψ's and ϕ's were characterized; but, if one had 'completely adequate and detailed knowledge of the *neural* processes in human brains, and the knowledge of the one–one, or at least one–many ψ–ϕ correlation laws', then, as he argues, 'a description of a neural state would be completely reliable evidence (or a genuine criterion) for the occurrence of the corresponding mental state'. (This argument presents a version of the so-called central-state identity theory.) He emphasizes, however, that there are statistical-mechanical limitations to the predictive power of knowledge about the isomorphism because other factors ('the relevant total initial conditions') besides the neural correlates are involved.[5]

Feigl's most intriguing thought about this isomorphism concerns a kind of particle/wave identity theory that seems potentially useful, would interest the poststructuralist, and should not prove disturbing to the functionalist. Observing that 'There is no plausible *scientific* theory anywhere in sight which would explain just why phenomenal states are associated with brain states' and that 'Many philosophers have resigned themselves to regard the ψ-ϕ correlations as "ultimate," "irreducible," "brute facts"', he proposes a strategy that 'removes the duality of the two sets of events, and replaces it by the much less puzzling duality of two ways of knowing the *same* event – one direct, the other indirect'. That '*same* event', of course, remains obscure. Thus there are 'brute facts' – though 'located differently' – in his theory also, as well as certain nomothetic limitations:

> this identity cannot be formulated in laws or law-like sentences or formulas. The identity amounts merely to the common reference of acquaintance terms on the one hand and unique physical descriptions on the other. Any other way of phrasing the relation creates gratuitous puzzles and avoidable perplexities. For example, it is misleading to ask, 'Why does a mental state "appear" as a brain state to the physiologist?' The brain-state-as-it-appears-to-the-physiologist is of course analyzable into phenomenal data forming part of the direct experience of the physiologist. The 'brute fact' simply consists in this, that the phenomenal qualities known by acquaintance to one person are known (indirectly) by description to another person on the basis of phenomenal (evidential) data which, in the vast majority of cases, are qualitatively quite different from the data had by, or ascribed to, the first person.

His move here involves trying to strip the medium-scale of false mysteries so that the '*same* event' can be considered differently. If his theory is correct – that is, if 'the configurational (Gestalt) features of immediate experience are isomorphic with certain global features of our brain processes'[6] (macro-states of the mind with statistical micro-states of the brain) – then one ought to be able to describe the structures and processes of the medium-scale.

Whether or not Feigl's theory will be corroborated remains to be seen. But he suggests an important method of inquiry concerning the medium-scale, one that deconstructs conventional methods. If it could help, as I believe it can, in describing and modelling the relations between brain and mind, then it might also help in describing and modelling those between syntax and semantics, word and concept, and so on – all those 'two ways of knowing the *same* event'.

It is predictable that future modelling of the brain/mind is going to proceed primarily through theories about information processing; such theories typically are readily instantiated in AI systems and are essentially linguistic in orientation – thus will the knowledges associated with each sector of the MLM circle continue to interanimate one another. But those undertaking such research must be aware that those sectors are equivalent and yet are not, that there are conjunctions among them and yet disjunctions as well; they must not rush to models that are too glibly comprehensive. (If philosophers want to be greatly helpful, they should develop a philosophy of models, a project engaged by structuralism but left inchoate. That project would necessarily explore the ways all cognition, verbal and nonverbal, is *always* articulated as modelling procedures.)

Francis Crick, in his concern with how 'a general theory of the brain' should be constructed, offers modellers some other advice as well. He suggests that they be aware of the various constraints determining the nature of the brain and not neglect empirical data, for 'There are so many possible ways in which our brains might process information that without considerable help from direct experimental facts (which are usually rather sparse) we are unlikely to hit on a correct theoretical description.' And he warns against 'the fallacy of the homunculus' (which attributes a false ontology to the overall cybernation of the brain) and 'the fallacy of the overwise neuron' (which attributes too deep a meaning to neural processes).[7]

Though Crick emphasizes some general empirical knowledge about the brain that must be taken into account, it is, as it stands, too simple to be useful and must be related to more problematic, less certain knowledge, especially that about brain circuitry. That circuitry appears to consist of both 'precision wiring' and 'associative nets' – the first found typically in small areas of intercellular connection and the second (much harder to describe in detail) typically in much larger ones – and is designed not only to extract 'particular features from the input' but also to establish associational patterns among them. He spins ingenious metaphors of mapping and stratified complexification to suggest how this 'exceedingly cunning combination' works to reflect 'both the structure of the world, external and internal, and our relation to it', but those metaphors remain merely provisional and will have to be related in turn to what is still to be learned about 'mechanisms for attention' and the 'overall control system'. Indeed, though he is

sceptical about achieving a full understanding of the brain, he
argues that, 'if a breakthrough in the study of the brain does come, it
is perhaps likely to be at the level of the overall control of the
system'. (He prophesies that 'the discovery that brain processing
was run phasically, by some kind of periodic clock, as a computer is,
would probably constitute a major breakthrough'.)[8]

An awareness of what is being modelled must be coupled with
an awareness of the constraints that govern the modelling process
itself, particularly if it is mathematically based. Any model, no
matter how comprehensive, is somehow less than (as Weizenbaum
would argue) or at least different from what it simulates, and it
necessarily involves a change of context (there is always an
implicit or explicit *ceteris paribus* clause in its premises). But there
are more specific constraints as well. Walter J. Karplus observes
that 'The construction of a mathematical model of a system entails
the utilization of two types of information: (1) knowledge and
insight about the system being modeled; (2) experimental data
constituting observations of system inputs and outputs. The
utilization of the former class of information involves deduction,
while modeling using empiric observations involves induction.'
Thus a purely deductive model 'can generally be considered a
unique solution to the modeling problem', but inductive methods –
which, of course, are now necessarily used in modelling the
brain/mind – always invite the familiar possibility of 'an
infinite number of models satisfying the observed input/output
relationships'. To be satisfactory at all, therefore, a model must be
deductively based as far as possible and, at best, must incorporate
'the knowledge of the types of elements which are present in the
system and how these elements are interconnected'[9] – a difficult
imperative in the case of the brain/mind. (If a black-box model is
purely inductive and a white-box one is purely deductive, then
present models of the brain/mind would have to be regarded as
being in the dark-gray-box range. I would speculate that, as the
shading shifts toward the white end of the spectrum, modellers
will increasingly, as it were, come out of their closets and admit
that they are interested in simulating that system not by any
arbitrary and practicable means but by a means that parallels it as
closely as possible. A secret wish is at play in their enterprise, one
as old as man's desire to be God.)

In other words, a built-in uncertainty is involved in modelling
the brain/mind, at least as long as the model retains even a trace

of inductive bias. That situation obviously has to do with problems encountered in discretizing variables and lumping parameters: computers demand considerable discretization, and parameter-lumping 'for biological systems' may involve 'a step in the direction of weaker and less reliable mathematical models'. The enterprise of modelling the brain/mind and its language acts therefore must increasingly emphasize the discretely quantitative, while at the same time enriching procedures for modelling the qualitative as generated by the quantitative. And those committed to that enterprise must realize, as they combine aspects of knowledge-based approaches (of the kind embraced by Feigenbaum's 'knowledge engineering'), method-based ones (of the kind embraced by John McCarthy's 'applied epistemology'), and others, that, in general, as Karplus warns, 'The ultimate use of the model must be in conformity with the expected validity of the model.'[10] A model, no matter what combination of theoretical languages (ways of 'seeing' [the unseen], to follow the etymology of *theory*) constitutes it, is, in a sense, only a gate through which assumptions are translated (however indirectly) into conclusions.

And there is a subtle, somewhat Gödelian dilemma implicated in all modelling. It is especially conspicuous in modelling the brain/mind. To model is to formalize, and, as Serres observes, 'to formalize is to carry out a process by which one passes from concrete modes of thinking to one or several abstract forms. It means to eliminate noise as well, in an optimal manner.' To model is thus also to exclude noise. (Or, as he otherwise puts it, 'To exclude the empirical is to exclude differentiation, the plurality of others that mask the same. It is the first movement of mathematization, of formalization.')[11] But to exclude noise is to exclude from the model an aspect of what is being modelled. In the case of the brain/mind this is a critical exclusion, for noise, in this information–theoretical sense, is one of the properties most obviously distinguishing it from computer hardware/software: it is far noisier. The dilemma thereby becomes particularly poignant because, like 'the meaning of a message', the model 'takes shape *only* against a background noise. . . . It requires the total exclusion of precisely what it needs to include, namely, background noise'.[12] Serres resolves the dilemma for information theory by personifying noise as a 'third man' who interrupts a dialogue between two others and whose role is required for their mutual co-operation, in trying to exclude him, as they play the game of communication.[13]

But it will not be resolved so easily by the modeller, for whom it raises the issue of how far simulation can be (or is desired to be) duplication.

In any case, modellers will have available for their research more and more powerful hardware (such as that under development by Seymour Cray and his associates) with performance characteristics that rub against the boundaries of physical law (consider, for example, Josephson-junction devices, superconducting logic circuits that can switch in a few picoseconds – though processing speed may well turn out to be only a secondary issue for modelling *per se*: the brain is, relatively speaking, a slow processor). Doubtless present hardware can be refined considerably; future hardware may include artificial neural systems that are precision-wired and associatively networked to imitate or outstrip their organic counterparts in many ways. Though there has not been a really remarkable advance in hardware since the invention of the microchip, that needed for the further evolution of AI systems, given research now in the offing, can *almost* be taken for granted. In so far as hardware can be differentiated from software, the modeller's problems, as has been seen, are with the latter; that will continue to be so. Those problems demand radical insights to spur and guide further software development.

I have discussed many insights that are valuable or potentially valuable in that regard, but there are several areas of research not usually associated with the kind of modelling I have been discussing that might yield further pertinent ones. Research on computer encryption is a case in point. Some of the difficult procedures involved in constructing cryptosystems may have analogs in the brain/mind, so that such research might suggest how, for example, the psychic ciphertext is produced from the neural plaintext – and vice versa. Also, Benoit B. Mandelbrot's research on fractals, a family of dimensionally irregular shapes that are ubiquitous in natural structures and may be statistically characterized and readily generated by a computer, may prove helpful.[14] Since they can be used to model so many phenomena, it would not be surprising if fractals, extending the topologies of Thom and MacKay, could be used to model, perhaps with cellular automata, certain 'irregular' aspects of structures in the brain/mind and natural language, especially those that are statistical or probabilistic, such as patterns of representation, of conceptual association, and of relation between syntax and semantics (because of processes of the latter, the former tends always to 'spill over' its one-dimensional organization).

Finally, Frederick W. Kantor's research on 'information mechanics' may be relevant to the exploration of some of the most far-reaching implications of the MLM metaphor. He is concerned with a 'conceptual picture' of the universe that involves the idea, perhaps even more ecumenical and holistic than similar ones from Thom and Hofstadter, that all physical phenomena occur in terms of informational relations. This idea (of *écriture* with a difference!), which he develops through and beyond nonrelativistic quantum mechanics, seems to be a further refinement of the translation, traditional since Ludwig Boltzmann began it, of thermodynamic theory into information theory, but, according to Kantor, it is not. In his account of such phenomena, he is interested in the interrelations of the information represented by physical systems and the 'code book' by which the representations are interpreted, but for him the processes of such systems are to be understood not merely as translatable into information-theoretical formulae but as *fundamentally* informational. Thus he describes gravity, for example, as follows:

What is gravity, and why are gravitational and inertial mass equivalent? A gross feature of gravity is that bringing two masses closer together releases energy. This gross feature appears understandable in terms of information. Each object may be regarded as a relatively localized time-like flow of information in a position representation, that is, in which information is represented by the object being in one of all the distinguishable places and/or combinations of places in which it might have been and/or among which it might have been divided. Two independent objects represent a total amount of information equal to the sum of their separate amounts of information. However, if two objects are required to be within some distance of each other, the number of possible configurations is reduced, so their being in any one such configuration represents less information. Some portion of their total information has been subsumed by nearness to each other. Energy is proportional to information, so a portion of their total mass energy is released in bringing them closer together.[15]

This description, here absent its mathematics, is doubtless

controversial, but it is electrically suggestive and derives from a notion, both revolutionary and obvious, that returns me to preoccupations with which I began this book: reality, that always emergent, never completed interpretive consensus, *is* information, is in the last analysis *already formalized*. Perhaps then the modeller's quest ought to be reconceived, by a subtle but definitive shift of perspective, as one not so much for a formalism as for the most comprehensive hermeneutic possible. Thus reconceived, that quest surely could avail itself more of poststructuralist ideas and strategies.

39

Ventriloquism, Indifference, Beyond

In the early 1960s Marshall McLuhan made the following argument about AI:

> Any process that approaches instant interrelation of a total field tends to raise itself to the level of conscious awareness, so that computers seem to 'think.' In fact, they are highly specialized at present, and quite lacking in the full process of interrelation that makes for consciousness. Obviously, they can be made to simulate the process of consciousness, just as our electric global networks now begin to simulate the condition of our central nervous system. But a conscious computer would still be one that was an extension of our consciousness, as a telescope is an extension of our eyes, or as a ventriloquist's dummy is an extension of the ventriloquist.[1]

His final point remains debatable and, in spite of the seeming intractibilities that confront AI work, is already qualified in a number of ways, as has been seen.

In the early 1970s Hubert L. Dreyfus, after a tediously repetitive examination of the problems that plague AI work, especially those concerning the formalization of context, declared that 'on the information processing level, as opposed to the level of the laws of physics, we cannot analyze human behavior in terms of a rule-governed manipulation of a set of elements'. In 1979, after another detailed look at such problems, he discerned little progress in dealing with them and reaffirmed his faith, this time by literary borrowings:

> Great artists have always sensed the truth, stubbornly denied by both philosophers and technologists, that the basis of human intelligence cannot be isolated and explicitly understood. In *Moby Dick* Melville wrote of the tattooed savage, Queequeg,

that he had 'written out on his body a complete theory of the heavens and earth, and a mystical treatise on the art of attaining truth; so that Queequeg in his own proper person was a riddle to unfold; a wondrous work in one volume; but whose mysteries not even himself could read . . . .' Yeats puts it even more succinctly: 'I have found what I wanted – to put it in a phrase, I say, "Man can embody the truth, but he cannot know it."'[2]

Dreyfus's argument is clever and considered (however much he needs to be disabused of misconceptions that lead him to this image of man himself as a kind of 'dummy'). He has a studied sense of the Achilles' heel of the AI enterprise. He is certainly correct that there are features of the brain/mind that present tenacious difficulties – though he admits that cognitive science can learn a great deal by exploring the implications of such difficulties. But, in his attention to the problems of representing knowledge, he fails to consider the possible capabilities of procedurally based, heuristically oriented programs in modelling natural language. He points out numerous paradoxes that beset attempts to model context, and he uses them to attempt to prove that the formalization of human behaviour, linguistic and otherwise, is impossible. His argument, however, seems finally to rely only on his notion of some mystery that is peculiarly human and beyond understanding. His position may or may not be vindicated in the future, but philosophical intuition alone will not engage the issues sufficiently: modelling will be required as well.

More recently, J. David Bolter has put forth another kind of argument about the limits of AI. It is more moralistic and nostalgic. His grasp of the AI enterprise has limits of its own (a belief that 'computer language is at every level univocal' by virtue of the discrete mathematics of circuit logic, a naïve view of the 'content' of language and its evacuation by the algebraizing of semantic-network theory, and so on), but he none the less boldly asserts that 'The goal of artificial intelligence is to demonstrate that man is all surface, that there is nothing dark or mysterious in the human condition . . . .' Indeed, he see AI work, in its obsession with formal systems, as typifying an age that is losing 'the Faustian concern with depth', one in which 'The programmer . . . does not discover his world so much as invent it.' He suggests that humanists in such an age must ask profound questions about the uses of computers, but he also tries to deal with those questions by complacent simplisms and to dismiss computers as mere appliances without important implications. In doing so he abdicates the humanist mission he has promoted and contributes to the fulfilment of his prophecy, to me far more troubling than McLuhan's or Dreyfus's (and not improbable), that 'the debate over the possibility of computer thought will never be won or lost; it will simply cease to be of interest, like the previous debate over man as a clockwork mechanism'.[3]

Bolter's prophecy troubles because it betrays an attitude not just of negativism but of indifference, on the part of many people, toward the 'depth' and importance of the issues that engage AI theorists and researchers. I have argued that in many respects they share with poststructuralists and others ideas and strategies for interrogating human cognition and language, for inventing a means (an 'anti-method') of discovering (*exactly*) how man 'does not discover his world so much as invent it'. Such an undertaking surely daunts the conservative and static-minded, but it must be continued. It opens a way toward the enlarged, more complex, though hardly less affirmative humanism that is now necessary.

And yet there is – and this I will grant McLuhan, Dreyfus, Bolter, Searle, Lucas, and all their ilk – for me (and surely for even the most dedicated member of the artificial intelligentsia) an unsuppressible doubt about the accessibility of some of the 'dark or mysterious' aspects of human consciousness, a wondering if there is not in the centre of the MLM circle a black hole that is, like the word in the mind of the dying Vergil at the end of Hermann Broch's *Der Tod des Vergil*, 'jenseits der Sprache [beyond language]'.[4]

Notes

Notes to Chapter 1   Mind, Language, Machine

1. Philip N. Johnson-Laird, review of *The Science of Mind* by Owen J. Flanagan, *Times Literary Supplement*, 14 Dec. 1984, p. 1441.
2. J. David Bolter, *Turing's Man: Western Culture in the Computer Age* (Chapel Hill: University of North Carolina Press, 1984), p. 150.
3. Jean-Jacques Rousseau, *Émile ou de l'éducation* (Paris: Garnier-Flammarion, 1966), p. 138. The translation is mine, as are all others herein – unless another translator is obviously indicated. On occasion, for various reasons, I quote from non-English texts in the original, with a parenthetical translation; most of the time, if there appear to be no serious translational problems, I simply quote from a published translation.
4. Josué V. Harari and David F. Bell, 'Introduction: Journal à plusieurs voies', in Michel Serres, *Hermes: Literature, Science, Philosophy*, ed. Josué V. Harari and David F. Bell (Baltimore, Md.: Johns Hopkins University Press, 1982), p. xxxvi.

Notes to Chapter 2   System, Text, Difference

1. Fredric Jameson, *The Prison-House of Language: A Critical Account of Structuralism and Russian Formalism* (Princeton, N.J.: Princeton University Press, 1972), p. 175. Having invoked the name of Jacques Derrida, as well as a term from his controversial poststructuralist thought, to which I will recur frequently, I should provide a distinction between poststructuralist (in his case, deconstructionist) and structuralist thought, to which also I will recur frequently (but without undue anxiety: structuralism and poststructuralism are interdependent, if mutually antagonistic, in many respects). According to Josué V. Harari, the 'common denominators' of the various aspects of structuralism, all of which descend from the work of Ferdinand de Saussure, are three:

> (1) the rejection of the concept of the 'full subject' to the benefit of that of structure; (2) the loss of pertinence of the traditional 'form/content' division insofar as for all structuralist theorists content derives its reality from its structure; and (3) at the methodological level, a stress on codification and systematization. . . . The most fundamental difference between the structuralist and post-structuralist enterprises can be seen in the shift from the problematic of the subject to the deconstruction of the concept of representation.

Thus, 'Using the tools furnished by structuralism', which relies on a 'conception of the sign as a closure', Derrida questioningly 'turns them, in a sense, *against* it', so that, as Harari says, borrowing a word from Roland Barthes, 'the trajectory from structuralism to post-structuralism' may be seen as that from '"semiology" to "semioclasty"' ('Critical Factions/Critical Fictions', in *Textual Strategies: Perspectives in Post-Structuralist Criticism*, ed. and intro. Josué V. Harari [Ithaca, N.Y.: Cornell University Press, 1979], pp. 27, 29, 30). A brief and balanced introduction to deconstruction may be found in Vincent B. Leitch, *Deconstructive Criticism: An Advanced Introduction* (New York: Columbia University Press, 1983). See also Christopher Norris, *Deconstruction: Theory and Practice* (New York: Methuen, 1982), which deftly outlines the Nietzschean and structuralist background of deconstruction, and G. Douglas Atkins, *Reading Deconstruction/Deconstructive Reading* (Lexington: University Press of Kentucky, 1983), which offers numerous examples of deconstruction as a praxis.

2. George Steiner, *After Babel: Aspects of Language and Translation* (New York: Oxford University Press, 1975), p. 26. On the play of the trace in temporality, see Jonathan Culler, *On Deconstruction: Theory and Criticism after Structuralism* (Ithaca, N.Y.: Cornell University Press, 1982), pp. 94–5.

3. Terence Hawkes, *Structuralism and Semiotics* (Berkeley and Los Angeles: University of California Press, 1977), pp. 77–8. The reader interested in pursuing Porzig's insight should see his *Wunder der Sprache: Probleme, Methoden und Ergebnisse der modernen Sprachwissenschaft* (Bern: Francke, 1950).

4. See Roland Barthes, 'Rhétorique de l'image', *Communications*, 4 (1964), 40.

5. Jonathan Culler, *Ferdinand de Saussure* (New York: Penguin Books, 1976), p. 122. The traditional logocentric 'metaphysics of presence' (which derives from the sense of self-presence illusorily reified by the inner 'voice') is as inadequate to a poststructuralist like Derrida as the traditional physics of space–time is to a post-Einsteinian physicist and for much the same reason: both involve culturally naturalized, conventional concepts that seem perfectly commonsensical and yet can be exposed readily.

6. This syzygy of signifier and signified might be conceived in terms of the verb *cleave*. It is one word and yet two with two distinct roots in Middle English and means 'split' (from *cleven*) and 'adhere' (from *clevien*) – the word itself is split into two that none the less adhere. Thus signifier and signified, by a projection of desire, adhere, and yet they are irrevocably split apart: they cleave. This situation is addressed also be Derrida's notion of the *brisure* that 'marks the impossibility that a sign, the unity of a signifier and a signified, be produced within the plentitude of a present and an absolute presence' (Jacques Derrida, *Of Grammatology*, trans. Gayatri Chakravorty Spivak [Baltimore, Md.: Johns Hopkins University Press, 1976], p. 69) – *brisure* meaning 'hinge', 'joint', as well as 'break' and, in heraldry, I

would add, 'difference' – a pertinent sememe of which Derrida seems not to be aware.

7. Culler, *Saussure*, p. 122.

8. The neural (and psychoneural) basis of difference, into which word Derrida inserts an *a* and spells as *différance* in order to emphasize its incorporating the senses (in terms of space/time) of both 'difference' and 'deferral' (of the signified, of presence), is suggested by him in his essay 'Differance':

> *Différance* is neither a *word* nor a *concept*. In it, however, we shall see the juncture – rather than the summation – of what has been most decisively inscribed in the thought of what is conveniently called our 'epoch': the difference of forces in Nietzsche, Saussure's principle of semiological difference, differing as the possibility of [neurone] facilitation, impression, and delayed effect in Freud. . . . ('*Speech and Phenomena' and Other Essays on Husserl's Theory of Signs*, trans. David B. Allison [Evanston, Ill.: Northwestern University Press, 1973], p. 130)

The bracketed word is the translator's. Here 'facilitation' denotes the increased conductivity (caused by a 'difference' in electrochemical potential), the increased capability for neurotransmission or the lowering of the threshold for conduction, along (an opening-up of) a neural pathway. (Freud's word is *Bahnung*; the French word is *frayage*: both denote 'pathbreaking', the 'opening of a way'.) For further discussion of this connection between neuropsychology and poststructuralism, see Derrida's essay 'Freud and the Scene of Writing' in his *Writing and Difference*, trans. and intro. by Alan Bass (Chicago, Ill.: University of Chicago Press, 1978), pp. 196–231, esp. 200–5.

9. Culler, *Saussure*, p. 122.

10. Ibid., p. 123. In more general cognitive-theoretical terms,

> The *content* . . . of a particular vehicle of information, a particular information-bearing event or state, is and must be a function of its function in the system. . . . The content of a psychological state or event is a function of its function, and its function is – in the end, must be – a function of the *structure* of the state or event and the system of which it is a part. (Daniel C. Dennett, *Brainstorms: Philosophical Essays on Mind and Psychology* [Montgomery, Vt.: Bradford Books, 1978], p. 163)

11. See Gérard Genette, 'Valéry and the Poetics of Language', in *Textual Strategies*, ed. and intro. Harari, pp. 359–73. According to him, the poet works against the arbitrariness of language to effect a seeming harmony between signifier and signified, an act involving a tension that he discusses in terms of the opposition of Hermogenes' and Cratylus' arguments (for the arbitrariness and non-arbitrariness of signs, respectively) as set out in Plato's *Cratylus*.

12. J. David Bolter, *Turing's Man: Western Culture in the Computer Age* (Chapel Hill: University of North Carolina Press, 1984), p. 15.
13. Culler, *Saussure*, p. 124.
14. Jameson, *Prison-House*, p. 172. This 'waiting' seems to begin quite early in the acquisition of language and to moderate Piagetian arguments about the child's egocentricity, for 'The whole of language learning is taking another person's position; it is finding out what words and expressions mean to another person' (John Macnamara, *Names for Things: A Study of Human Learning* [Cambridge, Mass.: MIT Press, 1982], p. 234) – an activity surely relevant to Mikhail Bakhtin's notion of the dialogicality of language and Derrida's of its equivocality.
15. Henry Miller, *Tropic of Cancer* (1961; reprint edn, New York: Ballantine Books, 1973), p. 54.
16. Michel Serres, 'The Origin of Language: Biology, Information Theory, and Thermodynamics', trans. Mark Anderson, in *Hermes: Literature, Science, Philosophy*, ed. Josué V. Harari and David F. Bell (Baltimore, Md.: Johns Hopkins University Press, 1982), p. 76.

Notes to Chapter 3   Relations, Origin, Silicon

1. Jonathan Culler, *Ferdinand de Saussure* (New York: Penguin Books, 1976), p. 126. This generalization applies with a vengeance to Roger Penrose's theory of 'twistors', which involves a mathematicization of subatomic 'particles' that attempts to discard consideration of space–time in its formulation of relationships, or to 'superstring' theory.
2. Ibid., p. 127. Though a phoneme is sometimes described as a sound that makes a difference in meaning – so that, for example, if the /p/ in *pit* is changed to a /b/, one gets *bit* – it is more accurately described as a *difference* in sound that makes a difference in meaning, the sound itself realizable only in various allophones. Thus it is more like a concept in a system of conceptual relations than like an isolable acoustic event.
3. See ibid., p. 128. Gregory L. Ulmer, discussing the 'Structural Differential', an apparatus for visually modelling conceptualizations developed by Alfred Korzybski (whose ideas Ulmer sees as anticipating deconstruction), echoes Braque's belief by understanding the purpose of that apparatus to be 'to reeducate people to think in a desubstantialized world consisting not of objects but of *events*' ('Textshop for Post(e)pedagogy', in *Writing and Reading Differently: Deconstruction and the Teaching of Composition and Literature*, ed. and intro. G. Douglas Atkins and Michael L. Johnson [Lawrence: University Press of Kansas, 1985], p. 51).
4. Thus Derrida 'shows that language is a "deconstructive" medium that serves to desseminate whatever is "heavy" by substituting itself' (Geoffrey H. Hartman, 'The Culture of Criticism', *Publications of the Modern Language Association*, 99 [1984], 383).
5. Paul Watzlawick, 'Epilogue', in *The Invented Reality*, ed. Paul Watzlawick (New York: Norton, 1984), p. 330.

6. John 1:1.

7. Ralph Waldo Emerson, *Nature*, in *The American Tradition in Literature*, 4th edn, ed. Sculley Bradley, Richmond Croom Beatty, E. Huson Long, and George Perkins (New York: Grosset & Dunlap, 1974), 1: 1050. Emerson is here exemplifying notions enshrined by the tradition of linguistic Adamicism, which ahistorically conceives of human language as the non-arbitrary and non-ideological vessel of 'natural' moral and spiritual values. For a witty discussion of this tradition, see Hans Aarsleff, 'Language and Victorian Ideology', *American Scholar*, 52 (1983), 365–72.

8. Ralph Waldo Emerson, 'The Poet', in *American Tradition*, ed. Bradley, Beatty, Long, and Perkins, 1: 1156.

9. Jacques Derrida, 'Structure, Sign, and Play in the Discourse of the Human Sciences', in *The Structuralist Controversy: The Languages of Criticism and the Sciences of Man*, ed. Richard Macksey and Eugenio Donato (Baltimore, Md.: Johns Hopkins University Press, 1972), pp. 247–8, 249.

10. Leonard Michaels, 'Bad Blood', *University Publishing*, no. 4 (Spring 1978), p. 3.

11. Friedrich Nietzsche, *Die fröhliche Wissenschaft*, in *Nietzsches Werke*, ed. Gerhard Stenzel (Salzburg: Verlag 'Das Bergland-Buch', n.d.), 2: 573.

12. See James H. Stam, *Inquiries into the Origin of Language: The Fate of a Question* (New York: Harper & Row, 1976).

13. See Julian Jaynes, *The Origin of Consciousness in the Breakdown of the Bicameral Mind* (Boston, Mass.: Houghton Mifflin, 1976), pp. 129–38. A more measured but no less inconclusive anthropological investigation may be found in Philip Lieberman, *On the Origins of Language: An Introduction to the Evolution of Human Speech* (New York: Macmillan, 1975). I should emphasize that I am not dismissing the search for the origin of human language in any simple way. That search has been a fascinating one that still should be taken seriously in some respects, as I do. But it has been marked by false assumptions, wrongheaded questions, and a paucity of empirical evidence. Furthermore, as poststructuralists, most notably Derrida, have argued, human language consists of so many interlocking systems (including the 'language' of painting and other nonverbal or quasi-verbal forms) that the search for the origin of language *per se* is necessarily doomed, a situation nineteenth-century linguists surely intuited when they turned from that search to the projects of philology. More generally, every origin, in Derridean terms, differs from itself: there is always a 'supplement' at the source. Origin and supplement, like a text and its gloss or nature and artifice, cannot be absolutely distinguished:

> Take, for example, masturbation, as in Derrida's case study of Rousseau in *Of Grammatology*. Masturbation is dangerous precisely because it supplements the 'natural' relationship; in other words, it is both added to and replaces nature. Each time nature fails us, the supplement is there to entice us, to restore through illusion the absent presence. Thus, the supplement, by definition external and

artificial, replaces nature and so becomes an integral part of it, to the point in fact where the artificial and the natural become inseparable, one and the same. Nature, in all its plentitude, then appears in its real form, that of myth *only*, and the pure origin, the metaphysical concept *par excellence*, is altogether undermined, since the supplement is no less originary than that which is natural. (Josué V. Harari, 'Critical Factions/Critical Fictions', in *Textual Strategies: Perspectives in Post-Structuralist Criticism*, ed. and intro. by Josué V. Harari [Ithaca, N.Y.: Cornell University Press, 1979] p. 35)

14. See Heinrich von Kleist, 'Über die allmähliche Verfertigung der Gedanken beim Reden', in *Werke in einem Band* (Munich: Hanser, 1966), pp. 810–14. Kleist's notion might be compared to Derrida's that *écriture* ('writing' in his special sense of the word) is virtually identical to thought itself or to Bakhtin's that consciousness is dialogically structured.

15. Richard E. Palmer, *Hermeneutics: Interpretation Theory in Schleiermacher, Dilthey, Heidegger, and Gadamer* (Evanston, Ill.: Northwestern University Press, 1969), p. 153.

16. Robert Jastrow, '*Penthouse* Interview: Robert Jastrow', *Penthouse*, Oct. 1978, p. 126. It is possible, of course, that at least some of the silicon now used in computer electronics will be superseded by other, more exotic materials (polymers, for example), but there are problems in their development and production that probably will delay that supersession for some time.

17. Obviously these questions speculate precariously about the personality traits of 'computer people'. The subject has been explored only limitedly. A slipshod but none the less interesting study is Sherry Turkle, *The Second Self: Computers and the Human Spirit* (New York: Granada, 1984).

Notes to Chapter 4   Writing, *Urtext*, Bullae

1. Denise Schmandt-Besserat, 'The Earliest Precursor of Writing', *Scientific American*, June 1978, p. 50.

2. It is worthwhile to note, lest there be any doubt that 'letter' means 'writing' in the quotation from the Authorized (King James) Version of 2 Corinthians 3:6, that *littera* in the Vulgate certainly means that and in the Revised Standard Version is translated as 'the written [as opposed to the spoken] code'. Derrida has a suggestive and relevant comment on the 'violence' of writing (which for him is not secondary to language as speech) as conceived by logocentrism:

> *Violence de l'oubli. L'écriture, moyen mnémotechnique, suppléant la bonne mémoire, la mémoire spontanée, signifie l'oubli. . . . Oubli parce que médiation et sortie hors de soi du logos. Sans l'écriture, celui-ci resterait en soi. L'écriture est la dissimulation de la présence naturelle et première et*

immédiate du sens à l'âme dans le logos. Sa violence survient à l'âme comme inconscience. (*De la grammatologie* [Paris: Minuit, 1967], p. 55)

[Violence of forgetfulness. Writing, mnemotechnic means, supplanting good memory, spontaneous memory, signifies forgetfulness. . . . Forgetfulness because mediation and departure of the logos outside itself. Without writing, the latter would remain in itself. Writing is the dissimulation of the natural and primary and immediate presence of meaning to the soul within the logos. Its violence befalls the soul as unconsciousness.]

See also Walter J. Ong, *Interfaces of the Word: Studies in the Evolution of Consciousness and Culture* (Ithaca, N.Y.: Cornell University Press, 1977), pp. 235, 240. He rehearses, in this book and others, all the clichés about phonic presence that Derrida attacks. Especially pregnable are his remarks on writing as 'mortmain', which derive from his distinction (a somewhat problematic one because children are exposed to writing before they 'learn' it) between speech as 'natural' ('mother') language and writing as 'artificial' and imposed ('father') language.

3. Schmandt-Besserat, 'Earliest Precursor', p. 50. Her discussion surely qualifies Derrida's assertion that 'It is now known, thanks to unquestionable and abundant information, that the birth of writing (in the colloquial sense) was nearly everywhere and most often linked to genealogical anxiety' (*Of Grammatology*, trans. Gayatri Chakravorty Spivak [Baltimore, Md.: Johns Hopkins University Press, 1976], p. 124). Though she suggests a link between writing and territoriality, very much a matter of 'genealogical anxiety', she does not explore it.

4. Schmandt-Besserat, 'Earliest Precursor', p. 59. See also 'From Reckoning to Writing', in 'Science and the Citizen', *Scientific American*, Mar. 1980, p. 96. I would suggest that this supplantation might well be interpreted in terms of Derrida's notion of the *supplément*, of which *écriture* is the supreme example. (See Derrida, *Of Grammatology*, pp. 141–64, 195–200, *et passim*.) Also, I should point out that, in the absence of spoken records, the connection between Schmandt-Besserat's writing and speech obviously is difficult to define; however, its symbols certainly may have evolved for some time without phonetic values.

Notes to Chapter 5   Invisibility, Children, Rules

1. Roger Brown, *A First Language: The Early Stages* (Cambridge, Mass.: Harvard University Press, 1973), p. 3.
2. Roger Brown, *Psycholinguistics* (New York: Free Press, 1970), p. 2.
3. Brown, *First Language*, p. 412.
4. See Jean-Marc-Gaspard Itard, *The Wild Boy of Aveyron*, trans. George Humphrey and Muriel Humphrey (1932; reprint edn, Englewood

Cliffs, N.J.: Prentice-Hall, 1962). For a more recent study of the language habits of such a child, see Susan R. Curtiss, *Genie: A Psycholinguistic Study of a Modern-Day 'Wild Child'* (New York: Academic Press, 1977).

5. Brown, *Psycholinguistics*, p. 99. Thus stimulus–response theory is only partially germane to the overarching question of how a child gains access to the power of the mind for linguistic purposes and then organizes it by those purposes. David Lightfoot, in *The Language Lottery: Toward a Biology of Grammars* (Cambridge, Mass.: MIT Press, 1982), offers cogent observations about the limits of behaviourist theories of language acquisition, specifically about their inability to account for 'how children attain systems that are so much underdetermined by the data available to them' (p. 210), and he argues more explicitly than Brown that the relation between experience and mental properties 'is mediated by genotypical structures' (p. 211). Subject to such mediation, the mind appears to develop by what psychologists call spreading activation – that is, a process, in this case, of proliferant analogizing.

6. Brown, *Psycholinguistics*, pp. 203–4.

7. Ibid., p. 204. The research of Derek Bickerton on creole languages – generically, languages that have evolved among the progeny of pidgin speakers – has yielded persuasive but still controversial results that may help to explain this 'mismatch'. His research, concerned mostly with Hawaiian Creole, shows that

> similarities among creoles cannot be accounted for by contact with other languages, either indigenous or imported. The finding suggests that what is common to creole languages may indeed form the basis of the acquisition of language by children everywhere. There is now an impressive body of evidence to support this hypothesis: between the ages of two and four the child born into a community of linguistically competent adults speaks a variety of language whose structure bears a deep resemblance to the structure of creole languages. . . . If there is a creole grammar somehow imprinted in the mind, creole languages should be easier to acquire than other languages. How is it, then, that not all children grow up speaking a creole language? The answer is that they do their best to do just that. People around them, however, persist in speaking English or French or some other language, and so the child must modify the grammar of the native creole until it conforms to that of the local language. (Derek Bickerton, 'Creole Languages', *Scientific American*, July 1983, pp. 116, 121)

Bickerton's work is quite suggestive, especially in its demonstration of the extent of grammatical similarities between the language of children born of English-speaking parents and English-based creole languages and in its arguments for the possibility that creole languages are almost directly reflective of an innate neural program for language (and hence of the base structure children learn to control), but a great deal remains to be done in order to corroborate and further particularize his primary hypothesis and its implications. In this connection see his exchange of letters with Richard Sproat in *Scientific American*, Dec. 1983, pp. 6–9.

8. Brown, *Psycholinguistics*, pp. 14, 204.

9. Breyne Arlene Moskowitz, 'The Acquisition of Language', *Scientific American*, Nov. 1978, p. 94B. This latter observation may be correlated with another: that the child in his hypothesizing must contend with the adult language as differing from his own since, unless he does, as Derrida says of the child as conceived by Rousseau in *Émile*, 'He has no language because he has only one' (Derrida, *Of Grammatology*, trans. Gayatri Chakravorty Spivak [Baltimore, Md.: Johns Hopkins University Press, 1976], p. 248). Also, though the point need not be laboured, the reader should be aware that the word *grammar*, as Moskowitz uses it here (and as I do here and elsewhere), denominates the patterns – or the knowledge about how to use the patterns – in which words are meaningfully arranged or, at other times, a system for describing, analysing, or formalizing such arrangements. It has little to do with 'linguistic etiquette'. For a pioneering discussion of the differences among these three (at least) grammars, see W. Nelson Francis, 'Revolution in Grammar', *Quarterly Journal of Speech*, 40 (1954), 299–312, esp. 300–1.

10. See Brown, *First Language*, pp. 90–111.

11. Moskowitz, 'Acquisition', pp. 95, 96, 98. She observes that 'The absence of a three-word stage has not been satisfactorily explained as yet; the answer may have to do with the fact that many basic semantic relations are binary and few are ternary' (p. 98). Indeed, all such relations are surely binary in the last analysis.

12. Ibid., p. 103.

13. Ibid., p. 106.

14. Ibid. I should note, in regard to my discussion of paired opposites, that, although one member of a pair may be marked in relation to the other, the meaning of either member still depends necessarily on its difference from the other. That mutual difference gives rise to the Derridean trace of each within the other; that 'hosting' determines a self-division of the signifier that is the condition of its meaning. Conversely, the trace is required for the difference to exist. Also, in regard to Moskowitz's point here, the research of Peter D. Eimas and his colleagues concerning how infants detect discrete phonemes demonstrates fairly conclusively that the mechanism for such detection is innate. See his 'Perception of Speech in Early Infancy', *Scientific American*, Jan. 1985, pp. 46–52.

Notes to Chapter 6   Chimpanzees, Gorillas, Fictionalization

1. See Lev Semenovich Vygotsky, *Thought and Language*, ed. and trans. Eugenia Hanfmann and Gertrude Vakar (Cambridge, Mass.: MIT Press, 1962), pp. 33–41 *passim*.

2. See Herbert S. Terrace, *Nim: A Chimpanzee Who Learned Sign Language* (New York: Alfred A. Knopf, 1979).

3. 'Hans, Sherman and Austin', in 'Science and the Citizen', *Scientific American*, Nov. 1978, p. 86. Though one should be mindful of the fallacies that can pertain to such comparisons between communication systems (especially since human language, continually and variously changeful, is much more than a mere extrapolation from relatively changeless animal signals), it is surely confirmed by now that the chimpanzee is capable of discerning and using the association of some arbitrary symbol with something else. That conclusion has been credited not only by many researchers concerned with language but also by some concerned more particularly with primatology, such as R. T. Passingham, a neurologist and psychologist whose research has been conducted mainly with monkeys. See his *Human Primate* (San Francisco, Calif.: Freeman, 1982).

4. See Steven Rose, *The Conscious Brain*, updated edn (New York: Random House, Vintage Books, 1976), p. 22.

5. Carl Sagan, *The Dragons of Eden: Speculations on the Evolution of Human Intelligence* (New York: Ballantine Books, 1978), p. 119.

6. Ibid., pp. 120, 114, 129, 130. It should be remembered that the DNA coding sequences of man and chimpanzee differ only slightly.

7. See Duane M. Rumbaugh, *Language Learning by a Chimpanzee: The Lana Project* (New York: Academic Press, 1977).

8. Francine Patterson, 'Conversations with a Gorilla', *National Geographic*, 154 (1978), 464. Perhaps I should remind the reader that American sign language is not at all a crude means of communication but a sophisticated system of signs that is only partially pictographic or iconic. It seems clumsily telegraphic and elliptical to the inexperienced user, but for the experienced user it is expressively flexible and capable of nuances that are difficult to translate into spoken or written form.

9. Ibid., p. 459.

10. Ibid.

11. Ibid., p. 464. Orangutans also apparently can sign with the same facility as Koko and her chimpanzee relatives. See Biruté M. F. Galdikas, 'Living with the Great Orange Apes', *National Geographic*, 157 (1980), 839.

Notes to Chapter 7   Alternity, Acquisition, Invariance

1. George Steiner, *After Babel: Aspects of Language and Translation* (New York: Oxford University Press, 1975), pp. 216, 217–18.

2. Wallace Stevens, 'The Man with the Blue Guitar', in *The Palm at the End of the Mind: Selected Poems and a Play by Wallace Stevens*, ed. Holly Stevens (New York: Random House, Vintage Books, 1972), p. 133.

3. Steiner, *After Babel*, p. 222.

4. Ibid., p. 228. As H. P. Grice and others have shown, the lie (insincerity) depends on the general pertinence of truth (sincerity) for its efficacy. The same could be said for Steiner's 'counter-statement'

and 'reality' ('very largely a linguistic product'). Indeed, the same could be said also for the *description* (what a text says in contradistinction to authorial intention) and *declaration* (what a text is intended to say) of Derridean deconstruction theory, each of which is in a sense the parasitic metalanguage of the other – an apt analog here especially, given Steiner's consideration of the ways language continually tropes/trips, counters, and subverts itself through its 'looseness'.

5. See George A. Miller, *Spontaneous Apprentices: Children and Language* (New York: Seabury Press, 1977).

6. Douglas R. Hofstadter, *Gödel, Escher, Bach: An Eternal Golden Braid* (New York: Basic Books, 1979), p. 616.

7. Roger Brown, 'The Development of Language in Children', in *Communication, Language, and Meaning: Psychological Perspectives*, ed. George A. Miller (New York: Basic Books, 1973), pp. 115, 116. I would hypothesize, from the general drift of Brown's discussion and from my own observations, that the child may first utilize metonymic capacities more than metaphoric ones (as perhaps did man, early in the evolution of language), but I know of no research that could affirm this hypothesis.

8. Lewis Thomas has gone so far as to speculate that what is unknown here may largely remain so by virtue of 'a scrambler someplace, maybe in the right hemisphere', which 'would be a protective device, preserving the delicate center of the mechanism of language against tinkering and meddling, shielding the mind against information with which it has no intention of getting involved' (Lewis Thomas, *The Medusa and the Snail: More Notes of a Biology Watcher* [New York: Viking, 1979], pp. 123, 124). Though I am in partial sympathy with the conservative humanism of such speculation, I think it is erroneous.

Notes to Chapter 8   Transformation, Discontinuity, Metalanguage

1. Carl Sagan, *The Dragons of Eden: Speculations on the Evolution of Human Intelligence* (New York: Ballantine Books, 1978), p. 49.

2. See ibid., pp. 100–2.

3. Ibid., p. 103.

4. Ibid., pp. 105, 106–7. The reader should remember, of course, that *Homo habilis* is a direct ancestor of *Homo sapiens*, who emerged about 100 000 years ago; modern man, *Homo sapiens sapiens*, did not emerge until much later.

5. Jacob Bronowski, *The Origins of Knowledge and Imagination* (New Haven, Conn.: Yale University Press, 1978), pp. 23–4, 25.

6. Ibid., pp. 25, 26.

7. Ibid., pp. 26, 27, 28, 30, 31, 32. The neural basis of this delay may be suggested by comparing the relatively small number of 'external' sensory receptors in the human organism (around 100 million) to the number of 'internal' synapses (around 10 trillion). See Heinz von

Foerster, 'On Constructing a Reality', in *The Invented Reality*, ed. Paul Watzlawick (New York: Norton, 1984), p. 52.

8. Bronowski, *Origins*, pp. 33, 34, 36, 38, 39.
9. Jacob Bronowski, *A Sense of the Future: Essays in Natural Philosophy*, ed. Piero E. Ariotti with Rita Bronowski (Cambridge, Mass.: MIT Press, 1977), pp. 105, 108.
10. Ibid., pp. 109, 111.
11. Ibid., p. 117. Jeremy Campbell relates this delay to the slow maturation rate of the brain (the slow expression of genes responsible for its development). See his *Grammatical Man: Information, Entropy, Language, and Life* (New York: Simon & Schuster, 1982), p. 141.
12. Bronowski, *Sense*, pp. 117–18, 119.
13. Ibid., p. 121. This 'layered structure' is, of course, ubiquitous in man's analytical activities – from Linnaean taxonomic nomenclature to computer-programming theory – and is therefore not surprisingly a salient feature of Derridean deconstruction, which involves not 'tearing a text apart', as some would have it, but rather

> more of the tracing of a path among textual strata in order to stir up and expose forgotten and dormant sediments of meaning which have accumulated and settled into the text's fabric. . . . Thus, deconstruction is really more of a technique of *de-sedimentation* (the word was first used by Derrida in *Of Grammatology* and later abandoned), a technique of de-sedimenting the text in order to allow what was *always already* inscribed in its texture to resurface. . . . The de-sedimentation process . . . should help to explain Derrida's view of textuality as a 'fabric of grafts' (*tissu de greffes*), of textual energy that is *dissemination*, as opposed to controlled polysemy. (Josué V. Harari, 'Critical Factions/Critical Fictions', in *Textual Strategies: Perspectives in Post-Structuralist Criticism*, ed. and intro. by Josué V. Harari [Ithaca, N.Y.: Cornell University Press, 1979], p. 37)

14. Roger Brown, *Psycholinguistics* (New York: Free Press, 1970), pp. 254–5, 255–6. Whorf himself was arguably more concerned with structural (grammatical) than lexical characteristics.
15. Bronowski, *Sense*, p. 122.
16. Ibid., pp. 127, 128.
17. Ibid., pp. 129, 131.

Notes to Chapter 9   Synergy, Neuroanatomy, Hemispheres

1. Jacob Bronowski, *A Sense of the Future: Essays in Natural Philosophy*, ed. Piero E. Ariotti with Rita Bronowski (Cambridge, Mass.: MIT Press, 1977), p. 134. For an illuminating treatment of this whole area of inquiry, see Mary-Louise Kean, 'The Linguistic Interpretation of Aphasic Syndromes', in *Explorations in the Biology of Language*, ed. Edward Walker (Montgomery, Vt.: Bradford Books, 1978), pp. 67–138. Also, for collections of relevant essays, see *Neural Models of*

Language Processes, ed. Michael A. Arbib, David Caplan, and John C. Marshall (New York: Academic Press, 1982), and *Language, Mind, and Brain*, ed. Thomas W. Simon and Robert J. Scholes (Hillsdale, N.J.: Erlbaum, 1982).

2. Bronowski, *Sense*, pp. 135–6. For a fuller discussion of this research, see Norman Geschwind, 'Specializations of the Human Brain', *Scientific American*, Sept. 1979, pp. 180–99.
3. Bronowski, *Sense*, p. 136.
4. Ibid., p. 135.
5. Ibid. pp. 136–7.
6. Carl Sagan, *The Dragons of Eden: Speculations on the Evolution of Human Intelligence* (New York: Ballantine Books, 1978), p. 177. See also R. W. Sperry, 'The Great Cerebral Commissure', *Scientific American*, Jan. 1964, pp. 42–52, and Michael S. Gazzaniga, 'The Split Brain in Man', *Scientific American*, Aug. 1967, pp. 24–9.
7. Bronowski, *Sense*, p. 152.

Notes to Chapter 10   Interconnectivity, Self-Consciousness, Excess

1. Carl Sagan, *The Dragons of Eden: Speculations on the Evolution of Human Intelligence* (New York: Ballantine Books, 1978), pp. 77, 181.
2. Ibid., p. 43.
3. Ibid., pp. 107–9.
4. George Steiner, *After Babel: Aspects of Language and Translation* (New York: Oxford University Press, 1975), pp. 223, 224.
5. E. F. Schumacher, *A Guide for the Perplexed* (New York: Harper & Row, Harper Colophon Books, 1978), pp. 16–17, 18, 23.
6. Steven Rose, *The Conscious Brain*, updated edn (New York: Random House, Vintage Books, 1976), p. 177. This excess may well have been occasioned by the sudden expression of an excess of unexpressed genes. See Jeremy Campbell, *Grammatical Man: Information, Entropy, Language, and Life* (New York: Simon & Schuster, 1982), p. 151.
7. Rose, *Conscious Brain*, p. 178.
8. Ibid., pp. 179, 180–1. For a brief discussion of the evolution of the architecture of interconnectivity, starting from internuncial neurons (which mediate between sensory and motor neurons), see Heinz von Foerster, 'On Constructing a Reality', in *The Invented Reality*, ed. Paul Watzlawick (New York: Norton, 1984), p. 50.

Notes to Chapter 11   Neocortex, Manifold, Catastrophe

1. Carl Sagan, *The Dragons of Eden: Speculations on the Evolution of Human Intelligence* (New York: Ballantine Books, 1978), p. 48.
2. René Thom, *Structural Stability and Morphogenesis: An Outline of a General Theory of Models*, trans. D. H. Fowler (Reading, Mass.: Benjamin, 1975), pp. 7, 8.
3. E. C. Zeeman, *Catastrophe Theory: Selected Papers, 1972–1977* (Reading, Mass.: Addison-Wesley, 1977), p. 23.

4. The question necessarily pertains only to spoken language, not written, for the acquisition of which there is no comparable threshold – largely because there is no comparable neural burgeoning. As Ong and others have noted, man is not prewired for writing; unlike the ability to speak, which develops in large measure autonomously, the ability to write is acquired mostly by formal education. (*Writing* is used here in the non-Derridean sense, of course, for Derrida's *écriture* – the structure, marked by the trace [*archi-écriture*], of *différance* – ultimately has to do with more fundamental processes that, while surely habilitated by the ontogenetic catastrophe, are in some sense prior to, though evolve along with – and themselves contribute manifoldly to the habilitation of – spoken language.) A similar distinction should be made in regard to the phylogenetic catastrophe.

Notes to Chapter 12   AI, Computers, Density

1. Margaret A. Boden, *Artificial Intelligence and Natural Man* (New York: Basic Books, 1977), p. 5.
2. 'Breaking a Barrier', *Time*, 30 Oct. 1978, pp. 109–11. It is also possible that optical circuitry, which switches photons rather than electrons, will supersede the electronic: it is faster and perhaps better suited for parallel processing.
3. Bolter suggests, by an ironic loop, that 'a computer will pass for human only when it begins to ask what are the differences between itself and a human being' (J. David Bolter, *Turing's Man: Western Culture in the Computer Age* [Chapel Hill: University of North Carolina Press, 1984], p. 191).

Notes to Chapter 13   Program, Game, Assembler

1. J. Z. Young, *Programs of the Brain* (New York: Oxford University Press, 1978), p. 2.
2. Joseph Weizenbaum, *Computer Power and Human Reason: From Judgment to Calculation* (San Francisco, Calif.: Freeman, 1976), p. 50. Wittgenstein, in his *Zettel* (ed. G. E. M. Anscombe and G. H. von Wright, trans. G. E. M. Anscombe [Berkeley and Los Angeles: University of California Press, 1967], p. 60), takes the figure a step further: '*Vergleiche: Ein Spiel erfinden – eine Sprache erfinden – eine Maschine erfinden* [Compare: inventing a game – inventing a language – inventing a machine].'
3. Ferdinand de Saussure, *Cours de linguistique générale*, ed. Rudolf Engler (Wiesbaden: Harrassowitz, 1967–74), 2: 194.
4. Weizenbaum, *Computer Power*, pp. 97, 68.
5. Ibid., pp. 98, 99.
6. Ibid., p. 103.

Notes to Chapter 14   Turing, More, Analogies

1. Joseph Weizenbaum, *Computer Power and Human Reason: From Judgment to Calculation* (San Francisco, Calif.: Freeman, 1976), p. 64. See A. M. Turing, 'On Computable Numbers, with an Application to the Entscheidungsproblem', *Proceedings of the London Mathematical Society*, 2nd ser. 42 (1937), 230–65. A less technical account may be found in his 'Computing Machinery and Intelligence', in *Minds and Machines*, ed. Alan Ross Anderson (Englewood Cliffs, N.J.: Prentice-Hall, 1964), pp. 4–30.

2. Larry J. Stockmeyer and Ashok K. Chandra, 'Intrinsically Difficult Problems', *Scientific American*, May 1979, p. 145.

3. Weizenbaum, *Computer Power*, pp. 64, 71.

4. The extent to which man transcends the universal Turing machine is at one extreme a matter of speculation about the soul, at the other typically a matter of speculation about intentionality. 'Intentional systems', as Dennett observes, 'are supposed to play a role in the legitimization of mentalistic predicates parallel to the role played by the abstract notion of a Turing machine in setting down the rules for the interpretation of artifacts as computational automata' (Daniel C. Dennett, *Brainstorms: Philosophical Essays on Mind and Psychology* [Montgomery, Vt.: Bradford Books, 1978], p. xvii). That supposition follows, obliquely at least, from Brentano's Thesis, which states that all mental phenomena manifest intentionality and that, obversely, no physical (nonmental) phenomena do; however, its usefulness in characterizing the differences between man and machine has proven problematic, not only because of the nonphysical nature of a 'machine' as an abstract system but also because of the difficulty of characterizing intentionality itself.

5. Weizenbaum, *Computer Power*, pp. 111–12.

6. J. Z. Young, *Programs of the Brain* (New York: Oxford University Press, 1978), pp. 8, 9.

7. Ibid., pp. 9, 10.

8. Ibid., pp. 10, 11.

9. René Thom, *Structural Stability and Morphogenesis: An Outline of a General Theory of Models*, trans. D. H. Fowler (Reading, Mass.: Benjamin, 1975), p. 11.

10. It might well be argued that the comparison outlined here, which is bolder, more detailed, and, perhaps, more debatable than Hofstadter's (see *Gödel, Escher, Bach: An Eternal Golden Braid* [New York: Basic Books, 1979], esp. p. 573), could include also a level higher (for software) than level 1 in my diagram. Such a level would be defined in the AI system by a 'higher-level' program, written in a language much closer to natural language than any now in use, that would be self-analytically flexible, logically 'imprecise', and discursively expansive. Such a level would be defined in the HI system by the 'program' of natural-language discourse, of statements interlinked into texts larger than the sentence. Indeed, research on higher-level programming, as it matures, may contribute insights helpful to the

construction of a thoroughgoing discourse grammar – and vice versa. For an overview of such research, see Terry Winograd, 'Beyond Programming Languages', *Communications of the ACM*, 22 (1979), 391–401.

11. Dennett, for example, observes that, when one is

> viewing AI as a species of top-down cognitive psychology, it is tempting to suppose that the decomposition of function in a computer is intended by AI to be somehow isomorphic to the decomposition of function in a brain. . . . This story is fine in principle, I think, and the day may come when this imagined isomorphism down to the neuronal level . . . is proclaimed, but in fact we see nothing remotely like this in current AI work. We see instead models that diverge from nature *very* early on the downward path. (Dennett, *Brainstorms*, pp. 113, 114)

Notes to Chapter 15   Form, Representation, Presence

1. J. Z. Young, *Programs of the Brain* (New York: Oxford University Press, 1978), pp. 39, 41.
2. Ibid., pp. 42, 41–2. Interestingly enough, a byte, a string of information eight bits long, is sometimes regarded as an 'electronic phoneme'.
3. René Thom, *Structural Stability and Morphogenesis: An Outline of a General Theory of Models*, trans. D. H. Fowler (Reading, Mass.: Benjamin, 1975), p. 127.
4. Young, *Programs*, p. 43.
5. Ibid., pp. 43, 46.
6. Daniel C. Dennett, *Brainstorms: Philosophical Essays on Mind and Psychology* (Montgomery, Vt.: Bradford Books, 1978), pp. 39, 42, 46, 47, 49, 50.
7. Ibid., pp. 90, 107–8, 122. The works by Jerry A. Fodor with which Dennett is principally concerned are *The Language of Thought* (New York: Crowell, 1975) and *Psychological Explanation: An Introduction to the Philosophy of Psychology* (New York: Random House, 1968).
8. Francisco J. Varela, 'The Creative Circle: Sketches on the Natural History of Circularity', in *The Invented Reality*, ed. Paul Watzlawick (New York: Norton, 1984), p. 320.
9. Dennett, *Brainstorms*, p. 123.
10. Ibid., pp. 123, 124–5.

Notes to Chapter 16   Recognition, Hypothesis, HEARSAY

1. J. Z. Young, *Programs of the Brain* (New York: Oxford University Press, 1978), pp. 48, 49–50.
2. Ibid., pp. 51–2.
3. Ibid., pp. 53, 54. My example is the classical axodendritic synapse,

but there are, of course, axoaxonic and dendrodendritic synapses as well.

4. Michel Serres, 'The Origin of Language: Biology, Information Theory, and Thermodynamics', trans. Mark Anderson, in *Hermes: Literature, Science, Philosophy,* ed. Josué V. Harari and David F. Bell (Baltimore, Md.: Johns Hopkins University Press, 1982), p. 80. He goes on to speculate that what is conventionally called the unconscious 'would seem to be the final black box, the clearest box for us since it has its own language in the full sense. Beyond it we plunge into the cloud of meaningless signals. Perhaps this box protects us from the deafening gasps of the stochastic; perhaps the box serves to turn them back into symbols' (pp. 80–1).

5. Young, *Programs,* p. 57. No matter how one may conceive of meaning being *produced,* it must surely be *recognitive,* and the 'action' involved is not only the obviously visible kind that beguiles the naïve behaviourist. (The play of thought here echoes Bohuslav Havránek's postulate that the response of the addressee determines the function of an utterance.) Also, I should note, in regard to Young's comparison (and my own, earlier) of switches and neurons (which are more flexible and probabilistic in their behaviour), that, if pushed, it quickly becomes untenable – unless one is considering logic gates that are far more sophisticated than those now in use.

6. David E. Rumelhart, *Introduction to Human Information Processing* (New York: Wiley, 1977), pp. 105–6.

7. Ibid., pp. 113, 116. Hearsay-II, the successor to Reddy's system discussed here, embodies some interesting, though not critically important, improvements. See Lee D. Erman, Frederick Hayes-Roth, Victor R. Lesser, and D. Raj Reddy, 'The Hearsay-II Speech-Understanding System: Integrating Knowledge to Resolve Uncertainty', *Computing Surveys,* 12 (1980), 213–53.

Notes to Chapter 17   ATN, Automata, Expectation

1. Philip C. Jackson, Jr, *Introduction to Artificial Intelligence* (New York: Petrocelli Books, 1974), pp. 297, 298.

2. Terry Winograd, *Understanding Natural Language* (New York: Academic Press, 1972), p. 44.

3. Jackson, *Artificial Intelligence,* p. 302.

4. Winograd, *Understanding,* p. 16.

5. Jackson, *Artificial Intelligence,* p. 303.

6. David E. Rumelhart, *Introduction to Human Information Processing* (New York: Wiley, 1977), pp. 117, 118.

7. Ibid., pp. 118–19.

8. Robert Wall, *Introduction to Mathematical Linguistics* (Englewood Cliffs, N.J.: Prentice-Hall, 1972), p. 254.

9. Winograd, *Understanding,* p. 43.

10. Ibid. Winograd's position here is open to question, specifically in regard to the psychological or neuropsychological reality of finite-

state systems, research on which began in the early 1940s with the work of Warren S. McCulloch and Walter Pitts. Though Stephen C. Kleene has tried brilliantly to demonstrate the equivalence of such systems and 'idealized neural networks', there is still considerable dispute, according to Brian Hayes, about whether the brain is such a system – not because the number of neurons is not finite (it obviously is) but because a neuron 'is far more complicated than a two-state cell' (and may behave in non-discrete ways) and because the mind is not simply 'a succession of instantaneous states' but includes contextualized 'knowledge of its own history'. Thus he is sceptical about the ability of automata, of whatever kind, to recognize and parse natural language and concludes that 'There are languages with grammars so preposterous that even a Turing machine cannot be counted on to recognize their statements in a finite amount of time. So far such languages have found little use in the world of computing machines, but people somehow manage to speak them' (Brian Hayes, 'Computer Recreations', *Scientific American*, Dec. 1983, pp. 20, 28).

11. Rumelhart, *Information Processing*, p. 121. I should add that there have been a few minor successes in building parsing systems that 'learn' to parse better as they parse more.

12. The term *context-free*, like its opposite, *context-sensitive*, pertains to the 'environmental' conditions under which, in a generative grammar, a symbol in a string may be rewritten by a rewrite rule. English, not being context-free, is subject to such conditions. Indeed, that sensitivity to context accounts for its 'excellent readability, even when distorted by misprints and mistakes', and, as a characteristic of redundancy at the level of DNA, correlates, as Lila L. Gatlin has observed, with the evolution of vertebrates from lower animals, whose genetic messages are higher in context-free redundancy (Jeremy Campbell, *Grammatical Man: Information, Entropy, Language, and Life* [New York: Simon & Schuster, 1982], p. 119).

13. Rumelhart, *Information Processing*, p. 122.

14. Ibid., pp. 127, 130.

15. Ibid., pp. 135, 136. The cloze test is based on the 'cloze [closure] procedure' developed by Wilson L. Taylor in the 1950s. Also, Rumelhart is, of course, correct in asserting that other constraints are involved in reading: they are manifold, complex, and only recently being thoroughly investigated – by researchers interested in everything from how semantic intention constrains the 'relative readability' of E. D. Hirsch, Jr, to how various kinds of 'implied readers' (readers as effects of the text) posited by the reader-response theories of Wolfgang Iser and others constrain comprehension. Such investigation demonstrates that reading is no mere passive process of receiving information but a very *active* one characterized by many interlocking interpretive procedures. Like listening, it involves a contstant guessing game (an internal speaking) in which the complexity of the game governs the degree of attention. Like writing, which necessarily involves reading, it is a compositional transaction between reader and text. For a brief survey of representative research, see Joseph J.

Comprone, 'Recent Research in Reading and Its Implications for the College Composition Curriculum', *Rhetoric Review*, 1 (1983), 122–37.
16. Rumelhart, *Information Processing*, pp. 137–8. There seems to be little doubt that both reading and listening involve top-down as well as bottom-up processing. After a review of research concerning closure in reading, E. D. Hirsch, Jr, concludes that

> language processing must entail some kind of reviewing procedure whereby everything must pass by the attention-monitor twice: perceived the first time as a sequence of not yet fully determined linguistic functions and perceived the second time more holistically and definitely as a semantic unit. . . . The maximum accurate reading rate is about 300 words per minute – or about ten syllables per second. This is just one-half our maximum processing rate of twenty times per second, suggesting that the maximum reading rate of even the easiest prose involves a scanning-plus-reviewing procedure through our attention-monitor. . . . Every clause that is read once is probably read twice.   (E. D. Hirsch, Jr, *The Philosophy of Composition* [Chicago, Ill.: University of Chicago Press, 1977], pp. 108–9)

Thus the guessing game of reading, like that of listening, entails anticipatively hypothesizing a whole (for example, the clause) before the consolidation of perceived parts (an act in which subvocalization or even vocal muttering, diminished greatly since Gutenberg, must play a part). The first activity seems to proceed in a mostly top-down fashion and the second in a mostly bottom-up fashion, though both activities probably proceed in fashions that are partly top-down and partly bottom-up and require semantic procedures that are hardly incorporated into a system of the kind discussed by Rumelhart. At any rate, Hirsch's conclusion is one that designers of language-comprehension systems would do well to heed. And it has important implications for the teaching of both reading and writing, for it suggests strongly that reading-comprehension problems have more to do with rereading ('reviewing') what is 'already read' than with reading ('scanning') and that much the same may be true of writing problems, given that the typical composition student is as inept at rereading (and hence revising) his own writing as he is at rereading that of others. Also, perhaps reading deconstructively should be understood, in these terms, as a refinement of rereading, a process attuned to the disjunctions and tensions that arise in comparing the interpretation of what is read to that of what is reread. (Reading is unstable: the monological continually dialogizes.) Indeed, the deconstructionist critic Barbara Johnson avers that 'Literary criticism as such can perhaps be called the art of rereading' (*The Critical Difference: Essays in the Contemporary Rhetoric of Reading* [Baltimore, Md.: Johns Hopkins University Press, 1980], p. 3).
17. Rumelhart, *Information Processing*, p. 146. There is an analogous situation in contemporary composition theory, which has developed some sophisticated ideas about 'syntactic fluency' but few of value

about its semantic counterpart. Recent efforts naïvely to use the former as an index of the latter in the evaluation of writing proficiency have been notably unsuccessful.

Notes to Chapter 18   Semantics, Components, Rapprochement

1. Manfred Bierwisch, 'Semantics', in *New Horizons in Linguistics*, ed. John Lyons (Baltimore, Md.: Penguin Books, 1970), pp. 167, 168. He does not make distinctions among syntax, semantics, and pragmatics as severely as someone like Charles Morris, who sees semantics as being concerned categorically with the relations between signs and their referents (and syntax with those between signs and other signs and pragmatics with those between signs and their users).
2. Ibid., pp. 168, 169, 170.
3. Ibid., pp. 170, 171. Bierwisch's redefinition may be glossed (redefined in turn) in terms of A. J. Greimas's conception of the sememe, here summarized by Jonathan Culler:

> Since the meaning of a lexical item can vary from one context to another, Greimas postulates that the semantic representation of a lexeme consists of an invariant core (*le noyau sémique*), made up of one or more semes [semantic features], and a series of contextual semes, each of which will be manifested only in specific contexts. To determine the semantic composition of a particular lexical item, one considers all the readings or 'semenes' that the lexeme has in a corpus and extracts, as components of the *noyau sémique*, those features shared by all sememes. The variations in meaning are reduced to a series of alternative contextual semes. (Jonathan Culler, *Structuralist Poetics: Structuralism, Linguistics, and the Study of Literature* [Ithaca, N.Y.: Cornell University Press, 1975], p. 77)

4. Bierwisch, 'Semantics', pp. 171–2. There is no doubt that selectional restrictions are functional, in a way of which human beings are generally conscious, in constraining semantic well-formedness in terms of the affinities of semantic components or features. However, those restrictions are regularly violated by processes of figuration (largely, I assume, deep-structural), especially metaphor, without risk to understanding – indeed, usually to its enrichment (precisely *because of* the disjunction of features). Thus, for example, the sentence *That man is a lizard* is not semantically well-formed since the predication involves an equation of *man*, with the intrinsic feature [+human], and *lizard*, with the intrinsic feature [−human]. Any person competent in English would sense the disjunction but would not find the sentence incoherent – in a certain context – and might find it quite informative, though narrowly speaking it is 'ungrammatical'. (See Rosemarie Gläser, 'The Application of Transformational Generative Grammar to the Analysis of Similes and Metaphors in Modern English', *Style*, 5 [1971], 265–83.) This kind of

violation is doubtless responsible, at least in part, for the 'ungrammaticality' that Michael Riffaterre sees as characteristic of poetic semiosis, which proceeds mostly during 'a second reading', the *'retroactive reading* . . . , the truly *hermeneutic* reading' (*Semiotics of Poetry* [Bloomington: Indiana University Press, 1978], pp. 3, 4, 5). Selectional restrictions account for 'ungrammatical' affinities only in a negative and undiscriminating way; the positive characterization of their range in terms of some criteria of 'acceptability' is perhaps no more susceptible to formalization than literary taste.

5. Bierwisch, 'Semantics', pp. 177, 178.
6. See Patrick Hartwell, 'Dialect Interference in Writing: A Critical View', *Research in the Teaching of English*, 14 (1980), 101–18, and Niels A. Lassen, David H. Ingvar, and Erik Skinhøj, 'Brain Function and Blood Flow', *Scientific American*, Oct. 1978, pp. 62–71.
7. Bierwisch, 'Semantics', pp. 178, 179.
8. Ibid., p. 179.
9. Ibid., p. 180.
10. Ibid.
11. Ibid., p. 181.
12. Ibid., pp. 181–2.
13. Ibid., p. 182.
14. Ibid., pp. 182, 183, 184.
15. See *Formal Philosophy: Selected Papers of Richard Montague*, ed. Richmond H. Thomason (New Haven, Conn.: Yale University Press, 1974), or *Montague Grammar*, ed. Barbara H. Partee (New York: Academic Press, 1976).

Notes to Chapter 19   Context, Reference, Schema

1. David E. Rumelhart, *Introduction to Human Information Processing* (New York: Wiley, 1977), p. 153.
2. Ibid., pp. 154, 158.
3. Robert Scholes, *Textual Power: Literary Theory and the Teaching of English* (New Haven, Conn.: Yale University Press, 1985), pp. 92, 94, 97, 85, 20.
4. See Rumelhart, *Information Processing*, pp. 158–60. See also Herbert H. Clark and Susan E. Haviland, 'Comprehension and the Given-New Contract', in *Discourse Production and Comprehension*, ed. Roy O. Freedle (Norwood, N.J.: Ablex, 1977), pp. 1–40. There is some evidence that the cerebral hemispheres divide the given-new task, with the right providing context for information stored in the left. See Jeremy Campbell, *Grammatical Man: Information, Entropy, Language, and Life* (New York: Simon & Schuster, 1982), pp. 248–9.
5. Rumelhart, *Information Processing*, pp. 162, 163. Using Clark's terms, one may see that the progress of discourse is similar to that of walking: walking involves a continual recovery from a forward fall; likewise, discourse continually risks incomprehension in the interpreter by presenting new information but then recovers understanding by turn-

ing it subsequently into given information through repetition of the given-new contract, of the predicational cycle whereby the 'content' of the comment (rheme) is translated into that of the next topic (theme). The process is not merely linear, however, and typically entails a 'spreading activation' whereby 'early' comments are recalled by 'later' topics, simple comments branch into complex and multiple topics, and so on.

6. Ibid., p. 165.
7. Roger C. Schank, 'Identification of Conceptualizations Underlying Natural Language', in *Computer Models of Thought and Language*, ed. Roger C. Schank and Kenneth Mark Colby (San Francisco, Calif.: Freeman, 1973), pp. 191, 192.
8. Rumelhart, *Information Processing*, pp. 165, 167. For a discussion of a slightly different short-story-interpreting program, see Eugene Charniak, *Toward a Model of Children's Story Comprehension*, Report 266 (Cambridge, Mass.: MIT Artifical Intelligence Laboratory, 1972). Charniak's investigation of that 'much more' has led him to be 'distinctly dissatisfied with the ad hoc nature of procedures for making and using text implications' and sceptical about extending them beyond the 'microworld' of his research (Robert F. Simmons, *Computations from the English: A Procedural Logic Approach for Representing and Understanding English Texts* [Englewood Cliffs, N.J.: Prentice-Hall, 1984], p. 8).
9. Rumelhart, *Information Processing*, pp. 167, 168.

Notes to Chapter 20   SHRDLU, Procedures, Mini-World

1. David E. Rumelhart, *Introduction to Human Information Processing* (New York: Wiley, 1977), p. 169.
2. Terry Winograd, *Understanding Natural Language* (New York: Academic Press, 1972), p. 26.
3. Ibid., p. ix. LISP, given its amazing facility for recursion, embedding, and manipulability, is a nearly ideal language for such programs. Developed in the late 1950s by John McCarthy, it is now the language of choice for AI and expert systems and has evolved to include the capabilities of an ultrahigh-level language: programs written in it are structured lists that can modify themselves, process one another as data, and so on. Still, it is surely only a precursor to a more powerful AI language and in some applications has been succeeded by PROLOG.
4. Ibid., pp. 23–4, 80.
5. Ibid., pp. 26–7.
6. Ibid., pp. 28, 29.
7. Ibid., p. 30. Relational databases, now in theoretical vogue but quite expensive to implement, also manifest a blur between procedures and data, one that is germane to Winograd's approach: processing that uses such databases can generate *new* information by juxtaposing files. If words could be represented as files, could not one then

construct a powerful relational (and poststructuralist?) grammar in terms of their possible juxtapositions?

8. Terry Winograd, 'A Procedural Model of Language Understanding', in *Computer Models of Thought and Language*, ed. Roger C. Schank and Kenneth Mark Colby (San Francisco, Calif.: Freeman, 1973), p. 170.

9. Winograd, *Understanding*, p. 31.

10. Douglas R. Hofstadter, *Gödel, Escher, Bach: An Eternal Golden Braid* (New York: Basic Books, 1973), p. 631.

11. Winograd, *Understanding*, pp. 31–2.

12. Ibid., pp. 32, 33.

13. Ibid., p. 40.

14. Ibid., pp. 40, 41, 89. Winograd's awareness of the limitations of procedural representations and of the blurred distinction between procedures and data has caused him to become interested in 'procedureless' or 'nonprocedural' languages in which control structures are implicitly incorporated into data-structures. See his 'Beyond Programming Languages', *Communications of the ACM*, 22 (1979), p. 399.

15. See, for example, Winograd, *Understanding*, pp. 8–15. None the less, it is sobering to realize, in regard to Dennett's earlier consideration of homunculi, that one of the most seemingly human responses from SHRDLU, 'BECAUSE YOU ASKED ME TO' (p. 13), is

> an example of how homuncular communications may fall short. . . . The context of production and the function of the utterance makes clear that this is a sophisticated communication and the product of a sophisticated representation, but it is not a full-fledged Gricean speech act. If it were, it would require too fancy a homunculus to use it'. (Dennett, *Brainstorms: Philosophical Essays on Mind and Psychology* [Montgomery, Vt.: Bradford Books, 1978], p. 124)

16. Winograd, 'Procedural Model', p. 183. One must be wary of being overly or inappropriately impressed by SHRDLU. Winograd has *not* created 'an English speaker and understander that is psychologically realistic at many different levels of analysis', but he has engaged some important problems and 'proposed ingenious and plausible *partial* solutions to them' – an achievement that 'stands quite unimpeached by the perfectly true but irrelevant charge that SHRDLU doesn't have a *rich* or human understanding of most of the words in its very restricted vocabulary, or is terribly slow' (Dennett, *Brainstorms*, p. 117).

17. Winograd, 'Procedural Model', p. 183. These limitations are exemplary of many that generally characterize AI systems and indicate that 'what artificial intelligence needs is a way to go beyond "delta function" programs: programs that are virtuosos in a very narrow domain but that have no flexibility or adaptability or tolerance for errors' (Douglas R. Hofstadter, 'Metamagical Themas', *Scientific American*, Sep. 1981, p. 30).

18. Winograd, 'Procedural Model', p. 184.

19. Ibid., pp. 185, 186. In simplest terms the problem of common sense in a system like SHRDLU is the severely limited extent to which it 'knows', as human beings know 'commonsensically', what it is 'talking about' – an astonishingly knotty conundrum of context discussed in David L. Waltz, 'Artificial Intelligence', *Scientific American*, Oct. 1982, pp. 118–33. Apparently this problem and others related to it (concerning constraints on syntactic analysis, the inherent metaphoricity of language, the formalization of context, the ineptitude of so-called co-ordinator systems in responding to speech acts) have recently tempered Winograd's already qualified optimism. See his 'Computer Software for Working with Language', *Scientific American*, Sep. 1984, pp. 130–45.

20. Winograd, 'Procedural Model', p. 154.
21. Hofstadter, *Gödel, Escher, Bach*, p. 628.
22. Winograd, 'Procedural Model', p. 175.
23. Hofstadter, *Gödel, Escher, Bach*, pp. 629–30.

Notes to Chapter 21   Correspondence, MARGIE, Concept

1. Roger C. Schank and Kenneth Mark Colby, Preface, *Computer Models of Thought and Language*, ed. Roger C. Schank and Kenneth Mark Colby (San Francisco, Calif.: Freeman, 1973), pp. vii, viii. Dennett has a relevant caveat about the casting of theories as programs:

> paying so much attention to the performance of SHRDLU (and similar systems) reveals a failure to recognize that AI programs are not *empirical* experiments but *thought*-experiments prosthetically regulated by computers. . . . Are computers . . . irrelevant to AI? 'In principle' they are irrelevant . . ., but in practice they are not. . . . computer simulation *forces* one to recognize all the costs of one's imagined design. (Daniel C. Dennett, *Brainstorms: Philosophical Essays on Mind and Psychology* [Montgomery, Vt.: Bradford Books, 1978], pp. 117–18)

2. Roger C. Schank, 'Identification of Conceptualizations Underlying Natural Language', in *Computer Models*, ed. Schank and Colby, p. 187.
3. Ibid., pp. 187, 188. This mapping has been variously schematized, though not in much psychological detail, by a number of contemporary rhetorical theorists. Most of them have been inspired by Frank J. D'Angelo's conceptual theory of rhetoric, which is inventional (in its pedagogical orientation) and builds upon hypotheses (derived from the work of Wolfgang Köhler, Donald O. Hebb, and others) that echo and, sometimes incautiously, extend beyond Schank's. Among them are the following:

> Rhetorical patterns [Aristotelian *topoi* and so on] could not be produced in speech or in writing unless they were based on underlying mental processes. . . . The structural properties which underlie our mental operations must be genetically inherited. In

generating discourse, the individual uses this underlying, abstract structure as a base. Then he supports this structure by filling in the details from the universe of discourse around him. . . . When they appear in discourse, these structural characteristics manifest themselves as grammatical patterns and as conceptual patterns. . . . A concept . . . has no objective reality. It is identical with the process of conceptualizing. . . . Words . . . represent and mediate concepts. (Frank J. D'Angelo, *A Conceptual Theory of Rhetoric* [Cambridge, Mass.: Winthrop, 1975], pp. 26, 28, 31)

4. Schank, 'Identification', pp. 189, 190.
5. Ibid., p. 192.
6. Ibid. Among such dependencies, I would suggest, might be included those involved in conceptual creativity, the generation of concepts by concepts or conceptualizations by conceptualizations, as in Kleist's *'allmähliche Verfertigung der Gedanken beim Reden'*. The inclusion of a generative dependency might advantageously qualify Schank's befuddled distinction.
7. Ibid., p. 194.
8. Ibid., pp. 228–9.
9. Ibid., pp. 232, 236.
10. Ibid., p. 242.
11. Margaret A. Boden, *Artificial Intelligence and Natural Man* (New York: Basic Books, 1977), pp. 150, 152, 153.
12. Ibid., pp. 155, 154, 155.
13. Ibid., pp. 156, 157.
14. Ibid., p. 158. Concerning M. Ross Quillian's point, see his 'Semantic Memory', in *Semantic Information Processing*, ed. Marvin L. Minsky (Cambridge, Mass.: MIT Press, 1968), pp. 227–70.
15. Boden, *Artificial Intelligence*, pp. 159, 160. Boden's argument has obvious bearing on a bedevilling problem in AI research, the 'frame problem'. (A *frame* is variously defined as a 'conceptual schema', an 'internal world-model', or an 'epistemological representation'. For an extended but naïve discussion of the notion, see Marvin L. Minsky, 'A Framework for Representing Knowledge', in *The Psychology of Computer Vision*, ed. Patrick Henry Winston [New York: McGraw-Hill, 1975], pp. 211–77.) It may be described as follows:

The frame problem is an abstract *epistemological* problem that was in effect discovered by AI thought-experimentation. When a cognitive creature, an entity with many beliefs about the world, performs an act, the world changes and many of the creature's beliefs must be revised or updated. How? It cannot be that we perceive and notice *all* the changes (for one thing, many of the changes we *know* to occur do not occur in our perceptual fields), and hence it cannot be that we rely entirely on perceptual input to revise our beliefs. So we must have internal ways of up-dating our beliefs that will fill in the gaps. . . . If one supposes, as philosophers traditionally have, that one's beliefs are a set of propositions, and reasoning is inference or deduction from members of the set, one is in for trouble, for it is quite clear (though still controversial) that systems relying only on such processes get swamped by combinatorial explosions in the updating effort. It seems that our entire conception of belief and reasoning must be radically revised if we are to explain the undeniable capacity of human beings to keep their beliefs roughly consonant with the reality they live in. (Dennett, *Brainstorms*, pp. 125–6)

16. Boden, *Artificial Intelligence*, pp. 160, 163.

Notes to Chapter 22   Flexibility, Networks, Maps

1. Eric Wanner and Michael Maratsos, 'An ATN Approach to Comprehension', in *Linguistic Theory and Psychological Reality*, ed. Morris Halle, Joan Bresnan, and George A. Miller (Cambridge, Mass.: MIT Press, 1978), p. 120.
2. R. F. Simmons, 'Semantic Networks: Their Computation and Use for Understanding English Sentences', in *Computer Models of Thought and Language*, ed. Roger C. Schank and Kenneth Mark Colby (San Francisco, Calif.: Freeman, 1973), p. 63.
3. Ibid., p. 64.
4. Ibid., pp. 64, 65.
5. Ibid., pp. 65, 66.
6. Ibid., p. 66.
7. Ibid., pp. 66, 67.
8. Ibid., p. 67.
9. Ibid., p. 70.
10. Ibid., p. 78.
11. Ibid., pp. 78, 80.
12. Ibid., pp. 80, 81.
13. Ibid., p. 82.
14. Ibid., p. 106.
15. Ibid., p. 108.

Notes to Chapter 23   MT, Linguistics, Logic

1. Ludwig Wittgenstein, *Zettel*, ed. G. E. M. Anscombe and G. H. von Wright, trans. G. E. M. Anscombe (Berkeley and Los Angeles: University of California Press, 1967), p. 121. Because of this 'joke' many now speak not of MT but only – and more humbly – of CAT (computer-aided translation).
2. Yorick Wilks, 'An Artificial Intelligence Approach to Machine Translation', in *Computer Models of Thought and Language*, ed. Roger C. Schank and Kenneth Mark Colby (San Francisco, Calif.: Freeman, 1973), pp. 114, 115.
3. Ibid., p. 115.

4. Ibid., p. 116.
5. Ibid., pp. 116, 118–19.
6. Ibid., p. 119.

Notes to Chapter 24   Interlingua, Thesaurus, Deduction

1. Yorick Wilks, 'An Artificial Intelligence Approach to Machine Translation', in *Computer Models of Thought and Language*, ed. Roger C. Schank and Kenneth Mark Colby (San Francisco, Calif.: Freeman, 1973), pp. 121, 122.
2. Ibid., p. 122.
3. Ibid., pp. 123, 124.
4. Ibid., pp. 142–3.
5. Margaret A. Boden, *Artificial Intelligence and Natural Man* (New York: Basic Books, 1977), p. 166.
6. Ibid., pp. 170–1, 316.
7. Ibid., p. 171.
8. Ibid., pp. 172–3, 174, 175.

Notes to Chapter 25   Translation, Universals, *Mystère*

1. George Steiner, *After Babel: Aspects of Language and Translation* (New York: Oxford University Press, 1975), pp. 8–9.
2. Ibid., pp. 28, 31, 45, 47. It is interesting to note, in regard to Steiner's last dictum here, that composition theorists have come to realize that, because of the kind and extent of differences between spoken and written languages, learning to write is a good deal like learning to speak a foreign language: in both cases the learner first translates, in Steiner's terms, 'between' the old language and the new one and only later assimilates the code of the new one sufficiently to translate 'inside' it.
3. Ibid., pp. 47, 45–6.
4. Ibid., pp. 47, 103–4.
5. Ibid., p. 195.
6. See Allan Calder, 'Constructive Mathematics', *Scientific American*, Oct. 1979, pp. 146–71.
7. Steiner, *After Babel*, pp. 105, 106. Bickerton's research on creole languages would seem to argue for universals that are not only more 'substantive' but also more 'specific' than any posited by Chomsky. His line of investigation, if followed far enough, may lead to a resolution of the uncertainty Steiner finds in Chomsky's theory. Bickerton acknowledges that Chomsky's arguments concerning an innate universal grammar are persuasive and supported by the studies of Eric H. Lenneberg; however, he also disagrees on one key point. He characterizes Chomsky's grammar as 'a computing device, somehow realized neurologically, that makes a wide range of grammatical models available to the child', who 'must then "select"

which of the available grammatical models matches the grammar of the language into which the child is born', but he argues that 'The evidence from creole languages suggests that first-language acquisition is mediated by an innate device of a rather different kind. Instead of making a range of grammatical models available, the device provides the child with a single and fairly specific grammatical model' (Derek Bickerton, 'Creole Languages', *Scientific American*, July 1983, p. 121).

8. Steiner, *After Babel*, pp. 106–7, 233–4.
9. Ibid., pp. 61, 110–11.
10. Ibid., pp. 111, 112, 113.
11. Ibid., pp. 113, 114.
12. Ibid., pp. 120, 128, 124, 125.

Notes to Chapter 26   Wiring, Conundrums, Topology

1. George Steiner, *After Babel: Aspects of Language and Translation* (New York: Oxford University Press, 1975), pp. 126–7.
2. Ibid., pp. 127, 128.
3. Ibid., pp. 199, 203, 202, 407, 204.
4. Ibid., pp. 221, 241, 249, 281.
5. Ibid., p. 284.
6. Ibid., pp. 288, 425, 426.

Notes to Chapter 27   Meaning, Discourse, Speech Act

1. George Steiner, *After Babel: Aspects of Language and Translation* (New York: Oxford University Press, 1975), p. 375. Aristotle's ἑρμηνεία is etymologically associated with the messenger-god Hermes as mediator between the known and the unknown who renders the unfamiliar intelligible. Verbal language seems to be particularly subject to the interpretive wavering between the known and the unknown, the revealed and the concealed – the interplay of text and context, figure and ground. Also, on Nietzsche's prototypically deconstructionist notion, see his *Wille zur Macht* and 'Über Wahrheit und Lüge im aussermoralischen Sinne'.
2. Samuel Guttenplan, Introduction, *Mind and Language: Wolfson College Lectures 1974*, ed. Samuel Guttenplan (Oxford: Clarendon Press, 1975), p. 5.
3. M. A. K. Halliday and Ruqaiya Hasan, *Cohesion in English* (London: Longman, 1976), pp. 1, 2, 4. The idea that a text as a unit of discourse (regarded by some as, like the utterance, a unit of *communication*) is different from a sentence is defensible and currently fashionable, but it is not unproblematic, especially in so far as it seems to be hardening into dogma. A text surely does differ from a sentence (and smaller syntactic structures); yet there are also similarities between them, as is persuasively demonstrated in Joseph E. Grimes, *The Thread of Discourse* (The Hague: Mouton, 1975), a work that also offers many

insights about discursive structures in languages other than English
that should sober anyone intent on making global generalizations
about texts on the basis of studies restricted to English.
4. Halliday and Hasan, *Cohesion in English*, pp. 10, 14, 25.
5. Ibid., pp. 27, 28. The lack of a thoroughgoing discourse grammar (or
text grammar) continues critically to limit the self-confidence of the
student of natural language. The necrology of theories that pretend
to deal with the problem grows annually. None of them – even those
based on the powerful generalities of extended tagmemic theory
(based on Kenneth L. Pike's emic approach to the study of language)
that once showed such promise – has proven adequate. James L.
Kinneavy, in his *Theory of Discourse: The Aims of Discourse* (Englewood
Cliffs, N.J.: Prentice-Hall, 1971), offers an admirable attempt, erudite
both historically and taxonomically, at describing and classifying
certain rhetorical aspects of the text, but his work does not deal
with grammatical issues and is also, with its beige positivism,
metaphysically naïve.
6. See Teun van Dijk: *Text and Context* (London: Longman, 1977), esp.
pp. 93–129; 'Text Grammar and Text Logic', in *Studies in Text
Grammar*, ed. J. S. Petöfi and H. Rieser (Dordrecht, Holland: Reidel,
1973), pp. 17–78 (an engaging consideration of the 'natural logic' of
the text); and *Some Aspects of Text Grammars* (The Hague: Mouton, 1972).
7. Anne E. Doyle, 'The Limits of Cohesion', in 'Notes and Comments',
Research in the Teaching of English, 16 (1982), 391.
8. Ibid., pp. 392–3. The quotations are from Robert de Beaugrande,
Text, Discourse and Process: Toward a Multidisciplinary Science of Texts
(Norwood, N.J.: Ablex, 1980), pp. 133, 77. See also – for an eclectic
overview of research on text dynamics, ATN-based simulation, and
other relvant matters – Robert de Beaugrande and Wolfgang Ulrich
Dressler, *Introduction to Text Linguistics*, updated and trans. Robert de
Beaugrande (New York: Longman, 1981).
9. See Thomas A. Sebeok, *The Sign and Its Masters* (Austin: University of
Texas Press, 1979), pp. viii, x.
10. Charles Morris, *Signification and Significance: A Study of the Relations of
Signs and Values* (Cambridge, Mass.: MIT Press, 1964), pp. 2, 3. The
reader should be aware that *interpretant* is one of the most slippery
words in semiotic theory. It may be used, of course, as Morris uses
it, but it may also be used to mean the 'interpreter', the 'response to
(effect of, meaning of) a sign', and the 'sign or set of signs that
interprets another sign'. It is used by Peirce, as Tzvetan Todorov
observes, in both of these last two senses: 'In the broad sense, the
interpretant is thus the meaning of the sign; in a narrower sense, it is
the paradigmatic relation between one sign and another [cf. Saussure's
notion of "value"]. The interpretant is thus always also a sign, which
will have its interpretant, and so on . . .' ('Semiotics', in Oswald
Ducrot and Tzvetan Todorov, *Encyclopedic Dictionary of the Sciences of
Language*, trans. Catherine Porter [Baltimore, Md.: Johns Hopkins
University Press, 1979], p. 85).
11. Morris, *Signification and Significance*, p. 9.

12. Louis Hjelmslev, *Prolegomena to a Theory of Language*, trans. Francis J. Whitfield (Madison: University of Wisconsin Press, 1961), pp. 34, 44, 45.

13. Paul Ricoeur, 'Structure, Word, Event', trans. Robert D. Sweeney, *Philosophy Today*, 12 (1968), 116, 117.

14. Ibid., pp. 118, 119.

15. Ibid., pp. 119.

16. Ibid., pp. 120–1, 123. Ricoeur's counter-presupposition that discourse 'consists in a series of choices' for selecting and excluding meanings, which obviously shimmers with implications for the modeller, is parallel to André Martinet's notion that communicative intention determines the 'monemes', the elementary lexical and grammatical choices, that constitute the message (see his 'Choix du locuteur', *Revue Philosophique*, 91 [1966], 271–82). Also, I should point out that Frege's distinction between *Sinn* and *Bedeutung* (which correspond more or less to Saussure's signified and referent) is preserved by a number of later writers, like Ricoeur, but sometimes in ways that are terminologically troubling. In his discussion of poetic texts, Riffaterre, for example, distinguishes between *significance* (the 'formal and semantic unity of the text') and *meaning* (the 'information conveyed by the text at the mimetic level') in a way that generally parallels Frege's distinction (Michael Riffaterre, *Semiotics of Poetry* [Bloomington: Indiana University Press, 1978], pp. 2, 3), but then Jean-Paul Sartre reverses the definitions of the two words (see his *Saint Genet: comédien et martyr* [Paris: Gallimard, 1952], p. 283). I tend to conflate them into *meaning*, though I appreciate the usefulness of the distinction – provided its problematic aspects are not forgotten.

17. Ricoeur, 'Structure, Word, Event', pp. 125, 126.

18. Paul Ricoeur, 'Creativity in Language: Word, Polysemy, Metaphor', trans. David Pellauer, *Philosophy Today*, 17 (1973), 97, 98.

19. Ibid., pp. 98, 99.

20. Ibid., pp. 99–100.

21. Ibid., pp. 101, 109, 102.

22. Ludwig Wittgenstein, *Zettel*, ed. G. E. M. Anscombe and G. H. von Wright, trans. G. E. M. Anscombe (Berkeley and Los Angeles: University of California Press, 1967), p. 43.

23. Ricoeur, 'Creativity', pp. 103, 104.

24. Ibid., pp. 104, 105.

25. John R. Searle, *Speech Acts: An Essay in the Philosophy of Language* (New York: Cambridge University Press, 1969), pp. 16, 17.

26. Ibid., pp. 19, 24, 25. There are various classifications for the kinds or 'dimensions' of speech acts. Cf. the slightly different one in Gerald Gazdar, *Pragmatics* (New York: Academic Press, 1978), pp. 5–18.

27. Searle, *Speech Acts*, pp. 42, 43–44.

28. Ibid., pp. 45, 48.

29. See, for example, John R. Searle, 'The Myth of the Computer', review of *The Mind's I: Fantasies and Reflections on Self and Soul*, composed and arranged by Douglas R. Hofstadter and Daniel C. Dennett, *New York Review of Books*, 29 Apr. 1982, pp. 3–6. Searle's

antipathies are more fully detailed in his *Minds, Brains and Science* (London: BBC Publications, 1984).

30. Rodolphe Gasché, '"Setzung" and "Übersetzung": Notes on Paul de Man', review of *Allegories of Reading: Figural Language in Rousseau, Nietzsche, Rilke, and Proust* by Paul de Man, *Diacritics*, 11 (1981), 39.

31. Searle's position seems especially ironic in view of Simmons's argument that his formulations 'have definite practical implications for natural-language processing programs' (Robert F. Simmons, *Computations from the English: A Procedural Logic Approach for Representing and Understanding English Texts* [Englewood Cliffs, N.J.: Prentice-Hall, 1984], p. 10). See also Barbara Johnson, *The Critical Difference: Essays in the Contemporary Rhetoric of Reading* (Baltimore, Md.: Johns Hopkins University Press, 1980), pp. 52–66. She, like Gasché, has applied to Austin's work the kind of Nietzschean strategy that dramatizes its revolutionary implications concerning reflexivity:

> if a performative utterance is originally a self-referential speech act, its production is simultaneously the production of a new referent into the world. This, however, is tantamount to a radical transformation of the notion of a referent, since, instead of pointing to an external object, language would then refer only to its own referring to itself in the act of referring, and the signifying chain would end in an infinitely self-duplicating loop. . . . The performative utterance is thus the *mise en abyme* ['placing in abyss', a term from heraldry] of reference itself. (p. 57)

I should note, in this regard, that some transformational grammarians argue that even nonperformative utterances are originally objects of performative verbs in the deep structure that are deleted in the surface structure. If that is somehow so, then all utterances would be performative and, following Johnson's argument, thereby self-referential. Such a possible result would have profound implications both for modellers and for deconstructionists seeking psycholinguistic sanctions for the interplay of the stated and the implicit, the grammatical and the rhetorical, the textual and the paratextual, and so on – all the processes of the text as an unstable hendiadys.

Notes to Chapter 28   Wittgenstein, Use, Functionalism

1. K. T. Fann, *Wittgenstein's Conception of Philosophy* (Berkeley and Los Angeles: University of California Press, 1971), pp. 63, 68.

2. Ibid., pp. 71, 70. This notion somewhat parallels the poststructuralist one that interpretation involves never a recovery of an absolute meaning but a play of possible meanings, that the text is always plural.

3. Ludwig Wittgenstein, *Zettel*, ed. G. E. M. Anscombe and G. H. von Wright, trans. G. E. M. Anscombe (Berkeley and Los Angeles: University of California Press, 1967), p. 32.

4. Geoffrey H. Hartman, 'The Culture of Criticism', *Publications of the Modern Language Association*, 99 (1984), 374, 386.
5. See, for example, Aaron Sloman, *The Computer Revolution in Philosophy: Philosophy, Science and Models of Mind* (Atlantic Highlands, N.J.: Humanities Press, 1978).
6. J. Z. Young, *Programs of the Brain* (New York: Oxford University Press, 1978), p. 295.
7. Wittgenstein, *Zettel*, p. 78.
8. Joseph Weizenbaum, *Computer Power and Human Reason: From Judgment to Calculation* (San Francisco, Calif.: Freeman, 1976), pp. 68, 97, 250.

Notes to Chapter 29   Entropy, Readiness, Probability

1. Philip C. Jackson, Jr, *Introduction to Artificial Intelligence* (New York: Petrocelli Books, 1974), pp. 274, 332.
2. Ibid., pp. 275, 281, 292, 294.
3. Donald M. MacKay, *Information, Mechanism and Meaning* (Cambridge, Mass.: MIT Press, 1969), pp. 10, 11, 13, 16–17. Actually there is another distinction in regard to MacKay's equating information and negative entropy: whereas energy cannot be created or destroyed, information can. Campbell uses this distinction to argue against deterministic models of the brain (like Freud's) and warns that one must be careful not to confuse energy and information transactions (see Jeremy Campbell, *Grammatical Man: Information, Entropy, Language, and Life* [New York: Simon and Schuster, 1982], p. 195). See also Michel Serres, 'The Origin of Language: Biology, Information Theory, and Thermodynamics', trans. Mark Anderson, in *Hermes: Literature, Science, Philosophy*, ed. Josué V. Harari and David F. Bell (Baltimore, Md.: Johns Hopkins University Press, 1982), p. 81, where he discusses writing the 'energy account' and the 'information account' of the system of a machine and that of a living organism. He argues that the complexity, miniaturization, and number of elements in the latter 'bring these two accounts closer and make them comparable', whereas in the case of the former 'the information account is negligible in relationship to the energy account . . .'. However, recent innovations in the theory of 'quantum-mechanical computers' appear to question such a comparison – see Charles H. Bennett and Rolf Landauer, 'The Fundamental Physical Limits of Computation', *Scientific American*, July 1985, p. 55.
4. MacKay, *Information*, pp. 19, 20, 21.
5. Ibid., pp. 22, 23, 24.
6. Campbell, *Grammatical Man*, pp. 160, 163. See Noam Chomsky, 'On the Nature of Language', *Annals of the New York Academy of Sciences*, 280 (1976), 46–57.
7. Josué V. Harari and David F. Bell, 'Introduction: Journal à plusieurs voies', in Serres, *Hermes*, p. xxxvii.
8. MacKay, *Information*, p. 26. The signal-box analogy suggests that all discourse is persuasive (its purpose, so to speak, is to set the

314 *Notes*

receiver's switches to match the configuration of the sender's). It is thus a kind of mechanistic version of Kenneth Burke's dramatistic doctrine of consubstantiality (see his *Rhetoric of Motives* [Berkeley and Los Angeles: University of California Press, 1969], pp. 20–3 *et passim*). The suggestion is ancient really and is certainly consonant with Gorgias' notion, as expounded in his *Helen*, of rhetoric as the art of using language to shape the psyche.
9. MacKay, *Information*, pp. 26, 28, 27–8, 30, 35, 41.
10. Ibid., pp. 42, 44–5, 47, 48, 49.
11. Ibid., pp. 49, 50, 51, 52.
12. Ibid., pp. 52, 53, 54.
13. Ibid., pp. 61, 72, 78, 77, 90–1, 84–5.

Notes to Chapter 30   Percept, Label, Core

1. George A. Miller and Philip N. Johnson-Laird, *Language and Perception* (Cambridge, Mass.: Harvard University Press, Belknap Press, 1976), p. 112.
2. Ibid., pp. 116, 118.
3. Ibid., pp. 124, 123–4, 164, 165.
4. Ibid., pp. 165–6, 167. I should remark here, in regard to both Miller and Johnson-Laird's compiler analogy and my own, that some of the functions involved may turn out to be like those of a compiler compiler or even a compiler compiler compiler – if the reader can imagine such functions. See Brian Hayes, 'Computer Recreations', *Scientific American*, Dec. 1983, p. 27.
5. Miller and Johnson-Laird, *Language and Perception*, p. 169.
6. Ibid., pp. 267–8.
7. Ibid., pp. 270, 291, 300–1.
8. Ibid., pp. 327, 328.
9. John R. Anderson, *Language, Memory, and Thought* (Hillsdale, N.J.: Erlbaum, 1976), p. 5.
10. Miller and Johnson-Laird, *Language and Perception*, pp. 372–3.
11. Ibid., pp. 702, 703.
12. Ibid., pp. 705, 706, 707.

Notes to Chapter 31   Isomorphism, Decipherment, Symbol

1. Douglas R. Hofstadter, *Gödel, Escher, Bach: An Eternal Golden Braid* (New York: Basic Books, 1979), pp. 49, 50.
2. Ibid., pp. 50–1, 52, 294, 53, 82.
3. Ibid., pp. 100–1, 159, 160. The metaphor of the cell as a manufacturing machine under the control of the DNA 'tape' recalls von Neumann's theorizations about such a machine that predate by several years the discovery of DNA. Also, Hofstadter's consideration of the implicitness of the 'meaning contained in the DNA' recalls the distinction, in regard to Winograd's work, between declarative and procedural

knowledge, for the 'knowledge' of the DNA, as Hofstadter conceives it, is declarative in nature. It is a distinction that, as he more recently observes, 'should remind biologists of the distinction between genes, which are relatively inert structures inside the cell, and enzymes, which are anything but inert' (Douglas R. Hofstadter, 'Metamagical Themas', *Scientific American*, Apr. 1983, p. 26).

4. Hofstadter, *Gödel, Escher, Bach*, pp. 166, 167, 169.
5. Ibid., pp. 170, 171.
6. Ibid., p. 267.
7. Ibid., pp. 337–8.
8. Ibid., 340, 343.
9. Ibid., pp. 347, 350, 349, 350.
10. Ibid., pp. 351, 350, 359, 356, 358, 359.
11. Ibid., pp. 360, 363, 371.
12. Ibid., pp. 575–7.
13. Ibid., p. 582.

Notes to Chapter 32 Formalism, Recursion, Gödel

1. Douglas R. Hofstadter, *Gödel, Escher, Bach: An Eternal Golden Braid* (New York: Basic Books, 1979), pp. 46, 17, 26. See Kurt Gödel, 'Über formal unentscheidbare Sätze der Principia Mathematica and verwandter Systeme, I,' *Monatshefte für Mathematik und Physik*, 38 (1931), 173–98, of which a good English version is *On Formally Undecidable Propositions of 'Principia Mathematica' and Related Systems*, trans. B. Meltzer (New York: Basic Books, 1962). A useful introduction to Gödel's thought is Nagel Muzzio and James R. Newman, *Gödel's Proof* (New York: New York University Press, 1958). Also, it is interesting, at the beginning of these Gödelian considerations, to ponder the extent to which deconstruction theory is shot with informal notions about undecidability and blind spots (see Paul de Man, *Blindness and Insight: Essays in the Rhetoric of Contemporary Criticism* [New York: Oxford University Press, 1971], *passim*) that have a Gödelian flavour. The deconstructionist is concerned with analysing how a text differs from (deconstructs) itself, is undecidable – a consequence of the action of the trace that makes impossible and illusory a univocal and closed reading. (And, of course, this situation does not pertain exclusively to texts that are, in the ordinary sense, written.) That undecidability involves a dialogical aporia of tropical play, an oscillation that may be variously codified (between declaration and description, textual closure/completeness and openness/incompleteness, grammatical weaving and rhetorical unravelling, and so on) and that is occasioned by the 'hole(s)' in what would otherwise seem to be a totalized text. Johnson, for instance, adduces a Gödelian (almost meta-Gödelian) sense of a text when she speaks of its 'oscillation between unequivocal statements of undecidability and ambiguous assertions of decidability' (Barbara Johnson, *The Critical Difference: Essays in the Contemporary Rhetoric of*

Reading [Baltimore, Md.: Johns Hopkins University Press, 1980], p. 146). (By the same logic, of course, the deconstructive reading that reveals such oscillation harbours the deconstructive reading of itself.)
2. Hofstadter, *Gödel, Escher, Bach*, pp. 53–4.
3. Ibid., pp. 60, 142, 145, 152. Heinz von Foerster characterizes 'cognitive processes as never-ending recursive processes of computation' ('On Constructing a Reality', in *The Invented Reality*, ed. Paul Watzlawick [New York: Norton, 1984], p. 49).
4. Hofstadter, *Gödel, Escher, Bach*, p. 302.
5. J. R. Lucas, 'Minds, Machines and Gödel', *Philosophy*, 36 (1961), 116.
6. Ibid., pp. 112, 113, 116, 117, 120, 121.
7. Ibid., pp. 125–6.
8. Hofstadter, *Gödel, Escher, Bach*, pp. 101, 470, 476. See also Daniel C. Dennett, *Brainstorms: Philosophical Essays on Mind and Psychology* (Montgomery, Vt.: Bradford Books, 1978), pp. 256–66. For a parallel argument concerning the Gödelian structure of the human nervous system, see Francisco J. Varela, 'The Creative Circle: Sketches on the Natural History of Circularity', in *Invented Reality*, ed. Watzlawick, p. 318.
9. See Margaret A. Boden, *Artificial Intelligence and Natural Man* (New York: Basic Books, 1977), pp. 434–41.
10. Hofstadter, *Gödel, Escher, Bach*, pp. 477, 478. See also Varela, 'Creative Circle', p. 320. Let me emphasize that Derrida, in trying, somewhat like Einstein grappling with the 'overriding system' of traditional physics, to open a different level of discourse – in his case metaphysical – can do that necessarily only in an emic fashion, within the system of ethnocentric Western metaphysics that he finds in place (in both his culture and himself). Indeed, 'Deconstruction has made us cautious about postulating a *topos noetos* (mind place), or logocentric vantage point. . . . There is no resting or reference point inside or outside language on which to set the Archimedean lever that would control the system' (Geoffrey H. Hartman, 'The Culture of Criticism', *Publications of the Modern Language Association*, 99 [1984], 387). He can, in other words, write the description of logocentric metaphysics only in terms of its declaration; there is no other system into which he can 'loop up' – any more than the reader can get outside the text to the transcendental signified or absolute presence. This situation accounts, in part at least, for the stylistic contortions of his thought/writing: he, like Nietzsche, is twisting language back on itself, trying in bootstrap fashion to wrench from it a seemingly impossible metalanguage.

Notes to Chapter 33 Loops, Self-Reference, Substrates

1. Douglas R. Hofstadter, *Gödel, Escher, Bach: An Eternal Golden Braid* (New York: Basic Books, 1979), pp. 502, 518–19, 531, 532.
2. Ibid., pp. 532, 533, 534, 10.
3. Ibid., pp. 547–8.

4. Ibid., p. 559.
5. Martin Gardner, review of *Gödel, Escher, Bach* by Hofstadter, in 'Mathematical Games', *Scientific American*, July 1979, pp. 22, 20. His observations are consonant with the generalization that, as Gödel demonstrated, systems grow in self-referentiality as they grow in complexity.
6. Hofstadter, *Gödel, Escher, Bach*, pp. 561, 562, 568.
7. Ibid., pp. 569, 570–1.
8. Ibid., p. 572. The functionalist theory involved here, like 'every cognitivist theory currently defended or envisaged, functionalist or not', is generally restricted to what Dennett calls 'the sub-personal level', a restriction that carries with it an implication of which the reader should be aware:

> the very feature that has been seen to recommend functionalism over cruder brands of materialism – its abstractness and hence neutrality with regard to what could 'realize' the functions deemed essential to sentient or intentional systems – permits a functionalist theory, however realistically biological or humanoid in flavor, to be instantiated not only by robots . . ., but by suprahuman organizations that would seem to have minds of their own only in the flimsiest metaphorical sense. (Daniel C. Dennett, *Brainstorms: Philosophical Essays on Mind and Psychology* [Montgomery, Vt.: Bradford Books, 1978], p. 153)

9. Hofstadter, *Gödel, Escher, Bach*, pp. 578–9, 584.
10. Ibid., pp. 686, 691, 692, 709.

Notes to Chapter 34 Disagreements, Problems, Possibilities

1. Philip C. Jackson, Jr, *Introduction to Artificial Intelligence* (New York: Petrocelli Books, 1974), p. 339.
2. Joseph Weizenbaum, *Computer Power and Human Reason: From Judgment to Calculation* (San Francisco, Calif.: Freeman, 1976), pp. 142, 145, 149, 200. Since formalization is a kind of translation, one might compare this argument to Derrida's (in his 'Des Tours de Babel', trans. Joseph F. Graham, in *Difference in Translation*, ed. and intro. Joseph F. Graham [Ithaca, N.Y.: Cornell University Press, 1985]) that 'There is . . . something like an internal limit to formalization, an incompletenes of the constructure. It would be easy and up to a point justified to see there the translation of a system in deconstruction' (p. 166).
3. Jacob Bronowski, *The Origins of Knowledge and Imagination* (New Haven, Conn.: Yale University Press, 1978), p. 103.
4. Jacob Bronowski, *A Sense of the Future: Essays in Natural Philosophy*, ed. Piero E. Ariotti with Rita Bronowski (Cambridge, Mass.: MIT Press, 1977), pp. 56, 57, 60, 61.
5. George A. Miller and Philip N. Johnson-Laird, *Language and Perception*

(Cambridge, Mass.: Harvard University Press, Belknap Press, 1976), pp. 270, 693.

6. Janet Dean Fodor, 'Formal Linguistics and Formal Logic', in *New Horizons in Linguistics*, ed. John Lyons (Baltimore, Md.: Penguin Books, 1970), pp. 199, 202, 207, 214. I should point out that there has been an attempt to formulate theorematically some such 'precise and explicit translation rules' by means of 'arc pair grammar', a radical outgrowth of 'relational grammar' that is quite different from and pretends to supplant transformational-generative grammar. But that attempt is problematic in a number of ways and certainly does not maximize 'the simplicity and generality of the grammar as a whole'. See David E. Johnson and Paul M. Postal, *Arc Pair Grammar* (Princeton, N.J.: Princeton University Press, 1980).

7. Ray Jackendoff, 'Grammar as Evidence for Conceptual Structure', in *Linguistic Theory and Psychological Reality*, ed. Morris Halle, Joan Bresnan, and George A. Miller (Cambridge, Mass.: MIT Press, 1978), pp. 202, 203.

8. Noam Chomsky, *Language and Mind*, enlarged edn (New York: Harcourt Brace Jovanovich, 1972), p. 99.

9. Robert Wall, *Introduction to Mathematical Linguistics* (Englewood Cliffs, N.J.: Prentice-Hall, 1972), p. 290.

10. Ibid.

11. See Seymour Ginsburg and Barbara Hall Partee, 'A Mathematical Model of Transformational Grammar', *Information and Control*, 15 (1969), 297–334, and P. Stanley Peters and R. W. Ritchie, 'On Restricting the Base Component of Transformational Grammars', *Information and Control*, 18 (1971), 483–501.

12. Wall, *Mathematical Linguistics*, pp. 295–6. See also P. Stanley Peters and R. W. Ritchie, 'A Note on the Universal Base Hypothesis', *Journal of Linguistics*, 5 (1969), 150–2, and P. Stanley Peters, 'Why There Are Many "Universal" Bases', *Papers in Linguistics*, 1 (1970), 27–43.

13. Paul Ziff, 'Natural and Formal Languages', in *Language and Philosophy: A Symposium*, ed. Sidney Hook (New York: New York University Press, 1969), pp. 224, 225, 226, 237, 239. Perhaps the most extravagant arguments against formalisms in the study of natural language may be found in G. P. Baker and P. M. S. Hacker, *Language, Sense and Nonsense: A Critical Investigation into Modern Theories of Language* (Oxford: Basil Blackwell, 1984). After criticizing the whole notion that natural language is a system of any kind, lambasting AI theory, labelling most formalists Fregeans, and ridiculing modellers, they wind up with a conclusion as absurd as Ziff's: 'There is no such thing as a theory of meaning for a language' (p. 387).

14. Richard M. Martin, 'On Ziff's "Natural and Formal Languages"', in *Language and Philosophy*, ed. Hook, p. 249.

15. Ibid., pp. 252, 255, 261–2.

16. Daniel C. Dennett, 'Computer Models and the Mind – a View from the East Pole', *Times Literary Supplement*, 14 Dec. 1984, p. 1453.

17. Ibid., p. 1454.

18. Ibid. See also W. Daniel Hillis, 'The Connection Machine', *Scientific American*, June 1987, pp. 108–15.
19. Douglas R. Hofstadter, 'Artificial Intelligence: Subcognition as Computation', in *The Study of Information: Interdisciplinary Messages*, ed. Fritz Machlup and Una Mansfield (New York: Wiley, 1983), pp. 279, 281, 283, 285.

Notes to Chapter 35   Memory, Learning, Self-Knowledge

1. Earl Hunt, 'The Memory We Must Have', in *Computer Models of Thought and Language*, ed. Roger C. Schank and Kenneth Mark Colby (San Francisco, Calif.: Freeman, 1973), pp. 370–1. For a diagram that suggests the role of memory functions in relation to others, see Daniel C. Dennett, *Brainstorms: Philosophical Essays on Mind and Psychology* (Montgomery, Vt.: Bradford Books, 1978), p. 155. Interestingly enough, Derrida reverses Hunt's question (and asks, in effect, 'What kind of man is the computer?') by discussing how the machine increasingly resembles 'the psychical apparatus', specifically memory, which he considers in terms of *écriture* (*Writing and Difference*, trans. and intro. by Alan Bass (Chicago, Ill.: University of Chicago Press, 1978), p. 228) – obviously a cogent perspective on the MLM metaphor.
2. J. Z. Young, *Programs of the Brain* (New York: Oxford University Press, 1978), pp. 81, 82, 83–4. I recognize that there are various ways of classifying memory functions, such as William James's *primary* and *secondary* memories, but none is unproblematic. Unable to offer a better alternative, I accept them – but only as tentative conveniences.
3. Ibid., p. 87.
4. Ibid., pp. 80, 93, 94.
5. Ibid., pp. 95, 96.
6. David E. Rumelhart, *Introduction to Human Information Processing* (New York: Wiley, 1977), pp. 177, 178, 196–7, 201, 202.
7. Ibid., pp. 203, 212, 213.
8. Ibid., pp. 215, 216, 217, 220.
9. Ibid., pp. 232–3, 234.
10. Ibid., pp. 236, 265.
11. George A. Miller and Philip N. Johnson-Laird, *Language and Perception* (Cambridge, Mass.: Harvard University Press, Belknap Press, 1976), pp. 143, 146, 147.
12. Ibid., pp. 271, 172. Umberto Eco conceives of such a network as a special kind of tangled labyrinth, one like a rhizome, in which all points are interconnected (see his *Semiotics and the Philosophy of Language* [Bloomington: Indiana University Press, 1984], pp. 81–2). The image suggests a mental ecology that correlates with the both/and logic, the operation of the trace, and other provisions of deconstruction theory.
13. Miller and Johnson-Laird, *Language and Perception*, p. 273.
14. Ibid., pp. 273, 274–5, 276. See also John R. Anderson, 'FRAN: A

Simulation Model of Free Recall', in *The Psychology of Learning and Motivation: Advances in Research and Theory*, ed. Gordon H. Bower (New York: Academic Press, 1972), 5: 315–78; John R. Anderson and Gordon H. Bower, *Human Associate Memory* (Washington: Winston, 1973); and James Moore and Allen Newell, 'How Can Merlin Understand?' in *Knowledge and Cognition*, ed. Lee W. Gregg (Potomac, Md.: Erlbaum, 1974), pp. 201–52.

15. Philip N. Johnson-Laird, 'The Perception and Memory of Sentences', in *New Horizons in Linguistics*, ed. John Lyons (Baltimore, Md.: Penguin Books, 1970), p. 269.

16. Jeremy Campbell, *Grammatical Man: Information, Entropy, Language, and Life* (New York: Simon & Schuster, 1982), pp. 228, 229.

17. E. D. Hirsch, Jr, *The Philosophy of Composition* (Chicago, Ill.: University of Chicago Press, 1977), pp. 109, 122.

18. Philip C. Jackson, Jr, *Introduction to Artificial Intelligence* (New York: Petrocelli Books, 1974), p. 336. Obviously there are many areas of memory research that I have not discussed, but there are two properties of memory, on which there has been only pioneering work, that should be mentioned: equipotentiality and multidimensionality. Holographic theories of equipotentiality have been proposed by Karl Pribram, Christopher Longuet-Higgins, and others. Those theories, tentative as they are, have a great deal to recommend them: they explain elegantly the particle/wave storage of memories both locally and globally, for example. But they lack sufficient empirical evidence. Very little has been accomplished in attempting to describe the multidimensionality of memory. Research on association has been stymied by the lack of such a description, though Zeeman offers an ingenious, albeit empirically troublesome, mathematical approach to it (see Steven Rose, *The Conscious Brain*, updated edn [New York: Random House, Vintage Books, 1976], p. 263, and E. C. Zeeman, *Catastrophe Theory: Selected Papers 1972–1977* [Reading, Mass.: Addison-Wesley, 1977], pp. 287–300).

Notes to Chapter 36   Dependency, Postsemantics, Paradigm

1. Gilbert Harman, Introduction, *On Noam Chomsky: Critical Essays*, ed. Gilbert Harman (Garden City, N.Y.: Doubleday, Anchor Books, 1974), pp. viii, ix–x, xi. From the years just after the publication of Chomsky's *Syntactic Structures* (The Hague: Mouton, 1957) until the present (a period that has witnessed the precarious fortunes of the so-called Katz-Postal hypothesis and other attempts at ironing out problems in Chomskyan syntactic theory), linguistic metatheory has been awash with debate about the extent to which transformations generate semantic values that are realized in surface structure and the extent to which meaning is the province of deep structure (that is, to which deep structure is the syntactic level required for input to be processed by rules of semantic interpretation) – problems obviously relevant to the issue of what deep structure 'contains' in the way of

representation. Recalling my earlier mention of affinities between Chomskyan and Derridean theory, I would propose that application of the latter might be advantageous here. One might hypothesize that the relation between declaration and description is largely defined by how the declarative surface structure harbours the trace of the descriptive surface structure. The meaning of the second thus would be implicit in the first, the meanings of the two arising from different deep structures. The transformations involved then could be seen not so much as generating semantic values but as *distinguishing* between those in the two deep structures so as to make some declarative and some descriptive. In this case the transformations, no matter what effects they otherwise have on meaning, would be meaning-preserving but in a way unpredicted by standard versions of either generative or interpretive semantics.

2. Philip C. Jackson, Jr, *Introduction to Artificial Intelligence* (New York: Petrocelli Books, 1974), p. 312. See also Ian Robinson, *The New Grammarians' Funeral: A Critique of Noam Chomsky's Linguistics* (Cambridge: Cambridge University Press, 1975), p. 173.

3. Jean Atchison, *The Articulate Mammal: An Introduction to Psycholinguistics* (1976; reprint edn New York: McGraw-Hill, 1978), pp. 232, 235. Brown observes that,

> Though no generative grammar can reasonably be considered a model of the process of sentence production or comprehension (it is much more like a set of axioms for testing whether a given string is or is not a sentence), generative grammars have, as their ultimate point, a distinctly psychological goal. They are intended to represent formally the knowledge that the native speaker must *somehow* utilize in producing and understanding sentences.

The *somehow*, however, still lacks specification. Furthermore, he contends, grammatical complexity, *if correlated with semantic complexity*, does do 'a good job of predicting order of acquisition'. But he contends also that 'We shall find, I think, that there are multiple "levels" of knowledge of structure, as revealed by various kinds of performance, and that there is no clear reason to enthrone any one of these as the child's true competence' (*A First Language: The Early Stages* (Cambridge, Mass.: Harvard University Press, 1973), pp. 406, 408, 413).

4. See Robin Campbell and Roger Wales, 'The Study of Language Acquisition', in *New Horizons in Linguistics*, ed. John Lyons (Baltimore, Md.: Penguin Books, 1970), pp. 242–60.

5. Judith Greene, *Psycholinguistics: Chomsky and Psychology* (New York: Penguin Books, 1972), p. 196.

6. Joan Bresnan, 'A Realistic Transformational Grammar', in *Linguistic Theory and Psychological Reality*, ed. Morris Halle, Joan Bresnan, and George A. Miller (Cambridge, Mass.: MIT Press, 1978), pp. 2, 59.

7. Jacob Bronowski, *A Sense of the Future: Essays in Natural Philosophy*, ed. Piero E. Ariotti with Rita Bronowski (Cambridge, Mass.: MIT

Press, 1977), pp. 140, 148. But see Campbell's speculation that 'the rules of expression for DNA', when discovered, will resemble those of transformational grammar (Jeremy Campbell, *Grammatical Man: Information, Entropy, Language, and Life* [New York: Simon & Schuster, 1982], p. 129).

8. Richard A. Hudson, *Arguments for a Non-Transformational Grammar* (Chicago, Ill.: University of Chicago Press, 1976), pp. 2, 3–4.

9. Ibid., pp. 4, 8–9, 14.

10. Ibid., pp. 14, 19.

11. Ibid., pp. 30, 23, 25, 26. A possible approach to untangling the issue of psychological reality here is suggested by a somewhat offhand remark made by Richard Ohmann, one whose implications have not been carefully pursued either theoretically or experimentally: 'the elusive intuition we have of *form* and *content* may turn out to be anchored in a distinction between the surface structures and the deep structures of sentences' ('Literature as Sentences', *College English*, 27 [1966], 267). The remark strikes me alternately as an annunciation of the obvious and as an insight that is novel and seductive, particularly to the poststructuralist.

12. Hudson, *Arguments*, p. 26.

13. Wallace L. Chafe, *Meaning and the Structure of Language* (Chicago, Ill.: University of Chicago Press, 1970), pp. 40, 54, 55.

14. Ibid., pp. 57, 59.

15. For some persuasive evidence concerning phonemic analysis and categorization in language comprehension, from research on a man who can talk backwards, see 'Reverse English', in 'Science and the Citizen', *Scientific American*, July 1980, pp. 76–7.

16. Chafe, *Meaning*, pp. 62, 65, 66, 68.

17. Ibid., pp. 346, 348, 351.

18. Given my readiness to consider the new formalism and related topics in terms of a 'new paradigm', I should point out that I am aware of the controversies about the application of Thomas Kuhn's paradigmatic interpretation of scientific revolution, as elaborated in his *Structure of Scientific Revolutions*, 2nd edn (Chicago, Ill.: University of Chicago Press, 1970), to the 'soft' sciences – or to any of them, for that matter. But the application in this case is at least analogically powerful and suggestive. (For a survey of those controversies, especially as they concern theories about language, see Robert J. Connors, 'Composition Studies and Science', *College English*, 45 [1983], 1–20. For a general retrospective survey see Frederick Suppe, 'The Waning of the *Weltanschauungen* Views', in *The Structure of Scientific Theories*, ed. Frederick Suppe, 2nd edn [Urbana: University of Illinois Press, 1977], pp. 633–48.) At any rate, there seems little doubt that a new paradigm, however it is schematized, is emerging. In various aspects it may be described, to follow Kuhn, as being in a 'preparadigmatic' phase. Evidence for that situation may be found widely, most notably in the preoccupation of composition theorists and others with the so-called New Rhetoric, with its emphasis on the interrelations of writing and reading, rhetoricity itself. For them the 'current-

traditional' paradigm is giving way to one that accommodates interdisciplinary theorizing and research, whose eclectic armamentarium includes neo-Gorgian rhetorical theory, deconstructive pedagogy, an enlarged pragmatics, Bakhtinian dialogism, reader-response theory, and so on. (See Maxine Hairston, 'The Winds of Change: Thomas Kuhn and the Revolution in the Teaching of Writing', *College Composition and Communication*, 33 [1982], 76–88; James A. Berlin, 'Contemporary Composition: The Major Pedagogical Theories', *College English*, 44 [1982], 765–77; and Sharon Crowley, 'Of Gorgias and Grammatology', *College Composition and Communication*, 30 [1979], 279–84.) Indeed, interdisciplinary exploration with its drive toward synthesis is crucial to transcending the ossified and confused compartmentalizations of the old paradigm and to developing the more holistic constructs that will constitute the new one:

> In its attempts to isolate single systems (phonology, morphology, syntax, etc.) and to keep language distinct from everything else, linguistic research may have remained on a superficial plane that *increased* complexity of study rather than reducing it. On a more powerful plane, a simpler and more unified account of human language may yet be forthcoming'. (Robert de Beaugrande and Wolfgang Ulrich Dressler, *Introduction to Text Linguistics*, updated and trans. Robert de Beaugrande [New York: Longman, 1981], p. 220)

Some aspects of that account may be presaged in Constance Weaver, 'Parallels Between New Paradigms in Science and in Reading and Literary Theories: An Essay Review', *Research in the Teaching of English*, 19 (1985), 298–316.

Notes to Chapter 37 Synthesis, Semiotics, Biology

1. Charles E. Osgood, 'Language Universals and Psycholinguistics', in *Universals of Language*, 2nd edn, ed. Joseph H. Greenberg (Cambridge, Mass.: MIT Press, 1966), pp. 309–10.
2. Ibid., pp. 311, 312–13.
3. Ibid., pp. 320–1, 322.
4. Fredric Jameson, *The Prison-House of Language: A Critical Account of Structuralism and Russian Formalism* (Princeton, N.J.: Princeton University Press, 1972), pp. 24, ix, 209, 210. It is perhaps worth noting that in Scholes's opinion (see *Textual Power: Literary Theory and the Teaching of English* [New Haven, Conn.: Yale University Press, 1985], p. 91) Jameson has more recently become trapped in 'the prison-house of language' – he has, in other words, become a poststructuralist of a kind.
5. Thomas A. Sebeok, *The Sign and Its Masters* (Austin: University of Texas Press, 1979), pp. x, xi.

6. Ibid., p. xiii.
7. Ibid., pp. 22, 24.
8. Ibid., pp. 28, 194, 195, 196.
9. Ibid., pp. 203–4, 205.
10. Ibid., pp. 44, 45.
11. Ibid., pp. 56, 57.
12. Ibid., pp. 57–8.
13. Ibid., pp. 67, viii.
14. Ibid., pp. 24, 25.
15. Ibid., pp. 34, 62, 122–3.
16. Ibid., p. 127.
17. E. C. Zeeman, *Catastrophe Theory: Selected Papers, 1972–1977* (Reading, Mass.: Addison-Wesley, 1977), p. 630.
18. René Thom, *Structural Stability and Morphogenesis: An Outline of a General Theory of Models*, trans. D. H. Fowler (Reading, Mass.: Benjamin, 1975), pp. 116, 117, 118.
19. Ibid., p. 118.
20. Ibid., p. 145. Thom's suggestion may be vivified by juxtaposition with one from Robert K. Lindsay in regard to modelling:

> One suggestion, which I have not seen sufficiently explored, is to represent continuous space in a digital computer through the formalizations of analysis. This suggestion would not have us store a continuous map in the quasi-literal way we store a discrete graph, but would employ an active memory which would construct new, discrete loci as they are called for, using the axioms which define, say, metric or topological spaces. From the 'outside,' to the program annexing or retrieving information, the map would act as a continuous store, but the physical representation would be digital. . . . The leap from a one-dimensional dense set to three-dimensional Euclidean space is rather large, but the leap to two-dimensional topological space might be manageable. ('In Defense of Ad Hoc Systems', in *Computer Models of Thought and Language*, ed. Roger C. Schank and Kenneth Mark Colby [San Francisco, Calif.: Freeman, 1973], pp. 393–4)

21. Thom, *Structural Stability*, pp. 157, 310–11.
22. Ibid., pp. 312, 313, 317.
23. Ibid., pp. 317–18, 323.
24. Ibid., pp. 321, 327, 328. For background on 'semantic density' and cumulative sentences, see Francis Christensen, *Notes Toward a New Rhetoric: Six Essays for Teachers* (New York: Harper & Row, 1967).

Notes to Chapter 38   Subsumption, Simulation, Information

1. Jacques Derrida, *Of Grammatology*, trans. Gayatri Chakravorty Spivak (Baltimore, Md.: Johns Hopkins University Press, 1976), p. 9.

2. E. C. Zeeman, *Catastrophe Theory: Selected Papers, 1972–1977* (Reading, Mass.: Addison-Wesley, 1977), p. 288.

3. Fredric Jameson, *The Prison-House of Language: A Critical Account of Structuralism and Russian Formalism* (Princeton, N.J.: Princeton University Press, 1972), p. 105.

4. Jeffrey Wine, 'The Brain: What We Know About It . . . and What We Don't Know', *Stanford Observer*, Nov. 1979, p. 3.

5. Herbert Feigl, *'The "Mental" and the "Physical"': The Essay and a Postscript* (Minneapolis: University of Minnesota Press, 1967), pp. 13–14, 63, 104.

6. Ibid., pp. 105, 106, 149. For a synoptic view of the intricacies of brain–mind interrelations as they have been variously delineated – by dualism, materialism, radical behaviourism, logical behaviourism, functionalism, and so on – see Jerry A. Fodor, 'The Mind-Body Problem', *Scientific American*, Jan. 1981, pp. 114–23. The mind–brain problem, a version of the classical mind–body problem (which in some ways resembles that occasioned by the commonplace notion that language, especially writing, is somehow separate from 'reality'), is increasingly being considered a pseudo-problem, like that entailed in distinguishing the logical and physical states of a computer: it arises only if one forgets that each kind of state can be related to – and is a version, in a different category, of – the other.

7. F. H. C. Crick, 'Thinking about the Brain', *Scientific American*, Sep. 1979, pp. 222, 224.

8. Ibid., pp. 229, 230, 232. The question of what kind of clock governs the brain (a version of which intrigued Bakhtin) is crucial, and the answer to it doubtless would have bearing on questions concerned with how parallel and serial processes are interrelated, how semantic structures are translated into sequential syntax, and so on. Though that answer is not yet within reach, there are some teasing clues. For instance, one's changing sense of time can be related to varying periodicities in the perceptual system (a fact that has important implications for research on semiosis and the aging process – information turning into noise – an enterprise of enduring interest to Sebeok), and a more-than-assonantal connection between synapse and syntax is suggested by the presumption that

> the individual brain states associated with memories must . . . be linked by synaptic logic into a sequence in which one follows almost inevitably from another – try stopping a stream of memory in midflow and the difficulty will become apparent. It is as if the arrow of time is located in the synapse, at least so far as memory is concerned.' (Steven Rose, *The Conscious Brain*, updated edn [New York: Random House, Vintage Books, 1976], p. 262)

9. Walter J. Karplus, 'The Spectrum of Mathematical Modeling and Systems Simulation', *Simuletter*, 9, no. 1 (1978), 33. There are, of course, problems involved in making any absolute distinction between deductive and inductive procedures, which in practice may be subtly

intermixed or entail abductive or other procedures as well, but his distinction seems useful as a way of generally classifying modeling methods, at least in terms of emphases.
10. Ibid., pp. 37, 38. Another version of Karplus's imperative might be that a model of a complex problem must be used in such a way as to maximize the extent to which the solution is inherent in the representation. A warning to accompany that imperative would be that the modeller must not confuse the *fit* of a model with its *match* (see Ernst von Glaserfeld, 'An Introduction to Radical Constructivism', in *The Invented Reality*, ed. Paul Watzlawick [New York: Norton, 1984], pp. 20–1).
11. Michel Serres, 'Platonic Dialogue', trans. Marilyn Sides, in *Hermes: Literature, Science, Philosophy*, ed. Josué V. Harari and David F. Bell, (Baltimore, Md.: Johns Hopkins University Press, 1982), pp. 68, 69.
12. Josué V. Harari and David F. Bell, 'Introduction: Journal à plusieurs voies', in *Hermes*, p. xxvi. They mention in passing that noise in this sense is *parasite* in French and thereby trigger for me a question, explored in deconstructive terms by J. Hillis Miller (in 'The Critic as Host', in Harold Bloom, Paul de Man, Jacques Derrida, Geoffrey H. Hartman, and J. Hillis Miller, *Deconstruction and Criticism* [New York: Seabury Press, 1979], pp. 217–53), about the conventional notion of the peripherality of the parasite (in this case, noise) in relation to the host (information). As is typically the case in parasitism, a both/and 'symbiosis', not a relationship of peripherality-centrality, is involved.
13. See Serres, 'Platonic Dialogue', pp. 66–7.
14. See Benoit B. Mandelbrot, *Fractals: Form, Chance, and Dimension* (San Francisco, Calif.: Freeman, 1977).
15. Frederick W. Kantor, *Information Mechanics* (New York: Wiley–Interscience, 1977), pp. vii, 2, 11–12.

Notes to Chapter 39   Ventriloquism, Indifference, Beyond

1. Marshall McLuhan, *Understanding Media: The Extensions of Man* (1964; reprint edn, New York: New American Library, Mentor Books, n.d.), pp. 304–5.
2. Hubert L. Dreyfus, *What Computers Can't Do: The Limits of Artificial Intelligence*, revised edn (New York: Harper & Row, Harper Colophon Books, 1979), pp. 226, 65–6. The quotation from Yeats is from his letter to Lady Elizabeth Pelham, 4 January 1939, which may be found in *The Letters of W. B. Yeats*, ed. Allan Wade (London: Hart-Davis, 1954), p. 922. Dreyfus and others of like persuasion have made much of the problem of modelling the tacit or implicit knowledge structures on which human cognition depends. But one should be careful not to attribute too much mysteriousness to such structures. Their tacitness or implicitness may come about, in part at least, for a reason similar to one that accounts for a similar phenomenon in generative grammars: if the system of rules is infinitely generative, then its (sentence-forming) processes can conceal those rules. But they are there and, by sufficient analysis, can be made explicit. Indeed, a proper role for the computer is that of a helpmate in such analysis, and the goal involved is defensible enough:

Researchers agree that presently operating models are simpler than their corresponding human processes by several degrees of magnitude . . ., but those models have already attained a complexity far beyond the scope of traditional theories in linguistics and psychology. Only the computer allows us to test immediately whether a mathematical or procedural theory of cognition or communication actually operates in real time; we can and must specify exact details that may remain hidden in human experiments. In short, computers can lead us from *understanding data* toward the broader domain of *understanding understanding*. (Robert de Beaugrande and Wolfgang Ulrich Dressler, *Introduction to Text Linguistics*, updated and trans. Robert de Beaugrande [New York: Longman, 1981], p. 220)

The same line of argument might be applied to the simulation of creativity, which is, quite apart from notions of 'inspiration' (and their something-from-nothing idiom), largely a matter of generative processes of thematic variation whose rules surely can be made explicit.

3. J. David Bolter, *Turing's Man: Western Culture in the Computer Age* (Chapel Hill: University of North Carolina Press, 1984), pp. 131, 221, 220, 224, 190.

4. Hermann Broch, *Der Tod des Vergil* (Zurich: Rhein-Verlag, 1947), p. 461. There is a quotation that might have served as a qualifying coda (and, since it is here, still does – as no less a part of my text for being the tail at the end of the subtext). It is from Charles H. Bennett:

Since Ω [an irrational number recently discovered by Gregory J. Chaitin] is defined as the overall halting probability of a computer with random input, it can be regarded as the sum of the probabilities of all halting computations. . . . Actually Ω is a totally informative message, one that appears to be random because all redundancy has been squeezed out of it, a message consisting only of information that can be obtained in no other way. . . . Ω is in many senses a Cabalistic number. It can be known of through human reason, but not known. To know it in detail one must accept its uncomputable sequence of digits on faith, like words of a sacred text. . . . Its first few thousand digits, which could be written on a small piece of paper, contain the answers to more mathematical questions than could be written down in the entire universe – among them all interesting finitely refutable conjectures. . . . The first few digits of Ω are probably already recorded somewhere in the universe. No mortal discoverer of this treasure, however, could verify its authority or make practical use of it. ('On Random and Hard-to-Describe Numbers', an unpublished paper quoted by Martin Gardner in 'Mathematical Games', *Scientific American*, Nov. 1979, pp. 28, 33–4)

The point (the sub-subtext) is that my black hole, like Broch's word or Chaitin's Ω – or even Queequeg's 'riddle' – though it may be 'beyond language' (or cannot be 'read'), is none the less still a(nother) signifier: 'Il n'y a pas de hors-texte.'

Index